Business Analytics Series

Risk Profiling of Organizations

Second Edition

Andrew D. Banasiewicz, Ph.D.

ERUDITE ANALYTICS

ABOUT THE AUTHOR

Dr. Andrew Banasiewicz is currently an Associate Professor of the Professional Practice in the department of Administrative Sciences at Boston University, where he also serves as the Director of the Master of Science in Enterprise Risk Management program. Additionally, he is the founder and a principle of Erudite Analytics, a data analytical consultancy. Prior to joining the faculty of Boston University, Banasiewicz spent over 15 years as a senior level analyst working with insurance and marketing organizations.

During his business tenure, Dr. Banasiewicz worked with numerous leading organizations, including The Coca-Cola Company, ConocoPhillips, Liberty Mutual Insurance, Nabisco, Kellogg, General Motors, GE Money, Nestle Purina, Nevada Power, Marriott International, The World Bank and others. His primary area of expertise is predictive analytics, particularly the design of decision support systems for risk management and marketing, as exemplified by a repurchase-predicting adaptive loyalty categorization methodology, or a multi-source data analytical system for estimating the likelihood of adverse development of casualty insurance claims. Banasiewicz wrote three analytics-focused books, in addition to multiple methodological journal articles and white papers; he is also a frequent speaker at national and international professional meetings. He holds Ph.D. in business from Louisiana State University.

FOREWORD

Risk is ubiquitous—it permeates virtually all aspects of our existence. In fact, it is so ever-present that we often implicitly discount its potential impact. For instance, even though each year over 40,000 individuals die in automobile accidents in the United States, surveys indicate that safety is among one of the least important or least considered factors in the automobile purchase process. Why? Obviously not because most car purchasers do not value their lives—rather, it is probably because we became so accustomed to those fatalities that we simply do not actively consider the potential hazard of automobile accidents. In general, it seems that the acuity with which we perceive many types of risk can be dulled by their commonplace.

A similar phenomenon is evident in organizational decision making. It is intuitively obvious that the conduct of business entails the assumption of a wide range of risks. Some of those risks, most notably credit or currency exposures received a considerable amount of attention, which ultimately led to the emergence and the proliferation of objective assessment tools. Even the inherently difficult to forecast natural disasters, such as violent storms or earthquakes, are being quantitatively modeled, albeit with a limited success. However, surprisingly little analytical effort has been put against other risk exposures. The case in point: Operational and strategic risks. Taken together, these broadly defined exposures have a very pronounced impact on the organization's present and future well-being, yet neither received adequate measurement attention. Instead, organizations tend to follow the "ignore or insure" philosophy, which can be overly costly at the very minimum, or even disastrous at times. This is both surprising and unwise given that not just success, but even the very survival of organizations hinges on making the "right" strategic and operational decisions.

The relative scantiness of operational and strategic risk assessment is only one of the limitations of how organizations tend to view risk—equally troubling is the tendency to liken "risk" to a "threat". The most commonly used definition of *risk* portrays it as the possibility of an adverse event taking place at some point in the future. A sudden rise in the cost of capital, a violent storm, unfavorable legislation or supply chain disruption are all examples of adverse developments, and indeed, all those—as well as many other negative events—pose a threat to the organization's well-being. However, so do forgone opportunities. "The road not taken", which could be a strategic partnership that the organization opted not to pursue, or a new technology, a

i

product line or a brand extension, all of which could have become a significant source of growth. Though their impact can be quite significant, strategic choices are rarely expressly incorporated into organizations' risk measurement processes. One of the leading reasons why forgone strategic options tend not to be viewed as threats, is because their consequences are less visible and their cost less obvious. From the standpoint of risk measurement and management, the possibility of something "bad" occurring is conceptually and operationally distinct from something "good" not occurring. And to the degree to which our perception of risk is tied to the former, we continue to overlook the potential impact of the latter.

Limiting the definition of "risk" to "the possibility of a negative outcome" can result in a skewed picture of the organization's overall risk exposure. To its owners, or shareholders, a business entity essentially represents a string of earnings, which tend to fluctuate over time as a result of the combination of internal decisions and external forces. Hence it follows that the definition of "risk" should encompass all internal and external factors that can materially impact the level of earnings, including both the "bad" outcomes materializing and the "good" ones not coming to fruition. Although on the one hand this will broaden the scope of what needs to be considered and evaluated, focusing only on those factors that can exert a measurable impact on earnings will have the effect of ultimately narrowing the scope of analysis. The resultant set of materially relevant risk exposures will comprise the organization's risk profile.

Each organization has a unique *risk profile*, which is a composite of the potentialities of bad and good outcomes. To understand the impact of risk on the organization's competitiveness, its risk profile needs to be compared with those of its key competitors, in the context of the total exposure and the total cost of risk. If the organization's total risk exposure is greater than that of its competitors, or if its total cost of risk is higher than that of its competitors, its earnings—and ultimately, its competitiveness—can be adverse effected. An objective, ongoing assessment of the likelihood and severity of the individual exposures comprising the overall profile offers the most direct and effective method of managing the impact of risk on earnings of organizations.

The *Risk Profile Measurement (RPM)* process outlined in this book details the analytical "how-to" of objectively estimating company-specific exposure to measurable risks that are most likely to impact its earnings. The focus of the measurement process is on estimating the likely impact of risk on the organization's earnings, in a manner that allows cross-exposure comparisons. Or stated differently, it is to estimate the net effect of individual risks. The resultant analytical proficiency carries with it a number of benefits that can be thought of as either strategic or tactical in nature. In terms of the former, the utilization of risk profile assessment makes possible an objective risk response determination. When confronted with the knowledge of a particular risk, organizations need to decide whether to accept, reduce, transfer or avoid it, doing which requires at least some knowledge of the risk type's occurrence probability and the expected severity, or cost. In terms of the latter, the RPM process contributes insights to further advise the implementation of the chosen course of action, once the most advantageous risk response has been selected. For instance, if the most appropriate response to a particular risk exposure is deemed to be "mitigation", RPM can contribute much of the needed information pinpointing the most pronounced drivers of risk, along with their relative impact, or elasticities. If "transfer" is the most appropriate response, the thorough assessment of the organization-specific risk profile will offer an estimate of the likelihood and the severity of a potential loss, which in turn will form the basis for framing the most economically-sound amount of insurance coverage for "intangible" risks, such professional liability or securities litigation.

Thus, this is a "how-to" book. Its primary focus is on detailing the step-by-step mechanics of estimating the organization's exposure to risks that can materially impact—both negatively as well as positively—its earnings. It is premised on the idea that systematic, ongoing utilization of the available data and proven statistical methodologies will materially enhance the efficacy of risk-related decisions, which will manifest itself in the strengthening of the organization's competitiveness.

ADB

Risk Profiling
of Organizations

ERUDITE ANALYTICS

To Alana, Katrina and Adam

Contents

FOREWORD   I

LIST OF ILLUSTRATIONS   XI

CHAPTER 1 - THE ART & SCIENCE OF KNOWING   1
   DATA, KNOWLEDGE & DECISIONS   3
KNOWLEDGE   5
   COMPONENTS OF KNOWLEDGE   6
   KNOWLEDGE CREATION   8
   THEORY OR DATA DRIVEN?   12
KNOWLEDGE AS A STRATEGIC ASSET   15
FROM DATA TO INFORMATION TO KNOWLEDGE   19
   SOURCES OF PROFICIENCY   21
THE PURSUIT OF KNOWLEDGE   30
   IS DATA AN ASSET?   31
   DATA AS A SOURCE OF COMPETITIVE ADVANTAGE   33
ABOUT THIS BOOK   38
   IN A NUTSHELL   38
   ORGANIZATION   39

CHAPTER 2 - KNOWLEDGE OF RISK   41
   RISK VS. UNCERTAINTY   43
   BROADENING THE SCOPE OF RISK   47
ASSESSMENT OF RISK   51
MANAGEMENT OF RISK   55
   RISK MAPPING   56
   RISK RESPONSE   58
   NOT EITHER OR   70
ENTERPRISE RISK MANAGEMENT TYPOLOGIES   72
   COSO FRAMEWORK   74
   ISO 31000 STANDARD   80
   ERM AND DEBT RATINGS   83

CHAPTER 3 - RISK MEASUREMENT   **86**
RISK PROFILING   88
    RISK PROFILE   88
    THE ECONOMICS OF RISK   90
THE RPM TYPOLOGY OF RISK   91
    UPSIDE RISK   93
    DOWNSIDE RISK   95
RISK QUANTIFICATION   98
    MEASURING VOLATILITY   98
    PROBABILITY AS A BUSINESS TOOL   102
    PROBABILITY ESTIMATION: DIVERGENT PHILOSOPHIES   103
    SEVERITY ESTIMATION   108
    A NOTE ON LIKELIHOOD—SEVERITY INDEPENDENCE   109
RISK PROFILE MANAGEMENT   110
    RISK ACCEPTANCE   112
    RISK TRANSFER   114
    RISK AVOIDANCE & REDUCTION   115

CHAPTER 4 - THE PROCESS OF RISK PROFILE MANAGEMENT   **120**
PROCESS & METHODS   121
    METHODS   122
    PROCESS VS. METHOD   126
THE OVERALL RISK ANALYTIC PROCESS   131

CHAPTER 5 - NEED IDENTIFICATION: INFORMATIONAL NEEDS   **133**
    DELINEATION OF STRATEGIC GOALS AND TACTICAL MEANS   136
    UNCOVERING INFORMATIONAL NEEDS   136
    ASSESSING DATA AND METHOD REQUIREMENTS   138

CHAPTER 6 - KNOWLEDGE CREATION: ANALYTIC PLANNING   **140**
    PLANNING VS. PLAN   141
ANALYTIC PLANNING FRAMEWORK   142
    GENERALIZABLE PLANNING TEMPLATE   143
    ADDITIONAL CONSIDERATIONS   143

CHAPTER 7 - KNOWLEDGE CREATION: UNDERSTANDING DATA   **145**
DATA FUNDAMENTALS   148
    EVENTS   148
    ATTRIBUTES   149
DATABASES IN A NUTSHELL   153
    THE SCOPE: DATA WAREHOUSE VS. DATA MART 153
BUT IT IS NOT ABOUT THE HARDWARE...   159
    THE DATA—INFORMATION—KNOWLEDGE CONTINUUM 160
    MORE ON REPORTING VS. ANALYTICS: TOOLS & APPLICATIONS 162
    SINGLE VS. MULTI-SOURCE ANALYSIS   167
FROM DATA TO KNOWLEDGE   169
    DATA CAPTURE INFRASTRUCTURE   170

CHAPTER 8 - KNOWLEDGE CREATION: ANALYTIC FILE   **171**
ANALYTICAL DATASET CREATION   173
    EXTRACTING A SUBSET OF THE DATABASE   173
    EXTRACT DATA ENRICHMENT   176
    DATA CLEANSING   177
    THE OUTLIER IDENTIFICATION PROCESS   180
    DATA REPAIRING   181
METADATA   188
    METADATA TEMPLATE   188
    USING METADATA   190

CHAPTER 9 - KNOWLEDGE CREATION: EXPLORATORY ANALYSES   **191**
    MORE ON DATA EXPLORATION TECHNIQUES   193
    DATA EXPLORATION PROCESS   195
THE EDA PROCESS   197
    EDA PART I: REVIEW PREVIOUS FINDINGS   197
    EDA PART II: ASSESS THE INFORMATIONAL QUALITY 201
    EDA PART III: DESCRIBE—ASSESS—EXPLAIN   206
CONFIDENCE INTERVALS   232
    INTERPRETATION   233

CHAPTER 10 - KNOWLEDGE CREATION: PREDICTIVE ANALYTICS   **235**
PREDICTIVE ANALYTICS   237
    FUTURE STATES' PARAMETERIZATION   238
    MORE ON MULTIVARIATE MODELING   242
    IMPACT QUANTIFICATION   244
    PREDICTION INTERVALS   245
    DEGREE-OF-SIMILARITY MODELING   247
ADDITIONAL MODELING CONSIDERATIONS   249
    DATA VS. STATISTICAL EFFECTS   249
    THE ROLE OF EFFECT TYPES IN IDS   253
    PREDICTIVE RELIABILITY OF INDICATORS   255
QUALITATIVE ANALYSES OF RISK   258
    WHEN NO HARD DATA EXISTS   258
    DELPHI METHOD   260
TEXT DATA   262
    STRUCTURED VS. UNSTRUCTURED DATA   262
    TEXT MINING APPROACHES   264

CHAPTER 11 - KNOWLEDGE CREATION: EVALUATING ALTERNATIVES   **272**
EXPERIMENTATION   273
    EXPERIMENTAL DESIGN   274
    SAMPLING REQUIREMENTS ASSESSMENT   277
    EFFECT ANALYSIS   279

CHAPTER 12 - KNOWLEDGE CREATION: FROM FINDINGS TO KNOWLEDGE   **284**
    EXPANSION OF THE KNOWLEDGE BASE   285
DEPLOYMENT   286
    TESTS' APPLICABILITY LIMITS   286
UPDATING   290

CHAPTER 13 - KNOWLEDGE DISSEMINATION   **293**
    BUSINESS INTELLIGENCE APPLICATIONS   294
INFORMATIONAL REFINEMENT   297
    DASHBOARDS VS. SCORECARDS   298
    EFFECTIVE PRESENTATION   299
THE NORMATIVE REPORT DESIGN FRAMEWORK   302

FUNCTION   302
FOCUS   303
METHOD   305

INDEX   **309**

BIBLIOGRAPHY   **315**

ENDNOTES   **318**

List of Illustrations

1.1 COMPONENTS OF KNOWLEDGE 7
1.2 CREATING EXPLICIT KNOWLEDGE 10
1.3 ANALYSIS OF DATA AS A KNOWLEDGE CREATION CONDUIT 11
1.4 THE RISK PROFILE MANAGEMENT PROCESS 30
2.1 KEY COMPONENTS OF THE DEFINITION OF RISK 49
2.2 CAUSAL VIEW OF RISK 50
2.3 RISK ESTIMATION PROCESS 51
2.4 HYPOTHETICAL RISK MAP 52
2.5 RESPONSE SELECTION 53
2.6 INTERDEPENDENCE OF RISK ACTIVITIES 56
2.7 INFORMATIONAL BASIS OF RISK PROFILE MANAGEMENT 64
2.8 THE COSO ENTERPRISE RISK MANAGEMENT FRAMEWORK 77
2.9 COSO RISK MEASUREMENT CONCEPTUALIZATION 78
2.10 ISO 31000 RISK MANAGEMENT: THE BUILDING BLOCKS 80
2.11 ISO 31000 RISK MANAGEMENT PROCESS: HIGH LEVEL VIEW 81
2.12 ISO 31000 RISK MANAGEMENT PROCESS 83
3.1 HYPOTHETICAL RISK PROFILE 89
3.2 RISK & COMPETITIVE ADVANTAGE 93
3.3 VARIANCE 99
3.4 DOWNSIDE VS. UPSIDE VARIANCE 101
3.5 UNIVARIATE FREQUENCY DISTRIBUTION 106
3.6 RESPONSE SURFACE 107
3.7 RISK RESPONSE ALTERNATIVES 110
3.8 INFORMATIONAL INPUTS & THEIR IMPACT 111
3.9 INFORMATIONAL BASIS OF RPM: LIKELIHOOD 115
3.10 INFORMATIONAL BASIS OF RPM: SEVERITY 116
3.11 SAMPLE ATTRIBUTE-BASED ASSESSMENT 118
4.1 GENERIC PROCESS OF RISK MODELING 121
4.2 PREDICTIVE ANALYTICAL PROCESS 123
4.3 DELPHI APPROXIMATIONS 124
4.4 HYPOTHETICAL BAYESIAN RISK NETWORK 125
4.5 PREDICTIVE ANALYTICS VS. DELPHI VS. BAYESIAN 126
4.6 LATENT CONSTRUCT MEASUREMENT 127

4.7 THE RISK PROFILE MANAGEMENT PROCESS — 131
6.1 GENERAL SYSTEM MODEL — 141
6.2 SYSTEM MODEL VS. RPM FRAMEWORK — 142
7.1 DATA WAREHOUSE VS. DATA MART — 155
7.2 ENTITY-RELATIONSHIP DATA MODEL — 156
7.3 RELATIONAL DATA MODEL — 157
7.4 OBJECT-ORIENTED DATA MODEL — 157
7.5 THE DATA-INFORMATION-KNOWLEDGE CONTINUUM — 160
7.6 DATA VALUE-ADD PROGRESSION — 161
7.7 FACTUAL VS. PROBABILISTIC DATA EXPLORATION — 164
7.8 DATABASE REPORRTING VS. ANALYSIS — 165
7.9 DATABASE EXPLORATION VENUES — 166
7.10 MULTI-SOURCE ANALYTICS AS A DRIVER OF UNIQUE KNOWLEDGE — 168
8.1 SAMPLE SCATTERPLOT — 179
8.2 STANDARD NORMAL DISTRIBUTION — 185
8.3 SAMPLE METADATA TEMPLATE — 190
8.4 USING METADATA TO ASSESS ANALYTIC PREPAREDNESS — 191
9.1 EXPLORATORY ANALYSES VS. ALL DATA ANALYSES — 194
9.2 EXPLORATORY DATA ANALYSES — 196
9.3 DESIRED VS. AVAILABLE DATA — 203
9.4 SAMPLE HISTOGRAM — 205
9.5 SAMPLE CORRELATION MATRIX — 220
9.6 NON-REDUNDANT ELEMENTS ONLY — 220
9.7 CORRELATION COEFFICIENT TYPES — 222
9.8 TWO-TAILED CORRELATIONS WITH SIGNIFICANCE TESTS — 223
9.9 CORRELATION & DEPENDENCE — 228
10.1 PREDICTIVE ANALYTICS — 240
10.2 STATISTICAL MODELING RATIONALE — 242
10.3 IMPACT-WEIGHTED MULTIVARIATE PREDICTIONS — 244
10.4 LINEAR VS. CURVILINEAR EFFECTS — 253
10.5 SUCCESSIVE APPROXIMATIONS AND THE DELPHI METHOD — 262
11.1 GENERALIZED TYPES OF EXPERIMENTAL TEST DESIGNS — 276
12.1 THE RPM ANALYTICAL PROCESS — 289
12.2 GENERAL TYPES OF UPDATABLE ANALYSES — 292
13.1 SCOPE VS. DETAIL — 299
13.2 SAMPLE SCORECARD — 302

Tables

2.1 SAMPLE LISTING OF RISK TYPES   60
2.2 CONTEXTUALIZING THE SAMPLE LISTING OF RISK TYPES   61
2.3 ALTERNATIVE FORMS OF RISK FINANCING   68
3.1 DOWNSIDE RISK TYPOLOGY   96
3.2 COMPETING LIKELIHOOD QUANTIFICATION APPROACHES   104
4.1 TYPES OF VALIDITY   129
6.1 SAMPLE ANALYTIC PLANNING TEMPLATE   143
7.1 CAUSALITY CRITERIA   150
7.2 CATEGORIES OF BUSINESS DATABASES   154
7.3 TYPES OF DATABASES   155
8.1 STRATIFIED SAMPLE SELECTION PROCESS   176
8.2 OUTLIER IDENTIFICATION PROCESS   182
8.3 MISSING DATA IMPUTATION: PHYSICAL REPLACEMENT OPTIONS   186
8.4 MISSING DATA IMPUTATION: NON-REPLACEMENT OPTIONS   187
9.1 EXPLORATORY DATA ANALYSIS PROCESS FOR RPM   197
9.2 COEFFICIENTS OF CORRELATION   219
9.3 INFORMATIONAL DOMAIN SPECIFICATION STRATEGIES   232
10.1 KEY MULTIVARIATE MODELING CONSIDERATIONS   245
10.2 THE DEGREE OF SIMILARITY MODELING PROCESS   249
10.3 THREE-TIER INDICATOR RELIABILITY ASSESSMENT   258
11.1 TEST DESIGN STEPS   275
12.1 UPDATE DECISION CRITERIA   294

1

The Art & Science of Knowing

There are some very hard to believe facts associated with folding an ordinary sheet of notebook paper. First, regardless of the size of a sheet, no one has been able to fold a sheet of paper more than twelve times[1]. However, what is even more extraordinary about paper folding is the height of the resultant stack. Starting with an appropriately sized sheet of ordinary notebook paper, folding it seven times (the number of folds once believed to constitute the upper limit) will result in a stack approximately equal in height to the thickness of an average notebook. Extra three folds will result in the stack height about the width of a hand (thumb included), and additional four (for a total of fourteen folds) would push the height of our stack to be roughly that of an average person. If we were to continue to fold our sheet of paper, the expected results become very hard to believe: Seventeen-fold would produce a stack the height of an average two story house; extra three folds (for a total of twenty) would yield a stack reaching approximately a quarter of the way up the Sears Tower. If folded over thirty times, the resultant stack would reach past the outer limits of Earth's atmosphere, and lastly, our ordinarily thin, albeit extraordinarily large in terms of area (to allow a large number of folds) sheet would produce a stack of paper reaching…all the way to the Sun. That is roughly 94 million miles!

For most of us, years of schooling imprinted our minds with a variety of abstract notions, while also conditioning our psyche to accept a considerable amount of intangible truths. So long as those scientific and other truths do not come in conflict with our "common sense" of reality, most of us are generally willing to accept even somewhat far-fetched claims. However, when that is not the case—that is, when a particular claim violates what we consider to be reasonable, the result is cognitive dissonance. We just can't accept a particular fact or a claim as being true. Even if the underlying rationale and the empirical method both seem acceptable and correct, it can be still very, very hard to believe a conclusion that "does not make sense". That is precisely the case with the paper folding exercise. It is an example of exponential growth, which is a phenomenon where the rate of growth rapidly increases as the quantity (e.g., the above stack of paper) gets larger. Since it is a well-defined mathematical property we can compute its values without the need for physical measurements, which is the reason we are able to estimate the height of the stack of paper, even though we are not physically able to fold a sheet of paper fifty times. I am going to venture to say that those of us who at some point in our educational journey were exposed to the notion of exponential growth found it to be intuitively clear and reasonable; furthermore, once properly explained, the computational steps also made sense, which is to say their logic does not clash with our view of the world. Yet when put to a bit of an extreme test, that otherwise acceptable concept can yield unacceptable conclusions. Folding a thin sheet of papers a relatively small number of times simply cannot result in such a staggeringly high stack…

This example underscores both the value and the challenge associated with using data analysis derived knowledge as the basis decision making. It is very easy to accept the findings which fall in line with our existing beliefs, though it could be argued that little incremental value comes out of such "discoveries". It is altogether a different story when findings contradict our a priori beliefs—Is there a problem with the data? Is the approach flawed? Are there any errors…? To be fair, data can be corrupted, an approach can be flawed and we all certainly make mistakes. At the same time, however, none of that could be the case—what then? Oftentimes, doubts linger and what could have become an inspiration for a competitively advantageous decision joins the repository of many other research initiatives, all dutifully written up, but never acted on.

Yet taking the leap of faith and acting in accordance with objectively validated insights can be quite beneficial. Much of information technology that permeates our professional and personal lives is "powered" by quantum

2

mechanical predictions; in fact, quantum theory is, in terms of the accuracy of its predictions, the most accurate scientific theory ever constructed[2]. At the same time, it is among the most bizarre, hard to believe frameworks in terms of its postulates. In quantum theoretical world objects can exist in two states or places simultaneously (a condition known as "superposition"), in addition to which, objects are also instantaneously "aware" of distant other objects (an effect known as "quantum teleportation"). It is akin to saying that a person can be simultaneously alive and dead and furthermore, that a person's physical existence is entangled with consciousness of others. What then determines whether someone is alive or dead? The act of looking, stipulates quantum mechanics. In other words, perception creates physical reality. Does that sound believable?

To Einstein these were "spooky interactions" which is a term he coined deriding the quantum theory. In fact, the great scientist spent more time trying to disprove the quantum theory than he did crafting his own theories of general and special relativity. But in the end, he failed. As much as it is hard to intuitively come to terms with the bizarre postulates of the quantum world, the equations describing its mechanics are extremely reliable. Microchip-powered computing devices, like the laptop on which I am typing this text, work undeniably well, because of the accuracy of quantum mechanical predictions, even though most of us have very hard time accepting the picture painted by the underlying theory.

Obviously, this is not a text on quantum mechanics or paper folding trivia. However, these two examples point to an interesting assertion: The believability of analytically derived explanations should not always be the ultimate determinant of whether or not we accept—and more importantly, act upon—the findings. This is not to say that we should totally disregard our intuition, for that would mean depriving ourselves of lifetime worth of accumulated, though not always well catalogued knowledge. Quite to the contrary—I am arguing that true edge producing knowledge needs to combine the elements of truths that might be intuitively obvious to us with those that may not make sense to us, but have been shown to be empirically true. In other words, why not try to get the best of both worlds?

Data, Knowledge & Decisions

As ably detailed by Quinn and his colleagues[3], success of organizations depends more on their intellectual and systems capabilities than physical assets. To a large degree, Quinn's conclusion is somewhat intuitively obvious: Physical assets are, for the most part, generic, thus it is the application or deployment of those assets that determines the overall success of organizations. Stated differently, it is the uniqueness of organizational "know-how", coupled with the ability to utilize that knowledge that are the greatest influencers of success. Hence it is of considerable importance to organizations to systematically develop competitively advantageous insights in a way that will aid their decision making processes.

It is not an easy task. Unlike the objectively measurable physical assets, knowledge is highly abstract and difficult to measure, both in terms of quality as well as quantity. In the organizational context, it is often either confounded with individuals or buried deep inside various reservoirs holding it. An even more fundamental challenge is that of knowing what we know, especially given the pervasiveness of the use of terms such as "data", "information", "facts", "insights" or "knowledge". When is what we know an inconsequential, as far as the ability to enhance the quality of decisions, informational tidbit and when is a true, difference making insight? The next section hopes to provide some clarification.

KNOWLEDGE

Plato[4] defined *knowledge* as "justified true belief." Oxford English Dictionary lists several different definitions of knowledge: 1. "expertise, and skills acquired by a person through experience or education; the theoretical or practical understanding of a subject", 2. "what is known in a particular field or in total; facts and information", and 3. "awareness or familiarity gained by experience of a fact or situation". Wikipedia offers probably the simplest definition, by equating knowledge with "what is known."

Oddly (in view of its 2,500 years or so vintage), Plato's definition of knowledge comes the closest to what it means to business decision making. In business in general, and risk management in particular, decision making is necessitated by plurality of alternatives—if there are no alternatives, defined here as substitutable courses of action, there are no decisions to be made. In view of that, knowledge can be construed as the degree of understanding (of relative advantages and disadvantages) of the competing options, or in Plato's terms, beliefs that are "justified and true" regarding the value of alternatives. The possession of such robust understanding leads to selecting the "best" alternative, or the option yielding the greatest net benefit[5]. Hence from the standpoint of risk management decisions, knowledge represents justified and true beliefs regarding the relative efficacy of competing courses of action.

Taking this line of reasoning a step further, knowing more will give rise to *informational advantage*, which is the ability to make more effective decisions stemming from better understanding of the potential outcomes of competing courses of action. In other words, deeper insights or better know-how on the part organizational risk management will contribute to the organization's competitiveness—in fact, under some circumstances, it could be a source of competitive advantage (a more in-depth description of the notions of "competition" and "competitive advantage" is offered in the *Risk Profile Measurement* chapter). However, in order to have that type of a profound impact, organizational knowledge has to exhibit several broadly defined characteristics—most notably it needs to be codifiable, teachable and systemic.

Codifiability of knowledge is its ability to objectively encode facts and inferences into clear behavioral guides. In a practical sense, it is a degree to which a particular set of insights or know-how can exist independently of those creating it. Examples of codifiable knowledge include multivariate statistical models-generated behavioral expectancies or propensities, such as the probability of adverse development of recently filed liability claims or the likelihood of securities or employment practices class action. On the other hand, risk manager's or claims adjuster's experience or intuition are not easily, if at all, codifiable. As discussed in the next section, not all knowledge can be encoded and as a result, communicated.

Teachability of knowledge reflects the degree to which it can be absorbed by the organization. In general, the more understandable and parsimonious the knowledge, the simpler it is to teach. That said, we sometimes do not draw a sufficiently clear line of demarcation between knowledge creation and its application, which is particularly the case in business analytics, where many potentially valuable insights are lost in the web of methodological complexities. In most circumstances, there is a significant difference between teaching how to conduct analyses and how to use the results, which is an important distinction explored in more detail in subsequent chapters. For now, let is suffice to say that insights communicated in a user-friendly format and dispensed in manageable quantities tend to be easy to absorb by the organization, which means that over the long haul will have more impact on decisions.

Lastly, knowledge has to be *systemic*, which is to say that it needs to permeate the organization. This is important simply because organizations are effectively systems of diverse functions that need to act in harmony to meet its stated objectives. For example, in order for the knowledge of expected future claim development to contribute to systematically reducing the total cost of risk, it needs to be made accessible (and taught) to multiple organizational functions, such as claims management, financial planning, human resources and others.

Components of Knowledge

Creation of knowledge will continue to be a largely human endeavor for the foreseeable future. I am not trying to say that information technology will not play a progressive bigger role in the development of organizational know-how; instead, I am trying to draw attention to an important distinction between *knowledge* and *information*, which are often used interchangeably (both notions are discussed in more detail in the *Understanding Data* chapter). Definitionally, information is best described as facts placed in a context, while knowledge is the sum of interpreted information—in other words, information constitutes input while knowledge is the final outcome. It means information is singular and for the most part non-evaluative (i.e., it contains no cause—effect delineation), while knowledge is cumulative and interpretive (i.e., observed outcomes are presented as results of specific actions). Hence, while information technology will certainly play an ever-increasing role in the generation and dissemination of information, the creation of decision-guiding, competitively advantageous knowledge is simply too complex, and to some degree too intangible to be automated, at least in the foreseeable future.

The cumulative character of knowledge gives rise to what is often called *explicit knowledge*, which is factual, objective and relatively easily codified and communicated. In essence, it is an analog to a database. The interpretive dimension, on the other hand, is evident in what is known as *tacit knowledge*. It is a subjective, hard to codify, teach and systematize though uniquely human aspect of knowing exemplified by skills, intuition and experience (hence the aforementioned intangibility of knowledge creation). In short, what we tend to regard as knowledge is essentially a product of the interplay between "hard facts" and "fungible interpretation", as shown below in Figure 1.1. Combining these two, quite different though equally important dimensions is the primary difficulty in automating the creation of knowledge processes, which is the reason for my earlier claim that the creation of knowledge will remain a largely human endeavor, at least in the foreseeable future.

Figure 1.1
Components of Knowledge

A somewhat different way of thinking about the building blocks of knowledge is to look at it from the standpoint of epistemology, which is a branch of philosophy concerned with the nature and scope of knowing. An epistemological definition points to four distinct types of knowledge: logical, semantic, systemic or empirical. Logical knowledge is the result of the understanding of how ideas relate to one another. Here, knowing manifests itself in applying accepted rules of logic, which stipulate additional truths. For example: All human beings are fallible. John is a human being, therefore, John is fallible. Semantic knowledge is the result of learning the meaning of words, which is simply the familiarity with definitions. The definition of epistemology mentioned earlier is an example of semantic knowledge. Systemic knowledge is the learning of a particular system, its symbols and their interpretations. For instance, one's mathematical skills are an example of systemic knowledge. Lastly, empirical knowledge is the learning resulting

7

from our senses. Much of the scientific knowledge falls under that umbrella—in the fact the scientific method discussed later relies heavily on empirically-derived understanding.

A yet another way of categorizing knowledge is to think of it in terms of a broadly defined purpose it serves, which can be either descriptive (also called declarative) vs. procedural. The former captures the essence of our understanding of "what is", while the latter encompasses our understanding of "how to" accomplish something. For example, knowing the frequency of certain types of loss-generating events and/or the severity of those events constitutes descriptive knowledge; knowing how to reduce the said frequency and/or severity exemplifies procedural knowledge. In the area of risk analytics, much of what falls under the umbrella of descriptive knowledge constitutes relatively generic information—the truly competitively advantageous insights usually exemplify procedural knowledge.

Knowledge Creation

How is knowledge created? Although specific mechanisms are probably too diverse and numerous to summarize here, knowledge creation can be either a conscious, end objective-guided endeavor or it can be a result of an unintended "accident". In other words, knowledge is created purposefully or incidentally. The former is quite familiar to most in the business world, as it is the primary mean of generating decision guiding insights in business. For instance, we notice a sudden upturn in the frequency of certain type of work related injuries, which then precipitates the question of "why". The process of answering this question is essentially the process of creating purposeful knowledge. On the other hand, the insight that ultimately led to the invention of the now-ubiquitous microwave oven was an unintended byproduct of unrelated research into physical properties of very short wavelengths, i.e., microwaves[6]. The researchers were not seeking to gain an understanding of the heating or cooking properties (they were researching radar properties of microwaves; in fact, the first commercially sold microwave oven was called Radar Range), and it was a pure accident that one of the researchers put a candy bar in his shirt pocket which began to melt as a result of direct exposure to microwave radiation…

Stories like the accidental microwave invention certainly stir our imagination, but, at least in business research, it is the often painstaking, systematic, purposeful pursuit of knowledge that can contribute to the creation and sustainment of competitive advantage. Stated differently, to be effective, analyses of business data should be directed toward answering specific questions. Thus as approached in this book, knowledge creation is a teleological[7] process which needs to be directed at a specific purpose to yield worthwhile results.

It all seems straightforward, though it is not. Most organizations are far more adept at capturing data than they are at turning it into decision aiding insights; in fact, the sheer volume and diversity of the available data can get in the way of using its informational content productively. Strategies often get lost in a sea of "interesting", albeit accidental findings generated and disseminated not because they support specific objectives, but simply because they are…well, interesting. More importantly, these often trivial informational pursuits tend to draw the same level of vigor (frankly, oftentimes even more as "interesting" tends to be more captivating than "important") as does the pursuit of insights to guide the firm's stated strategic goals. Hence in some instances it is not the scarcity but the overabundance of data that impedes the creation of competitively advantageous knowledge, which when coupled with ineffective information filtering processes can significantly diminish the potential value of corporate data.

And thus the challenge: To create hard to imitate knowledge base to serve as a foundation of sustainable competitive advantage, by means of injecting unique insights into the organization's decision-making processes. As pointed out earlier, it means pulling together of the two, frankly quite different dimensions of knowledge: explicit and tacit.

Starting with the former, the creation of a robust *explicit knowledge* reservoir requires the translation of data-derived information into higher level insights. This entails two somewhat different and temporally sequential steps. First is the informational reduction, which is a set of statistical procedures-based activities (discussed in more detail in subsequent chapters), designed to expressly differentiate between facts that are critical to reaching the stated strategic objectives and those that are not. The second step is that of *meta analyses,* which entail summarizing the critical, based on informational reduction results, but still too granular information into higher-order insights. The entire data—to explicit knowledge process is depicted in Figure 1.2

Figure 1.2
Creating Explicit Knowledge

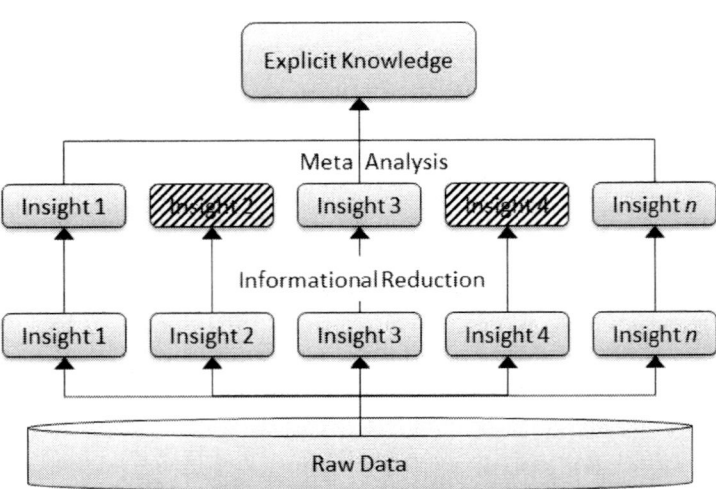

Explicit knowledge alone, however, rarely gives rise to competitive advantage because it is still devoid of experience based fact interpretation, thus it is usually not sufficiently indicative of the most advantageous courses of action. In other words, the absence of the experiential dimension, such as an experience in a particular industry to help contextualize company-specific loss experience, or hands-on claim management or loss prevention experience may both limit the potential applicability of the fact-only based explicit knowledge. This is particularly important considering that in many industries most of the competitors have access to a wide array of fundamentally the same information; hence, working from the same factual base, they are likely to arrive at similar insights, if their knowledge creation pursuits are limited to the explicit dimension of knowledge.

Adding the experiential or tacit component of knowledge into the knowledge creation mix helps to draw attention to what matters from a competitive standpoint. Thus to gain informational advantage over its competitors, an organization has to develop proprietary sources of factual information or find an effective method of "personalizing" its factual knowledge by combining it with the elements of *tacit knowledge*. There are numerous examples of successfully pursuing both alternatives. The world's largest retailer, Wal-Mart, in contrast to most of its competitors has consistently refused to sell its store movement data (i.e., sales data collected from the point-of-sale devices) to the outside syndicated information aggregators (most notably, AC Nielsen and Information Resources) to assure the uniqueness of its knowledge. The results are self-evident...On the other hand, Capital One Bank, working fundamentally with the same type of data as its competitors invested heavily in its own, proprietary data analytical processes (i.e., tacit knowledge) which enabled it to consistently deliver above average financial results. The competitive and other circumstances in which these two companies operate pushed them in somewhat different directions, but both organizations made the most of their circumstances, largely because they were purposeful and systematic.

Harnessing the value of tacit knowledge is in many regards more challenging as so much of it is subjective and difficult to codify. That said, a systematic process, framed in the larger context of risk analytics can serve as a conduit to extracting, normalizing and ultimately, incorporating the tacit dimension into the overall organizational knowledge base. The recommended process is depicted in Figure 1.3.

Figure 1.3
Analysis of Data as a Knowledge Creation Conduit

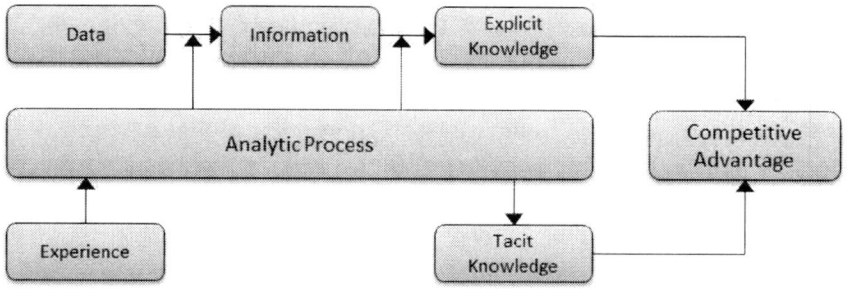

As suggested earlier and graphically shown in Figure 1.3, the broadly defined analytical process is a conduit to systematically transforming data into information and, ultimately, (explicit) knowledge. Furthermore, it is also as a source of the more experience-based tacit knowledge, which is important from the standpoint of maintaining the objectivity of the resultant insights. In other words, the data analytical skill set (*analytical process*), coupled with accumulated industry and related expertise (*experience*) support both the process of extracting explicit knowledge out of data (*data* → *information* → *explicit knowledge* progression) and the accumulation of tacit knowledge. The end goal of the knowledge creation efforts—which is sustainable *competitive advantage*—is the product of a unique combination of explicit and tacit knowledge at the organization level. In a conceptual sense, the entire process outlined above it is a reflection of the teleological nature of the business knowledge creation and accumulation: competitively useful knowledge creation is directed at a specific purpose, rather than "fishing" for whatever can be found in the seemingly endless ocean of data.

Theory or Data Driven?

How do we know that we know? Ascertaining the validity and reliability of what is considered "knowledge" is probably one of the oldest controversies in science. At issues here is not only the availability of objective evidence—i.e., knowledge, but also its believability. In other words, how do we separate facts from fiction? Consider the so-called "Galileo Affair[8]" to appreciate the potential difficulty of distinguishing between objectively verifiable facts and subjective beliefs. The Galileo Affair is anchored in the idea of empirically testing the key postulates of the heliocentric system proposed by Copernicus. As the inventor of telescope, Galileo was the first to be able to gather closer celestial observations and more precise measurements empirically verifying the accuracy of Copernican thesis. Yet lacking an appreciable understanding of optics, many of Galileo's contemporaries were skeptical of his findings, suspecting the apparent celestial phenomenon to be tricks of the lenses. And so in their eyes, a great scientist was a heretic.

Obviously, our understanding of the world in which we live has increased immensely over the nearly four centuries that elapsed since Galileo's struggles. Yet as we continue to push the limits of our knowledge, we continue to struggle with the same basic task of being able to differentiate between objectively verifiable knowledge and subjective beliefs.

From the standpoint of philosophy of science, the creation of objective knowledge can be either *theory* or *data laden*. The former is carried out by means of hypothesis testing, which is a method of empirically assessing specific theory-derived claims. It means that theory laden knowledge creation springs from the foundation provided by a particular conceptual and rational paradigm—and, it is limited to testing specific claims of predictions derived from that framework. It also means that results of empirical analyses are interpreted within the confines of the theory being tested. There is a certain amount of intuitive appeal associated with that stance, but more importantly, it is supported by neuroscience studies detailing the "mechanics" of the functioning of the brain. These studies suggest that cognitive processing of information requires that our brains hold some beliefs about reality, as absent those, we would be unable to learn from the available information[9]. In other words, the human knowledge creation process appears to be somewhat confirmatory, i.e., theory laden, in nature.

In the way of contrast, the *data laden* approach assumes no existence of an underlying theory and instead approaches the analysis of the available data as a purely exploratory endeavor. Hence the resultant knowledge is built "from scratch", as it is cobbled together from individual insights found while exploring the available data. The data laden approach certainly has merit, but at the same time it is more likely (than the theory laden approach) to be blotted by data imperfections, which is a significant drawback, both in science and in business.

Business analysts need to carefully consider the strengths and weaknesses of these two competing knowledge creation frameworks. The theory laden method requires the availability of a somewhat "mature"—i.e., testable theoretical framework. It is important to keep in mind that a handful of loosely stated suppositions or insights generated by past analyses do not necessarily constitute a "theory", at least not one that can offer an adequate explanation and/or prediction of the phenomenon of interest. On the other hand, often there can be multiple competing theoretical frameworks available, which can be confusing, to say the least. This brings us back to the earlier-made distinction between "purposeful" and "incidental" knowledge. Directing knowledge creation efforts toward clearly stated objectives, analysts can usually take advantage of conceptually robust and empirically validated conceptual frameworks emanating from a long list of business-related disciplines, such as psychology, economics and neuroscience. In fact, the risk analytical framework outlined in this book makes a heavy use of several such frameworks, most of all the persuasion theory, the theory of reasoned action (both "imported" from psychology) and the equimarginal principle ("borrowed" from economics).

The challenges faced by the data laden approach to knowledge creation are more formidable, which is a result of the combination of heightened dependence on the accuracy of data associated with this approach and the inherent imperfections of most databases. As it is intuitively obvious, greater dependence on open-ended exploration of data will create significantly more stringent data quality requirements. In purely exploratory (i.e., open-ended) data analyses, the absence of a supporting theoretical framework makes the task of differentiating between actual and spurious relationships particularly difficult, at times even impossible. Hence the question asked earlier—how do we know that we know?—becomes particularly difficult to answer.

Especially important to the assessment of the overall informational correctness of data are the notions of quality and representativeness. The *quality of data* manifests itself through data accuracy and completeness. The former represents the degree to which the coded values comprising a dataset are error-free, while the latter communicates the availability of actual (as opposed to "missing") data values for all records contained in a file. *Representativeness of data*, on the other hand, is an outgrowth of the inherent "incompleteness" of virtually all business databases. Even the largest data reservoirs contain, in effect, only a subset of all events of a particular type (such as workplace accidents or insurance claims), which then raises the question: How representative is a particular sample of the overall universe? However, unlike the previously discussed data quality which tends to limit the reliability of overall findings, the representativeness of data plays a role in the generalizability of insights.

All of these considerations can be distilled to a few key takeaways. First and foremost, of the two competing knowledge creation approaches, data laden knowledge creation is significantly more demanding in terms of data quality and representativeness. Hence, relying on this approach to the creation of business knowledge will result in a higher likelihood of arriving at erroneous conclusions, when the available data is imperfect either in terms of quality or representativeness. This limitation is well illustrated by the drawbacks of automated data mining applications frequently used in conjunction with large event-tracking databases. It is one thing to flag statistically significant effects, it is yet another (and a significantly more difficult task) to reliably differentiate between persistent relationships and spurious ones.

Theory laden knowledge creation is certainly not immune to the dangers presented by poor data quality, but it is significantly less impacted by it, for a number of reasons. First, virtually no theory is ever validated or refuted on the basis of a single test, or even a handful of tests, which obviously reduces the danger associated with a single, low quality dataset. Second, a single study typically tests multiple hypotheses derived from the theory of interest and under most circumstances, not all of those hypotheses would be impacted in the same fashion by data imperfections. Perhaps most importantly, theory laden approach takes fuller advantage of the cumulative nature of knowledge creation, by offering a way of leveraging previously uncovered insights and building on that base with the help of additional analyses.

KNOWLEDGE AS A STRATEGIC ASSET

An organization that "knows" how to produce something at a lower cost than other producers will enjoy cost advantage over its competitors. If its goal is to grow market share, the cost advantage will give it the ability to do so without sacrificing profitability, or it can simply enjoy higher margins and use the resultant profits elsewhere. Either way, being able to make the same product for less is clearly advantageous—does the same reasoning hold true for an organization that knows how to reduce its total cost of risk? I believe so.

From an accounting standpoint, the cost of risk represents an expense. Insurance premiums, which are a common component of the overall cost of risk, have no appreciable residual value[10] past their effective time horizon, nor do most other risk financing mechanisms. The same generally holds true for captive insurance[11], though it is possible, at least in principle, to structure a captive to be a profit-seeking entity. Of course, contractual risk transfer costs are not the only risk-related expenses; in fact, for some companies that particular aspect of the total cost of risk represents a relatively minor portion of the total. Organizations in heavy manufacturing, retail and hospitality industries, to name a few, employ large numbers of workers engaged in activities which are conducive to physical injuries—many of the larger firms in those industries spend tens of millions of dollars annually on work-related accidents. These costs are as much a part of the total cost of risk as commercial insurance premiums. And furthermore, these costs usually have a direct, and obviously adverse impact on earnings. Hence it follows that knowing how to systematically and sustainably reduce the total cost of risk will enhance the organization's competitiveness.

Much of the decision-aiding knowledge comes from insights derived from event-tracking data, which encompasses a wide range of business-to-consumers and business-to-business interactions[12]. Thanks in a large part to the brisk growth of electronic transaction processing (ETP) systems, event-tracking data became ubiquitous over the past couple of decades. Starting with the introduction and subsequent proliferation of bar code-reading electronic scanners (first used in an Ohio supermarket in 1974), followed by digitization of inter- and intra-company record-creating events and further fueled by rapid advances in computing and data storage technologies, the ETP systems now generate enormous amounts of relatively accurate and detailed data describing just about every aspect of business, risk management included.

ETP was taken to a new level by the explosive growth of internet-based connectivity, which contributed not seen before volumes of event-tracking information. In addition, it also created a natural venue for broader data cross-pollination, by enabling organizations to more readily gain access to broader swaths of data from the outside.

Another important aspect of the wide spread adoption of ETP as the primary mode of processing business transactions has been the commoditization of the resultant data. Stated differently, most organizations competing in a given industry have comparable data assets, hence it follows that any cross-organization data-related knowledge differences are most likely a function of data analytical advantages. Just about every organization has lots of data, but some are simply better at squeezing competitively advantageous insights out of it.

It seems fair to say that, at an organization level, data crunching capabilities evolve primarily in response to organizational priorities and the growth in the availability of data. It follows that as more data becomes available, data crunching capabilities of organizations will also steadily expand. However, since the expansion of data analytic capabilities is also contingent on organizational priorities, not all companies will develop at the same pace. In the end, a common pool of data brought about by the proliferation of electronic transaction processing systems (such as computerized casualty claim processing systems) will bring about some common-to-all, generic data analytical capabilities, while at the same time creating competitive disparity in terms of more advanced data analytical competencies.

This trend is particularly evident in the area of marketing promotion evaluation. The vast majority of organizations that have access to the requisite data will typically also have "basic" data analytical capabilities, usually built around data summarization and reporting. Chances are that risk managers at firms competing in the same industry are looking at very similar claims reports. Much of that basic informational parity can be attributed to the proliferation of third-party developed reporting applications, such as the widely-used "business intelligence" tools offered by a number of different vendors, such as Business Objects, Cognos or MicroStrategy.

By all accounts, the convergence of wide-spread data availability and reporting capabilities should have produced a leveled informational playing field—in other words; most firms competing in a particular area ought to have comparable informational competencies. Yet, that is not the case. In virtually all industries only a handful of firms are able to consistently use data—readily available to most—to their advantage. To paraphrase an old cliché: Most companies are data-rich, but (still) information-poor. So even though data is accessible to the vast majority of organizations, it tends to widen the competitive divide rather than narrowing it. As discussed in a growing number of popular business texts, such as Davenport and Harris' *Competing on Analytics,* Levitt and Dubner's *Freakonomics,* Ayres' *Super Crunchers,* or Baker's *The Numerati,* advanced analytical "know-how" has become one of the key determinants of firms' marketplace competitiveness.

As noted earlier, in the knowledge-intensive environment, informationally competent firms are able to consistently outperform their competitors, primarily because they are able to make better use of organizational resources. Whether it is better understanding of consumers' needs and preferences, a more accurate assessment of the impact of competitive actions or more reliable estimation of likelihood and severity of major risk exposures, better information typically leads to better decisions. Knowing less, on the other hand, tends to introduce an element of randomness into the organization's decision making process (as the shortage of robust information necessitates guessing), which over the long run translates into a more uneven performance, often reflected in more volatile stock. And last but not least, informational competency enables organizations to take a more proactive decision making stance, which is generally viewed as a prerequisite to both winning and maintaining market leadership. The lack of reliable decision insights tends to impose a more reactive decision making mode, which tends to force organizations into playing catch-up with their better informed rivals.

It is important to note that persistent informational deficiency does not just negatively impact the organization's performance—it may actually pose a threat to its very survival. The steadily accelerating pace of globalization coupled with the broadening trend of de-regulation continues to stiffen the competitiveness of markets, which in effect is raising the cost of poor decisions. Under most circumstance, there is simply too little time and too much competition to practice "trial and error" decision making.

As demonstrated by the likes of Microsoft, Proctor & Gamble or Marriott, timely, accurate and unique business insights are among the key pathways to sustainable competitive advantage. IBM takes those ideas even further, by building mathematical models of its employees, with the goal of improving productivity and automating management. The degree to which market leaders are able to consistently outperform their competitors is now inextricably tied to their proficiency in translating large volumes of data into decision-guiding insights. The speed and precision with which an organization can translate raw data into decision-guiding insights determines whether it will be able to pinpoint competitive weaknesses and to identify the most advantageous courses of action, or be among the first to spot and take advantage of emerging trends and opportunities. And as the marketplace competition continues to heat up, fueled by growing privatization, accelerating product innovations and the widening trend of deregulation, it is not just the success, but even the very survival of organizations that is becoming increasingly more dependent on their ability to make sound and effective decisions. In a sense, all organizations are now in the information business but their competencies in that area are highly uneven.

In view of the enormous scope and the depth of what can be included under the broad label of "business analytics", this book does not pretend to offer a "one size fits all" solution that could be applied to all data analysis-related business problems. My focus is on one particular aspect of business informatics: risk analytics. More specifically, it is on delineating a clear, operationalizable process of using the readily available data for the purpose of developing cost-effective methods of protecting earnings of non-financial organizations. A lot has been written in the area of quantitative credit and market risk, but disproportionately little effort has been put into the development of similarly robust analytical frameworks in the area of strategic and operational risk. The goal of this book is to contribute toward filling that gap.

An old Taoist proverb teaches that "a journey of a thousand miles begins with a single step"; here, the journey toward the development of a robust analytical framework starts with an explicit recognition of the tacit differences separating raw data, information and finally, decision-aiding knowledge.

FROM DATA TO INFORMATION TO KNOWLEDGE

Although often used interchangeably, the notions of *data, information* and *knowledge* all convey fundamentally different meaning. From the standpoint of decision making utility, data is potential information—information is potential knowledge—and knowledge is potential competitive advantage. Implicit in these differences is a tacit value creation progression, where the initially low value *raw* data is being transformed into higher value information, and ultimately into the "finished product", which usually takes the form competitively advantageous knowledge. Hence the notions of data, information and knowledge are all linked together by the value-adding transformation of the low impact, generic commodity (data) into high value, decision-aiding corporate asset (knowledge). The earlier mentioned cross-firm invariance in informational proficiency is in itself a manifestation of differences in firms' analytic capabilities. An analytically proficient organization has the requisite skills and processes allowing it to reliably and consistently turn the competitively generic data into competitively unique and advantageous knowledge, while an analytically deficient organization lacks either the necessary skills or processes. Hence the attainment of informational proficiency is rooted in the development of a *knowledge creation process* as the primary conduit to the establishment of a fact-based decision making framework.

Within the confines of business—and specifically, the management of risk, the knowledge creation process is defined as a set of operationally-clear data analytical activities aimed at extracting unique, competitively advantageous insights out of the otherwise generic raw data. The operationally-clear data analytical activities are further defined as *specific* statistical techniques or computational algorithms[13] offering the most effective and efficient means of transforming specific types of data into well-defined decision inputs. As implied in the above definitions, the data analytical process makes an extensive use of a variety of quantitative techniques, with the goal of bringing about edge-producing insights, not readily available to others in the marketplace. Culled together into a single reservoir, the collection of these insights comprises the organizational knowledge base, which is an increasingly important component of organizational equity. As it is intuitively obvious, the quality of the organizational knowledge base is highly dependent on the robustness of the process producing it, which as discussed later, is one of the primary drivers of cross-firm informational inequalities. Perhaps less intuitively obvious is that the ultimate measure of its efficacy is the degree to which the results attributed to that knowledge contribute to the establishment or maintenance of sustainable competitive advantage.

Some of the most revolutionary and admired companies, including General Electric, Wal-Mart, Microsoft, Google or Amazon can attribute much of their success to informational proficiency and the impact it has had on their decision making. Although operating in vastly different industries and governed by considerably dissimilar operating models, these organizations nonetheless have one thing in common: They excel at extracting knowledge out of data and using it to their advantage. In fact, in most industries, knowledge leaders are also performance leaders, because knowing more means making better decisions in anything from resource allocation to opportunity identification. It is important, however, to consider their informational proficiency in the confines of their respective industries to account for cross-industry data inequalities. Some sectors of the economy, such as retailing, financial services or hotel and hospitality are event-tracking data-richer than some other ones, such as energy or materials. (This difference is primarily due to the dominant transaction type distinctiveness—e.g., retail entails business-to-consumer sales of specific items, while the materials industry is most often characterized by bulk business-to-business sales.)

In addition to data availability inequalities, the individual segments of the economy are also characterized by dissimilar levels of competitive intensity. Retail, hospitality, consumer package goods, financial services or gaming and entertainment sectors tend to be among the most competitive, in terms of the sheer number of firms offering directly substitutable products. Operating in more competitively intense environments results in firms having a greater incentive to invest early and invest more in data-supported decision-aiding infrastructure. Not surprisingly, the best known and probably the most compelling and talked about examples of unique knowledge-driven competitive advantage come from those industries. Household names, including Wal-Mart, Capital One, Proctor & Gamble or Marriott became recognized performance leaders in their respective industries as a direct consequence of first becoming data-based knowledge leaders. These companies had the foresight to invest in the development of superior business intelligence systems and also had the discipline to make objective information the bedrock of their decision making. They have been able to consistently outperform their competitors because they are in a position to better read the marketplace and make more effective use of their resources. To them, as well as a host of other, analytically-advanced data users, informational proficiency simply diminishes the amount of guesswork in such critical areas as pricing,

20

merchandising, promotional allocation or new product design, which offers ample competitive cushion to knowledge-enabled firms.

It is remarkable that in spite of the compelling evidence pointing to significant competitive benefits associated with superior, fact-based knowledge, so many organizations continue to bet their future on intuition of individual decision makers. Obviously, there is value in the accumulated experience, but its impact can be considerably more pronounced when coupled with broader learnings stemming from objective data. The goal of building a robust organizational knowledge base is not to replace the decision maker, but rather to enhance his/her efficacy by systematically reducing the level of uncertainty inherent in virtually all decisions. Knowing more enables one to spot and take quicker and fuller advantage of emerging marketplace opportunities and it is well-known that the "first mover" advantage often translates into higher profits (which is an obvious consequence of no or very few competitors). And last, but certainly not least: Superior knowledge is also more difficult to replicate by the competition than other sources of competitive advantage. Successful products can be copied relatively quickly, just as eye-catching promotional campaigns can be mimicked and winning strategies imitated, but because superior information is the "invisible" force behind better products or more effective campaigns, it is extremely difficult for others to replicate. Not surprisingly, firms that mastered turning data into better decisions continue to outpace their peers.

Sources of Proficiency

Informational competency is rarely, if ever, a product of an accident. Its genesis can be usually traced to careful planning of data capture/acquisition, strong execution of data analytical strategies and disciplined, system-wide embrace of fact based decision making. It all translates into a well-defined set of "hard" and "soft" assets. In terms of the former, superior knowledge requires robust computer hardware and software, both of which are needed to support data capture or acquisition, compilation and the initial processing of the accumulated data as well as the subsequent in-depth analyses. The latter entails the availability of an appropriate data analytical skill set, without which, even the "best of breed" hardware and software will not catapult the organization to informational competency. In other words, it is entirely possible that an organization could make substantial investments in information technology and still only keep up with the competition. That is because getting ahead of the competition in terms of decision-aiding knowledge—i.e., gaining and sustaining informational, and ultimately, competitive advantage—demands looking beyond the "common-to-many" data analytic mindset in search of unique, advantage creating insights. It means pursuing a more ambitious, forward-looking informational vision.

But what does a "forward-looking informational vision" mean? In broad, conceptual terms it amounts to looking at a right problem in a right way. In more precise analytical terms, it is simply the creativity surrounding the analysis of the available data.

Knowledge leaders work at being at the forefront of informational proficiency by molding data to questions posed by critical business challenges, rather allowing computational convenience to dictate what type of information is extracted from the data on hand. They seek specific, decision-aiding insights into such key competitive edge producing problems as quantification of incremental sales or revenue impact of competing price and promotion strategies. They understand that in many regards, the pursuit of business knowledge is the antithesis of mass-producing generic reports that capture every imaginable nuance and detail contained in the raw data, while answering few if any of the outcome-deciding questions. That is why organizations that ultimately become performance leaders have the drive, conviction and skills to enable them to leave the comfort of the "tried and true" traditional—i.e., generic—data reporting and analyses to look for answers not yet found by their competitors. They are not satisfied with knowing as much as their competitors—instead, they search for unique, competitive edge producing insights. That, in a nutshell, is the essence of a "forward-looking informational vision."

Similar to other mold-breaking behaviors, analytic innovation has its own share of impediments that need to be overcome. Probably the most significant, at least from the behavior-changing standpoint is the organization's ability to sharpen its informational focus. In short, there is a fundamental difference between the *availability* and *applicability* of information. This distinction is important when thinking about data analysis—i.e., information creation—vs. data usage—i.e., information deployment. In principle, edge-producing analytics entail the inclusion of all available data, but the effective use of the resultant insights is contingent on focusing on only the sub-set of all available knowledge that is directly related to the decision at hand. Quite often, to know more at the decision time demands "setting aside" the bulk of the available information. Frankly, this is among the reasons the previously discussed broad-base reporting tends to be an ineffective decision aid. Organizations that become knowledge leaders cultivate not only robust

22

knowledge creation, but also rational and disciplined information usage guidelines. In a nutshell, making better decisions calls for specific, decision-related set of insights—everything else, interesting or not, is superfluous to that process.

It is a lot easier said than done, though. Many organizations' MIS/IT functions are permeated by the "volume production" mentality, which usually manifests itself in a string of detailed reports that overwhelm most, while informing only a few. It is the unspoken, though enduring belief that generating large volumes of information represents a "return" on the often hefty data infrastructure expenditures. In one form or another, the emphasis on volume is quite common, which is in a large part due to the often significant divide separating those who create information from those ultimately using it. This analyst—user divide is one of the reasons that the often significant investments in database and reporting technologies rarely translate into noticeable marketplace benefits. Stated differently, technologically advanced database management systems (DBMS) can be a source of informational parity, but not of competitively advantageous knowledge. This is a critical distinction and one of the key reasons behind the development of the analytical process outlined in this book.

In a strange sort of a way, the trend toward DBMS application standardization is to some degree "responsible" for the low business impact of many of these often pricey data management systems. The ever more robust capabilities of the off-the-shelf applications along with their progressively greater ease of usage, vis-à-vis the mounting technological challenges of the custom-built data processing solutions[14] have led to the virtual disappearance of the latter. Though otherwise a very positive development, the widespread adoption of generic decision support systems also carries with it some not-so-positive consequences, such as the informational conversion. Simply put, similar (at times, identical) data combined with generic data management and analysis systems often lead to very similar informational bases, quite unintentionally "shared" by organizations competing in a given industry. In the end, multiple firms competing for more-or-less the same customers and offering functionally very similar products often end up trying to out-wit each other with the help of fundamentally the same information.

Still, as mentioned earlier, a relatively small but highly successful segment of companies have found a way to consistently extract competitively unique insight out of the otherwise generic data. Their data and data management systems are usually quite similar to their competitors', but their knowledge creation is typically far ahead of the rest. The key to those organizations' success lies in how they approach the task of mining data. Unlike their less able peers, the analytically-proficient firms tend to look beyond the *retrospective* (i.e., a detailing of past results), metric-centric report generation, instead focusing on *prospective* (projections supporting future decisions), business issue-centric and decision-directing insights. Reflecting fundamentally different informational paradigms, the retrospective and prospective data analytical postures differ on a number of key dimensions, with the two most important being the degree of informational specificity, or the volume of the resultant information.

It is axiomatic that the more tailored the information is to the business problem at hand and the specifics of the organization, the more it will benefit the organization's decision making. Particularly, in order for data analyses to make positive contributions to the firm's success, its outcomes have to be objectively evaluative of competing courses of action. This means that the resultant knowledge should be sufficient to point the decision maker in the direction of the greatest anticipated benefit. Although it seems like a simple enough task, making this conceptual goal an operational reality can be complex. The reasons behind the complexity are rather apparent: Many of the "traditional" data analytic techniques are ill-suited to the realities of modern event-tracking databases and the informational demands the fact-based decision making. As shown throughout this book, some of the more basic techniques, such as statistical significance testing or impact (i.e., lift) quantification, are at odds with the intended use of the resultant insights—in other words, usage limitations imposed by computational processes conflict with the intended or desired business applications. Some other techniques, such as experimentation, are not per se at odds with business applications, but their usability limits are often outstretched by informational demands placed on them.

The area demanding perhaps the most fundamental re-evaluation is the broadly defined results or outcomes reporting. Virtually all organizations rely on tabulating and trending their period-by-period revenues and expenses, which are often "sliced and diced" in a myriad of ways. Although it is certainly important to keep abreast of historical performance metrics, this information is of little help in forward-looking decision making. Choosing among competing courses of action, such as competing risk financing alternatives, requires the decision maker to be able to quantify option-specific expected impact. It ought to be done in a way that will enable the decision maker to estimate the net benefit associated with each option. Stated differently, making better choices demands objective estimates of *cause-*

attributable effects, which is the ultimate measure of the *worthiness* of individual, competing alternatives. This is fundamentally different then topline cost or aggregate outcome based comparison, hence a closer look seems warranted.

Cause-Attributable Effect

Basic reporting is best exemplified by what has come to be known as *management dashboards*, which are reader-friendly, graphics-intensive[15] summarizations of key performance indicators. These reports are typically built around outcome tabulations, such as frequency and severity of certain types of losses aided by side-by-side comparisons, with metrics of interest typically broken down by type or geography. Management dashboards are clearly beneficial to decision makers insofar as they can—if well designed— present a relatively comprehensive snapshot of specific aspects of business, in a highly parsimonious format. The vast majority of dashboards, however, tend to be inconclusive. They focus on easy to measure outcomes, such frequency of the total cost, while failing to address the underlying *causes*. This is a considerable limitation. Most losses can have numerous causal explanations, which means that knowing which—if any—of those factors had a measurable impact on the outcome of interest is quite important to future risk mitigation and cost containment efforts.

To be of more benefit to their users, management dashboards should be built around *effect attribution*. In terms of the previously mentioned knowledge creation continuum, knowing the magnitude of the impact associated with specific causes will arm the decision makers with future action guiding knowledge by linking specific outcomes with the most important causes. It is, however, considerably more complex methodologically. It also represents a shift in information generation philosophy: The traditional "observable outcome oriented reporting" is focused on churning out reports encompassing all that *can be known*, while the "cause-attributable effect quantification focused reporting" advocated here is focused on specific insights into *critical to know* areas.

In practice, the difference between these two methodologically and substantively distinct result measurement approaches translates into two fundamentally dissimilar sets of activities: The former are typically built around simple metric-by-metric tabulation and summarization of aggregate results, while the latter emphasize translating of large volumes of either inconclusive or incomplete pieces of data into probabilistic cause—effect estimates. From the analytical standpoint, the observable outcome based reporting is computationally straightforward and nowadays the task is almost always handled by highly automated, functionally elegant data reporting software packages. The opposite is true for effect attribution based reporting, which demands highly involved, often complex and manual statistical modeling preceded by a considerable amount of data preparation. Although some parts of the requisite process are prone to standardization (hence this book), cause—effect estimation is considerably more effort and expertise intensive. The payback however, as illustrated later in this book, can be substantial.

Volume

The volume of information also matters. Interestingly, more often than not there tends to be an inverse relationship between the sheer amount of information and its business utility. This may sound counterintuitive, particularly considering our enduring belief that it is better to know more rather than less. The pitfall in this line of thinking, however, is the implicit assumption that more information translates into deeper knowledge. This is simply not true, mainly because a considerable amount of the available information often has very little to do with a particular business decision (or any decision, for that matter). For instance, the decision as to which of several competing risk financing alternatives should be selected requires an objective assessment of the net present value of each option. Other information, such as the last year's claims trends or cross risk type cost distribution comparisons might be deemed "interesting", but ultimately will offer little-to-no help in identifying the most economically appropriate option. In short, one can have lots of information but little-to-no knowledge. It follows that to yield the maximum benefit, information creation needs to be rooted in the give-and-take considerations of quality over quantity and need-directed problem solving over propagating spurious informational details. Frankly, it is counterproductive to disseminate interesting but not decision aiding informational tidbits, simply because processing it takes time and attention away from the task at hand, while making no substantive contributions to decisions at hand.

From the viewpoint of science, there is nothing new about the notion of less being more. As one of the key tenets of scientific inquiry, this idea traces its philosophical roots to Ockham's Razor[16], which is a centuries-old axiom guiding the process of scientific theory building. Better known as the *principle of parsimony*, this basic "keep it simple" prescription tells us that the best explanations are those that involve the fewest number of concepts or informational details. A business decision maker will benefit much more from a relatively few, but highly action-directing insights than from a large number of mostly inconclusive and often unrelated details.

This is not to say that whatever information is not applicable to an issue at hand should be discarded—quite to the contrary, more effort should be put into cataloging and meta analysis as the means of making effective use of all informational assets (more on those in later chapters). Of the two, the latter can be particularly beneficial, though it is rarely used in applied business research. Operationally, *meta analysis* is data about data, which in essence is the exploration of results of data analysis in search of underlying patterns and other communalities. It can be particularly beneficial to database analyses because it offers a robust and an objective method of summarizing the often quite voluminous basic insights. It can serve both as the means of uncovering of new insights as well as succinctly communicating of the otherwise excessively detail findings.

Clearly, informational excellence can be quite beneficial to firms' economic well-being which brings us to an obvious question: What is required of an organization for it to develop a high level of informational proficiency? Or, stated differently: What separates informationally-advanced organizations from the rest of the pack?

Impact of Analytics

Informational competency is rarely, if ever, a result of data access inequalities. As previously discussed, most of the same-industry organizations today have access to more-or-less that same type of raw data, largely due to the fact that the vast majority of it comes from functionally generic sources[17]. For instance, the bulk of Wal-Mart's data comes from its point-of-sale systems which are functionally quite the same—i.e., capture the same type of basic data—as are those used by K-Mart or other major discounters (after all, these are standard applications sold and developed by outside vendors). In that sense, Wal-Mart's informational superiority should not be attributed to (raw) data inequalities. The previously-noted standardization of electronic transaction processing systems just about guarantees that most competitors in an industry will have access to the same types of event-tracking data.

That is not to say that there are no instances of firms enjoying access to unique sources of data. A handful of organizations (the names of which I am, unfortunately, not at liberty to disclose) supplement their worker compensation claims data files with not only the basic employee demographics, which is relatively common, but with in-depth behavioral and attitudinal profiles collected with the help of detailed employee surveys. Hence, not only do these organizations have at their disposal the "standard" event-tracking claim details passively collected by claims management systems, but they are able to augment it with behavioral and attitudinal data. Of course, taking that extra step is often contingent on highly specialized skill set, which means that organizations pursuing the collection of such data are typically already far more informationally proficient than their competitors. In other words, the capture of the "special purpose data" is more a result of informational competency than its precursor.

Another possible source of informational proficiency could be the broadly defined data infrastructure, which is comprised of data storage as well as data processing hardware and software. Probably even more than data access, the data processing infrastructure is extremely unlikely to be the source of informational advantage for two basic reasons: First, over the last several years the widespread standardization of warehousing and reporting applications has led to a certain degree of functional conversion, which means that differently branded applications are nonetheless quite similar in terms of their capabilities. Secondly, even the largest organizations more-or-less abandoned the earlier trend of developing from scratch their uniquely own (and thus different) decision support systems in favor of standardized, outside vendor-supplied solutions. In other words, there is little-to-no cross-user infrastructure differentiation.

In the end, neither the mere access to raw data, nor the availability of a "state-of-the-art" data processing infrastructure are likely to be a source of a sustainable informational advantage. This leaves only two other plausible explanations: 1. organizational culture, and 2. the data analytical *know-how*.

Culture, defined here as the institutionalization of fact-based decision making, holds quite a bit of intuitive appeal as the source of the cross-firms knowledge disparity. After all, if an organization does not value information, in the sense of embracing data-driven decision making, it could not possibly develop a superior data-based knowledge foundation. However, one could also argue the flip side of this reasoning, namely, that it is unrealistic to expect a rational firm to value anything prior to the existence of convincing evidence. Since both sides of this argument have merit, this has the characteristics of the proverbial "chicken and egg" circular argument, with no clear way of settling "which came first". However, looking to organizational culture as the source of informational proficiency implicitly assumes that the organization has the skills required to extract uncommon insights out of the otherwise common data. And this indeed could be the crux of the problem—many firms do not.

To put it simply, the biggest single source of informational advantage is the superior knowledge creation know-how. Overall, the most significant factor that consistently explains why some data-rich organizations are also knowledge-rich while other, equally data-rich and technologically-enabled firms are comparatively knowledge-poorer is the advanced data analytical skill set of the former. At the time when data is ubiquitous and the basic data processing increasingly informationally-generic, it is the ability to go beyond the basic data crunching functionality that is the key determinant of the value of the resultant information.

Though manifestly important, the knowledge creation know-how is arguably the least developed and certainly the least formalized aspect of the new, digital world. Many will balk at this statement, as after all, quantitative data analysis itself is a well-established, long-standing field of study. And indeed it is, in the academic sense. However, as shown throughout this book, it is not in the practical, particularly business sense. Similarly to a number of other fields of study, quantitative methods tend to be inwardly oriented and primarily focused on methods, rather than outcomes. Those trained in it tend to acquire substantial amounts of domain-specific knowledge, but very little understanding of the contextualizing influences of different data types or business objectives. Analysts' understanding of even the most rudimentary characteristics of modern business databases tends to lag far behind their comprehension of the specific inner-workings of the individual quantitative analysis methods, which is to some degree a reflection of many academics' limited exposure to the more complex business data sources. Frankly, that poses a problem as extracting unique and competitively advantageous insights is as dependent on the in-depth knowledge of statistical techniques as it is on the comparable knowledge of data.

THE PURSUIT OF KNOWLEDGE

In his 1969 book, *The Age of Discontinuity; Guidelines to Our Changing Society*, Peter Drucker wrote about knowledge-based economy, which is the use of knowledge technologies (e.g., data management and reporting; predictive analytics) to produce economic benefits. The essence of Drucker's argument was that industrial society was being gradually replaced by information society, where the creation, diffusion and integration of information became the thrust of political, cultural and business activities. His conception of knowledge economy, as the economic equivalent of information society, was one where wealth was created through the exploitation of understanding, rather than the traditional means of land, labor and capital. Some of the most admired companies today, such as Google, Microsoft, Apple or eBay are a testament to the astuteness of Drucker's observations.

One of the most persistent indicators of the informational maturity of organizations is their outlook on data. Though virtually all firms recognize the importance of raw data as a source of information, not all take a full advantage of its informational content. To the vast majority, event-tracking data needs to be *reduced* to be of value, which means tabulated, summarized, described and distributed via a wide range of reports, such as those showing total number of losses, losses per geography, time period, etc. On the other hand, a relatively smaller set of organizations take a far more expansive and exploratory approach to data. Their more inquisitive stance stems from the desire to understand the causes of the observed outcomes, rather than merely tabulating unexplained results. Not surprisingly, their data mining capabilities are, almost always, far more developed, particularly in the sense of a wide-scale (i.e., organization-wide) use of multivariate statistical analyses and experimental design. These are the knowledge leaders discussed earlier—the organizations whose "data crunching" capabilities evolved beyond the often pointless report propagation in search of unique, competitive edge producing knowledge.

Interestingly, both types of organizations, the "causal knowledge seekers" and the "result summarizers" tend to speak of data as a corporate asset. In case of the former, exemplified by firms such as Capital One, Marriott, Proctor & Gamble or Wal-Mart, data is clearly a corporate asset—after all, those firms were able to gain and maintain competitive advantage through an innovative and an effective use of it. Looking at data's "asset-worthiness" through that prism, it is hard to see how the latter category of companies, the "result summarizers", can make the same claim. If the firm's competitive position has not been enhanced by data, is that data really an asset to the organization? Probably not.

The reason for that is simple: Data, as a digital representation of certain outcomes (e.g., losses or claims) or states (e.g., demographics) is merely a raw material with a *potential* to inform the firm's decision making. Absent the know-how necessary to extract competitive edge-producing insights out of it, raw data offers little-to-no utility to an organization, in addition to which, its informational (and any monetary) value diminishes over time[18]. For instance, 10 years old workers' compensation claim details offer little in a way of insight into present-day likelihood of adverse claim development. In other words, virtually all business data have a certain period of applicability, beyond which its informational contents become simply too dated and in effect, obsolete. At the same time, just "having" data (i.e., its capture, storage and ongoing maintenance) can be quite costly, often requiring millions of dollars of capital expenditures on computer hardware and software, not to mention dedicated stuff (database administrators, programmers, etc.). These considerations point to the question of business value: If the data residing in our IT systems does not make clear and consistent contributions to revenue-generation or cost savings, why should it be considered an asset? After all, basic business logic suggests that an asset should not consume more than it either currently or potentially can contribute. Let's take a closer look.

Is Data an Asset?

An *asset* is defined as something of economic value that the organization owns and controls and that is expected to provide future benefits. In an investment sense, an asset increases the value of a firm or benefits the firm's operations. Although data can be viewed as having intrinsic economic value, since in many instances it could be sold in the marketplace, that argument is only applicable to a certain sub-set of firms (e.g., retailers often sell their event-tracking data to outside vendors, such as AC Nielsen or IRI, who then re-sell it, typically as packaged solutions to manufacturers) and data types. In a broader context, it is fair to say that few if any organizations would be willing to sell their claims, loss history or product sales data, as any potential monetary gains would be far outweighed by the potential competitive self-hindrance. Furthermore, there are a number of regulations governing sharing of certain types of data, such as the recently-enacted Shelby Act which places severe limitations on the use of vehicle registration data, or the Health Insurance Portability and Accountability Act of 1996 which sets limits around accessing and sharing individuals' health information. All considered, outside of the data service provider industry, few companies decide to invest in data capture and its ongoing maintenance capabilities because of the expectation of deriving an income stream from future sales of that data.

Under most circumstances, the real "asset-worthiness" of data stems from its potential to improve the firm's operations through the generation of unique knowledge, which in turn can give rise to competitively advantageous decisions. This leads to an obvious conclusion that data that do not contribute, meaningfully, to the development of competitive advantage should not be considered an asset. In fact, keeping in mind the often high cost of its capture and maintenance, poorly utilized data could even be viewed as an expense from a strictly cashflow point of view. There simply is no getting around the obvious conclusion that unless properly used, data investments can lead to an economic loss when evaluated in the confines of basic cost—benefit analysis.

All considered, it is then more realistic to think of data as a *potential* asset; as such a categorization highlights the importance of the analysis of the available data. This more tenuous expression of data's asset-worthiness underscores the obvious fact that without a significant amount of effort put into analytics; even the "best" data will not contribute enough to the organization's well-being to warrant an unconditional asset designation. Also, thinking of data as a potential, rather than an actual asset also draws attention to the importance of taking steps to extract economic benefits out of data that are at least equal to data's "cost of ownership."

Thinking of data as a potential asset also has a secondary benefit of redirecting the emphasis away from storage and maintenance infrastructure and toward the usage. Since the 1980's, organizations across industries have been investing heavily into data capture and maintenance related infrastructure, while dedicating disproportionately little effort and resources to data exploration. It has been estimated that approximately 85%-90% of total data related expenditures were directed at the hardware and software infrastructure, with only the remainder going toward extracting insights out of data. In other words, only about 10¢ out of every $1 of data related spending went toward actually making data into a true organizational asset. As a result, the well-known expression of a firm being "data-rich, but information-poor" is often quite true.

But even the 10% or so of the total information technology expenditures that in one way or another was dedicated to data exploration has not always been utilized as much as possible. Oftentimes, a good part of that spending went toward the production of generic information (e.g., the standard, measurable outcome focused management dashboard reports discussed earlier) that could bring the organization up to the level of competitive parity, though not sustainable competitive advantage. Some of that is due to the previously discussed convergence of technological data capture and storage platforms combined with a generic approach to data analysis, together leading to further informational convergence. Further fueling the informational convergence is the recent proliferation of third-party analytics, or data analysis vendors offering fundamentally the same type of information to multiple competitors in an industry. Unlike the technological standardization, however, the degree of analytical convergence varies across industries, as it tends to reflect of the availability of data to vendors. Nonetheless, there is a distinct trend of relatively few, large data providers and aggregators providing informationally-non-distinct analytical products and services to a wide cross-section of the marketplace.

The slow but persistent process of technological and informational convergence underscores the importance of the earlier discussed forward-looking informational vision built around analytically-innovative approaches to data analysis. Raw data has the potential of becoming an asset, but its asset-worthiness hinges on the organization's analytical skills. Data is an asset to organizations that are able to systematically extract competitive edge producing insights out of it. To others, specifically those whose data crunching capabilities are limited to standard, off-the-shelf tools and whose informational vision does not extend beyond basic outcome reporting, data is yet another component of the cost of doing business.

Data as a Source of Competitive Advantage

The last couple of decades have been particularly eventful from the standpoint of business information. Some of the more noteworthy trends, from the standpoint of knowledge creation, include the following:

> ▷ A combination of rapid gains in data processing capabilities, decreases in storage and processing costs and the proliferation of powerful software applications resulting in database technology become affordable to an ever growing number of organizations. *Result*: Leveraging the organization's own and competitive data became a key ingredient of firms' business strategies.

> The growing digitalization of business processes, including event and transaction processing, spawns an overabundance of event-tracking data often leading to potential users "drowning in data but lacking information."
>
> *Result*: Organizations spent large sums on customer data warehouses, yet to-date only a handful truly leverage their data assets.

> The forces of deregulations coupled with growing business globalization lead to the heightening of competition, ultimately amplifying the importance of timely, accurate and "on point" information.
>
> *Result*: Increasing competition accentuated the need for speedy extraction of actionable business insights from databases.

> Information availability and immersion become a part of everyday business culture and data analysis techniques, slowly making their way into the common business lexicon.
>
> *Result*: As database analytics is no longer a domain of a few, large organizations, the demand of skilled analysts exploded.

Taken as a group, these developments are to a large degree responsible for the growing importance of unique (to the organization), fact-based knowledge in building and sustaining competitive advantage. In a sense, all organizations are now in the information business, to the degree to which their competitive well-being has increasingly grown dependent on the access to timely and accurate decision guiding insights. Stated differently, knowledge surrounding the key decisions, such as product design (i.e., what is the most desirable bundling of product attributes?), promotional mix allocation (i.e., how should the finite promotional dollars be allocated across the available promotional alternatives to deliver the highest incremental benefit?) or the total cost of risk management (i.e., how to provide sound protection against loss-causing events at the lowest possible total cost?) is now among the most pronounced determinant of firms' success.

In a recent, insightful look at the impact that the persistent and well thought out data analysis—defined as reliable conversion of raw data into competitively advantageous knowledge—can have on organizations' long-term success, Thomas Davenport delineated a number of key factors characterizing information-driven organizations[19]. These included the widespread use of modeling and optimization, enterprise-wide deployment of data-derived insights and solid support from the top echelons of management. Of those, the *widespread use of modeling and optimization* comprises the general set of skills needed to translate the mounds of often dissimilar raw data into useful information. As detailed by Davenport, the quality of the resultant analyses requires the coming together of three key components: the right focus, the right people and the right technology. Implicit in the interplay of those three information quality shaping forces is the analytic know-how, which is that somewhat intangible quality that on one hand calls for a strong quantitative methodological skills, while at the same time contributing a healthy amount of problem solving creativity. A disciplined and rational left brain meets the spontaneous and untamed right brain...not impossible, but at the same time, not an everyday occurrence either.

As previously outlined, organizations that excel at extracting competitively advantageous knowledge out of the otherwise generic data are able to do so because of their data analytical prowess and the organization-wide fact-based decision making discipline. Processes ranging from high level strategic planning to tactical decisions surrounding product mix, logistics, inventory and distribution or promotional mix spending allocation are all making increasingly better use of the available data. To that end, one of the key drivers that fueled Wal-Mart's growth and its eventual ascendance to the world's largest retailer (and the #1 ranking on the Fortune Magazine listing of the largest U.S companies, based on gross revenue[20]) was its early embrace of the information-driven decision model. While its competitors continued their march forward, or so they believed, guided mostly by their intuition, anecdotal evidence and rarely empirically-validated generalizations, Wal-Mart looked to objective and representative data insights for decision cues. As a result, its merchandising mix consistently outperformed its peers, while its simulation and optimization based supply chain management mercilessly squeezed unnecessary inventory and stock-out costs, enabling it to offer competitive prices while still generating attractive returns for its shareholders. It is no surprise that the now industry-leading organizations such as Dell and Amazon emulated Wal-Mart's supply chain philosophy as one of the engines catapulting them to the position of prominence.

But Wal-Mart's way is not the only way—frankly, blindly copying methods of successful companies' practices can be a slippery slope, as it cannot be assumed that just because a particular practice or a method works well in one instance, it will work equally well for others. Inherent in the development of effective data analytical capabilities is a certain element of organizational self-discovery, which entails the identification of the most adaptable (to the specific of the organization) ways the organization can use data to gain and sustain competitive advantage. After all, the retail industry's dynamics are quite different from the pharmaceutical, financial or other sectors of the economy, as is the available data, Neither are any two firms in a given industry exactly the same, particularly in the cultural sense (for instance, some firms are highly centralized while others are de-centralized in terms of their decision making models; some are overt risk takers in terms of heavy emphasis on new, trend-setting products, while others are risk avoiders, preferring instead to focus on the "tried and true" ideas or technologies). Therefore, the specifics of "what" data and "how" it can be used effectively are shaped by both industry-wide forces (e.g., what type of data and data insights can offer the greatest potential competitive levers?), as well as by company-specific competencies and goals (e.g., company's intrinsic capabilities and its organizational culture).

Capital One, as one of the leading credit card issuers in the U.S and one of the leading credit card industry innovators has consistently delivered above average results by an almost religious dedication to objective data analysis, especially customer mix optimization. Harrah's, a major casino entertainment organization and a relative risk-taker in its industry, systematically improved its profitability by using data analysis to attract and retain customers with the greatest profit potential. A resource-constrained baseball club, the Oakland A's consistently posted one of the league's best regular season records by identifying the otherwise undervalued players that could perform the desired assortment of tasks, something Oakland was able to do in spite of working with a far below average budget. Honda developed a second-to-none brand loyalty by using data for early detection of potential problems, thus greatly increasing the reliability of their automobiles. A leading hotel chain, Marriott, uses advanced analytics to optimize the price-profitability relationship, while Novartis, the giant pharmaceutical firm leverages data analysis to improve the quality and the efficacy of its R&D efforts. Last but not least, Procter and Gamble, a leading consumer packaged goods manufacturer continues to prosper in a very competitive, mature industry segment in a large part due to organization-wide embrace of data-driven new product development, as well as promotional mix allocations and evaluation practices. Progressive's market capitalization grew more than four-fold as a result of the insurer's deployment of statistical models-based automotive policy underwriting technology.

Yes overall, the use of advanced statistical modeling techniques has been comparatively slow in a broadly defined area of risk management. While many organizations, as exemplified above, readily recognize the value of using data as one of the basis of consistent revenue growth, considerably fewer see statistical data analyses as an effective mean of cost containment. This is beginning to change, however. In his recent book, *The Numerati*, Stephen Baker discusses IBM's efforts to use behavioral modeling techniques to improve the productivity of its vast legion of business process consultants and technologist, as well as to automate project management.

There are numerous other areas where behavioral modeling can be a vehicle of systematic cost reduction. The bulk of larger retailers and manufacturers, among others, spend tens of millions of dollars on workers' compensation and/or general liability claims. As detailed later in this book, considerable savings can be realized by deploying organization-tailored predictive modeling technologies to automate claim processing, "flag" individual claims deemed to be most at risk of adverse development and delineate specific causal factors leading to higher costs. By taking these steps, an organization will be able to effectively process larger volumes of claims more expeditiously and with fewer resources, take proactive steps (e.g., more aggressive claim management and monitoring) against specific, potentially explosive claims and develop more effective cost containment and safety protocols.

In a similar vein, organizations routinely allocate $millions to insurance coverage procurement without sound informational foundation relating the actual cost to anticipated benefits. In many instances insurance coverage is clearly needed, but in all instances it is an expense with little-to-no residual value. Stated differently, the amount of coverage purchased should reflect both the company specific likelihood and severity—it should also contemplate the threshold impact of loss on earnings. Furthermore, what if, through diligent analysis of the available data (which, by the way, is readily available for risk analysis, and it is quite rich) it could be discerned that an organization would be better off to pursue altogether different means of risk protection?

ABOUT THIS BOOK

First and foremost, this book is about knowledge creation—or more specifically, it is about utilizing objective data and established analytic methodologies to create competitively advantageous, decision guiding insights. My desire to write this book is rooted in my experience and observation that although companies tend to be quite diligent about collecting and cataloguing the available data, few come anywhere near taking the full advantage of that resource.

In a Nutshell

This is a "how-to" book: How to use commonly available data to get unique insights into commonly asked risk management related questions. Given its analytical focus, the bulk of the book's contents are related to quantitative data modeling. That said, non-statistical modeling issues are explored with a comparable level of depth and care, as the creation of truly unique and valuable business insights necessitates a solid understanding of elements of other supporting domains, such as strategic planning, data warehousing and economics.

The bulk of the ideas presented here stem from hands-on practical experience of working with numerous, large organizations from a cross-section of industries, including financial, energy, automotive, packaged goods, insurance, banking, telecommunications, high tech, retail, consumer durables and hospitality. The overall analytical process and its individual components are expressly "calibrated" to take into account the most commonly used data sources, with the primary emphasis on large event-tracking data warehouses, exemplified by risk management systems. Also explicitly considered are other common business sources of data including sample based behavioral surveys; data aggregator-compiled "causal overlays" exemplified by consumer geodemographics; public financial filings and disclosures, such as the Standard & Poor's Compustat database tracking quarterly and annual financial filings that are required of publicly traded companies. In the data sense, the basic premise of the data analytical processes presented in this book, represents an amalgamation of dissimilar sources to form the basis for creating the otherwise beyond reach knowledge.

Content-wise, I draw upon the work of multiple disciplines, including statistics, business strategy, database technology and management and to a lesser degree from other areas, such as industrial psychology. In my discussion and recommendations I rely heavily on practical database analytical consulting experience, based on my work with large corporate databases of Fortune 500 organizations from a wide cross section of industries mentioned earlier. I make extensive use of database analytical examples drawn from real-life analysis and modeling projects to illustrate the shortcomings of some methods and processes and to underscore the advantages of other approaches.

As stated above, this book is about the "how-to" of database analytics. Although it offers theoretical descriptions and rationales behind the recommended approaches, the focus throughout this text is on hands-on, systematic process of answering specific business questions. It is important to note that the end goal of the risk analytical process detailed here is not a mere translation of data into information, but rather it is the establishment of a source of unique and thus competitively advantageous organizational knowledge, added-to and updated on ongoing basis.

My secondary objective is to contribute to re-focusing of analysts' attention away from the "modeling" part of the process and toward the "usage" of the resultant knowledge. This is not to say that I am advocating modeling carelessness, far from it, as the subsequent chapters show. I am merely trying to shine the spotlight on the utility of the end product of analysis—an abstractly defined statistical model rarely communicates as much to its intended users as it does to the analysts who crafted it, unless the results are properly framed and communicated.

It has also been my experience that technical analysts tend to work in a relative "vacuum", far removed from both the business initiators of analyses and users of the resultant information. At times that might be necessary, but it still dilutes the impact of analytic results, in part due to analysts' somewhat superficial understanding of the anticipated informational outcomes (i.e., specific inputs into business decision making). Although to some degree information will always be shaped by analysts' subjectivity, steps should be taken, however, to temper that with objectively derived organizational goals and objectives.

Organization

The central theme of this book is the risk analytical process offering the means of systematically and objectively assessing the organization's risk profile. Figure 1.4 below depicts the overall outline of this process.

Figure 1.4
The Risk Profile Management Process

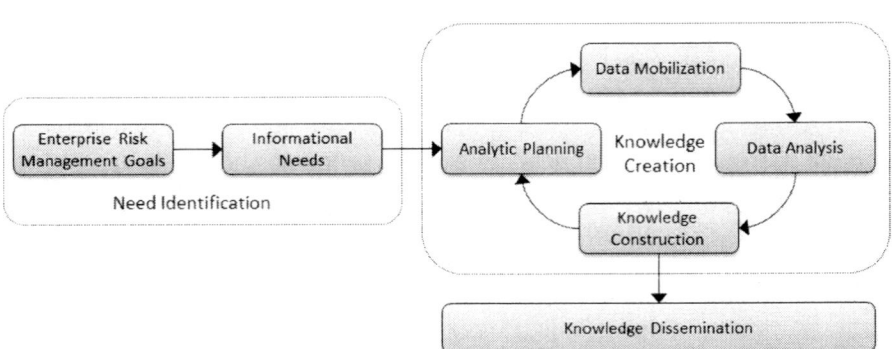

As illustrated above, the overall process can be divided into three broad dimensions: 1. *Need Identification* (comprised of *Enterprise Risk Management Goals* and *Informational Needs*), 2. *Knowledge Creation* (comprised of *Analytic Planning, Data Mobilization, Data Analysis* and *Knowledge Construction*) and 3. *Knowledge Dissemination.* The entire process is termed *Risk Profile Management,* or *RPM,* and it is detailed in chapters 4 through 13, with chapters 2 and 3 providing a high level overview of the key concepts and frameworks encompassed within the broadly defined realm of risk management (Chapter 2), and an overview of the key technical / statistical considerations relating to risk measurement (Chapter 3)..

It is important to note that while the bulk of the RPM process (the *Knowledge Creation* dimension in Figure 1.4) is focused on "measurement" related considerations such as statistical data analysis, the overall scope of the process transcends the technical, estimation-related matters. For that reason, though much of the ensuing discussion refers to the aforementioned "measurement" considerations, the RPM process as such encircles a broader, "management" related set of topics.

2

Knowledge of Risk

Merriam-Webster dictionary defines *risk* as a "...possibility of loss or injury", positing that the term dates back to the latter part of the 17th century. The dictionary also suggests that the notion of risk stems from an older term (dating back to the 13th century) peril, which it defines as "...exposure to the risk of being injured, destroyed, or lost." The notion of peril is itself related to the chronologically contemporary (also dating back to the 13th century) concept of danger, defined as "...exposure or liability to injury, pain, harm, or loss".

It seems odd that something that clearly has been an inseparable part of mankind since the dawn of our civilization has not gotten a formal recognition until just a few centuries ago. Common sense tells us that *risk* did not enter the realm of human experience at some arbitrary point, such as the aforementioned 13th or 17th centuries—it has shadowed us throughout our history. It was the conception of risk it took quite a while longer to develop in our cognitive awareness. In a sense, the evolution of what we now describe as risk ran parallel to the maturation of our social and economic structures, both in terms of the types of risk as well as the acuity of our perception of it. As these structures grew in complexity, so did our awareness and fear of adverse outcomes.

Building on the Merriam-Webster definitions cited earlier, I start by defining risk as the possibility of adverse events occurring at some point in the future. It is a very broad definition, both conceptually and operationally. It is a combination of old and new, natural and man-made as well as tangible and abstract. There are many forms of risk that existed throughout the history and have been recognized as such, others that existed in principle, but did not become recognized as threats until relatively recently, and still others that are a direct byproduct of the socio-political-legal fiber of our society. For instance, the various forms of natural catastrophes, such as wind, floods or earthquakes have been our constant companion since the dawn of our civilization. At the same time, the possibility of a person getting injured while on someone else's premises certainly existed for many centuries, but it did not become a recognizable risk until relatively recent (in the sense of historical chronology) tort law developments. Similarly, corporations, as independent, legal business entities with outside shareholders and independent management have also been in existence for centuries[1], yet securities class action litigation (civil suits filed by shareholders alleging dishonest and/or deceptive practices on the part of management) did not become a threat until 1980's. Similarly, intellectual property or technological risks did not exist (as a concept and a form of threat) before the advent of the industrial age.

It is important to note that, in the strict sense of the word, we do not create or eliminate risk—rather, risk is a consequence of our actions. The action of erecting a building carries with it the possibility of property damage, by wind, fire or other means—in other words, the risk of man-made property damage[2] is a result of the decision to put up or otherwise assemble a property. In a more general sense, the risk of damage represents a liability associated with all damageable assets. This is also true in less tangible situations. For instance, if we enter into a service agreement with another party, that action gives rise to the potentiality of non-performance or non-payment. In this instance, risk is a consequence of the decision to enter into a service agreement with another party. The examples are virtually endless, all pointing to the same conclusion: The development of thorough understanding of risk starts with a careful delineation and study of specific risk-spawning actions.

This is particularly true of economic risk. Business interactions are ultimately about exchanging elements of value. Looking back in time, what is known as business transactions today started as barter trades, which are exchanges of goods or services not involving the use of money. There is no way of knowing when the first barter exchange took place (nor is it particularly important to be able to pinpoint the exact instance), though it is safe to say that it goes all the way back to the dawn of our civilization. What is important to note is that from the very first barter exchange, both parties assumed the risks associated with giving up what they had (the benefits of which were quite well-known to the owner) for something else (the benefits of which were less know to the prospective owner). It was that uncertainty gap that gave rise to the *exchange risk.* Conceptually, the action of economic exchange is rooted in properly valuing the anticipated benefits associated with what is being acquired, which means that the most rudimentary aspect of risk is that of over-valuing of the acquisition. Hence in the sense of risk analysis, a barter transaction can be described in the context of expected vs. realized utility, as shown below:

Exchange Risk = (Expected Utility - Realized Utility)

As time passed, barter trade gave way to monetary exchanges, i.e., buying and selling, and a good portion of individual traders began to group together to form business organizations. And as the economic plenty of an evolving society continued to expand, along with the socio-economic-political infrastructure, so did the varieties of economic threats. Stated differently, our conception of risk grew beyond its initial nucleus of (barter) exchange risk to become a function of assets, both tangible, such as factories, inventories or real estate, and intangible, such as rights or intellectual property and the environment affecting those assets, such as socio-political, regulatory or physical.

So, is risk simply the uncertainty regarding the future events and outcomes? As it tends to be the case with numerous other abstract notions, this too gave rise to a healthy debate. The analysis of some of the key points and conclusions follows.

Risk vs. Uncertainty

Intuitively, risk and uncertainty are noticeably different. The former implies more specificity in terms of what might happen, while the latter is a reflection of a general state of ambiguity regarding the future. In more concrete terms, the key risk consideration is whether or not the (known) event will occur, while uncertainty connotes a non-specific insecurity or ambiguity regarding the future in general. Not surprisingly, risk theorists tend to conclude that it is extremely important to draw a clear line of demarcation between risk and uncertainty. Perhaps the best set of original ideas trying to differentiate between these two concepts can be traced back to the work of

Frank Knight, dating back to the early 1900's. In his seminal book, *Risk, Uncertainty & Profit*, published in 1921, Knight comes to following conclusions: *"... Uncertainty must be taken in a sense radically distinct from the familiar notion of Risk, from which it has never been properly separated. The term "risk," as loosely used in everyday speech and in economic discussion, really covers two things which, functionally at least, in their causal relations to the phenomena of economic organization, are categorically different. ... The essential fact is that "risk" means in some cases a quantity susceptible of measurement, while at other times it is something distinctly not of this character; and there are far-reaching and crucial differences in the bearings of the phenomenon depending on which of the two is really present and operating. ... It will appear that a measurable uncertainty, or "risk" proper, as we shall use the term, is so far different from an unmeasurable one that it is not in effect an uncertainty at all. We ... accordingly restrict the term "uncertainty" to cases of the non-quantitative type."*

Building upon Knight's work, Hubbard offered a more operationally clear differentiation between risk and uncertainty[3]. According to him, risk always implies uncertainty, but not the other way around—uncertainty does not necessarily imply risk, which is in keeping with the definition of risk offered in the opening paragraph of this chapter. More specifically, Hubbard offers the following risk vs. uncertainty tests: An event of a circumstance can be categorized as uncertainty if:

Definition: The lack of complete certainty, that is, the existence of more than one possibility. The "true" outcome/state/result/value is not known.

Measurement: A set of probabilities assigned to a set of possibilities. Example: "There is a 60% chance this market will double in five years"

Otherwise, an event or a circumstance can be categorized as risk if:

Definition: A state of uncertainty where some of the possibilities involve a loss, catastrophe, or other undesirable outcome.

Measurement: A set of possibilities each with quantified probabilities and quantified losses. Example: "There is a 40% chance the proposed oil well will be dry with a loss of $12 million in exploratory drilling costs".

Knight's and Hubbard's reasoning has a strong appeal, considering that the goal of managing threats confronting business organizations is to minimize the organization's exposure to potentially economically damaging events, or to support the attainment of stated strategic objectives. Uncertainty is undeniably ubiquitous and as such, very difficult—if not altogether impossible—to manage effectively. Risk, on the other hand, can be construed as a special case of uncertainty, further contextualized by the stated organizational strategic objectives.

It is also true, however, that much has changed since Knight published his insightful ideas. Most notably, the global economy is now leaning toward service, rather than manufacturing industries – in fact, according to the most recent figures available from the World Bank, of the twenty largest economies – i.e., the so-called G-20 – only three (China, Indonesia and Saudi Arabia) derive more than 50% of their gross domestic product from manufacturing. Hence it follows that a considerable number of business organizations are engaged in activities where the primary—meaning, of most concern—source of threat are events that both Knight and Hubbard would classify as uncertainty, rather than risk. For instance, a financial services organization, such as a bank or a mutual fund manager, can certainly be adversely impacted by natural catastrophes, but the potential peril would more than likely pale by comparison to the impact that mismanaged or miscalculated market or credit exposures would have on those organizations[4]. Secondly, in a more methodological sense the notions of risk and uncertainty do not exhibit the necessary discriminant validity[5], as these two concepts are confounded and situation-dependent. For instance, two otherwise similar organizations could have considerably different analytical capabilities, so much so that what might be un-measurable (and thus considered "uncertainty") to one might be measurable (and thus considered "risk") to the other.

In view of the above, what is the value of differentiating between risk and uncertainty, in the context of risk management? Are we getting too entangled in semantic considerations?

Let's go back to the basic definition of risk compiled by Merriam-Webster: Risk is a possibility of loss or injury. A loss can be a result of property damage caused by a natural disaster, it can be a result of a lawsuit brought by customers (product liability), shareholders (executive liability) or regulators (non-compliance), or it can stem from a decline in value of market securities. It can take on a number of other forms as well, but in all cases it will manifest itself as adverse impact on the organization's earnings. Furthermore, just because the outcome itself appears more tangible does not mean that the potential threat is more measurable. Each year, several hurricanes move along the Gulf Coast of the United States, and even though many follow very similar paths, their impact varies considerably. With that in mind, let's consider Hubbard's definitions of risk and uncertainty, presented earlier. The author defines uncertainty as "...the lack of complete certainty, that is, the existence of more than one possibility; the "true" outcome / state / result / value is not known." At the same time, he defines risk as "...a state of uncertainty where some of the possibilities involve a loss, catastrophe, or other undesirable outcome." Are these definitions meaningful, or sufficiently distinct, in the context of the aforementioned Gulf Coast hurricanes? Not at all and here is why.

Whether our focus is on hurricanes or any other type of a natural or a man-made threat, it is hard to envision a situation other than "the lack of complete certainty", to use Hubbard's words. Short of being able to gaze into the proverbial crystal ball, the lack of complete certainty is a ubiquitous property of future events, as prior to materializing the future state of any outcome is probabilistic in nature. Even if we now that the onslaught of a bad storm is unavoidable or the shareholder suit imminent – we do not have complete certainty regarding the ultimate consequence of either of these two, and countless other threats. The reason that Knight's and Hubbard's uncertainty vs. risk differentiation lacks operational clarity and definitional distinctiveness is because they do not expressly consider the *degree of knowability* of individual threats.

The key to being knowable, for a particular threat, is to be estimable using objectively sourced information. Furthermore, to be estimable a threat has to be assessed in the context of two key dimensions that jointly determine its expected consequences: 1. how likely is it to occur, and 2. how severe will be its impact. Recalling an earlier-made assertion that all future events are speculative (probabilistic), the distinction between the likelihood (#1) and the severity (#2) helps to illustrate why that is the case: From the standpoint of managing the organization's risk exposure, it is imperative to not only know the expected chances (likelihood) of a particular threat occurring, but it is also critical to know the force of its impact (severity). For example, if threats A and B have 90% and 10%, respectively, probability of occurrence, threat A appears to be clearly more worrisome – however, if A's severity is estimated at $10,000, while B's at $1,000,000 a different conclusion emerges[6].

Keeping the above in mind and turning our attention to the uncertainty vs. risk distinction and the notion of the degree of knowability, I define *uncertainty* to include all threats that have non-estimable likelihood and severity, and I define *risk* to include all threats that have estimable likelihood and severity. Furthermore, both likelihood and severity will be deemed non-estimable when the requisite data either do not exist or are insufficient, in view of an estimation methodology under consideration. Lastly, given the multiplicative nature of the two threat-defining dimensions of likelihood and severity, to be estimable a particular threat has to have the requisite data available for both dimensions.

Broadening the Scope of Risk

As discussed in the preceding section, the term "risk" denotes a *threat*, which is a reflection of certain amount of linguistic conditioning causing us to think of risk as a possibility of an undesirable event taking place. And certainly, every business organization faces a considerable amount of *downside*—defined here as asset-damaging or loss-generating events—risk. The same organizations, however, also face a wide array of *upside risks*, defined here as an unrealized growth opportunity. For example, an electric utility with power generating plants located in the Gulf of Mexico region faces the downside risk of hurricane related wind damage, while at the same time is faces the upside risk associated with the decision to invest or not in renewable power generation assets. To truly appreciate the risk exposure of the said utility, it is necessary to assess both its downside as well as upside risks, hence our conception of risk needs to be framed in the context that includes both the avoidance of undesirable events, i.e., downside risks, as well purposeful pursuit of desired states, i.e., upside risks.

Downside risk is the possibility of asset-damaging or loss-generating events taking place, while *upside risk* reflects the chances of anticipated growth not materializing. Both can adversely impact the organization's earnings.

It follows that risk is not necessarily something to be avoided—in fact, good risk taking can have a very positive impact on the organization. Microsoft took a risk by tying its success, in terms of its core operating system, to the proliferation of personal computers, just as Google took a risk by deviating from an established practice of charging advertisers based on the actual visits to their websites, rather than total traffic (which was an established practice at that time). These are examples of companies that successfully increased their exposure to upside risks—of course, there are numerous examples of ineffective upside risk taking, such as the much-anticipated entrance of IBM into the personal computer industry in the 1980's (which turned out to be unprofitable for the company, ultimately causing it to exit out of that business) or the ill-advised decision by Gateway in the 1990's to vertically integrate by expanding into retail. Although the anecdotal evidence is mixed, the aggregate results overwhelmingly point to the desirability of increasing the exposure to the upside risk, as evidenced by the higher overall returns realized by investors (both individuals and organizations) who put their money in equities, rather than government and corporate bonds.

There is an important nuance, however, that needs to be addressed—risk taking recklessness. First reported by Bowman[7], and subsequently coined the "Bowman Paradox", the positive risk-return relationship does not hold for organizations engaging in poor risk taking. Specifically, firms earning below average returns tend to exhibit negative risk-return relationship, while those earning above average returns tend to exhibit the (expected) positive risk-return relationship. In other words, good risk taking will advantageously increase the upside risk, while limiting the downside risk.

Overall, at any given time the organization-specific total risk exposure will be a sum of net present value of both the downside and upside risk, or

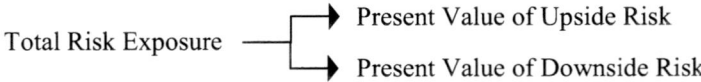

Total Risk Exposure → Present Value of Upside Risk
→ Present Value of Downside Risk

It is competitively advantageous to an organization to thoughtfully increase its exposure to upside risk, while systematically lowering the potential impact of downside risk. Increasing the spread between the two types of risks will systematically enhance the organization's competitive advantage. It follows that management of upside risk entails systematic evaluation of risks to be taken, while management of downside risk calls for systematic reduction of risk exposure.

Aside from considering "what" types of events should fall within our conception of risk, it is also important explicitly estimate "the possibility" of both the upside and downside risks impacting the organization. It is intuitively obvious that risk potential is a function of two, usually independent dimensions of *likelihood/probability* and cost, usually referred to as *severity*. Risk is inherently probabilistic because it reflects uncertainty associated with the future. Events that have not yet occurred but whose future occurrence is known with certainty are not risks—they are more accurately described as either assets or liabilities. For instance, a lease payment that is to be made on a periodic basis is a liability, because its occurrence (or rather, its recurrence) and amount are known exactly ahead of time. On the other hand, future wind or flood related property damage is a risk because neither its occurrence nor the amount of damage are known ahead of time. Both good and bad outcomes, or upside and downside risks, respectively, can be expressed in terms of the likelihood of occurrence and the magnitude or severity of the resultant gains or losses.

The third and final component of the definition of risk, in the organizational context, should the "standardized impact" estimation. This is most important when dissimilar risks are evaluated in a holistic, or enterprise-wide setting, and when resource allocation decisions are based on those evaluations. The most reasonable benchmark for cross-risk types impact comparisons is the net earnings impact assessment. Stated differently, to adequately communicate the magnitude of an upside or downside risk, and to make rational (i.e., reflecting risk type-specific impact) resource allocations, the assessment of risk needs to be expressed in terms of the impact on the organization's revenues or earnings. Figure 2.1 summarizes the three key definitional components of risk.

Figure 2.1
Key Components of the Definition of Risk

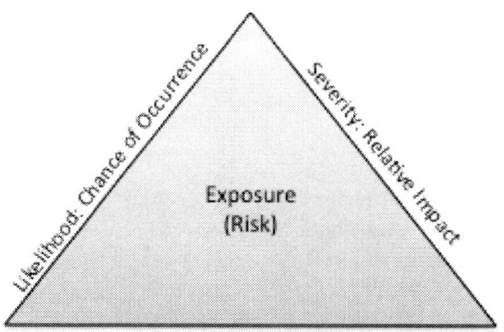

Type: Upside vs. Downside

Although nominally the type of risk, the possibility of occurrence and the relative impact all play a role in framing individual risk types, their roles are not the same. More specifically, the type of risk and the possibility of the risk event materializing are both antecedents (i.e., they precede) the risk event, while its impact follows the risk event. Hence from a causal standpoint, it is more appropriate to express risk in the following manner:

Figure 2.2
Causal View of Risk

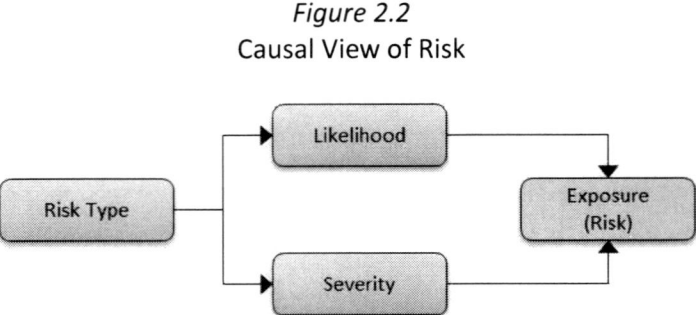

The causal view of risk is essential to the development of a holistic risk management approach, or active management of the organization's risk profile, because it draws attention to the distinctiveness of managing the underlying root causes of risk and the capitalization of the possible risk outcomes. Stated differently, to actively manage the organization's exposure to risk, explicit steps need to be taken to mitigate the possibility of unfavorable outcomes and to put in place economically-optimal capital provisions, in the event the possibility materializes.

ASSESSMENT OF RISK

Accepting the dual face—upside vs. downside—of risk stretches the conceptual boundary of our conception of risk and so by extension, it also expands the requisite operationalization of it. Intuitively, there are considerable measurement differences separating risks as diverse as hurricanes, fraud, cost of capital fluctuations or strategic missteps. The risk estimation process, however, will tend to follow a similar set of steps, as depicted in Figure 2.3 below.

Figure 2.3
Risk Estimation Process

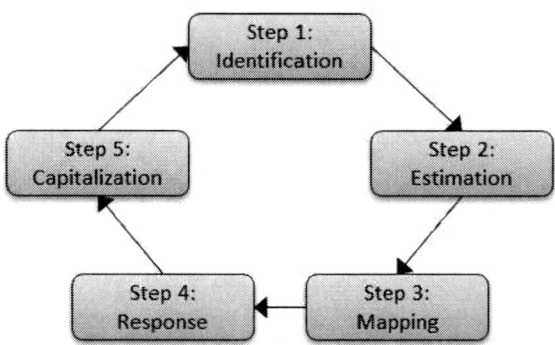

First and foremost, individual risks need to be clearly identified. As detailed later, there is a long list of upside and especially downside risks that could potentially have a material impact on the organization's financial well-being. Once clearly delineated, the potential impact of each of the risks needs to be estimated, in terms of the probability of the event taking place as well as its severity. The *Estimation* stage is usually most readily associated with the notion of risk analytics, as it tends to be the most "analytical" part of the overall process, however, just presenting the likelihood and severity estimates outside of the earnings impact can be of limited utility to the decision makers because it does not expressly contemplate the net impact of risk on earnings.

Mapping of the individually identified and estimated risks is the next step in the risk analytics process. It is, in effect, putting together of a "risk puzzle", or a matrix of individual risks categorized in the context of estimated likelihood and severity. Figure 2.4 offers a generic example of a risk map:

Figure 2.4
Hypothetical Risk Map

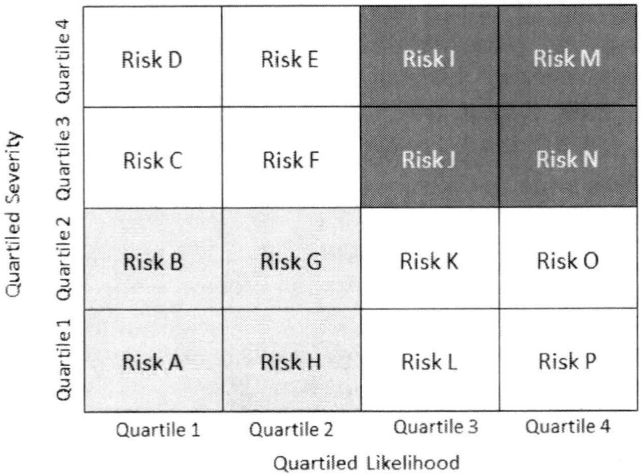

	Quartile 1	Quartile 2	Quartile 3	Quartile 4
Quartile 4	Risk D	Risk E	Risk I	Risk M
Quartile 3	Risk C	Risk F	Risk J	Risk N
Quartile 2	Risk B	Risk G	Risk K	Risk O
Quartile 1	Risk A	Risk H	Risk L	Risk P

Quartiled Severity (vertical axis)

Quartiled Likelihood (horizontal axis)

In the illustration shown above in Figure 2.4, each individual risk is plotted on the likelihood—severity grid, with each risk dimension being broken out into four magnitude-based quartiles. In effect, the probability and the estimated cost of each event are used as basis for placing individual risks into an appropriate cell. In the resultant 16-cell matrix used here, the four cells falling at the intersection of the top two likelihood and the top two severity quartiles are highlighted (in red) as the high risk region, while the four cells falling at the intersection of the bottom two likelihood and bottom two severity quartiles are highlighted (in red) as the low risk region. Using quartile-based likelihood and severity is somewhat of an arbitrary choice, as circumstances might warrant a more granular (such as decile-based) or more coarse view— the important point here is that an single categorization schema should be applied to all risk to enable robust and objective side-by-side risk impact comparisons.

The next step in the risk analytics process is that of determining the most appropriate response. Consider Figure 2.5.

Figure 2.5
Response Selection

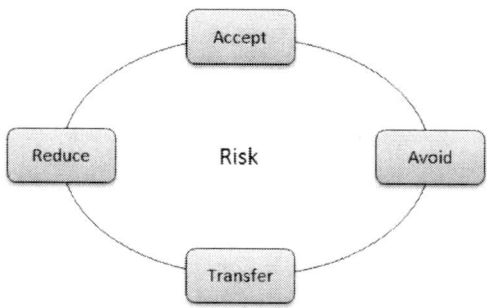

There are four distinct risk responses: *acceptance, reduction, transfer* and *avoidance* (more on each later in this chapter). The goal of this stage of the risk analytics process is to overlay the impact on earnings-adjusted efficacy of each of the four options onto the risk map develop in the previous stage, which leads to the final stage of the process: *Capitalization.* Virtually all non-zero likelihood risks, both upside and downside have capital implications ranging from setting aside funds for insurance coverage acquisition to contingent capital planning to product infrastructure investments.

Exposure

It is intuitively obvious that the degree of risk exposure will vary, at time significantly, across companies. Upon a bit more reflection, it also becomes intuitively obvious that cross-company risk exposure will depend primarily on the degree of business spread (the number of distinct product or service types offered) and geographic spread (the number of physical locations). A business entity that is comprised of multiple, dissimilar business units—i.e., a diversified conglomerate—will tend to be exposed to a wider array of risks than an entity operating a single business unit. For example, a vertically integrated electronics manufacturer (i.e., a company engaged both in manufacturing and retail) will bear the risks associated with manufacturing as well as retailing, while a company engaged only in manufacturing will only bear the risks associated with manufacturing.

In a similar manner, an organization that operates in multiple geographic locations and/or jurisdictions will face more risks than a single location organization. For example, a multinational firm is exposed to proportionally more regulatory, environmental, contractual and physical risks than an organization operating in a single location/jurisdiction.

Of course, that is not to say that it is more advantageous to only compete in a single product line or a single location as this type of concentration carries its own perils—the assumption of risk needs to be evaluated in the context of return it generates. In other words, the risk "posture" of an organization needs to be commensurate with the organization's economic returns. Furthermore, any incremental risk associated with the contemplated course of action needs to be contrasted with the expected incremental economic gain. For example, building an oil refinery in the coastal region of the Gulf of Mexico heightens the risk of hurricane-related wind damage, while at the same time it is advantageous from the standpoint of crude oil access and transportation costs. To make a rational "build vs. not build" decision, one has to be able to objectively estimate the incremental economic values of both sides of the risk—return relationship. Doing so, however, will amount to just a single step in the multi-step enterprise risk management process. In addition to wind damage related risk, what other risks need to be taken into account to make a more holistic risk assessment of this particular project. And what is the nature of any cross-risk type interdependencies?

MANAGEMENT OF RISK

In 1956, Harvard Business Review published "Risk Management: A New Phase of Cost Control", which posited that a professional insurance management should be the domain of a risk manager. Roughly two decades later, The American Society of Insurance Management changed its name to Risk and Insurance Management Society, and about a year later, in 1976, Fortune magazine published a seminal article titled "The Risk Management Revolution", which discussed "...the coordination of formerly unconnected risk management functions with an organization with oversight by the board of directors." In many regards, these events marked the rise of formal (i.e., department-based) corporate risk management functions. The creation of the first-ever Chief Risk Officer position by GE Capital in 1993 brought even a greater level of recognition of the importance of organization-wide, senior management level risk exposure oversight.

Risk management as an attempt at diminishing the exposure to risk, rather than a structured organizational function, has a far longer history. Interest rates, which started to emerge roughly 5,000 years ago in Babylon, are the earliest known form of a specific, definable way of treating risk. The Code of Hammurabi, circa 1755 BC, contains the first formal form of risk shielding, or insurance. By creating the concepts of "bottomry" (i.e., ship bottoms) and "respondentia" (or cargo), it laid the foundation for marine insurance which was built around the three key components: 1. a loan on a vessel or cargo, 2. an interest rate, and 3. a surcharge to cover the possibility of loss. In effect, ship owners were the insured and lenders were the underwriters. By about 750 BC, the concepts first introduced in the Code of Hammurabi were refined into the notion of "general average", which became a fundamental notion underlying marine and other forms of insurance coverage.

Modern day insurance based risk management dates back to 12th century Italian ports, most notably, Venice (in fact, the term "policy" is derived from Italian "polizza", meaning a "promise" or "an undertaking"). Roughly five centuries later, insurance began to take hold in the Great Britain, with the Great Fire of London of 1666 giving rise to the first insurance company, The Insurance Office, formed a year later.

As noted earlier, however, risk management goes far beyond insurance coverage acquisition—more specifically, it encompasses the following set of activities:

Risk type identification.
Specific and distinct threats to the organization need to be singled out in an operationally clear manner.

Risk type impact estimation.
The two distinct and independent dimensions of risk—likelihood and severity—need to be estimated in terms of their potential impact.

Aggregate risk mapping.
Individual risks need to be pulled together into a single, coherent picture of the overall threat to the organization.

Response optimization.
Taking action is a logic consequence of the previous three steps.

These four sets of activities are causally related, as shown in Figure 2.6 below.

Figure 2.6
Interdependence of Risk Activities

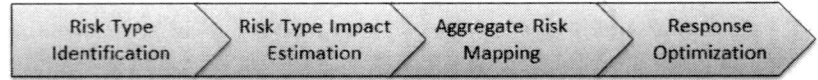

| Risk Type Identification | Risk Type Impact Estimation | Aggregate Risk Mapping | Response Optimization |

Risk Mapping

The delineation of individual risk types and the estimation of their impact should be framed in the context of *risk mapping*, which is simply the process of explicitly identifying and assessing specific areas of risk exposure. The most pronounced benefit of risk mapping is that it helps to pull together a variety of otherwise dissimilar aspects of the organization's overall risk exposure, thus yielding the first step in the enterprise-wide risk assessment process.

To yield thorough and credible outcomes, the risk mapping process should encompass two interconnected sets of activities: 1. Identification of all pertinent risks in the context of the "known vs. knowable" clarification, and 2. Meta analytic assessment.

Known vs. Knowable

All potential risks facing an organization should be clearly listed and for each, assess what is already "known" and what else might be "knowable". The importance of the "known—knowable" dichotomy is primarily of methodological nature. More specifically, there are two, somewhat methodologically distinct approaches to risk quantification: 1. trend extrapolation-based outcome simulation, and 2. multivariate modeling. The goal of the former is to estimate the most likely outcomes by means of simulating a large number of potential outcomes and comparing the probabilities of different scenarios. The latter approach, on the other hand, is in principle a two-step process of explaining the past by means of identifying the key influencers and estimating their relative impact (step 1), followed by the construction of a forward-looking predictive function (step 2). Depending on the risk category, i.e., variability in known events vs. possibility of an unknown event, either of the two approaches may be more appealing or plausible. In general, the less manageable the risk, the lower the benefit of the explanatory approach, for the somewhat intuitive reason: Even if robust explanation is feasible, the return on the investment needed to craft an adequate explanation may simply not be there for risks over which the organization ultimately exercises little-to-no control. On the other hand, the return may be quite high for risks over which the management yields a meaningful degree of control.

Meta Analysis

Derivation-wise, the prefix "meta" is a Greek-derived term meaning "after", "beyond" or "adjacent". Epistemologically, the term "meta" is used to denote "being about something"—such as *metadata* is data about data (i.e., description of informational contents of a particular data file) or metamemory refers to individuals' knowledge about whether they could remember something if they concentrated their efforts on trying to remember. Hence *meta analysis* is about knowledge extracted from the analysis of multiple other analyses. Sounds tautological, but the essence of meta analysis is to distil and summarize specific insights into a broader knowledge base.

Initially, meta analysis was used to circumvent sample size limitations for studies with sample sizes deemed too small to support broader generalizations; in that context, analyzing the results from a group of studies was believed to lead to greater reliability and generalizability of findings.

According to Wikipedia, the first reported use of meta analysis dates back to 1904 and is attributed to Karl Pearson, one of the early pioneers of modern statistics; however, the term "meta analysis" did not become formally recognized as a statistical term until the mid-1970's, as noted in Oxford English Dictionary. Interestingly, in contrast to the early goals of meta analysis, which was to overcome sample size inadequacies of individual studies, the current interest in meta analytic research is driven by the opposite problem—an overwhelmingly large volumes of data and research studies necessitate the creation of "high order" knowledge, which is the derivation of macro conclusions from more micro-focused research initiatives.

From the methodological standpoint, meta analysis imposes measurement uniformity in evaluating related, though somewhat dissimilar pieces of information. This is not a technique per se, but rather a loosely defined approach to distilling multiple sources of information into a singular, summary-like set of findings. The main benefit of meta analysis is that it draws attention to the key validity, reliability and generalizability related descriptors of individual sources of information or research studies. This is usually accomplished by cross-tabulating such a priori delineated evaluation criteria, followed by systematically assessing each source of information in terms of those evaluative dimensions. A more in-depth detailing of meta analysis is offered in later chapters.

How will meta analysis contribute to risk mapping? By bringing about two specific outcomes: First, it will result in the creation of an objective and robust evaluative template, which in turn will form the basis for consistent, risk type specific evaluation of the available information. Second, it will yield a summary of the available risk exposure information—in a sense, it will contribute an enterprise-wide summary of risk types and risk exposure, in the context of reliability of the current level of knowledge.

Risk Response

Establishing definitional and operational clarity with regard to risk types and risk exposure necessitates crafting an effective risk management plans. Stated differently, risks need to be dealt with, hence careful risk definition and cataloging needs to be followed by an equally thorough assessment of risk type specific response strategies. In general, an organization has four distinct risk response options available:

Avoidance.	In most situations, this translates into exiting out of activities that give rise to risks that are to be avoided.
Reduction.	Taking specific steps, often referred to as "risk mitigation", to reduce the likelihood and/or severity of specific risk types.
Transfer.	Insuring, sharing or otherwise outsourcing specific risks.
Acceptance.	For the most part, it entails no action, either as a result of explicit cost-benefit analysis or because no other options are available.

Avoidance

"Don't do it" is often the easiest recommendation to issues and the hardest one to implement. As noted earlier, risk is a consequence of our, or in a broader sense, organizational actions, hence risk avoidance is ultimately directed at actions that precipitate risks to be avoided. Under most circumstances, risk avoidance is the most appropriate strategy for risks falling under the general umbrella of regulatory risks. An officer or a director of a company should not knowingly mislead investors or governmental officials; the same executives should not attempt to bribe foreign or domestic officials; a company should not engage in anti-competitive, price-fixing schemas, etc. As taxing, in terms of time and effort, as regulatory compliance can be (e.g., there is a mounting opposition to the reporting burden imposed by the enforcement of the Sarbanes-Oxley Act), it is nonetheless a relatively uncomplicated risk management task: Regulated behaviors are usually explicitly defined and penalties are equally clearly laid out. Contrasted with other types of business risks, such as the possibility of a hurricane damaging a particular facility, absolution of key technologies or the probability of a major product liability suit, identifying and avoiding regulatory risks is relatively easy. Why? Largely because unlike hurricanes or market forces, regulatory requirements are perfectly knowable (after all, that is the exactly the goal of governmental regulations), which also makes this a very atypical type of a threat.

Conceptually, there are other types of risks that can be avoided, to a larger or a greater degree, but are not knowable in advance, as is the case with regulatory threats. For instance, a decision to enter a particular geographic market or product category is generally under the company's control, though potential dangers that might be associated with those decisions are rarely, if ever, known in advance. Are those risks avoidable? In principle, yes, because they stem from the company-controlled factors.

To generalize beyond the above examples, there are two, mutually independent (i.e., either—or) prerequisites for avoidance being a viable risk management strategy: 1. a particular risk type is *knowable*, as is the case with regulatory risk, or 2. actions giving rise to a particular risk type are *controllable* by the company, as is the case with operational risks. If neither of the two conditions is true, avoidance is likely not a viable strategy.

In practice, how many risk types are then avoidable, at least in principle? Consider the earlier-delineated risk types shown below in Table 2.1.

Table 2.1
Sample Listing of Risk Types

Risk Type	Description
Market	Significant change in supply & demand function, including raw materials;
Competitive	Entry of new competitors;
Technological	Obsolescence of current technologies; cost of acquiring new ones;
Financial	Increase in the cost of capital; unfavorable exchange rate changes;
Operational	A broad category of threats relating to strategic and tactical decisions;
Regulatory	Changes in public policy and governmental regulation;
Environmental	Changing pollution, carbon emissions & disposal standards;
Supply Chain	Failure of contractor to deliver on time, schedule or for agreed price;
Physical/Property	Natural disasters, crime, vandalism or arson;
Socio-Cultural	Changes in the demographic makeup of the marketplace;
Reputational	Negative publicity adversely impact brand equity;
Professional	Changes in the ability to attract and retain skilled human resources;

The twelve different risk types listed and briefly defined in Table 2.1 can be considered in the context of the two key avoidance prerequisites named earlier: 1. being knowable, and/or 2. being controllable. Implicit in these two notions is the source of the specific actions giving rise to particular risk types. Hence the information presented in Table 2.1 can be further contextualized by expressly considering the source of each type of risk and ascertaining whether or not it is knowable and/or controllable. Consider Table 2.2.

Table 2.2
Contextualizing the Sample Listing of Risk Types

Risk Type	Source	Knowable	Controllable
Market	External	No	No
Competitive	External	No	No
Technological	External	No	No
Financial	External	No	No
Operational	*Internal*	No	*Yes*
Regulatory	External	*Yes*	*Yes*
Environmental	External	*Yes*	No
Supply Chain	External	No	No
Physical/Property	External	No	No
Socio-Cultural	External	*Yes*	No
Reputational	*Internal*	No	*Yes*
Professional	*Internal*	*Yes*	*Yes*

The risk type cross tabulation shown in Table 2.2 draws attention to several important conclusions. First, the idea of a risk type being "knowable" can be better understood in the qualifying context of *time* and *information*. Internally-sourced risk type are knowable because the requisite information is readily available—at the same time, socio-cultural or environmental risks are knowable because these phenomenon usually unfold very slowly, and though information may be imperfect, an interested observer will nonetheless be able to discern these trends by carefully studying their indicators. Second, the idea of risk creating actions being "controllable" can be further refined in relation to specific control mechanism, which can take the form of either policy-driven efforts, or risk profile management.

Policy-driven risk avoidance is the process of crafting, instituting and enforcing of rules of conduct expressly designed to avoid specific types of risks. For instance, putting in place and enforcing a clear, well-informed and compliance-minded hiring and promotion policies is one of the viable strategies for avoiding claims of unfair workplace practices. *Risk profile management* is a risk avoidance strategy built around purposeful analysis of key risk indicators (defined here as unambiguous and objectively measurable factors that are highly correlated with specific events), targeted at risk-adjusting the organization's decision making processes. In contrast to highly deterministic, rule-based policy-driven risk avoidance, risk profile management is highly probabilistic in nature. For instance, thorough analysis of securities class action litigation might reveal that certain traits of organizational behavior, such as high frequency of financial restatement coupled with aggressive revenue accruing and highly volatile share price might be highly correlated with the risk of securities class action litigation. Active profile risk management efforts geared at avoiding the possibility of costly securities litigation would leverage this knowledge and use to risk-adjust decisions touching upon the above mentioned factors.

Turning our attention back to Table 2.2 brings to light the third key conclusion stemming from the analysis of risk type specific viability of risk avoidance. Roughly half of the twelve risk types listed above stem from external actions and are neither knowable nor controllable. In other words, for these risk types, avoidance is generally not going to be a viable strategy. In a broader sense, this suggests that a significant proportion of threats confronting organizations ought to be considered from the standpoint of financial management of risk exposure. This is saying that when it comes to some risks, the emphasis should be placed on objective assessment of the organization's exposure to those risk, expressed in terms of the probability of occurrence as well as the expected cost, and taking specific steps to either reduce or altogether transfer not so much the possibility of occurrence, but the resultant financial consequences.

Reduction

The distinction between risk avoidance and risk reduction is not always clear. Taking the regulation-mandated reporting steps does not guarantee regulatory compliance per se, most notably because the accuracy may be suspect. Similarly, a sound workforce practices policy will not immunize the organization from the possibility of discrimination or sexual harassment claims as rogue employees can willfully disregard the stated policy. The point is that risk reduction can, in many instances, be viewed as practical consequence of what might overtly be believed to be risk avoidance efforts. However, conceptually there are a number of distinctions separating these two risk response postures.

First and foremost, risk reduction does not necessitate risk type being knowable or controllable—it does, however, necessitate some degree of understanding of key risk indicators, which in turn necessitates the risk type being estimable. To be estimable, a risk type has to be operationally distinct and measurable, in a manner allowing cross-occurrence comparisons. In short, there has to be sufficiently sized and representative sampling of the event's occurrences to enable the estimation of the key dimensions of risk: likelihood and severity.

Risk reduction efforts need to be considered in the context of the two dimensions of risk—likelihood and severity. Stated differently, reducing the likelihood of a particular undesirable event might entail considerably different set of activities than reducing the severity of the same event.

Reducing Likelihood

There are two, briefly discussed earlier, broadly defined sets of activities that are available for reducing the likelihood of a particular risk type: 1. policy setting, and 2. risk profile management.

As implied in the name, *policy setting* is the creation, implementation and enforcement of specific rules of conduct aimed at diminishing the likelihood of undesirable events. Doing so is predicated upon the availability of appropriate knowledge regarding risk increasing activities. More often than not, policy setting is prohibitive in nature, which is a direct consequence of the character of the policy-shaping knowledge. The risk estimation is in effect the analysis of historical occurrences of the event (i.e., risk type) which means that the resultant knowledge is going to be focused primarily on the event precipitating behaviors and other traits. As a result, the bulk of organizational policies designed to reduce the likelihood of specific risks are focused on prohibiting the undesirable event likelihood increasing behaviors and activities. This can be an effective tool for lowering the probability of certain types of risk, particularly those falling under the broad umbrella of reputational risks.

Risk profile management is an alternative likelihood lowering approach (discussed in the upcoming two chapters). It is rooted in the modern information theory[8], or more specifically, in multivariate probabilistic models leveraging large corporate and third-party (organizations maintaining large, usually national databases compiling behavioral, demographic, psychographic or attitudinal data) data sources. It is defined as the utilization of probabilistic, event predicting insights to risk-adjust organizational decisions. As implied in its description, risk profile management is not quite as "cut and dry" as the policy setting outlined earlier. It generally does not produce prohibitive behaviors or activities—instead, it provides an objective, quantifiable method of estimating incremental effects of actions or behaviors that have been shown to be associated with heightened likelihood of undesirable events. The informational basis of risk profile management is graphically depicted in Figure 2.7.

Figure 2.7
Informational Basis of Risk Profile Management

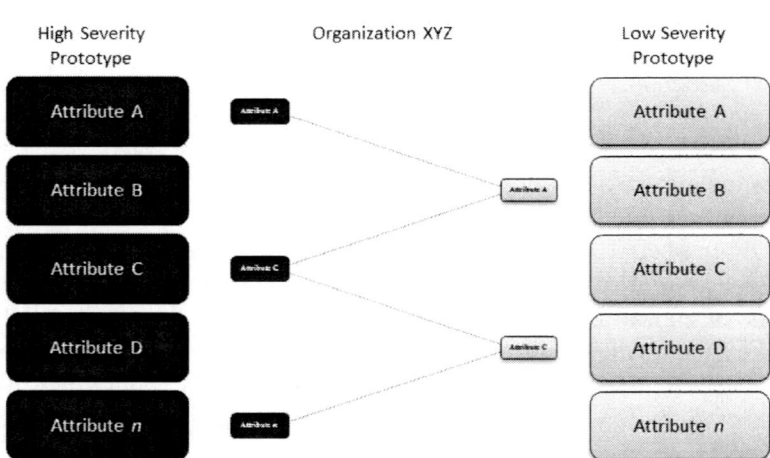

The "High Likelihood of Undesirable Event" represents a prototype of a high risk organization, expressed in terms of specific, risk-increasing attributes, A thru *n*. The "Low Likelihood of Undesirable Event" represents a prototype of a low risk organization, expressed in terms of risk-reducing attributes. The line in the center of the chart shows the similarity of Company XYZ to either the high or low risk profile on each of the delineated attributes. The high and low risk profiles are expressed in term of probabilities, where the former exhibits significantly above average likelihood of the undesirable event taking place, while the latter embodies significantly below average chance. Active risk management entails a deliberate examination of the company's "positioning" on each of the risk exposure (likelihood) determining attributes, followed by making appropriate, informed decisions.

Transfer

Going back to Table 2.2, roughly half of the risk types identified there are externally driven events that are neither controllable, in terms of their likelihood or severity, nor knowable, at least no sufficiently ahead of their occurrence. The financial meltdown rapidly and dramatically unfolding at the time of writing of this book (2008-2009) is an example of such risks. On a more micro scale, a company can unexpectedly be confronted with a failure of a key supplier (supply chain risk), an introduction of a market-changing technological innovation by one of its competitors or the entry of a large, dominant organization into its product category. In short, there are multiple types of undesirable events that exhibit some, usually unknown probability of occurrence, possibly resulting in a wide range of economic losses. For those types of losses, the risk management efforts are—as they should be—focused almost entirely on the severity dimension, or the likely financial fallout. Stated differently, when confronted with "unmanageable" (i.e., those that cannot be either avoided or systematically reduced) risks, they seek to transfer all or some of those risks, largely with the goal of insulating their earnings from unexpected and potentially highly dramatic jolts. Insurance coverage is the most often sought remedy for dealing with unmanageable risks.

The acquisition of insurance coverage by an organization is often described as "risk transfer." That is technically incorrect. Considering that any risk is defined in the context of two independent dimensions of likelihood and severity, transference of risk should be reflected in changes to both dimensions. In other words, in order for an organization to transfer a particular of risk to another entity, the recipient, or transferee, has to assume both the likelihood of the threat materializing as well as the severity of the risk type being transferred. That is not the case with insurance coverage, which affects only the severity aspect of risk, while having no impact on likelihood. This leads to an obvious conclusion that commercial insurance should not be described as risk transfer, but rather as a post-event compensatory mechanism. This line of reasoning is intuitively obvious to most of us: Buying flood insurance, for instance, does not remove the possibility of our homes getting flooded—it only offers financial compensation in the event of that threat materializing.

Definitional issues notwithstanding, let's go down the path of treating that insurance coverage does indeed constitutes risk transfer. Broadly speaking, an organization considering procuring insurance has two basic options: 1. to buy specific type and amount of coverage from a commercial insurance provider, or 2. In the case of the first of the two options, the decision amounts to selecting the type of coverage, the amount of coverage (i.e., the "limits") and the attachment point, also called "self-insured retention". Having made those decisions, all that's left is to shop around for the best terms (i.e., price) and conditions (coverage inclusions, exclusions, etc.)[9]. The key advantage to using commercial insurance is that, under most circumstances, it is readily available, which means that a desired amount of protection can be put in place relatively quickly. The key disadvantage to relying on commercial insurance coverage is that it represents, from a financial standpoint, an expense yielding no residual value[10]. And although an insurance policy is technically an asset, as it represents a contingent form of capital, purchasing it creates a drag on earnings.

An alternative to commercial insurance is the so-called "captive insurance." *Captive insurance* companies are insurance companies established with the specific objective of financing risks stemming their parent company, or a group of companies. In essence, it amounts to a particular organization choosing to establish its own insurance company, rather than relying on commercial coverage. The term "captive" was coined by F. Reiss in the 1950's. Working (as a consultant) with Youngstown Sheet & Tube Company, Reiss was looking for a risk financing solution which would enable his client to put in place the required coverage, but in a more financially economical manner. His client company had a series of mining operations and its management referred to the mines whose output was put solely to the corporation's use as "captive mines". When Reiss helped them incorporate their own insurance subsidiaries, they were referred to as captive insurance companies because they wrote insurance exclusively for the captive mines[11]. The key advantage to owning a captive is financial—unlike commercial insurance premiums which are paid to an outside entity, payments made into a captive stay within the parent organization, which means that if the captive's operating costs combined with incurred losses are less than the paid premiums, the effective cost of coverage is reduced by the amount of residual value. The key disadvantage to owning a captive is twofold: 1. Added complexity to the risk management (or more specifically, financing) function, and 2. Increased risk exposure—captive, after all, is an insurance company, which means it too faces the possibility of incurring abnormally large losses[12].

Turning our attention back to more broadly defined risk transfer considerations, in a true risk transfer, the other party assumes both dimensions of risk, either by means of a contract or a hedge. A *contract,* in the context of risk transfer, is defined as a voluntary, deliberate and legally binding agreement between two or more competent parties, while a *hedge* is defined as an investment made by taking a trading position in a futures or options market to minimize the impact of adverse changes in interest rates or in the prices of commodities or securities[13].

Contractual risk transfer shifts the responsibility for claims, loss and damages to the other party, with the goal of shielding the organization from any responsibility relating to the risk being transferred. Risk transfer contracts are relatively common in construction, where the owner of the project being constructed may transfer all responsibility to the project's manager, or in supply chain management, where the risk may be transferred to a major vendor. Conversely, these types of arrangements are rarely seen in the realm of professional liability (e.g., professional malpractice or directors' and officers' liability).

Unlike the explicit and somewhat tangible contractual risk transference, *hedging* is more of a broad risk transfer strategy aiming to minimize, rather than altogether eliminate exposure to certain types of business risks. There are different types of hedges available, reflecting varying amounts of speculative decision making. One of the most straightforward and least speculative types is the so-called "natural hedge" which is based on pairing of naturally co-existing phenomenon. For instance, one of the safest methods of limiting a multinational company's exposure to currency exchange fluctuation is to establish production facilities in a country in which a given product is being sold (doing so, of course, may expose the organization to other risks, such as socio-political or regulatory ones).

There are a number of alternatives to the above outlined "traditional" risk transfer approaches; as a group, these fall under the umbrella of *alternative risk transfer*, or ART. Given the proliferation of those methods, it is worthwhile to take a closer look.

The ART of Risk Transfer

Perhaps the first known alternative risk transfer mechanism was Tanker Insurance Company Ltd., which was the first captive insurance company formed in 1920. Self-funded insurance, as exemplified by captives, became more widely spread following Douglas Barlow pioneering the notion of "cost-at-risk" (introduced in 1962) which offered an objective method of comparing the total cost of insurance to the total cost of risk self-funding. Many of the alternative risk transfer mechanisms in use today grew out of series of insurance capacity crises in the 1970's through the 1990's. As a group, most of the ART techniques allow investors in capital markets to play a more direct role in providing insurance-like protection, effectively contributing to the blurring of the distinction between insurance and financial markets. The most frequently used alternative risk financing alternatives are shown below.

67

Table 2.3
Alternative Forms of Risk Financing

Form	Description
Self-Funded Insurance	Frequently taking the form of captive insurance or financial reinsurance; both captives and financial reinsurance come in a variety of different forms, such as single parent, association, group, agency or rent-a-captive; or finite, surplus relief, funded (for reinsurance).
Risk Securitization	Exemplified by the so-called special purpose vehicles best known for offering catastrophe & reinsurance bonds.
Non-Indemnity Trading	Best exemplified by industry loss warranties.
Insurance Hedge Funds	Investment vehicle which function like fully collateralized reinsurance but take the form of hedge funds.
Fronting Arrangements	Under most circumstances, these are a specialized form of reinsurance where a commercial insurance company which is licensed in a particular jurisdiction to issue a policy acts as a front, but the risk is then fully transferred to a captive insurance company through a reinsurance agreement.
Loss Portfolio Transfer	Negotiated arrangements which mitigate accrued liabilities by converting future liabilities to present day fixed price.
Reciprocal Insurance	It represents an interchange among subscribers of reciprocal agreement of indemnity thru a common attorney-in-fact.
Finite Risk Reinsurance	Built around matching of current and potential liabilities against assets over an appropriate length of time (under finite risk a company ends paying most of its losses over time, but if it has a favorable loss experience it also shares in the underwriting profit, inclusive of investment income).
Contingent Capital	Often used to provide financial coverage for statistically improbable losses without incurring the cost of maintaining excess (over and above realized severity) insurance limits; it is a form of securitized capital based on option contracting.
Retrospective Ratings	A mechanism for adjusting insurance premium, retrospectively, on the basis of losses incurred during the insurance period.

On average, about 40% of the total cost of risk in North America is handled by the variety of alternative risk financing solutions outlined above. Naturally, in view of the combination of buyer-specific risk transfer needs, the prevailing marketplace conditions (most notably, the availability of capital) and the risk transfer mechanism specific characteristics, the "best" alternative risk transfer solution will be highly situational. That said, expressly considering the available ART options should be a standard risk management practice.

<u>Acceptance</u>

Not everything that is worth knowing is knowable. And similarly, not every imaginable potential threat should be acted on. It is simply not economically feasible to "do something" about each and every conceivable threat. But how does the organization decide which risks it should actively manage (i.e., avoid, reduce or transfer) and which it should, in effect, do nothing about? The answer can be found in the nature of the impact of a given risk type, specifically, the *competitive parity* of impact. In essence, the key determining factor governing the risk acceptance decisioning is whether or not a particular risk type is expected to have a disproportionately large impact on the organization, or can the expected impact be assumed to be proportionate to the impact on other organizations?

Consider the threat of a large asteroid striking Earth. According to the scientists, the likelihood of it happening is far less than 1-in-1,000,000, but nonetheless, it is a possibility and hence it poses a potential threat to an organization (and obviously the mankind at large, but I shall only consider the impact on organizations). If it materialized, would it be significantly more damaging to Company A than to Company B? Obviously, nobody really knows, but as far-fetched as it may seem, the fate of dinosaurs can give us a hint. The dominant, at this point in time, theory explaining the relatively sudden disappearance of dinosaurs points to a large asteroid colliding with Earth, which resulted in a huge dust cloud being kicked up shutting off much of solar radiation needed for plant photosynthesis, ultimately resulting in cutting off the dinosaurs' food supply. Of interest to us is that it was not just one, two or a few dinosaur species that disappeared—essentially the entire dinosaur ecosystem vanished. The risk associated with this particular event (i.e., an asteroid colliding with Earth) was essentially the same for all species of dinosaurs, hence accepting that risk did not disadvantage any of the individual species.

In the context of (human) risk management, financing threats that do not expose the company to a disproportionate, vis-à-vis the competitors, amount of risk amounts to unnecessarily reducing the firm's earnings, in effect imposing an excessive risk tax on shareholders. Hence the decision to accept certain risks should be based on comparative exposure assessment, rather than the often-recommended cost-benefit analysis[14]. Comparative assessment analysis examines the potential impact of a risk type in the context of the organization's set of competitors to determine if the potential impact, in term of its consequences, would vary across individual companies. The analysis itself is highly contextualized, shaped largely by the nature of specific types of risk and industry characteristics. For instance, the potential impact of global warming driven changes in carbon dioxide emission standards (a type of regulatory risk) would be far more pronounced in "large emission footprint" industries, such as electric utilities or manufacturing, than in (relatively) "low emission footprint" industries, such as financial services or healthcare.

More so than in the case other three risk response modalities (avoidance, reduction and transfer), risk acceptance can be a reflection of the organization's culture. A conservative, risk-avoiding entity might have a significantly different view of a particular risk, such as carbon emission related potential regulatory changes, than an aggressive, risk-taking organization. Neither view is inherently better or worse than the other, though expressly taking it into account is an important part of the due diligence process. It is important to note that the character of an organization tends to be a reflection of natural biases of the key decision makers. According to the cultural theory[15], there are four major perceptual biases relating to the perception of risk: Individualist, Egalitarian, Hierarchist and Fatalist. *Individualists* are those whose decisions are generally unconstrained by the demands of the organization at large; *Egalitarians* are those favoring a more democratic decision making; *Hierarchists* tend to ascribe value and importance based on the input-provider's position in the organization; *Fatalists* tend to believe that little can be done to mitigate risks. In the somewhat subjective assessment of hard-to-measure risks, the evaluation of the type of risk that is deemed acceptable will be influenced by the bias of the key decision makers.

Not Either Or

It is common to think of the alternative risk responses in the context of "one or the other" choice. That is not correct. As shown in Figure 2.2, the causal view of risk shows a clear line demarcation between the antecedent causes and the resultant outcomes, which suggests that risk mitigation and risk transfer efforts should proceed concurrently. To a large degree, that is because it is not reasonable to believe that risk mitigation alone will eliminate the

70

possibility of an undesirable event taking place, while on the other hand, it is unwise and economically reckless to forego risk mitigation efforts once some financial protections have been put in place. An ideal risk management approach, which is also at the heart of the risk profile management framework presented in this book, calls for combining risk mitigation and risk capitalization efforts in such a way as to deliver the greatest possible earnings' protection, at the least cost. Conceptually, the framework borrows from some of the key tenets of enterprise risk management (ERM), a broad outline of which is offered next.

ENTERPRISE RISK MANAGEMENT TYPOLOGIES

The continuing maturating of risk management as a distinct organizational function prompted a number of organizations to start to think in terms of the overall, or organization-wide risk exposure, a notion that has come to be known as *enterprise risk management*, or ERM. The impetus behind ERM is twofold: First, as the scope of risk management efforts continued to grow, it became progressively more and more important to develop a coherent organizational framework to organize the overall efforts in terms of the decision making processes. Second, as the cost associated with organizational responses to individual risks grew, it became progressively more challenging to make sound financial decisions in regard to risk management expenditures. Hence, the imperative to systematically evaluate the organization's exposure to clearly delineated threats and to identify the most effective remedies prompted many organizations to consider a more holistic view of risk.

The emerging "discipline" of enterprise risk management is being shaped by the forces of the evolving regulatory environment, the ongoing development of internal control standards and the growing informational/analytic efficacy. Those forces, in turn, are themselves driven by the seemingly never-ending succession of corporate scandals and—by extension—risk management failures. The collapse of the savings-and-loan sector in the late 1980's and early 1990's, the 1991 Salomon Brothers bond scandal, the Bearings derivatives fiasco of the mid-1990's, the Enron, WorldCom and other corporate governance scandals of the early 2000's, the stock option back-dating that following shortly after, the subprime lending disaster that already racked up over half a trillion of U.S dollars of financial institutions' write-offs (as the writing of this book) and it is still believed to be far from over…

It is hard to pinpoint a specific time when ERM entered the corporate stage. In fact, it is probably more appropriate to look at its emergence as a gradual phenomenon, a product of the evolution the corporate conception of risk and the risk management practice. The emergence of the modern portfolio theory, marked by Markowitz's seminal work on portfolio allocation under uncertainty[16] is generally believed to mark the starting point of modern, corporate risk management efforts. The subsequent introduction of the Capital Assets Pricing Model (CAPM) as a tool for determining a theoretically appropriate required rate of return of an asset[17] and particularly, Black and Scholes' options pricing model[18], laid the foundations for major risk transfer jump-started systematic risk evaluation and management efforts. The passing of the Foreign Corrupt Practices Act in 1977, which came on the hills on SEC investigations in the mid-1970's where over 400 U.S. companies admitted to making questionable or illegal payments (in excess of $300 million) to foreign officials, acted as yet another force prompting organization to consider a more formal risk management efforts. Initially, that led to strengthening of focus on compliance and internal controls, but eventually, starting in the mid-1980's companies began to form risk management departments.

The 1985 formation of COSO (Committee of Sponsoring Organizations[19]) tasked with sponsoring the National Commission on Fraudulent Financial Reporting opened a new chapter in structured risk management efforts—a formal study of causal factors precipitating fraudulent financial reporting. Several years after its formation, COSO published its first official risk management framework: *Internal Control – Integrated Framework* (1992). Several waves of corporate scandals later and on the heels of the 2002 Sarbanes-Oxley Act, which established new or enhanced standards for all U.S public company boards, management and public accounting firms, COSO published a broadened and significantly revised version of its original framework, described in more detail in the next section.

Though many of the ideas imbedded into it are universal in nature, the inner-logic of the COSO framework primarily reflects North American regulatory priorities and marketplace realities, all of which makes this framework less applicable outside of North America. The *ISO 31000 Standard*, published by the International Organization for Standardization[20] in 2009, is both more universal and more contemporary (the aforementioned revised COSO framework was released in 2004), which means it explicitly considers threats accentuated by more recent events, such as the financial crisis of 2008. Thus, even though North American risk management community might be more familiar with the COSO framework, the ever-accelerating globalization trend points toward the ISO 31000 standard as s more universally appropriate conceptualization.

Although some components of the enterprise risk management may reflect binding governmental regulations (e.g., Basel II capital requirements for financial institutions or Sarbanes-Oxley Act's Section 404 imposing risk assessment and reporting requirements for publicly traded companies), enterprise risk management is fundamentally a self-governing endeavor. In other words, beyond adherence to applicable regulations, companies are in essence free to embrace – or not – an enterprise approach to risk management and for those that do, to design their own ERM infrastructure. An organization interested in instituting sound ERM practices should seek the guidance of one or more of the established frameworks: 1. Committee of Sponsoring Organizations, or COSO, *Enterprise Risk Management – Integrated Framework* (2004); or 2. International Organization for Standardization, or ISO, *Standard 31000*, commonly referred to as ISO 31000: 2009. I should point out that the latter of the two frameworks is a replacement to the Australian/New Zealand Standard (*Risk Management, AS/NZS 4360*: 2004, itself a revision of AS/NZS 4360: 1999 standard), so although some literature might cite three distinct general ERM conceptualizations, effectively there are only two current ones. In addition, financial organizations might also want to refer to the Bank for International Settlements: Basel II standard (*International Convergence of Capital Measurement and Capital Standards: A Revised Framework*[21]), which addresses systemic risks that are unique to financial intermediaries, such as liquidity or capital adequacy (given the idiosyncratic character of the Basel II standard it will not be covered here).

COSO Framework

In September of 2004, the Committee of Sponsoring Organizations of the Treadway Commission issued an expanded version of its 1992 framework (*Internal Controls – Integrated Framework*), under a new heading of *Enterprise Risk Management – Integrated Framework*. The *COSO ERM Framework*, as it is commonly known, has since gained wide acceptance among U.S-based companies, but not so outside of the United States.

COSO defines enterprise risk management as "…a process, effected by an entity's board of directors, management and other personnel, applied in strategy setting and across the enterprise, designed to identify potential events that may affect the entity, and manage risk to be within its risk appetite, to provide reasonable assurance regarding the achievement of entity objectives." Among the most noteworthy notions put forth in the aforementioned definition is the emphasis of the role of ERM as a strategic tool, rather than a mere means of demonstrating compliance. In other words, risk management should be viewed—and more importantly, practice—as a contributor to the enterprise's value creation. To do that, ERM needs to be able to deal effectively with potential future events that could be a source of economically-impactful uncertainty, and it needs to provide means of reducing the likelihood of negative and increase the likelihood of positive outcomes.

Application-wise, the COSO framework attempts to help organizations accomplish four risk management related core organizational objectives of strategic planning, operational management, reporting and compliance. As expressly noted in the language of the framework, those objectives need to be evaluated at all levels of the organization, inclusive of division, business unit or subsidiary. In more explicit terms, COSO defines those as follows:

> ➢ *Strategic planning.*
> Those aligned with and supporting attainment of the organization's high level goals. Focused on the question of "What we are trying to accomplish?"
> ➢ *Operational management.*
> More tactically oriented outcomes, such as performance or profitability. Focused on the question of "How are we going to accomplish our strategic goals?"
> ➢ *Reporting.*
> Communication means and processes. Focused on the question of "How are we going to communicate with our internal and external stakeholders?"
> ➢ *Compliance.*
> The organization's adherence to applicable laws and regulations. Focused on the question of "What are we going to do to make sure we comply with all laws and regulations affecting us?"

Regardless of the organizational level of analysis (i.e., entity-wide vs. division, etc.), the assessment should be built around a portfolio view of risk, in a sense in which "portfolio" is used in the Modern Portfolio Theory (MPT) in finance. (Very briefly, MPT describes how rational investors can use diversification to optimize their portfolios and how risky assets should be priced.) The basic provisions of the Modern Portfolio Theory yield two key, ERM-related implications: 1. portfolio risk is not the simple sum of the individual risk elements, and 2. to understand portfolio risk, one must understand the risks of the individual elements and their interactions.

Stated differently, each risk needs to be evaluated independently of all other risks, in addition to which, cross-risk interrelationships need to be estimated. In other words, one of the basic provisions of the COSO framework is to estimate, at the level of individual business units as well as entity-wide, the impact of individual risks and the interdependencies among those risks. Having done so, the organization is then in position to explicitly consider its overall risk exposure vis-à-vis its risk appetite and make appropriate risk type specific decision: to avoid, reduce, share or accept.

The overall enterprise risk management process is embodied in the following eight components (see Figure 2.8 for a visual depiction):

- *Internal Environment.*
  It sets a philosophy for how risks and controls are viewed and addressed by the organization; it sets and reflects the management's risk bearing philosophy.
- *Objective Setting.*
  A delineation of the entity business goals, which is an essential prerequisite to identifying events that may potentially impede reaching of those objectives.
- *Event Identification.*
  Singling out of specific factors, both internal as well as external, that may affect strategy implementation and the attainment of stated organizational objectives. Ideally, this step an explicit differentiation between potential threats and opportunities.
- *Risk Assessment.*
  Evaluation of the above-delineated risk factors in terms of their expected likelihood and severity.
- *Risk Response.*
  Selection of a set of actions to align assessed risks with the entity's risk appetite, in the context of the strategy and objectives.
- *Control Activities.*
  Selection and execution of policies and procedures tasked with ascertaining that the selected risk responses are adequately carried out.
- *Information Sharing.*
  The development of a process to capture and disseminate pertinent information.
- *Monitoring.*
  An ongoing oversight of the risk management process, inclusive of any modifications that may be deemed necessary.

Figure 2.8
The COSO Enterprise Risk Management Framework

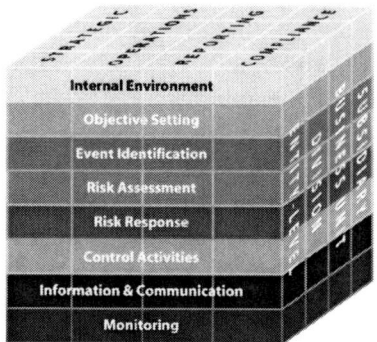

The COSO framework presents a compelling depiction of risk management which is not viewed just as a "necessary evil" imposed by various regulatory burdens, but a contributor to the attainment of the entity's stated strategic goals. At the same time, it also paints a relatively methodologically complex picture. If risk portfolio cannot be assumed to be a simple sum of its parts, enterprise risk management measurement has to encompass the means of empirically estimating the nature of cross-risk interdependencies. To be informationally complete, these estimates ought to be framed in the context of risk-specific likelihood and severity assessment.

Impact of the COSO Framework

The vast majority of organizations that embrace the idea of enterprise risk management also embrace the COSO framework is the primary conceptualization. In view of that, the COSO framework should have had a considerable impact on the practice of risk management; yet, the evidence does not necessarily support that assertion.

An informal survey conducted among risk managers representing a cross section of energy, hospitality and entertainment, healthcare and technology organizations suggests that, on the one hand, COSO-expressed ERM initiatives garnered a lot of attention and interest, but, on the other hand, to-date tangible benefits are far and few in-between. The findings suggested two key reasons behind the lack of noticeable business impact of the COSO framework:

⊳ *The framework's complexity, coupled with its breadth.*
The implications of the Figure 2.8 are intellectually compelling, but equally operationally daunting. In theory, it is hard to argue with the vision where the totality of the organization's risks is systematically evaluated at all levels of the organization and results communicated to the appropriate stakeholders. Making that happen is a different story altogether. Perhaps the framework is too all-encompassing. A large organization, comprised of multiple, often quite dissimilar business unit would face a gargantuan task, if it were to pool the universe of its risks together into a singular framework. This is not to say that, if done successfully, the COSO-communicated vision would not be beneficial to the organization. However, the overt complexity of the proposed framework might be as much an impediment as it is a roadmap for an organization.

⊳ *The lack of clear operationalization—no measurement clarity.*
The COSO's framework is surprisingly mute on the topic of measurement. Specifically, it provides no appreciable guidance regarding how the individual risks it delineates are to be measured, in effect, pushing that responsibility onto the users of the framework. However, as discussed later in this chapter, not only is the number of risk types quite large, the very "measurability" (i.e., the availability of objective data) of individual risks varies considerably. In other words, while the "what" to measure is important, "how" to measure is critical. Consider Figure 2.9.

Figure 2.9
COSO Risk Measurement Conceptualization

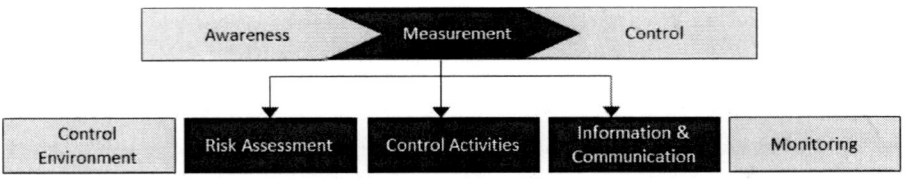

As shown in the above, COSO-derived conceptualization, measurement plays a pivotal role in the efficacy of the overall framework—after all, control activities are predicated upon objective assessment of the viability of risk events. It is simply hard to understand why risk measurement is given so little attention in the context of the overall framework, unless this silence can be taken as an implicit admission of intractability of the ideas embodied by the COSO process. Or perhaps in its drive to be all-encompassing, COSO failed to take into account the issue of risk type specific measurability. As it is intuitively obvious, some risk types are much prone to being estimated than some others. For instance, the probability of an organization incurring securities class action litigation can be more precisely estimated than the probability of its technology becoming obsolete. Specific reasons notwithstanding, the efficacy of the enterprise-wide risk assessment promoted by the COSO framework is suspect as a direct consequence of its failure to take into account inherent measurement differences separating individual risk types. So while it puts forth some very worthwhile conceptual ideas, the COSO ERM framework is not likely to become the agent of change for the risk management practice.

Beyond the insights revealed by the aforementioned survey, the COSO framework suffers from a couple of additional, somewhat more subtle limitations. First, it implicitly anchors risk in the possibility of an adverse event taking place or not. In other words, risk is viewed as having either a negative (an adverse event materializes) or a neutral (an adverse event does not materialize) outcome—i.e., it equates risk with downside risk. As discussed earlier, a complete definition of risk needs to also include upside risk, such as those exemplified by introducing a new product, new technology or venturing into a new market. Just as storm or civil litigation, both examples of downside risk, can have costly consequences, investing in a new product launch can have equally (or even greater) significant negative consequences. Hence both downside and upside risks can negatively impact the organization's earnings, in addition to which, upside risk can have a positive impact on earnings. This is to say that in order to be truly "enterprise-wide", a risk assessment framework needs to encompass both the downside as well as upside risks.

Secondly, COSO invites a certain amount of reductionism. More specifically, there is a tendency to use it a "check box" tool for internal reporting or compliance-related needs. In some way, this is yet another consequence of the framework's complexity, coupled with lack of clear operationalization. Nonetheless, there is a temptation to reduce the risk investigatory power of the framework to that of superficial compliance. Stated differently, in order to be truly effective, a risk assessment framework cannot be reduced to a superficial compliance tool.

ISO 31000 Standard

The current Standard traces its origin to the *AS/NZS* (Australia / New Zealand) *4360, Risk Management* framework published in 2004, itself a third revision of the framework bearing the same designation originally released in 1995 (and subsequently revised in 1999). The overall goal of the Australian/New Zealand Standard is to outline a rational context for identifying, analyzing, evaluating, treating, monitoring and communicating risk in a manner geared toward reaching a balance between the pursuit of growth and avoidance of losses. The risk management approach the Standard promotes is built around an iterative process consisting of sequentially-ordered steps that encourage continuous improvement in risk-related decision-making efficacy. The process is intentionally generic, so that it can be applied to a wide range of activities or decisions in public, private or community (e.g., not-for-profit) enterprises.

Continuing the AS/NZS 4360's spirit of universal applicability, the ISO *Standard 31000: 2009* outlines a framework for implementing risk management, rather than a framework for supporting the risk management processes (which is the case with the earlier-discussed COSO framework). Stated, differently, the intent of the Standard is to enable individual organizations to shape their own risk management-supporting frameworks by way of expressly defining their risk architecture, risk strategy and risk protocol related preferences, as graphically depicted in figure 2.10.

Figure 2.10
ISO 31000 Risk Management: The Building Blocks

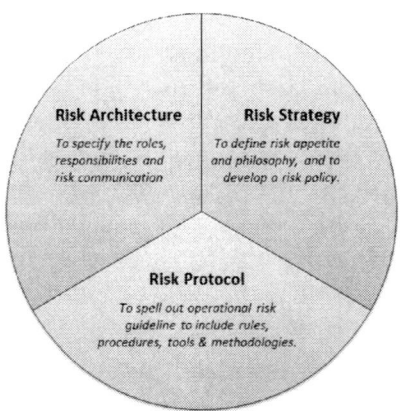

80

Understandably, the greater (than COSO) ambiguity of the Standard can be unsettling, but there is wisdom in it that should not be missed: To be universally applicable, which is to say to be meaningful to public, private or community enterprises, across types of endeavors and/or industries, a framework has to be devoid of any specifics that are meaningful in one context but not in another. At the same time, to be useful, an approach has to offer insights or guidance that would otherwise not be available, which raises an obvious question: What specific guidance does ISO 31000 Standard offer?

First and foremost, the Standard makes it clear that to yield material gains, the embrace of ERM by an organization has to be rooted in a leadership (board of directors and executive management) mandate and an express commitment. Once that has been secured, the next step is to design a framework tailored to the specifics of the organization's circumstances, with a particular emphasis on its risk philosophy and risk appetite. Once designed, the framework needs to be operationalized, or implemented, which has wide ranging implications from the, somewhat intangible process design to more concrete rules, procedures, tools, techniques and methodologies. Once implemented, the effectiveness of those processes, and the framework as such, needs to be monitored and, periodically, reviewed. Inevitably, the ongoing monitoring is likely to produce framework enhancement ideas, thus the next step suggested by the Standard is that of improving the framework, at which point the risk management process loop starts anew...Figure 2.11 shows the schematic of the process.

Figure 2.11
ISO 31000 Risk Management Process: High Level View

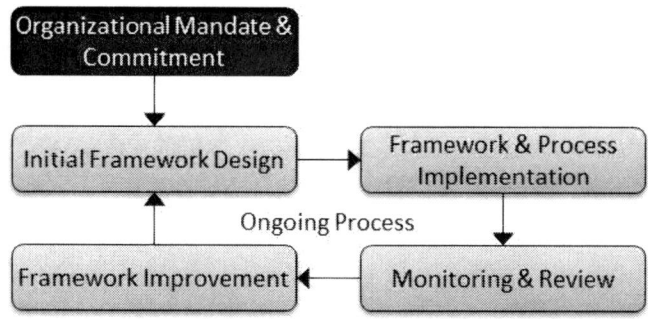

Perhaps one of the more controversial aspects of the ISO 31000 conceptualization is that it departs from a traditional definition of risk which defines it as "probability of loss"- using the Standard's terminology (ISO Guide 73), risk is "the effect of uncertainty on objectives." In doing so, the Standard explicitly incorporates the earlier discussed notions of upside and downside risk, which is an important consideration in establishing the view of risk management as a function which aids the attainment of organizational objectives, rather than merely contributing to the minimization of the impact of adverse developments.

The "heart" of the ISO 31000 process outlined in Figure 2.11 is the process geared at objective, ongoing and systematic risk assessment, treatment and response. Using the Standard's terminology, the process – which takes place within the risk management context of the organization (i.e., is adapted to the uniqueness of the organization) – is comprised of two main elements: 1. Risk assessment, and 2. Risk treatment. The former entails *risk identification*, which establishes the exposure of the organization to identifiable (upside and downside) risks, all in the context of uniqueness of the organization's legal, political, social, cultural and economic circumstances, *risk analysis*, the goal of which is to produce a risk profile of the organization to aid in the risk prioritization and treatment efforts, and *risk evaluation*, the goal of which is to map individual risks to the part of the organization effected by those exposures and to describe the available control mechanisms. The latter of the two key elements of the process – risk treatment – is conceptualized as an activity of selecting and implementing the appropriate response mechanism, which encompass the earlier-discussed options of risk avoidance, mitigation, transfer and financing. Lastly, the ISO 31000 process acknowledges the importance of feedback, for which it suggests two distinct mechanisms: 1. communication & consultation, and 2. monitoring & review. Figure 2.12 shows a graphical depiction of the ISO 31000 process.

Figure 2.12
ISO 31000 Risk Management Process

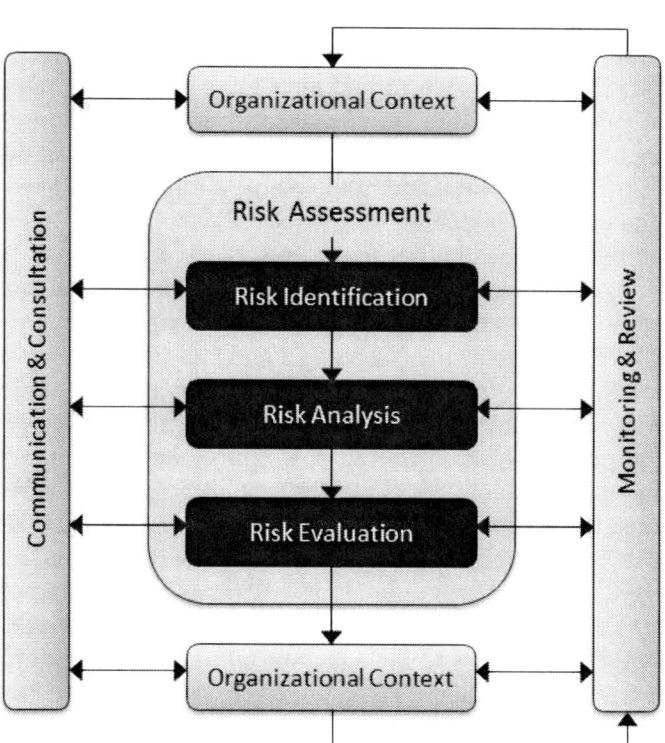

ERM and Debt Ratings

One of the major rating houses, Standard & Poor's (S&P), recently announced that it was planning to expand its current assessment framework to also include an evaluation of the state of enterprise risk management. The outside commentators, such as various consultancies and auditors, had a generally positive reaction to S&P's announcement, as at least on the surface it appears to be a formal acknowledgement of an important aspect of organizational management. Again, it is a compelling argument—that said, there are serious questions surrounding the efficacy of such assessments.

To start, I should point out that Standard & Poor's embraces the COSO framework as the model for ERM construction and implementation. Naturally, the earlier noted operational shortcomings of the COSO model need to be taken into account while contemplating the efficacy of S&P's assessment of corporations' ERM practices. Given the considerable operational ambiguity characterizing the COSO framework, and more specifically the framework's largely undefined measurement specifics, what exactly will be the target of S&P's assessment? Stated differently, if the COSO conceptualization does not offer tangible guidelines spelling out the specific steps and actions that an ERM-implementing organization is to take, what exactly will the S&P (or any other entity) assess? How valid and reliable will such an assessment be and what will be its ultimate value?

Secondly, it seems obvious that being an assessor requires a considerable degree of demonstrated expertise in the area. What qualifies Standard & Poor's to be the evaluator of the adequacy of companies' ERM adequacy? A skeptic would say that being a baseball umpire does not make one a qualified football referee—why should it be any different in this context? Furthermore, has Standard & Poor's demonstrated a great deal of proficiency in mastering its core skill set, to warrant it venturing into becoming the evaluator of yet another, not very closely related dimension of organizational efficacy? Consider the 2008 financial crisis, an event which, to a large degree, was triggered by catastrophic losses in the US markets connected to a broadly defined area of securitized debt obligations. S&P, as well as other major rating agencies put what amounted to a "stamp of approval" on billions of dollars of debt obligations that, contrary to the agency's ratings, were built on dangerously shaky foundations…To be fair, there were multiple other entities, both private and governmental, that were just as blindsided by the said collapse – of course, it is also fair to say that S&P is in the business of knowing and the mere fact that their failure was accompanied by failures of others does not make it any less of a failure. All of this goes to say that healthy skepticism seems warranted when it comes to an organization which seeks to broaden its evaluative scope, while manifestly still has not perfected its core capabilities.

Thirdly, the COSO framework embraced by S&P is skewed toward North American considerations while more and more companies are operating globally. Although a number the North American regulatory philosophies and practices have been adapted in other parts of the world, considerable cross-market differences endure, which means that an assessment of a particular company's enterprise risk management practices ought to be carried out in the context of a more universal framework, which in this case is ISO 31000 Standard discussed earlier.

All considered, is an assessment of the organization-specific enterprise risk management embrace and implementation feasible, regardless of what entity is doing it? I believe so, provided a more explicit operationalization of the conceptually sound ERM ideas spelled out in the aforementioned Standard, especially the notion of "risk profile" addressed by the ISO 31000 guidelines.

3

Risk Measurement

Much like individuals, organizations are bundles of individual attributes. An organization can be described in terms of its business (i.e., products or services and it produces and markets), size (revenue, market capitalization, number of employees), the degree of diversification, location, growth, means of ownership (private vs. public), etc. The resultant description can be relatively broad or quite specific, which means that the list of descriptors can be relatively short or quite long.

A special type of a description is *profiling*. Although "profiling" and "describing" are often used interchangeably, these two activities are considerably different. The main thrust of this difference is the idea of distinctiveness, or the degree to which a particular entity stands out. Generally speaking, to describe means to paint a complete picture, without regard to whether or not the individual components making up the description give rise to distinctiveness of individual entities. For instance, a description of an organization will include traits that are unique to it, as well as those it shares in common with other organizations. On the other hand, to profile means to assemble a sub-set of all available characteristics, specifically, those that are unique to a given entity, thus enabling cross-entity differentiation. In that sense, a profile is almost comprised of a sub-set of traits making up a broader description.

An obvious benefit of profiling is that is focuses on a smaller number of difference-communicating metrics. An equally important, though somewhat less obvious benefit of profiling is disambiguation.

Let's consider a business organization. We can provide a very general description of our hypothetical organization in terms of the type of business, size, products/services, number of locations, means of ownership. At the same time, we can create a far more detailed description by including specific financial, accounting, governance and other details, which quite conceivably (especially for a public company) can entail hundreds of individual metrics. Although relatively simple operationally, the task of compiling an adequate description can be somewhat complex in the sense of deciding just how much detail to include.

Profiling offers a natural solution to the above problem by re-redirecting the efforts away from informational completeness and toward the aforementioned distinctiveness. It amounts to asking: "In the universe of all available descriptors, which ones make this organization stand out?" In other words, all available descriptors can be grouped into distinctive and non-distinctive traits. The former are those that give rise to differences, while the latter are a source of similarities. Of course, being classified in one group or the other is context-dependent, as under one set of circumstances a set of attributes can be a source of differences, while in a different situation it can be a source of similarities. It sounds a bit confusing, but it is quite straightforward: Since information—and ultimately, knowledge—is compiled for a purpose, it stands to reason that its efficacy is tied to context, meaning that all worthwhile information is necessarily contextualized.

RISK PROFILING

Profiling is ideally suited to the analysis or risk because it helps to focus attention on the most pertinent areas of the organization's exposure to risk. This may not seem very clear at first, but let's consider another important concept briefly discussed in the opening chapter, namely the notion of *competitive advantage*.

The vast majority of business organizations have competitors and thus the vast majority of business decisions are, to some degree, shaped by competitive considerations; risk management related decisions are certainly not an exception to that rule. Let's consider the decision process of choosing the amount of directors' and officers' insurance coverage to purchase: It is almost a matter of habit for organizations to expressly consider the amount of coverage purchased by their peers, as most insurance buyers do not want to materially deviate from the peer-defined norm. Similarly, when evaluating the efficacy of their risk mitigation efforts, organizations tend to benchmark their results against peer groups, again, to make sure their outcomes compare favorably to those of their competitors.

Risk Profile

Although the vast majority of risk-related decisions are made in the context of a particular exposure – such as physical damage to buildings and equipment, supply chain or cyber related business interruption or regulatory investigation – from an organization-wide perspective, the basic tenets of the earlier discussed enterprise risk management are suggestive of the need to simultaneously consider the totality of the organization's exposures to all identifiable threats. Conceptually, from the standpoint of risk management any business organization can be viewed as a "bundle of risks"; hence, the totality of risk exposures facing a firm can be thought of as its *risk profile*, defined here as a composite of the organization's exposures to identifiable and meaningful threats. Risk profiling of organizations has a wide range of goals, some of the most common of which include clearly, objectively and unambiguously compiling and communicating the totality of the organization's exposures to all knowable and material threats; drawing comparisons among individual threats; and suggesting optimal risk management choices.

Risk profiling is implicitly selective, insofar as its intent is to draw attention to organizational characteristics that are capable of materially impacting shareholder value. Manifestly, the overt goal of compiling and

88

focusing on the organization's risk profile is to reduce the complexity of managing risk at the enterprise level by narrowing the focus what matters the most. The rationale behind *risk profile management* is as follows: In order to ensure an operational feasibility of the holistic management of the totality of the organization's threat exposures, the analytical scope has to be reduced to a manageable set of factors. To be manageable, a particular threat has to be knowable, which is to say that it has to be estimable (recall the earlier made distinction between uncertainty and risk). To be estimable, both the likelihood and the severity of a threat have to be objectively quantifiable, which means that a statistically adequate past occurrence and outcome data has to be available[1]. Lastly, the magnitude of earnings impact ought to be strong enough to have a measurable impact on the organization's competitiveness, which in this context is operationalized as the impact on the firm's earnings. Hence, the management of the organization's risk profile is ultimately focused on the identification and estimation of specific factors that are capable of materially impacting the organization's competitiveness.

Figure 3.1
Hypothetical Risk Profile

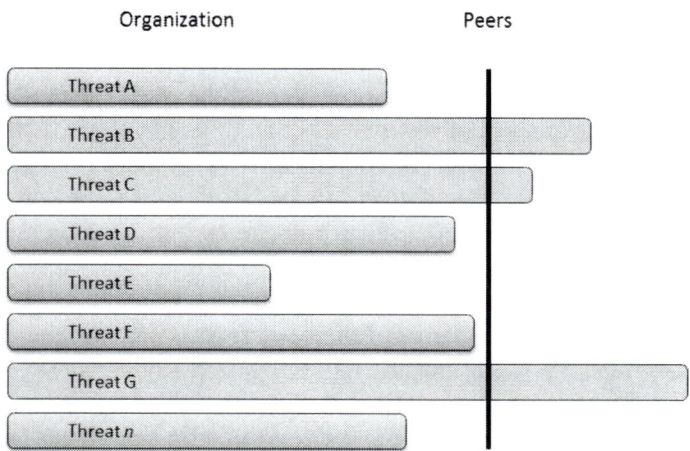

As graphically illustrated in Figure 3.1, there are two key components of a risk profile: 1. a peer group average, and 2. the organization-specific assessment, which imply two points of comparison. The first is the threat-by-threat assessment of the organization vs. the peer group defined average, which offers insights into which of the individual exposures could be deemed "abnormal". In the hypothetical example shown in Figure 3.1, Threat B, C and G all could be deemed abnormally large, as their organization-specific levels are noticeably greater than the peer-wide average. The second point of comparison is the within the organization threat-by-threat assessment, the goal of which is to provide an objective threat response / management prioritization. Again referring to Figure 3.1, Threat G, followed by B and C should be place at the top of the "need to manage / determine appropriate response" list. More on that in later chapters.

The Economics of Risk

It is important to note that the economics of risk necessitates carefully considering the costs (e.g., insurance premiums) and the benefits (e.g., loss protection) of each of the four risk response options discussed in the previous chapter. In that sense, the organization's risk profile can be viewed as one of the key influencers of that organization's competitiveness, as each of the four risk response alternatives discussed in the previous chapter have either near-term and definitive (e.g., insurance premium) or longer-term and speculative (e.g., unexpected and high loss) cost consequences. For instance, assuming a greater amount of risk can effectively enhance the firm's near-term profitability (by foregoing the expense of insurance premiums), and thus its competitiveness; at the same time, however, will expose the firm to the possibility of a larger future loss and a resultant erosion of competitiveness. Transfer of a greater amount of risk will have an opposite effect, which underscores the key risk transfer interdependence: The cost of risk transfer is definitive—its benefits are speculative, but the latter tends to be considerably greater (by, on average, about 50:1 ratio) than the former. And therein lies the challenge: In order for a business organization to have a competitively advantageous risk profile, it has to find an optimal balance between near-term earnings dampening risk transfer or mitigation efforts (e.g., commercial insurance coverage, the use of outside risk mitigation advisors, etc.) and potential longer-term earnings volatility increasing risk acceptance. The remainder of this book is focused on providing specific analytical insights into how to effectively balance these opposing considerations.

THE RPM TYPOLOGY OF RISK

Einstein believed that "…solutions should be simple, but not too simple." In other words, it is important to properly balance the desire to simplify our explanation of a phenomenon, but not to the point of foregoing to communicate the degree of intricacy of a system. This is a very true of risk analytics, where two, often opposing considerations need to be balanced: 1. the desire to simplify the explanation to make it more "workable", and 2. the need for it to be sufficiently complete to be beneficial. Hence the challenge lies in finding the optimum tradeoff between the completeness of the estimation process, which is necessary to yield valid and reliable likelihood and severity of impact estimates, and the explanatory simplicity, which is needed in order to formulate and implement risk reduction or avoidance strategies. Echoing Einstein's belief, I am convinced that the best solution is to meet half-way: Analysts should strive to de-mystify the often esoteric risk modeling methodologies, while at the same time, risk management practitioners should strive to gain a base level of proficiency in risk quantification methodology.

With that in mind, let's turn our attention to risk categorization. As noted in the previous chapter, from the standpoint of an organization, risk encompasses the possibility of asset-damaging or loss-generating events taking place, and the chances of the anticipated growth not materializing. The former is called "downside" risk, primarily because it is associated either with loss or the absence of it, but no gain. The latter, on the other hand, is called "upside" risk because it is associated with the possibility of a gain. In many regards, these two types of risk are quite different, but ultimately, both can be expressed in terms of their expected impact on earnings. Hence the efficacy of upside and downside risk assessment, in terms of the likelihood of occurrence and the severity of impact, will have a pronounced impact on the overall financial well-being of the organization. That said, the manner in which upside and downside risks impact the organization's earnings are quite different.

Upside risk is, to a large degree, a reflection of an organization's strategic posture. It is well known that the earning power of even the most successful products will tend to diminish with time due to competitive forces, changing tastes and other factors. In other words, an organization that wants to not even grow, but just maintain its earnings level simply has to bet on new products and other growth-spurring initiatives. These bets represent upside risk; these are decisions involving choices among competing resource allocation options and the risk is a measure of likelihood and degree of success. It follows that growth is a function of successfully increasing the organization's upside risk, which means selecting options boasting the greatest likelihood of success and the greatest payout.

When looked at from the standpoint of financial well-being, downside risks are a potential drag on earnings. In general, that is a result of either actual losses and damages or inefficient risk capitalization structure. The former is relatively self-evident: A damaging event such as a hurricane can cause a considerable amount of wind and flood related physical damage to factories, offices and other structures, in addition to business interruption costs. Somewhat less visible, but potentially also quite costly are financial losses related to high accident-related injury rates.

The second of the two downside risk related sources of earnings drag, an inefficient risk capitalization structure, is considerably less obvious. The essence of the impact of risk capitalization structure on earnings is as follows: An organization that is lacking effective downside risk assessment functionality is usually forced to adapt a conservative—meaning, costly—capital structure, which amounts to using equity as a cushion against possible financial distress. On the other hand, an organization with more robust risk assessment functionality is able to adapt a more financially aggressive and less costly capital structure. More specifically, by using debt to finance specific risks, the organization will be able to lower its weighted cost of capital[2].

Putting the two together—the potential revenue/earnings gains associated with placing thoroughly considered upside bets, coupled with systematically reducing the potential downside costs of risk—will results in improving the organization's overall competitive position. Stated differently, the goal of risk profile management is to systematically increase the upside risk (i.e., to maximize the organization's growth opportunities), while, simultaneously systematically reducing the downside risk (i.e., minimizing the likelihood of loss generating events). In such broadly defined role, of risk management becomes a direct contributor to the organization's competitiveness, as shown in Figure 3.2.

Figure 3.2
Risk and Competitive Advantage

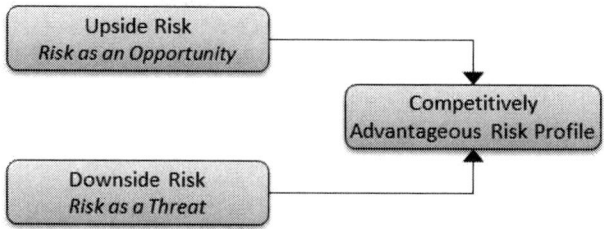

Upside Risk

Perhaps the best way to frame the notion of "upside risk" is to relate it to the well-known economic concept of "opportunity cost", which is the amount of foregone value associated with choosing one alternative over another. Opportunity cost suggests the choice between two mutually exclusive, but desirable options—in a sense, it is a measure of efficiency, as it assures that scarce resources, financial, human and other, are deployed against the most beneficial of multiple alternatives. The scope of opportunity cost stretches beyond the explicit financial expenditure focused notion of accounting cost, insofar as it attempts to take into account monetary as well as non-monetary (or at least, hard to express in monetary terms) costs associated with different alternatives. The rationale imbedded in the idea of opportunity cost is an essential component of the marginal theory of value, which captures the amount of change associated with competing alternatives. In that sense, it is one of the key considerations underpinning the strategic decision making process.

Broadly speaking, strategic planning can be viewed as the process of evaluating competing capital investment decisions geared toward identifying the courses of action that will result in the greatest increase in shareholder value. A key part of the strategic planning process is the assessment of risk and return associated with each alternative being considered. In more operationally-clear terms, strategic risk can be defined as "…the risk to earnings or capital arising from adverse business decisions or improper implementation of those decisions…it is a function of the comparability between an organization's strategic goals, the business strategies developed to achieve those goals, the resources deployed against those goals and the quality of implementation " (Office of the Comptroller of Currency, 1998). According to a recent Booz Allen Hamilton's Shareholder Value Destruction study which analyzed 1,200 global companies with market capitalization greater than $1 billion, strategic failures (such as poor brand or customer relationship management, emergence of disruptive technologies or industry cannibalization) accounted for approximately 60% of the reasons behind the loss of shareholder value[3]. These findings are in keeping with another research conclusion, a 2002 Academy of Competitive Intelligence survey of 140 corporate strategists which concluded that about two out of every three organizations have been surprised by as many as three high impact events in the preceding five years, which does not seem surprising given that 97% of the surveyed organizations indicated having no "early warning" systems in place.

Not surprisingly, issues relating to strategic risk assessment have been receiving increasingly more attention, both from academics and practitioners alike. In their 2005 Harvard Business Review article[4], Slywotzky and Drzik identified seven distinct classes of strategic risk:

> *Industry*: Margin squeeze, overcapacity, commoditization, deregulation, etc.
> *Technology*: Patent expiration, process obsolescence or shifts in technology.
> *Brand*: Erosion of value or outright collapse.
> *Competitors*: Emergence of global rivals or one-of-a-kind competitor.
> *Customers*: Shifting preferences or over-reliance on a few customers.
> *Project*: R&D, M&A or IT failures.
> *Stagnation*: Flat or declining sales volume, unfavorable shift in volume-price relationship.

Is strategic risk synonymous with upside risk? In effect, yes. Simply put, *upside risk* is a strategic failure relating to the assessment of the available courses of action and the resultant plan of action. More specifically, it represents the possibility of failing to achieve revenues or earnings growth due to misalignments of strategic goals, external forces impacting those goals, the strategies developed to achieve them, the resources deployed against them and the quality of implementation.

One of the more striking characteristics of upside risk is that it does not lend itself to easy objective (i.e., numerical) codification. In other words, one should not expect to be able to devise a robust rule-based strategic risk evaluation schema. On the one hand, that certainly contributes to the complexity of evaluating strategic risks; however, it has the positive benefit of removing the temptation of transforming risk analytics into a box-checking set of activities. Instead, the assessment of upside risk needs to take an interdisciplinary view combining the traditional risk quantification approaches with the real options framework and the cultural theory rooted assessment of revealed or expressed preferences. More on that later.

Downside Risk

Although it is intuitively obvious as an idea, the notion of downside risk can be operationally amorphous and highly context dependent, as it encompasses a seemingly infinite number of threats, while also being subject to evolving regulatory and broader societal forces. Still, it is possible to arrive at a general risk typology by systematically moving down the level of threat generalization. In that sense, downside risks can be either external or internal; the former can be sub-divided into controllable and not controllable, while the latter fall under the general umbrella of managerially controlled activities. Each of the resultant risk categories is made up of multiple, more narrowly defined risk types, briefly defined below:

> *Economic*: The effect of global economy on "localized" (i.e., of interest to a particular organization) economy. Risk type: External—Not Controllable.
> *Market*: A significant change in supply and demand functions, including prices of raw materials and other production inputs. Risk type: External—Not Controllable.
> *Competitive*: Entry of new competitors. Risk type: External—Not Controllable.
> *Technological*: Obsolescence of current technologies / costs of acquiring and instituting new technologies. Risk type: External—Not Controllable.
> *Financial*: Cost of capital and exchange rates. Risk type: External—Not Controllable.
> *Operational*: A broad category of risks arising out of the organization's implementation of its strategy and tactics. Risk type: Internal—Controllable.
> *Regulatory*: Changes in public policy and governmental regulations. Risk type: External—Controllable.

95

- *Environmental*: Changing pollution, carbon emission or disposal standards. Risk type: External—Not Controllable.
- *Supply Chain*: Also known as "contractual" risk, this pertains to contractor failure to deliver on time, schedule or for agreed upon price. Risk type: External—Controllable.
- *Professional*: Change in the firm's ability to attract and retain skilled human resources. Risk type: Internal—Controllable.
- *Natural*: Natural disasters, such as wind and flood dangers; crime, such as theft, vandalism or arson. Risk type: External—Not Controllable.
- *Socio-Cultural*: Demographic changes affecting the demand for the organization's goods or services. Risk type: External—Not Controllable.
- *Reputational*: Negative publicity in media, word-of-mouth and other sources, potentially adversely impacting the firm's brand equity. Risk type: Internal—Controllable.

This is a relatively long list—and quite varied. However, upon a closer examination, these risk types can be grouped into a more coherent downside risk typology shown below in Table 3.1.

Table 3.1
Downside Risk Typology

Downside Risk		
External		Internal
Not Controllable	Controllable	Managerially-Controlled
Financial	Regulatory	Compliance
Market	Professional	Operational
Political	Supply Chain	Reputational
Economic		
Natural		
Socio-Cultural		
Environmental		
Technological		

All downside risk types are either *external* or *internal* in terms of their source. The former represent outside ongoing forces, such as regulatory frameworks, or isolated events, such as natural catastrophes, impacting the organization and potentially causing financial distress (i.e., adversely impacting earnings). The latter represent the failures of management to exercise proper control, as exemplified by failure to comply with applicable laws or regulations. External risk types, which are far more numerous and diverse, can be further subdivided into *controllable* and *not controllable*. As implied by the label, controllable external risks are those whose possibility of occurrence or adverse impact can be actively managed either by adapting organizational behavior or contractually. Conversely, not controllable external risks are those over which an organization exercises little-to-no control.

What is a common thread connecting all of these diverse types of risk? There are several. First, regardless of type, all risks are probabilistic in nature. In other words, the cost of capital will not definitely increase (it could stay the same or decrease), new regulations are not necessarily imminent or competitively unfavorable, nor is natural disaster-rooted property damage guaranteed. Second, risk refers to negative outcomes—e.g., changes in competitive, technological, market or financial circumstances that may benefit the organization are a source of opportunity, not risk. Third, risk has tangible economic consequences, usually expressed as a loss of monetary value. For instance, an unfavorable (to a US firm) change in the U.S dollar—euro exchange rate does not constitute a risk for a company with no European market, production or asset exposure. And fourth, and perhaps the most obvious communality is that risk refers to the future. Stated differently, risk is a reflection of uncertainty stemming from a lack of control over future developments.

Tying these three common threads together yields the following, generic definition: Downside risk reflects a probability of a negative outcome stemming from a future event and relating to something that is of value. In the context of competitive advantage, downside risk represents the probability of an adverse impact on the level or the stability of earnings.

RISK QUANTIFICATION

As noted in the previous section, what is broadly defined as "risk" represents the possibility of occurrence of an undesirable event or an outcome. Furthermore, as illustrated in Figure 2.2, the "possibility of occurrence" is itself a function of likelihood and severity of the individual undesirable events and outcomes. Hence, risk quantification should be viewed as a task of estimating the said two dimensions of risk—likelihood and severity—for each event or outcome that is of interest or concern.

The typology of risk outlined in the previous section (*Typology of Risk*) stressed the importance of evaluating the individual risk types as potential sources of drag on earnings, which means evaluating risk in the context of its potential impact on the organization's competitive advantage. Put another way, it is important to consider the relative (to competitors, or otherwise defined peer group) impact of risk types, which calls for estimating the "average" impact and organization-specific deviation from that average. This adds a yet another aspect to the evaluation of risk, namely the notion of volatility.

The next few pages are dedicated to a general overview of measurement aspects of concepts of *volatility, likelihood* and *severity*. The goal of this overview is to bring to light the most important measurement considerations associated with each of these concepts.

Measuring Volatility

A concept of considerable important to the quantification of both the likelihood and severity dimensions of risk is *volatility*, which is defined as the degree of unpredictable change in a variable over a period of time. In finance, volatility captures the essence of risk, or fluctuations in returns generated by financial instruments. In statistical analysis, volatility is expressed through the notion of *variance*, which is a measure of statistical dispersion, computed by averaging the squared distance of possible (i.e., observed) values of a random variable from the expected value, or mean. Consider Figure 3.3.

Figure 3.3
Variance

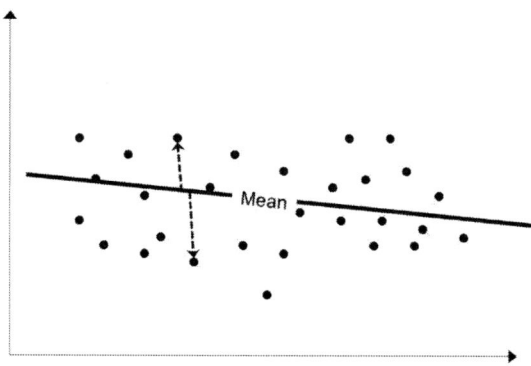

The above diagram shows a scattering of data points casted in the context of a 2-dimensional space. Let's say that these points represent monthly generation output of a hydroelectric utility, with the vertical axis capturing the magnitude of the said generation. The "mean line" drawn through the middle of the distribution represents the average production for a particular time period (e.g., the past five years) and each "dot" denotes monthly output. The points, or dots, falling both above and below the mean line, can be expressed in terms of relative deviation from the average, as shown by the two dotted arrows.

In the above illustration, variance is the total or combined—i.e., above as well as below the mean—amount of deviation from the expected, or mean, value. Mathematically, variance can be expressed as follows:

$$Variance = \sum_{i=1}^{n}(x_i - \bar{x})^2$$

where,

   n is the number of observations
   x_i is an observed value i
   $\bar{x}$ is the mean value

Although mathematically useful, variance has relatively little practical informational value, as it confounds the unit of measurement with the total amount of variability in a given data set. However, once standardized, variance can be a very telling indicator. Standardizing variance simply amounts to taking a square root of it; its derivative is called "standard deviation" and it is computed as follows:

$$Standard\ Deviation = \sqrt{\frac{\sum_{i=1}^{n}(x_i - \bar{x})^2}{n}}$$

where,

n is the number of observations
x_i is an observed value i
$\bar{x}$ is the mean value

The key advantage of standard deviation (over variance) is that it standardizes the measurement of volatility by factoring out the magnitude of the unit of measurement, while retaining the proportional aspect of the assessment. The net effect of this simple transformation is the enablement of direct cross-variable comparisons.

Just standardizing the measurement scale is not enough, as in the analysis of risk it is usually not the total, but directional volatility that matters. Consider the example of a hydroelectric utility mentioned earlier. The generation of hydroelectric power is highly dependent on the level of river flows—in particular, it is impacted by declining flows. In other words, as the amount of water in a particular river diminishes (which might be a result of a relatively dry winter resulting in a diminished amount of snow to be melted) the hydroelectric output will fall. Since electricity is generally consumed as it is being produced, diminished output may necessitate "gap purchases" in the electricity marketplace, which not only requires the availability of funds, but itself is also a subject to potential market price volatility. In short, the same amount of gap electricity purchase can carry a different cost, depending on the spot market prices at the time of the purchase. Hence a hydroelectric utility is faced, in this scenario, with two distinct and directionally different risks: The possibility of diminished flows-related generation <u>decrease</u> and the potential <u>upward</u> volatility in electricity market prices. Clearly, the worst case scenario is a simultaneous decline in generation and an increase in market prices.

As illustrated by the above example, the notion of variance and its derivative the standard deviation can be too general to capture the true amount of risk-related volatility in an outcome of interest, because these measures do not expressly differentiate between the upward and downward variability. Hence in situations where risk is reflected in either upward or downward deviation from the base, or mean, values, it might be more applicable to consider only a part of the overall variability, as shown in Figure 3.4.

Figure 3.4
Downside vs. Upside Variance

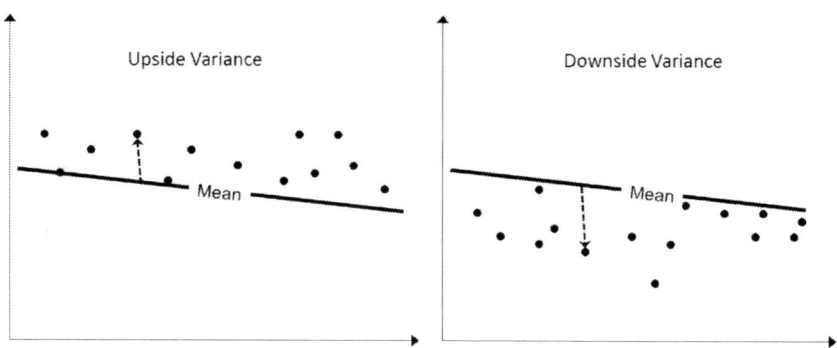

If that is the case, *semi-variance* should be used in place of variance. More specifically, *positive semi-variance* should be computed when risk is reflected in an increase over the mean baseline, which is computed as follows:

$$Positive\ Semi-Variance = \frac{1}{n}\left(\sum_{x_i>\bar{x}}^{n}(x_i - \bar{x})^2\right)$$

where,

        n is the number of observations above the mean
        x_i is an observed value i
        $\bar{x}$ is the mean value

Alternative, *negative semi-variance* should be computed in situations where risk is reflected in an decrease below the mean level:

$$Negative\ Semi-Variance = \frac{1}{n}\left(\sum_{x_i<\bar{x}}^{n}(x_i - \bar{x})^2\right)$$

where,

        n is the number of observations below the mean
        x_i is an observed value i
        $\bar{x}$ is the mean value

As is the case with variance, both the positive and negative semi-variance can be standardized to enable direct cross-variable or cross-effect comparisons. The resultant measures, positive and negative semi-standard deviations, respectively, are computed as follows:

$$Positive\ Semi-Standard\ Deviation = \sqrt{\frac{1}{n}\left(\sum_{\substack{i \\ x_i > \bar{x}}}^{n}(x_i - \bar{x})^2\right)}$$

$$Negative\ Semi-Standard\ Deviation = \sqrt{\frac{1}{n}\left(\sum_{\substack{i \\ x_i < \bar{x}}}^{n}(x_i - \bar{x})^2\right)}$$

where,

n is the number of observations above or below (for positive or negative semi-standard deviation, respectively) the mean
x_i is an observed value i
$\bar{x}$ is the mean value

The above shown operationalizations of semi-variance and semi-standard deviation are uniquely suited to the analysis of risk, because they underscore the fact that risk, in the sense of a possible loss, is usually a manifestation of directional volatility. Specifically, in situations where risk increases as a function of negative deviation from the mean, negative semi-variance and its derivative, the negative semi-standard deviation should be used. On the other hand, in situations where risk increases as a function of positive deviation from the mean, positive semi-variance and its derivative, the positive semi-standard deviation should be employed.

Variance estimation is a mean to an end, which is the estimation of the probability of an event of interest taking place. The next section takes a closer look at the notion of probability[5].

Probability as a Business Tool

In the everyday language of business, likelihood is synonymous with probability, which is simply an attempt to predict unknown outcomes based on known parameters. Weather forecasters strive to predict (unknown) outcomes such as the future air temperature, the amount of precipitation or sunshine, based on known parameters, which are historical trends and interdependencies. In a more technical sense, the deployment of statistical likelihood estimation techniques allows us to estimate the unknown parameters based on known (i.e., historical) outcomes. In other words, by leveraging historical data, likelihood estimation enables us to create empirical bases for making forward-looking predictions. In the context of risk, the probability dimension reflects an attempt at quantifying the chance that a particular undesirable event will take place.

In business analyses, we are concerned with three basic types of probability: marginal, joint and conditional. *Marginal probability* is the probability of a given variable assuming a specific value, irrespective of the values of other variables. In the context of the automotive insurance claims example cited earlier, marginal probability could be computed to estimate, for instance, the probability of the total accident cost exceeding $5,000. Marginal probability, along with the equimarginal principle discussed later, forms the foundation for the approach for estimating the unique amount of total risk exposure to a specific factor, or the notion of "effect attribution."

Joint probability is the probability of two or more events occurring together. Consider the probability of an automotive accident, in inclement weather conditions, involving three of more vehicles. In the statistical modeling context, joint probability forms the basis for estimating "interaction effects", which is a co-occurrence of two or more events.

Conditional probability is the probability that a given event (such an automotive accident) will occur given that one or more other events (such as inclement weather or speeding) have occurred. The notion of condition probability provides a conceptual rooting for the area of business analytics that has come to be known as "predictive analytics", which focuses on making forward-looking estimates of outcomes of interest based on an a priori assessment of causal interdependencies.

Probability Estimation: Divergent Philosophies

According to Jeffrey[6], "before the middle of the seventeenth century, the term 'probable' (derived from Latin *probabilis*) meant approvable, and was applied in that sense, univocally, to opinion and to action. A probable action or opinion was one such as sensible people would undertake or hold, in the circumstances". The more formalized, or mathematical treatment of probability (i.e., the Probability Theory) can be traced as far back as the sixteenth century and the first attempts to analyze the games of chance[7]. Hence initially the probability theory focused almost exclusively on discrete events, later expanded to include continuous variable, largely in response to the growth of calculus-rooted analytical applications[8]. The seminal work of Kolmogorov[9] laid the foundation for modern probability theory.

Risk analyses historically made a heavy usage of one of the key contributions of the probability theory: probability distributions. It has been observed than the occurrence of variety of natural or physical phenomenon and processes can be well described with the help of a range of probability distributions. A probability distribution captures a range of possible values that a random variable can attain and the probability that the value of the random variable is within a measurable subset of that range. Some of the more frequently used (in actuarial analyses and elsewhere) discrete variable distributions include binomial, negative binomial, Poisson and Bernoulli, while the most frequently utilized continuous distributions include normal, exponential, gamma and beta.

Interpretation-wise, there are two somewhat distinct (and dissimilar) approaches: Bayesians and Frequentist. The basic tenets of these competing approaches are briefly summarized in Table 3.2.

Table 3.2
Competing Likelihood Quantification Approaches

Approach	Description
Bayesian	Named after Thomas Bayes, who proved what is known called "Bayes' Theorem", which relates conditional and marginal probabilities of two random events, which is often used in estimating the likely underlying causes of an observed outcome (or posterior probabilities). Broadly speaking, Bayesian Probability treats likelihood as measure of a state of knowledge; in other words, probabilities are a function of beliefs and uncertainty. However, that interpretation can be further segmented into two somewhat distinct schools of thought: the objective school, which relies on logical interpretation, akin to Aristotelian logic; and the subjectivist school, which promotes the view that the state of knowledge should correspond to personal belief. Needless to say, the former is easier to codify, hence it is used extensively in data mining applications.
Frequentist	As implied in the name, this is a strictly observation-based, empirical approach. Relying on objective data collected by means of experiments or recorded historical occurrences, the probability of random variable reflects the relative frequency of occurrence of the observed outcome. Under the Frequentist view, if 2% of publicly traded companies end up entangled in securities class action litigation on annual basis, on average, a given publicly traded company faces 2% chance of incurring this type of litigation.

Both the Bayesian and Frequentist approaches have quite a bit to contribute to the risk management efforts. For risk types of which robust historical event data is available, the Frequentist approach can provide a good approximation of the average, expected future probability of a particular event taking place. For example, an insurance company writing automotive coverage will almost always have ample historical accident data, which will enable to empirically estimate the likelihood of different types of accidents, etc. Not surprisingly, the Frequentist approach has been used extensively in the insurance industry.

At the same time, there are a number of important risks for which transaction-type quantitative data is not readily available. Evian flu, terrorism, ransom and kidnapping, reactor meltdown at a nuclear power plant are among the examples of such risks. Even if data on such events is available, it is usually too sparse to be generalizable for forecasting purposes. In those situations, Bayesian approach, combining expert knowledge and uncertainty can yield estimates superior to pure guessing.

The analytic framework outlined in this book aims to incorporate the elements of the two competing probability approaches—the Frequentist method is used with (relatively) high frequency risks for which robust quantitative data is available and the Bayesian approach is employed when risk types lack the requisite objective data.

The above discussion focuses on likelihood as a single measure problem. A particular event of interest, such as hurricane, an automotive insurance claim or the availability of capital, is viewed more-or-less in isolation from everything else. For instance, a frequency distribution of automotive accidents of single, male drivers between ages of 18 and 25 shows a cumulative frequency counts in the context of their probability of occurrence. It offers no insights regarding the underlying causal factors—in other words, it is a descriptive tool showing "what is", without providing any explanation as to "why."

Multivariate Probability

In business analyses, we often try to understand the inner-workings of a particular micro-system, many of which are comprised of multiple variables and a web of interdependencies. The behavior of each of the elements of such a system can be described in terms of its (univariate) probabilities; however, to understand the system as a whole requires the assessment of the combination of all component probabilities, or multivariate probability.

Conceptually, *multivariate probability* is a generalization of a univariate probability to higher dimensions, where 1 variable = 1 dimension. It means that unlike a single variable (i.e., univariate) probability which entails an assessment of a single value frequency distribution, multivariate probability entails a single-value assessment of a product of multiple frequency distributions. Consider the sample contrast: The economic cost associated with auto accidents can be expressed as a frequency distribution, where different dollar intervals represent different frequency of occurrence, as shown in Figure 3.5 below.

Figure 3.5
Univariate Frequency Distribution

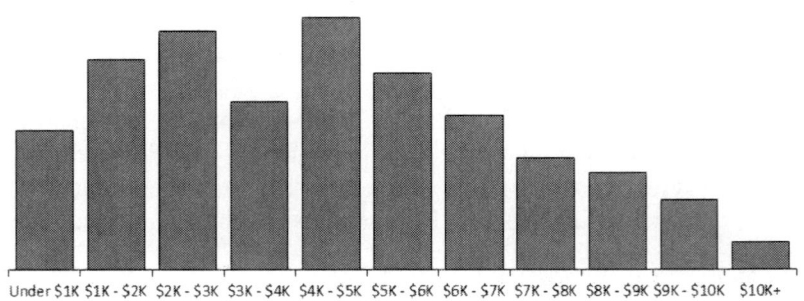

Under $1K $1K - $2K $2K - $3K $3K - $4K $4K - $5K $5K - $6K $6K - $7K $7K - $8K $8K - $9K $9K - $10K $10K+

Utilizing the Frequentist approach outlined earlier, the above frequency distribution can be easily converted into probabilities associated with each cost interval (e.g., under $1K, $2k - $3k, etc.) by computing relative frequencies, which is a given interval's share of the total frequencies.

The picture becomes a lot more complex when the above example is extended to jointly consider a couple of additional measures, such as the age of the driver and the time of day. The resultant multivariate distribution can no longer be depicted in the context of the familiar Cartesian (i.e., X-Y) coordinates used in figures 3.3 and 3.4; instead, it needs to be presented as a far harder to visually interpret response plane or a multivariate density function, exemplified in Figure 3.6.

Figure 3.6
Response Surface

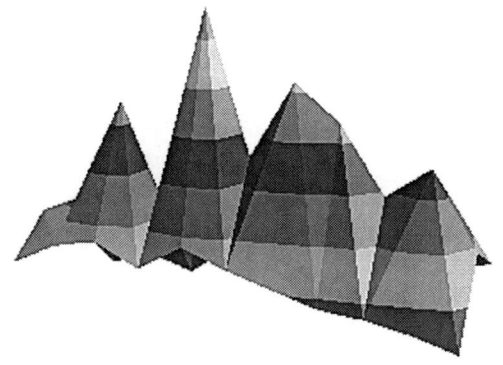

An important notion associated with multivariate probability is that of *dependence vs. independence* of the constituent variables. In a technical sense, any two (or more) variables are considered to be independent if their conditional probability is equal to their unconditional probability. Or stated differently, when the occurrence or non-occurrence of one of the variables does not affect the occurrence or non-occurrence of the other(s), the variables can be considered to be independent.

This is an important consideration, both from the data modeling and practical standpoints. Modeling-wise, independence of individual measures is a reflection of their non-redundancy and it is among the requirements of some of the more commonly used multivariate statistical modeling techniques, such as regression discussed in later chapters. The independence assumption, as an attribute of multivariate probability, carries some very real implications for risk management practices. Risk mitigation efforts can be greatly enhanced by the delineation of drivers of risk, or factors that have been shown to either heighten or lower the organization's exposure to specific risks. In order to establish actionable and effective risk mitigation efforts, the organization must be able to estimate factor-specific impact, or the degree to which "pulling a specific lever" (i.e., acting upon an individual risk factor) is going to have a desired impact.

Severity Estimation

In many respects, severity is a far simpler notion than likelihood. In essence, *severity* is an estimate of the magnitude of economic impact associated with a particular risk; it is typically expressed in terms of cost.

Much like probability, severity estimates are highly dependent on the availability of historical loss data. Depending on the type of risk, historical losses can come in the form of (relatively) exact insurance claims and the resulting payouts (e.g., securities litigation claims), internal company records (e.g., workers' compensation claims), coverage provider (e.g., automotive accidents) or outside private or governmental sources (e.g., terrorism). Consequently, the accuracy of the resultant estimates may vary quite widely.

There are three important considerations that need to be addressed in the context of severity estimation: attribution, recency and projectability.

Attribution is a measure of accuracy of the cause—effect linkage. Is the particular loss figure attributed, or assigned to a correct cause? It is intuitively obvious that attributing correct amounts to correct causes is essential to making reliable forward projections, though the available data may not necessarily exhibit the requisite coding discipline.

Recency reflects the "newness" of the historical loss data. For some types of risks, such as operational risks falling under the umbrella of general liability or workers' compensation, an organization might have 10, 15 or even 20 years of data available, which poses the question—how far back should an analyst reach to make reliable forward-looking projections? This issue is further complicated by the notion of *claim development*, which is a measure of the maturation of individual losses[10]. All considered, what constitutes appropriate, from the practical standpoint, and adequate, from the data modeling standpoint, recency will vary across situations.

Projectability addresses the fundamental question of usability—is the available historical cost data going to form a valid foundation for making future projections? There are numerous reasons for why the available data may not be projectable. First, it could be non-generalizable. In other words, while the data may reflect a particular sub-set of the overall population, the goal might be to make population-wide projections (or vice-versa). Second, it could be too sparse. A case in point is the growing threat of pandemic risks (such as avian flu) and terrorism, neither of which has enough data points to substantiate robust projections (a potential qualitative remedy, the Delphi method, is discussed later). Third, it could be either too specific or too broad. For example, the much talked about global warming patterns and the supporting numerical evidence might form an appropriate background for setting global CO_2 emission standards, but would likely be too coarse to help a single utility organization risk-adjust considerations surrounding the construction of a new power plant.

A Note on Likelihood—Severity Independence

For methodological and practical purposes, the two risk dimensions—likelihood and severity—are almost always estimated individually. At times, it might be beneficial to combine the two sets of estimates into a single "expected value of risk" figure. The ability to do that hinges on the degree to which the two sets of estimates are mathematically independent of one another.

In a data analytical sense, independence = additivity, which in turn supports computing of a product of likelihood and severity, i.e., the aforementioned "expected value of risk". As used in this book, the notion of likelihood—severity independence is a binary consideration, meaning that the two risk dimensions either are or are not independent. Measurement-wise, that determination is based on computing of a correlation coefficient and the corresponding statistical significance testing (both concepts are discussed at length in later chapters). A lack of statistically significant correlation between likelihood and severity is taken as an indication of likelihood—severity independence. On the other hand, the finding some degree of interdependence between the two attests to interdependence between the two risk dimensions, with the magnitude of the correlation coefficient providing an estimate of the strength of the said relationship. Since that points to an informational overlap between likelihood and severity (i.e., some degree of redundancy), combining of the two dimensions into the aforementioned expected value of risk estimate should not be undertaken.

RISK PROFILE MANAGEMENT

Estimation is, generally, a mean to an end. The point made repeatedly throughout this book is that objectively-derived, robust information increases the quality of decisions, ultimately positively impacting the organization's competitiveness. In the context of risk management, objectively estimated likelihood and severity of individual threats are the foundation of risk profile management (note the distinction between "management" and "measurement"- the latter can be considered an enablement of the former).

Risk Profile Management (RPM) was first briefly discussed in the preceding chapter, in the context of risk reduction. It represents an application of multivariate modeling (a family of statistical techniques for simultaneous analysis of multiple metrics) to the problem of likelihood and/severity estimation. Although I initially talked about it in the context of reducing downside risk, RPM should in fact be generalized to a broader definition of risk, which includes both downside as well as upside risks.

Recall the earlier discussed risk response alternative, graphically summarized in Figure 3.7 below.

Figure 3.7
Risk Response Alternatives

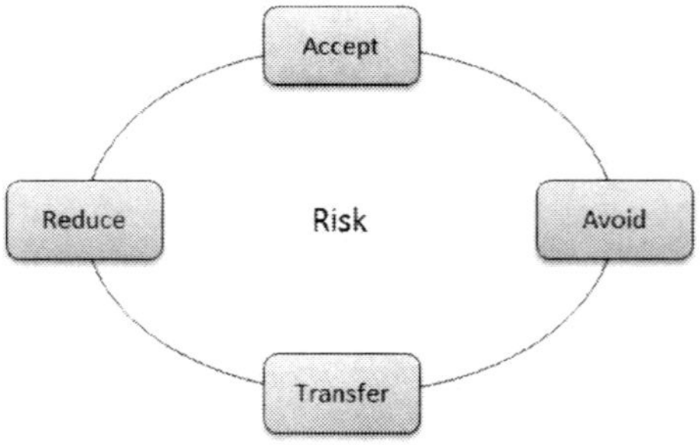

The essence of RPM is to minimize the adverse impact on earnings stemming from the organization's exposure to identifiable and measurable risk types. Each of the four broad responses, acceptance, reduction, transfer and avoidance, entails a different set of risk management activities. That should be intuitively obvious. Somewhat less obvious, however, might be an assertion that the type of information that is available will also play a role. Of course, in order for that effect to be discernable, the continuum of possible informational inputs needs to be broken out into a manageable number of discrete, non-overlapping categories. The proposed information type categorization schema is shown in Figure 3.8.

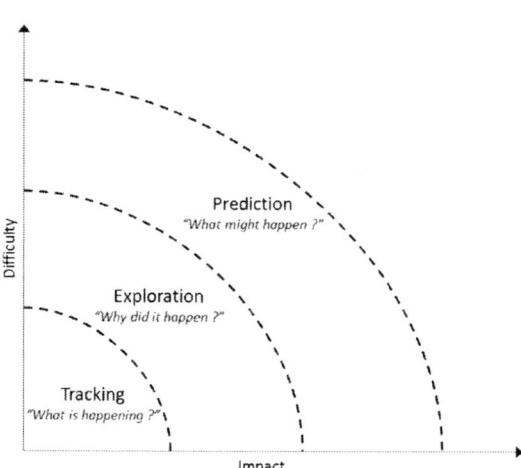

Figure 3.8
Informational Inputs and Their Impact

There are three distinct types of informational inputs: tracking, exploration and prediction. Their relationship can be captured in terms of analytical "difficulty" and business "impact", which comprise the vertical and horizontal dimensions, respectively. *Tracking*, which entails actively capturing information regarding a phenomenon of interest, is analytically the least involved of the three, but it also delivers the least amount of business value or impact, because it focuses on generic (i.e., not a source of competitively advantageous insight) information, which is also rarely suggestive of the underlying root causes. *Exploration*, which is the conduct of analysis the goal of which is to discern the root causes of the observed (i.e., tracked) outcomes, is more analytically involved, but it also deliver greater impact to the organization, in the form of knowledge of factors influencing the phenomenon of interest. Lastly, *prediction* is the most analytically involved of the three types of informational inputs, while also delivering the greatest amount of impact on the organizational decision making. It entails making forward-looking predictions regarding the outcomes of interest, built on the foundation of rigorous cause-effect analysis.

The importance of the above outlined continuity of informational inputs to RPM is paramount, as it provides the informational basis for an ongoing monitoring and adjustment. Information is not uniformly distributed across risk types, which means that the type of assessment—i.e., tracking vs. exploration vs. prediction—will vary across the types of risk. That said, it is the goal of Risk Profile management to gather the best available information, on ongoing basis and in a format that contributes to shaping risk response decisions.

Ultimately, any risk response decision should be considered in the context of a risk-return tradeoff. At least in theory, it is possible for an organization to enter into a large number of financial contracts which would either outright transfer the risk or provide post-event compensatory mechanisms, so much so that the said organization would be shielded against a vast majority of loss causing events. However, the overall cost would be more than likely prohibitively high, so that from the economic standpoint, that would not be a plausible scenario. Hence basic economics, in effect, force organizations into deciding which risks to transfer, which ones should be considered avoidable, or at least mitigatable, and which ones simply need to be accepted. In order to not imperil the organization, this decision needs to be rooted in the explicit analysis of clearly defined risk type—risk response conjoints, such as storm damage—transfer vs. storm damage--accept. It is another way of saying that organizations need to make economically rational decisions regarding the most economically appropriate response to each delineated risk. Insurance coverage offers protection against certain types of insurable events, but it can be costly, which means that buying large amounts of insurance can be a drag on earnings. At the same time, an un-insured adverse loss can be a source of even a greater shock to earnings. Hence an objective and reliable evaluation of the aforementioned risk type—risk response conjoints is at the heart of Risk Profile management.

Risk Acceptance

The willingness to participate in a competitive marketplace implies willingness to accept a certain amount of risk. More specifically, it entails the acceptance of the upside component of the overall risk (see the *Defining Risk* section in the previous chapter), which is a set of risks surrounding the organization's strategic decisions. For instance, an auto manufacturer developing (i.e., investing in) an electricity-powered automobile implicitly assumes the (strategic) risk associated with future viability of this particular alternative fuel approach. In other words, the organization makes a strategic decision and then it implicitly assumes the risk of that being the "wrong move".

At the same time, a successful business organization will also actively hedge against a number of other risks, discussed earlier under a broad umbrella of downside risks. As a whole, downside risks are events or outcomes threatening to bring about an economic loss or otherwise defined cost, which means that, true to their name, there are no potential benefits to downside risks. Storm related damage either occurs or not; employment practices or securities class action either happens or not; unfavorable (to the organization) legislation is either enacted or not, etc.

In addition to upside risks, there is a handful of downside risks that an organization may choose to accept. Consider the "external, not controllable" risk types delineated in Table 3.1—virtually all of those broadly defined risk types fall outside of the organization's sphere of control. Of course, it does not mean that the organization should accept all of those risks, in the sense of assuming a "do nothing" posture; in fact, by doing so, it would have likely increased the potential adverse impact (of those exposures) on earnings. At the same time, some of those exposures, such as socio-cultural, political or economic present very few, if any, real options.

Well, that is not entirely true. Just because certain types of risk exposure are not "manageable", in the sense of being changeable likelihood or severity-wise, does not mean that the organization needs to become a victim of its circumstances. Aggressive intelligence gathering and incorporating the so-collected insights into decision making can be an effective risk reducing mechanism. The essence of Risk Profile Management is that every delineated risk—without regard to whether or not internal or external, controllable or not—needs to be actively managed in a way that is most appropriate, given the risk type's inherent characteristics. It means that while an organization may have to accept certain types of risk, it should actively track important and knowable manifestations of those risks with the goal of adjusting its decisions, as appropriate.

Recall the Figure 3.8 shown earlier. In the context of the three types of information inputs outlined in that illustration, risk acceptance entails that—at a minimum—the organization puts in place a process to track and disseminate (to the appropriate stakeholders) information pertaining to risk types it chooses to accept. In essence, this amounts to saying that there are external factors, which are not controllable yet pose a potential threat to the organization; if the organization chooses or is otherwise forced into accepting those risks it should actively track them and incorporate those insights into its overall risk management process.

Risk Transfer

This is probably the most intuitively obvious risk response mechanism. At the same time, it is also the most costly, in terms of near-term financial cost, risk response alternative. Essentially, risk transfer entails the use of a wide range of financial tools to provide "protection" against , ranging from traditional insurance coverage to an array of alternative risk transfer mechanisms, such as captive insurance, hedge funds, contingent capital, securitization and other, discussed in more depth in the previous chapter (even though, as pointed out earlier, insurance coverage is technically not a risk "transfer" but a post-event compensatory mechanism, since it affects the severity, but not the likelihood dimension of risk, it is commonly thought of as a risk transfer tool).

In the event-tracking sense, risk transfer is the most involved risk response decision, as it involves a two-part consideration: 1. Is it economically desirable to transfer a particular risk?, and, 2. What specific monetary value should be pursued?

The ultimate determinant of the extent of the potential damage associated with a given risk type is its estimated impact on earnings. In terms of the three broad types of informational inputs, the risk transfer decision calls for the prediction of risk type-specific likelihood and severity. This is, of course, one of the key difficulties associated with effective risk transfer, namely, the availability of quantitatively sound, rational informational basis. For some types of risk, such as physical, i.e., property, damage, the needed information may be easier to obtain than for other types, where objective valuation is not plausible. Let's consider two typical cases: physical damage and executive liability to illustrate the difference.

In the case of physical damage, such as the threat to physical structures (e.g., manufacturing plants, office buildings, hotels, etc.) posed by wind, flood or earthquake, the extrinsic value of the property provides a key set of objective inputs into severity estimation, while historic event occurrence records will yield another set of inputs, namely the frequency estimates. Obviously, the extent of damage is a range in itself (i.e., it could range from very minor damage to complete destruction of a property), and the historical tend-derived frequency estimate represents an average of past occurrences, nonetheless, the appropriateness of entering into a risk transfer contract (question #1 above) and the value of the said contract (question #2 above) can be estimated from a sound informational basis.

That is not the case for executive liability considerations. The core executive liability risk is that faced by directors and officers of the organization who might stand accused of "causing" financial losses to investors by virtue of improper or inadequate communications. The result can be a securities class action, which is a legal action taken by shareholders against directors and officers of the company[11]. Although the basis for those suits is a decline in the company valuation, the ultimate cost (which typically takes the form of a settlement for non-dismissed cases) is not very closely tied to settling companies' market capitalization, so much so that a large company may end up with a relatively modest settlement, while a significantly smaller company may end up with a considerably larger one[12]. Hence in contrast to the physical damage example, when it comes to less tangible threats organizations do not necessarily have readily available informational input that could be used to substantiate the appropriateness of their risk transfer decisions.

Risk Avoidance & Reduction

From the informational standpoint, the essence of Risk Profile Management is the notion of "explanation by prediction", fully explored in the next chapter. In broad terms, it emphasizes the identification of specific risk factors, which can be used as indicators of likelihood or severity of individual risk types. Consider Figure 3.9.

Figure 3.9
Informational Basis of RPM: Likelihood

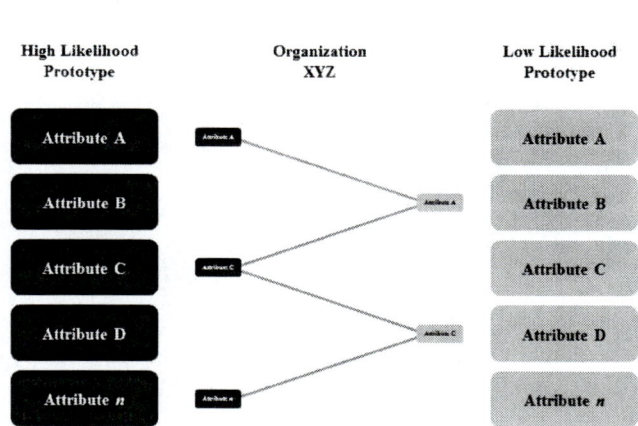

The "High Likelihood of Undesirable Event" represents a prototype of a high risk organization, expressed in terms of specific, risk-increasing attributes, A thru *n*. The "Low Likelihood of Undesirable Event" represents a prototype of a low risk—in a sense of the likelihood of occurrence— organization, expressed in terms of risk-reducing attributes. The line in the center of the chart shows the similarity of Company XYZ to either the high or low risk profile on each of the delineated attributes. The high and low risk profiles are expressed in terms of probabilities, where the former exhibits significantly above average likelihood of the undesirable event taking place, while the latter embodies significantly below average chance. RPM entails a deliberate examination of the company's "positioning" on each of the risk exposure (likelihood) determining attributes, followed by making appropriate, informed decisions.

Although the example shown in Figure 3.9 focuses on *likelihood* of an undesirable event, the same rationale applies to the *severity* aspect of risk. A given type of risk, such as storm-related property damage, securities class action litigation or workers' injuries can vary significantly in terms of its financial impact, both in terms of absolute costs and its effect on earnings. Hence, the same type of assessment can be carried out in the context of severity, as shown below.

Figure 3.10
Informational Basis of RPM: Severity Dimension

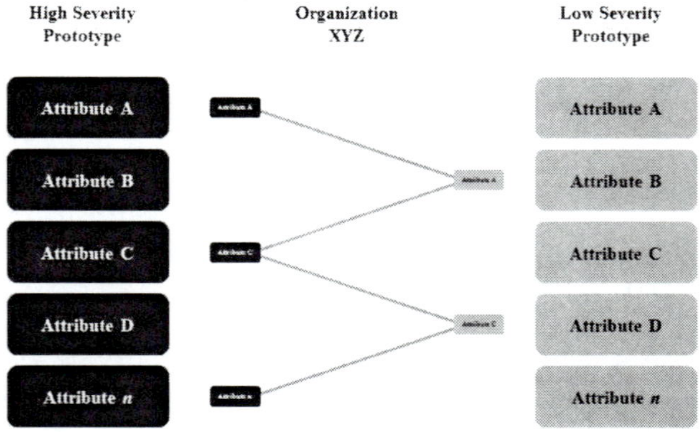

There are two key aspects of risk profiling that define active profile management: 1. identification of actionable attributes, and 2. assessment of partial, or attribute-specific impact.

116

Actionable Attributes

Just as every one of us has multiple characteristics over which we have little-to-no control, there are aspects of organizations that are not subject to their direct control. A publicly traded company controls the number of shares of its stock that it sells to the public, but it has virtually no control over the trading price of its shares. Similarly, an organization has quite a bit of control over the direct or absolute pricing of its products, but it has considerably less control over relative prices of its products, as the latter are heavily influenced by competitors' prices (and ultimately, most organizations are constrained by their input prices). As a result, some aspects of the organization's risk profile will not be directly controllable, which means that a critical part of RPM is the identification of specific risk-related traits over which the organization does have a reasonable degree of control.

Attribute-Specific Impact

As noted earlier, risk profile is a mix of risk exposure-effecting organizational traits. To the degree to which risk profiling is based on similarity (to prototypical high and low risk exposure entities) analysis, some of those attributes will be those that are shared with high risk prototype, while some others will be shared with low risk prototype. Hence it follows that some of the organization's characteristics will increase its risk exposure, while some others will lower it. Furthermore, both the risk heightening and risk lowering attributes will vary in terms of the strength of their impact. Consider the following generic example:

Figure 3.11
Sample Attribute-Based Assessment

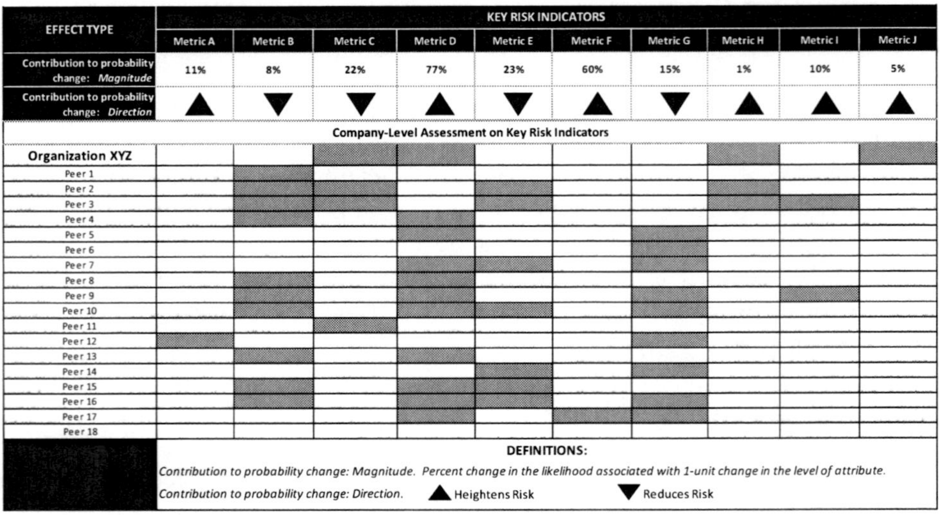

EFFECT TYPE	KEY RISK INDICATORS									
	Metric A	Metric B	Metric C	Metric D	Metric E	Metric F	Metric G	Metric H	Metric I	Metric J
Contribution to probability change: *Magnitude*	11%	8%	22%	77%	23%	60%	15%	1%	10%	5%
Contribution to probability change: *Direction*	▲	▼	▼	▲	▼	▲	▼	▲	▲	▲
Company-Level Assessment on Key Risk Indicators										
Organization XYZ										
Peer 1										
Peer 2										
Peer 3										
Peer 4										
Peer 5										
Peer 6										
Peer 7										
Peer 8										
Peer 9										
Peer 10										
Peer 11										
Peer 12										
Peer 13										
Peer 14										
Peer 15										
Peer 16										
Peer 17										
Peer 18										

DEFINITIONS:

Contribution to probability change: Magnitude. Percent change in the likelihood associated with 1-unit change in the level of attribute.

Contribution to probability change: Direction. ▲ Heightens Risk ▼ Reduces Risk

Key risk indicators (Metric A, Metric B, etc.) are presented in the context of two effect types: 1. Contribution to probability change: Magnitude, which shows the standardized impact of a metric on risk dimension (likelihood in the above example), and 2. Contribution to probability change: Direction, which depicts the nature of impact of a metric on a particular risk dimension. The former is a measure of elasticity, or responsiveness of either likelihood or severity to the level, in changes in it, of a particular predictor of risk, such as Metric A, Metric B, etc. The latter encapsulates the direction of change, where each predictor of risk can either heighten or reduce the probability of its occurrence or its severity.

The second part of the assessment illustrated in Figure 3.11 above is focused on contrasting the focal company's metric-by-metric exposure with that of a set of pre-selected peers. This part of the evaluation attempts to pinpoint specific aspects of the company's risk profile that contribute unfavorably to its risk exposure. There are two distinct aspects to that assessment: First, each organization (i.e., the company as well as each of the peers) are compared to the overall size and industry type adjusted "average" to determine whether each entity is above, below, or within the average, across all metrics that have been identified to be predictive of a particular risk (jointly labeled as "Key Risk Indicators" above). Second, if a particular attribute (e.g.,

Metric A) heightens the company's risk exposure, it is beneficial to be below average on that metric; hence if any of the entities evaluated is above average on that attribute. The reverse logic applies to all predictors of risk which lower the exposure to risk, such as Metric B: It is advantageous to be above average on a measure which reduces risk, while the instances where an entity is below average.

4

The Process of Risk Profile Management

The ideas outlined in this book are rooted in the belief that analyses of business data in general—and risk analytics in particular—are most effective when framed in the context of *explanation-based prediction* and *entity- specific estimation*. To appreciate the importance of former it is important to consider it from the standpoint of epistemology, which is the study of nature of knowledge and processes that create it, while the latter of the two considerations is a reflection of the unit of analysis, or the level of aggregation of analytic conclusions. In a more applied sense, the informational benefits of entity-specific, explanation-based predictions are most evident when contrasted with the widely used, in the analyses of risk, alternative, which is the extrapolation of past trends into the future. Commonly used in actuarial analyses, this broadly considered approach generalizes past patterns without expressly considering any underlying causes – for instance, insurance loss reserving is based on past, aggregate outcomes such as past losses and loss development factors to estimate the value of future liabilities. While such approaches yield adequate insights for some information seekers (e.g., insurance carriers), they fall short in other contexts where deeper knowledge is needed to support activities such as risk mitigation.

PROCESS & METHODS

Taking a closer look at the issues relating to epistemology, it is important to keep in mind some of fundamental differences between the purely scientific goal of theory creation and testing and the focus of applied risk analytics, which is that of estimating the likelihood and severity of specific outcomes (i.e., individual risk factors) along with the delineation and parameterization of key risk drivers. Hence, the goal of risk analytics is not to search for universally true and longitudinally invariant (i.e., unchanging over time) generalizations, but rather, to make reasonably accurate estimates in relation to future states of certain outcomes that are of interest to us. In fact, it is usually assumed that much of what we find today is going to change in the future given the dynamic nature of market behaviors. Hence process-wise, the logic of risk analytics can be depicted as follows:

Figure 4.1
Generic Process of Risk Modeling

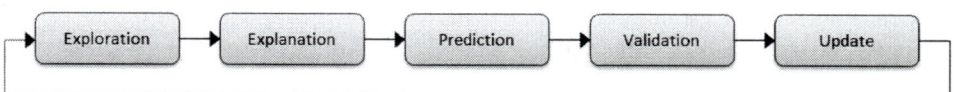

The process depicted in Figure 4.1 illustrates the notion of explanation-based prediction: Exploratory analysis-generated prediction gives rise to a prediction, which is followed by validation. In practice, exploratory analyses will yield a causal model which in turn forms the basis for a scoring equation which generates forward-looking (likelihood and severity) estimates, which are validated against the known outcomes. Once the new batch of behavioral data is available, the analytical process is re-started to take into account any changes in (data-contained) behavioral patterns. This process is inherently reductive, which is to say it analyzes individual risk types into their constituent, lower level components, all with the goal of identifying specific indicators that can be used to estimate future outcomes and to mitigate their likelihood and/or severity, when possible.

Somewhat more hidden is the second of the two previously mentioned characteristics of the risk analytical approach described in this book is the notion of entity-specific estimation. This might seem self-evident, but there are a lot of aspects of risk management where that is not the case. For instance, when assessing exposure to executive liability, which is one of the major components of compliance risk, it is common to make use of group attributes such as industry membership, size (i.e., its market capitalization or revenue) and a handful of somewhat more esoteric characteristics, such as accounting accruals. Companies with shared communalities on those attributes form risk clusters which may include as few as several dozen and as many as several hundred of individual organizations, all of which are assumed to exhibit essentially the same exposure to, in this example, executive liability (or other threats). In the absence of more specific information, these types of approximations might be deemed reasonable—and indeed they are, but only to the extent to which the available data does not support more detailed, entity-specific analyses[1].

Methods

The two framing aspects of the risk analytics approach described in this book—explanation-based prediction and entity-specific estimation—carry a number of implications. First, the estimation of the likelihood and severity of outcomes of interest will encompass the use of multiple metrics, both quantitative and qualitative, to enhance the accuracy of future states' predictions and the completeness of the underlying causal explanation. Second, analytic conclusions will be geared toward improving the business efficacy of future decisions, measured in terms of the expected impact on earnings. Third, the interrelationships among the individually-estimated risk types will be assessed in the context of a dynamic system capable of propagating future changes. Method-wise, these translate into the following considerations:

> ⊳ *Focus on multi-source, multivariate analyses.*
> Risk types vary widely in terms of their nature, the overall frequency of occurrence and the availability of ready-to-use data. Frankly, some risks are significantly easier to measure than some other ones, a fact which obviously contributes to very uneven enterprise risk operationalization landscape. The approach outlined in this book is expressly focused on developing all-inclusive, in terms of the individual risk types, risk assessment capabilities. In more operational terms, the risk analytic methodology presented here is built around multivariate, or multi-variable, analyses of dissimilar sources of data. Multi-source analyses are a necessary prerequisite to a simultaneous assessment of the totality of the organization's risk exposure. Multivariate

122

analyses, on the other hand, are necessary to the development of reliable explanation-sourced forward-looking prediction of likelihood and severity of individual risk types. The basic tenets of modern measurement theory[2] stipulate the use of multiple indicators in situations where the phenomenon of interest is illusive in nature (i.e., the so-called "latent" or unobservable constructs) or when no single indicator is a perfect predictor of the outcome of interest. With that in mind, multivariate statistical analyses can be thought of as a family of mathematical techniques designed to simultaneously estimate the effects of multiple measures, in such a way as to allow to: 1. take into account possible cross-variable interdependencies, and 2. quantify the net effect that can be attributed to each measure. In a context of a specific risk type, such as exposure to securities class action litigation, multivariate analyses will yield insights that are both maximally complete (given data limitations), while containing minimum amount of explanatory redundancies. Hence extended over a number of different risk types, i.e., multi-source data analysis, multivariate analytical techniques will yield maximally explanatory and the most accurate predictive capability. In this book, multivariate statistical modeling will be jointly referred to as *Predictive Analytics* (PA). Figure 4.2 offers a graphical summary of the predictive analytical risk estimation processes detailed in Chapter 10.

Figure 4.2
Predictive Analytical Process

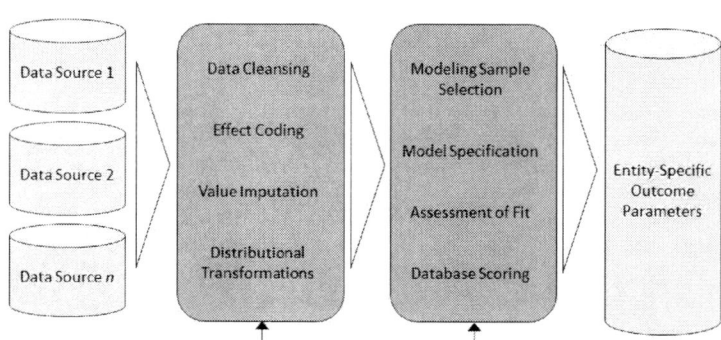

> *Qualitative estimation of risk types for which no reliable quantitative data exists.*

Recently, a number of organizations became increasingly concerned with a threat of pandemic, which is an outbreak of an infectious disease, infecting humans and causing serious illness that spreads easily across a large area, such as a continent or worldwide. There is very limited, at best, data available to use as basis for estimating likelihood and severity of a major epidemic, such as the much talked about avian flu, yet to a number of organizations (particularly healthcare providers who would incur a heightened inflow of patients while facing their own staffing shortages) this is a risk worth considering. In situations such as that and similar, the requisite likelihood and severity estimates need to be derived via alternative means, the most appropriate of which is the Delphi method. Also known as "jury of expert opinion", this approach takes advantage of a cross-section of subject matter experts by funneling their judgment and experience into stress-tested set of qualitative estimates. Hence in this book, qualitative risk assessment will be referred to as *Delphi Approximations* (DA), graphically depicted in Figure 4.3 below and detailed in Chapter 10.

Figure 4.3
Delphi Approximations

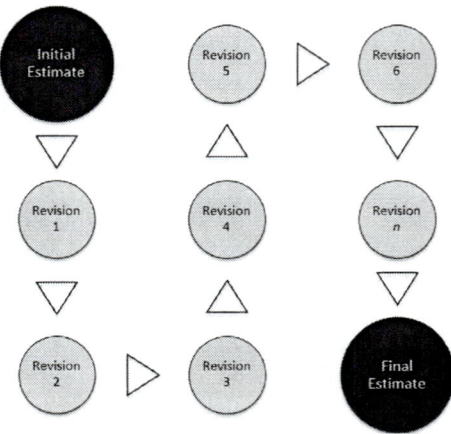

> *Estimation of cross-risk interrelationships, supporting system-wide propagation of future changes.*
> As noted earlier, the individually estimated risk types are subsequently integrated into an overall system combining risk type impact enumeration with the assessment of interdependencies among the individual risks. Furthermore, in order to be able to accommodate the ongoing updates called for by the analytical approach discussed in this book, the risk assessment system needs to be capable of propagating changes to one or more "connections" onto the entire network. Consider Figure 4.4.

Figure 4.4
Hypothetical Bayesian Risk Network

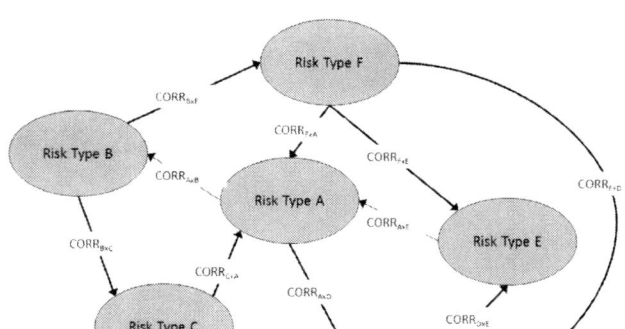

In the hypothetical risk network depicted above, the individual risks—Risk Type A, Risk Type B, etc.—are connected by lines showing their interdependencies, along with magnitudes of those interdependencies (CORR$_{AxB}$, etc.). The interdependencies are measured in terms of bivariate correlations, which are non-directional. The arrow-expressed directional cross risk type connections denote future propagation of changes to any of the bivariate relationships onto the entire network. This is a basic outline of a Bayesian belief network, which is the methodological foundation of the cross risk type integration framework discussed later. Consequently, the overall risk type integration methodology will be referred to as *Bayesian Networks* (BN).

Process vs. Method

The overall risk analytical process depicted in Figure 4.1 suggests a deterministic lock-step progression of *exploratory analysis* being followed by *explanation*, then *prediction* and then *validation*. However, in view of considerable differences separating Predictive Analytics (PA), Delphi Approximations (DA) and Bayesian Networks (BN), the meaning of each of the analytical stages will take on a significantly different meaning for each of the three methodologies.

Figure 4.5
Predictive Analytics vs. Delphi vs. Bayesian

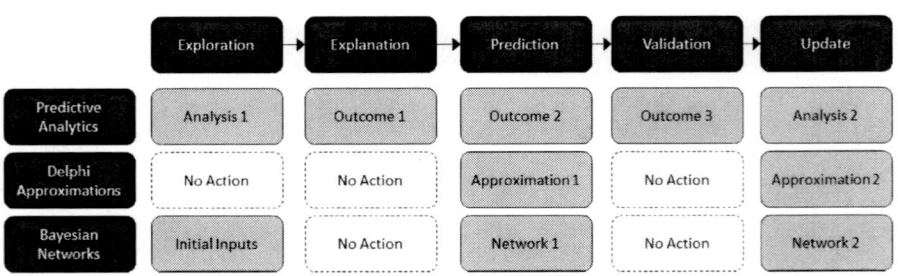

	Exploration	Explanation	Prediction	Validation	Update
Predictive Analytics	Analysis 1	Outcome 1	Outcome 2	Outcome 3	Analysis 2
Delphi Approximations	No Action	No Action	Approximation 1	No Action	Approximation 2
Bayesian Networks	Initial Inputs	No Action	Network 1	No Action	Network 2

As highlighted in Figure 4.5, the fundamental difference between PA, DA and BN, in the context of the data analytical process, is that Predictive Analytics is a continuous endeavor while Delphi Approximations and Bayesian Networks are in essence discrete events. More specifically, within the realm of PA, data and the analysis of it are two separate entities, where externally-sourced data is gradually transformed into evidence and knowledge, with the help of data analytical techniques. Stated differently, data and data analytic techniques are independent of one another, which is in contrast to DA and BN, where data and the analysis of it are indistinguishable from one another. In the case of Delphi Approximations, there is no external data—instead, it is created by the technique itself. In fact, DA is synonymous with outcome parameterization by means of subjective estimates, while PA is synonymous with parameterization of external outcomes based on objective, past frequencies.

Bayesian Networks' development structure follows yet a different pattern. As an integrative framework amalgamating outcomes of Predictive Analytics and Delphi Approximations, it becomes "active" when either PA or

DA make appropriate inputs—or more specifically, likelihood and severity estimates—available. The initial network (Network 1 in Figure 4.4) is completed when either evidence-based, or objective (Predictive Analytics) or belief-based, or subjective (Delphi Approximations) probabilities are made available.

Considering the substantial differences in the development paths separating PA, DA and BN, it is important to ascertain their respective validity and reliability. The next section considers these notions in more detail.

Validity & Reliability

The concepts of validity and reliability are often used somewhat interchangeably, mostly because both are tools that are useful in ascertaining the efficacy of measurement qualities of indicators of abstract, latent constructs. Consider the following measurement challenge: A group of political scientists is trying to estimate the possibility of a politically destabilizing event taking place at a particular part of the world in the next 12 months. What are their respective definitions of a "politically destabilizing event"? Restated in more operational terms, the problem at hand can be phrased as follows: "What tangible benchmarks or indicators could be used by the group of political scientists to estimate the probability of a politically destabilizing event taking place in the part of the word of interest, in the next 12 months?" Graphically, this can be expressed as follows:

Figure 4.6
Latent Construct Measurement

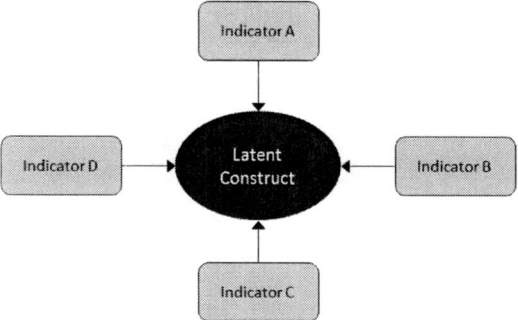

In essence, the challenge of quantifying the likelihood or the severity of somewhat abstractly expressed events is twofold: First, it is of identifying the "right" indicators (Indicator A, Indicator B, etc., in Figure 4.6), which are the tangible, easier to assess proxies for the event in question. Second, it is that of ascertaining the accuracy of those indicators—in other words, how good a proxy Indicator A is the latent construct of interest. These considerations are of considerable importance to the informational robustness of Delphi Approximations.

There are two distinct dimensions characterizing the quality of measurement of the Latent Construct depicted in Figure 4.4—reliability and validity. *Reliability* captures the repeatability or consistency of a particular operationalization. A measure (such as Indicator A or Indicator B) is considered reliable if it gives us the same result over and over again, of course assuming that what we're measuring (Latent Construct) is not changing. Conceptually, reliability can be thought of as a ratio of "true level of the measure" to the "entire measure". In practice, however, the "true" measure is rarely known, hence in an applied sense the best way of estimating reliability is to express it as a correlation among multiple observations of the same measure. There are several different types of reliability—internal consistency, test-retest reliability, parallel forms and inter-rater reliability—however, in the context of risk measurement it is the inter-rater reliability that is of greatest importance.

In the context of Delphi Approximations, the *inter-rater reliability* is operationalized by correlating single item responses across responders. In other words, responses of all experts to Indicator A would be correlated to estimate the reliability of Indicator A, responses of all experts to Indicator B would be correlated to estimate the reliability of Indicator B, and so on. Computationally, this would be accomplished as follows (the following assumes that individual expert's responses are continuous—if not, see Chapter 9 for a more in-depth discussion of other types of coefficients of correlation):

$$IRR = \sqrt{\frac{\sum_{i=1}^{n}(X_i - \bar{X})^2}{n - 1}}$$

where,

      IRR is Inter-Rater Reliability
      X_i is response of expert 1

As a general rule, to conclude that there indeed is a sufficient level of inter-rater reliability, the following decision rule can be employed:

$$|IRR| \geq \frac{2}{\sqrt{n}}$$

where,

128

n is the number of individual experts/opinions

For example, if IRR = 0.80 and there are 15 individual experts, then the measurement can be deemed reliable if IRR is 0.52 or higher.

The other of the two key aspects of latent construct measurement is *validity*, which captures the degree to which the construct's conceptualization and operationalization are in agreement. Simply put, it is the quality of measurement. Conceptually, validity is both broader and a somewhat more elusive idea, hence it can be looked at from a number of different angles, which reflect two key underlying questions: 1. Is the operationalization a good reflection of the construct? 2. How will the operationalization perform? These two broad questions can be broken down into several, more specific question-expressed types of validity considerations:

Table 4.1

Types of Validity

Type	Description
Face Validity	On their face value, are the indicators (Indicator A, Indicator B, etc., in Figure 3.5) as a whole a good reflection of the latent construct?
Content Validity	Is the informational content of individual indicators in keeping with the meaning of the latent construct?
Discriminant Validity	Are these measures of the latent construct operationally different from other sets of measures?
Predictive Validity	Will the operationalization be able to predict the outcome of interest with a reasonable degree of accuracy?
Convergent Validity	Do predictions generated by the operationalization converge with other, related predictions?
Concurrent Validity	Can the operationalization distinguish among types of outcomes?

Clearly, validity-related considerations represent a mix of qualitative and quantifiable considerations. The goal behind the assessment of Delphi Approximations related validity considerations is not necessarily to attempt to provide a numeric assessment of the different faces of validity outlined above. Rather, it is to draw attention to potential pitfalls and thus to invite a thorough due diligence of the measurement approach.

In terms of more tangible outcomes, a thorough consideration of the two key aspects of latent construct measurement—validity and reliability—will contribute to more accurate estimates. More specifically, the measurement of risk types for which no readily available quantitative data is available will be expressed as an additive composite of two components: a true estimated value and an error associated with that estimate. Formally, that can be expressed as follows:

Risk Type Estimate = True Value + Random Error

More specifically, the likelihood and severity of occurrence of an event of interest can be expressed as:

Likelihood Risk Type$_A$ = variability(Risk Type$_A$ Frequency) + error
Severity Risk Type$_A$ = variability(Risk Type$_A$ Cost) + error

The RPM Process: Management vs. Measurement

It is important to note that the earlier discussed RPM Process encircles the broad *management* considerations, comprised of Need Identification, Knowledge Creation and Knowledge Dissemination facets (see Figure 1.4 in Chapter 1 and Figure 4.7 in the next section); at the same time, the bulk of the ensuing discussion will be focused on the more narrowly scoped *measurement,* or analytical considerations. Hence the "RPM Process" label will be used in reference to both the overall management process, as well as the more narrowly defined measurement topics.

THE OVERALL RISK ANALYTIC PROCESS

The process-based approach to effective analyses of large volumes of multi-sourced data is captured in the RPM process depicted below.

Figure 4.7
The Risk Profile Management Process

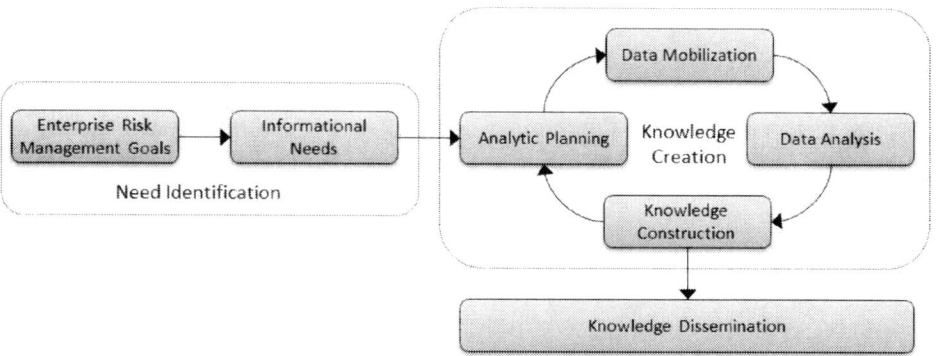

As depicted in Figure 4.7, the overall risk analytical process is comprised of seven distinct components, which are grouped into three explicit categories: 1. *Need Identification*, 2. *Knowledge Creation*, and 3. *Knowledge Dissemination*. The goal of the *Need Identification* part of the overall risk analytical process is twofold: First, it is to bring forth the agreed upon risk management goals and priorities of the organization. To be clear, the focus of this step is simply on delineating – as opposed to deriving – the individual objectives that have been embraced by the organization. Second, it is to translate the delineated strategic objectives into specific informational goals. Implicitly, this step recognizes that a successful achievement of the organizational goals is, to a large degree, dependent on the attainment of a high degree of decision making clarity. Hence, the overall objective of the Need Identification stage of the risk analytical process is to distill the agreed upon risk management goals into a clear set of informational demands.

The goal of the second, broad stage of the risk analytical process— *Knowledge Creation*—is that of fulfilling the informational demands identified earlier. That is both a tall order and a very broadly scoped endeavor. As graphically shown in Figure 4.7, it encompasses four distinct process-linked components: *Analytic Planning, Data Mobilization, Data Analysis* and

Knowledge Construction. It is an iterative process which continues to refresh data-derived knowledge supporting current goals, or generates new knowledge for updated or newly established goals. In a sense, this is the "engine" of the risk measurement process outlined in this book hence the bulk of the remaining chapters will be focused on an in-depth discussion of each of the four general stages comprising the Knowledge Creation process.

Lastly, the risk analytical process culminates in the *Knowledge Dissemination* step, a deceptively simple, logical conclusion to the overall progression. To say that it is deceptively simple is akin to saying that its importance is frequently overlooked, which can lead to informationally-rich insights having unjustifiably little decision-guiding impact. Hence, it is the purpose of the Knowledge Dissemination chapter to draw attention to the importance of this step and to offer best practices-inspired suggestions.

5

Need Identification:
Informational Needs

One of the biggest challenges facing risk analytics is that those who create the information, namely quantitative analysts, rarely have the requisite understanding of users' needs, and conversely, the latter rarely have an adequate understanding of "data crunching" considerations. It is natural for an analyst to view data modeling as a technical task governed by data and method characteristics—in fact, it is necessary to have that mindset in order to assure the validity and reliability of results. At the same time, the users of the resultant information are generally focused almost entirely on practical implications, paying little attention to methods. These focal point differences are usually explained by a combination of skill set and job responsibilities, in which case they can be viewed as a consequence of an organization having a diverse and at times highly specialized pool of skilled resources. That notwithstanding, these non-overlapping skill sets and areas of responsibility can have negative consequences. More specifically, the often limited understanding of each other's priorities and critical issues can, and often does, lead to analysts guessing their way through projects' practical substance-related considerations, at the same time as the future business users are glazing over the results' research methodology-related limitations. In essence, the analysts charged with creating information and the users of it speak different languages. That state of affairs did not work out particularly well for the Babylonians building their Biblical tower, and it works equally poorly for modern organizations trying to establish competitively advantageous knowledge base. The lack of effective risk analyst—risk manager communication destroys shareholder value, as the impact of poorly thought out analytical insights is likely to be minimal vis-à-vis the costs incurred in generating those insights.

So what can be done about it? To paraphrase an age-old question: Should kings become philosophers, or should philosophers become kings? In other words, should the (future) users of information expect that analysts attain high levels of practical business proficiency, or should the analysts expect that those using the results of their work attain adequate levels of technical savvy? It is my experience-derived belief that neither is a viable scenario. For the most part, given the depth and the relative complexity of quantitative data analytical methodologies it is simply unreasonable to expect users of analyses-derived insights to become methodological experts, or even attain "working knowledge" of analytical methods. At the same time, considering the typical detachment (in terms of day-to-day involvement and responsibilities) of analysts from practical applications of their analyses, it is not likely that they will reach the users' level of practical business proficiency. That leaves only one feasible avenue to improving the less than ideal analyst—business user level of cooperation; namely, to put in place a systematic process of defining informational needs which can reliably "translate" business informational needs into operationalizable analytical activities. Unfortunately, it is not quite as easy as it may sound.

There are a couple of general, highly interrelated challenges that need to be surmounted. The first one can be broadly described as the level of informational precision. While business needs are typically stated in somewhat general, if not ambiguous terms, data analysis needs precision and specificity, if it is to hit the informational bull's eye. For example, let's consider a question commonly asked by claim managers or adjusters: "What is the likelihood of particular claim exceeding a given cost threshold?" To a business user this seems to be a perfectly clear, self-explanatory question, yet to an analyst, its meaning is far from obvious. Looking at it from a standpoint of having to make the most appropriate data and method selection, an analyst will realize that there are numerous, operationally distinct approaches that can be used here, each yielding a considerably different answer. In the end, what might seem to be a clear-cut business question can have multiple data analytical "translations", each leading to a somewhat dissimilar end result.

The second obstacle is even more fundamental, as it involves timely and complete a priori delineation of business informational needs. As defined here, it is a relatively broad endeavor encompassing the distilling of the big strategic picture into more granular tactical components, clearly stating data and methodological requirements, followed by the sketching out of an analytical roadmap. Taken together, the component parts of the a priori delineation of business informational needs can be thought of as a continuum to which both the analysts and business users of information can contribute.

Business users are responsible for putting forth strategic and tactical objectives, which is the point of departure in developing a robust informational foundation. At this point, the emphasis is on presenting a comprehensive picture of the high-level business objectives. Next, the strategic and tactical objectives need to be translated into specific informational requirements. For instance, the high level strategic goal of reducing the total cost of risk may translate into, among other things, the need to estimate the likelihood of encountering securities class action litigation (informational need #1), the most likely cost associated with the threat of securities litigation (informational need #2), or the identification of the most pronounced leading indicators of costly liability claims (informational need #3). The success of this endeavor will depend on the business users and analysts working together earnestly to add a dimension of analytical precision to the stated informational needs.

Once the informational needs have been defined and operationalized, the analysts are then responsible for addressing data and methodological requirements. It all boils down to answering a basic question: What are the data and methodological requirements that are necessary to deliver against the stated informational needs? The last step in the process—the development of an analytic roadmap—puts forth a clear plan for how those goals will be accomplished, spelling out the timeline, resource requirements, means and dependencies as well as the final deliverables. It makes it possible for analysts to describe the upcoming deliverable and solicit feedback before committing to a specific analytical course of action.

Each of the steps in the informational needs delineation process should be viewed as somewhat broadly defined set of activities, rather than a singular action. A more in-depth description of each step follows.

Delineation of Strategic Goals and Tactical Means

Baldrige defines strategic objectives as "...an organization's articulated aims or responses to address major change or improvement, competitive issues, and business advantages." Paralleling an advertising slogan, business analytics does not "make" strategic objectives—it "helps" to turn abstract objectives into operational reality.

A well-defined set of strategic goals includes the appropriate operationalizations, or tactical means by which the stated objectives are to be reached. For instance, the goal of reducing the total cost of risk can be tactically reached by increasing retention limits, imposing a ceiling on insurable losses, more effective pre-emptive identification of claims with heightened likelihood of adverse development or targeting specific causes of losses with policy changes. In fact, it is the tactical means to the organization's stated strategic goals that are the true point of departure in the analytical planning process, simply because tactics are more tangible and as such, more indicative of the requisite informational needs. In that sense, the goal of risk analytics is to aid in the identification and execution of tactics driving the stated strategic objectives.

The task of delineating the focal strategies and tactics belongs to business users, with a particular emphasis on those accountable for reaching the stated goals. Goal specificity is highly desired.

Uncovering Informational Needs

Once the organization's overall strategic goals and their tactical means have been clearly enunciated, specific informational needs can be identified. In general, those will fall into one of the following two categories: 1. exploratory and predictive capabilities, and 2. ongoing assessment capabilities.

Exploratory and Predictive Capabilities

This is a broad category of potential analyses, ranging from relatively simple univariate (i.e., one variable at a time) descriptive investigations to complex multivariate (i.e., simultaneously considering multiple variables) predictive models and simulations. Exploratory analyses represent a broad family of approaches focused on describing and profiling trends, characteristics and outcomes of interest. Consider the aforementioned task of managing the total cost of risk. For a number of organizations (particularly those in manufacturing, retail, hotel and restaurant industries), workers' compensation and general liability represent the lion's share of the overall cost of risk, which is due to a combination of high frequency and (potentially) high severity of individual claims. However, in most cases, the true culprit is the latter—the potentially high cost of individual claims[1]. The challenge, of course, is to be able to explain the causes of high cost claims, as well as to predict adverse claim development. Basic exploratory analyses are an effective starting point in developing a clear picture of the total cost of risk by providing structured outcome tabulation. Distributions of aggregate frequency, severity and causal outcomes, resulting from the said univariate analyses can offer a revealing picture of the overall cost of risk, thus providing an objective starting point in risk mitigation and cost reduction efforts. In practical risk management terms, exploratory analyses can be a rich source of policy (e.g., safety, claim management, etc.) shaping decisions.

Predictive analytics go beyond describing the *past*—these methods are expressly focused on estimating *future* outcomes, all with the goal of identifying specific cases (e.g., claims) that should be treated differentially. The rationale behind predictive analytical methodologies is rooted in the basic economics of risk management, which postulates that the amount of effort and resource allocation should be proportional to either the cost of benefit associated with a particular outcome. For instance, a high cost claim should be allocated proportionately more resources than a low cost claim. This is generally an intuitively obvious rationale, but the problem is that the future cost of most claims is not known ahead of time. This is where predictive analytics comes in: A set of multivariate statistical techniques, deployed against a representative sample of fully-developed (those with known total, or closing cost) claims with the goal of deriving a probabilistic scoring functionality capable of estimating expected future cost of current, recently filed claims. There are numerous other examples of using predictive analytics in risk management, but the general idea is that past interdependencies and patterns can be used to estimate the most likely future outcomes, which in turn can support a more productive allocation of risk management resources.

In general, exploratory and predictive analytical capabilities supply decision-making inputs prior to taking a particular risk management action—in other words, they are helpful in making better informed decisions. In the way of contrast, the ongoing performance assessment set of capabilities discussed below helps to assess the impact of decisions that were made by objectively quantifying their impact. As discussed throughout the subsequent chapters, the two sets of capabilities are the cornerstones of the database analytical process described in this book.

Ongoing Assessment Capabilities

The general task of assessing the impact of analytic-inspired actions entails a family of methods focused on objective quantification of the impact of specific decisions. Depending on data availability and the level of methodological sophistication, it can range from a simple tallying to a relatively involved quantification of cause-attributable effect size. In contrast to the innovation focused exploratory and predictive capabilities, the ongoing impact assessment values cross-time and cross-treatment standardization. In other words, one of the desired qualities of ongoing assessment is the comparability of outcomes across different types of initiatives and across time.

Both the exploratory and predictive capabilities, as well as the ongoing impact assessment are most effectively planned through a close cooperation between business users and analysts. Combining the knowledge of the two early in the analytical planning process will likely bring about greater efficiencies later by zeroing in on what questions should be asked and which ones can actually be answered in view of the ever-present data and methodological limitations.

Assessing Data and Method Requirements

The notions of data availability and methodological readiness are best depicted as continuums, representing the *degree of* data availability or methodological readiness. Consider the earlier-described event-tracking data, best exemplified by various types of insurance claims (e.g., workers' compensation or general liability). Oftentimes, these data are readily available for use, as it will either reside in the organization's own data systems (in the case of organizations handling their own claims), or it will be managed by a third-party administrator, or TPA. Generally, in either case, the extraction and deployment of the claims data can be handled very quickly. By the same token, data representing an enhancement offered by an outside vendor, such as consumer credit bureaus, geodemographic or behavioral research/profiling firm, may take longer to be made available[2]. (In addition to the operational steps, using outside data vendors entails an extra step of charge validation, which is a result of a standard practice of using the "highest variable match rate[3] as the basis for cost calculation.) Often glazed over as banal or mundane, these details should be expressly considered as a part of the analytical planning because as uninteresting (to both analysts and business users of information) as they tend to be, they have the potential of derailing the timing of even the simplest analyses. And gaining a leg up on the competition means not only having the right insights, but also having that knowledge available at a time when using it can make a difference.

On the methodological readiness side, it is important to acknowledge that the depth of expertise and the methodology-specific experience can vary— at time substantially—across analysts. Keeping that in mind is not only one of the key prerequisites to effective analytical planning (discussed next), but may also lead to questions surrounding the "do in-house" vs. "outsource" decisions.

An often overlooked consideration involves tool requirements. As the available statistical analysis software grew more powerful over the years, it also grew more expensive, modularized (i.e., divided into a base system plus add-on modules) and specialized (i.e., the general purpose SAS and SPSS statistical analysis packages vs. a limited purpose tools, such as MARS or CART). Consequently, many organizations opt to initially purchase scaled down versions of the more expensive software and add additional modules as the need arises. Again, it is worthwhile to consider the informational objectives in the context of the required tools to avoid last minute surprises.

6

Knowledge Creation: Analytic Planning

Planning is one of the essential building blocks of rational, intelligent behavior. There are two key aspect of planning: The first is the psychological process of thinking about future states or outcomes, as well as the means and impediments of getting there. The second is the creation of a structured action map, or a plan, aimed at achieving stated goals.

The process of planning has several benefits. Thinking focused on future states or outcomes of interest spurs the identification of numerous considerations that might not have otherwise been noticed. Structuring of an action plan, on the other hand, brings about procedural clarity through the delineation of process steps, dependencies and the timeline.

Probably the most productive way of looking at analytic planning is through a system approach. A *system*, defined here as an organized set of interrelated elements, is comprised of inputs, processes, outputs and outcomes, all linearly organized as shown below.

Figure 6.1
General System Model

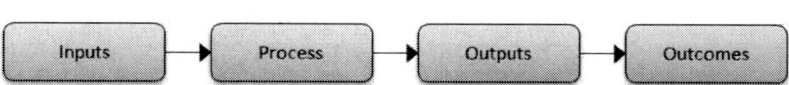

Inputs include both resources (human, capital, etc.) as well as the stated organizational objectives, discussed in earlier chapters. *Process* is a collection of means of transforming inputs into something else, namely, outputs. *Outputs* are tangible results produced by the processes embodied by the system. And lastly, *outcomes* are the benefits derived by end users.

The Risk Profile Measurement (RPM) approach detailed in this book is well suited to the systems-based analytic planning because of the implicit determinism imbedded in its logic, as evidenced by a priori delineation of threats to the organization's revenue stream. When coupled with the limited scope of risk management endeavors, which are focused on identifying the most appropriate risk response or a combination of responses (see the *Knowledge of Risk* chapter), it can be seen the goal of an *analytic system* is to generate maximally effective, decision aiding knowledge.

Planning vs. Plan

Sometimes we confuse the "how" something is produced with "what" is being produced. Naturally, the process of planning should produce a plan— that much is obvious. What gets overlooked, however, is the implicit temporal distinction between the two, namely, that the process of planning should be viewed as being antecedent to the outcome, which is a plan. This is not just a semantic distinction – the ongoing nature of the RPM process detailed in this book demands both flexibility and longitudinal consistency. Stated differently, to be effective, an analytic plan has to stem from a robust planning framework, capable of supporting the ongoing risk analytical changes and corrections in a manner which will retain the requisite measurement consistency across time.

An important requirement of the planning framework is that it incorporates the key elements of the RPM framework: objective informational need identification, data considerations, method selection and the creation of competitively advantageous knowledge. An RPM-tailored planning framework is discussed next.

ANALYTIC PLANNING FRAMEWORK

Consider the general systems model depicted in Figure 6.1 above—it is composed of several, serially arranged elements: Inputs, Process, Outputs & Outcomes. Now, consider the Risk Profile Measurement framework, first depicted in Figure 1.4. As shown in Figure 6.2 below, the two conceptualizations are closely related.

Figure 6.2
System Model vs. Risk Profile Measurement

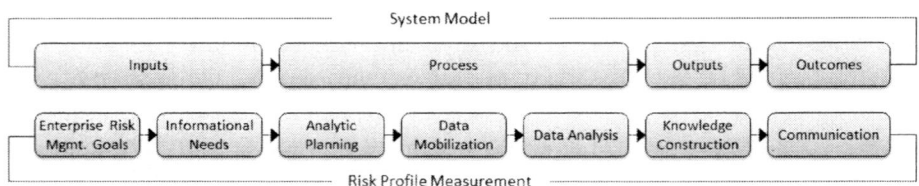

Let's dig deeper into the above graphically-depicted conceptualization. Considering the tenets of the general systems model in the context of the RPM process, we can establish the following interdependencies:

Inputs ➔ Informational Objectives and Data
The creation of decision aiding knowledge is, to a large degree, shaped by two mutually independent forces: 1. Stated information objectives, which essentially represent questions in need of answers, and 2. The available data, which effectively constrains the validity and the reliability of the resultant insights.

Process ➔ Methods
In many regards, this is the most straightforward part of the analytical plan development—it entails the identification of the most appropriate data analytical methodology or methodologies, given the stated informational objectives and constraints imposed by the available data.

Outputs ➔ Analytic Results
The purpose of this stage is the delineation of expected analytical (statistical) outputs and the ascertaining of the validity and reliability of those outputs. In

particular, it is to "spell out" specific means or tests for establishing non-spuriousness of inferences drawn from data.

Outcomes ➔ *Decision Inputs*
From the standpoint of end user value, this is a particularly important aspect of the analytic planning process: What steps should be taken to "translate" the often highly abstract, esoteric data analytical outcomes into unambiguous decision aiding knowledge? It is often both the most overlooked and challenging aspect of the overall data analytical endeavor.

Generalizable Planning Template

Although the specifics of any initially developed analytic plan will more than likely change over time, a considerable amount of objectivity and consistently can be instilled by setting up a general planning template. An example of an analytic planning template is shown below – it is important to note that the essence of the template exemplified below is to bring about a reasonable amount of standardization, which is particularly important in view of potential team discontinuity.

Table 6.1
Sample Analytic Planning Template

Input	Analysis	Outcomes
Information Needed:		Anticipated analytical/statistical outcomes
Exploratory	Most appropriate analytical methods	
Predictive		
Available Data		Reliability & validity checks
Limitations		
Business Insights		
Anticipated decision aiding knowledge		

Additional Considerations

A helpful way of thinking about analytic planning is to consider the resultant plan to be a contract between the analysts and the end user community. Hence in addition to the above delineated system consideration, a well-crafted analytic plan might also contain the following:

> ⯈ An explicit delineation of the individual analytic initiatives with a clear linkage to specific informational needs and ultimately, the organization's strategic objectives.
> ⯈ An overall completion timeline showing the starting and completion dates for each analytic project.
> ⯈ An explicit description of how each initiative will improve the decision-making process.
> ⯈ Analytic and business owners of each initiative, along with their respective roles and responsibilities.

It is worthwhile to remember that the purpose of an analytic plan, or a roadmap is twofold: On the one hand, it sets clear expectations among the ultimate business users of the to-be-derived insights, both in terms of the specific upcoming deliverables as well as the approximate completion time. In that sense, it serves to minimize disruptive clarification demands, thus allowing analysts to concentrate on the task at hand.

The second key purpose of preparing an explicit analytic roadmap is efficiency. Clear directions go a long way toward streamlining the actual conduct of analyses and reducing potential re-work. Perhaps even more importantly, clarity enhances the quality of data analyst—business user communication, which is the key to timely and cost effective analytics.

7

Knowledge Creation: Understanding Data

D ata is not only a potential organizational asset—it is a centerpiece of a thriving industry encompassing capture and storage hardware, manipulation and reporting software and exploration-focused consulting. Business organizations tend to view database infrastructure as a competitive necessity, investing heavily in ever larger and more complex data systems. However, the result of billions of dollars of aggregate database infrastructure spending, coupled with large scale capture and cataloguing of data are all too often disappointing, as the hoped-for informational enlightenment is reduced to just a barrage of inconclusive reports, contributing more to clutter than to the quality of decision making.

Nowadays, virtually all mid-size and larger business organizations either already have in their possession or have a ready access to a variety of transaction-recording and/or descriptive data. In fact, the vast majority of these organizations own multiple databases, maintained and used by a variety of functional areas, such as sales, claims management, human resources, industry analysis, marketing and so on. And, as pointed out in the opening chapter, most organizations subscribe to the flawed belief that data is an asset, which is to say that the, often considerable expense required to capture, store and maintain the ever-growing volumes of diverse data is absolutely justifiable. Underscoring that unwavering conviction is the fact that, in total, over the past 25 years or so, businesses in the U.S alone invested in excess of $1 trillion in data-related infrastructure, with mixed results. Some, including Wal-Mart, Google, Capital One, Harrah's or Marriott, to name just a few, clearly benefited from their data-related investments; many others put a lot more into the database endeavor then they ever were able to get out of it. In fact, it could be argued that, overall, the database revolution did more for the fortunes of data service suppliers than it for the competitiveness of an average database using organization.

Let me reiterate the point I made in the opening chapter: Data is not an asset—it is a potential asset. It means it is a resource, a raw material of sorts which needs to be made into something useful before it can denote value. Wal-Mart did not overtake K-Mart because it had more data—it was because Wal-Mart made systematic and purposeful analysis of their data (which, by the way, was not meaningfully different than K-Mart's data) the very heart and soul of their decision making. In other words, Wal-Mart managed to squeeze a lot more out of its data, which in turn greatly increased the efficacy of the company's decisions.

Getting more out of data is a function of two, somewhat related considerations. First, it requires what could be called an intimate knowledge of data sources. Do not forget—the vast majority of data capture is a byproduct of business process digitization, particularly what is broadly termed electronic transaction processing. It means business databases tend to be large in terms of size and esoteric in terms of content. Typically, they encompass millions of records and hundreds or even thousands of individual metrics, many of which are far from being intuitively obvious. The bottom line: The attainment of robust knowledge of a particular database requires dedicated effort, which is perhaps why an average user will just "scratch the surface"…

The second prerequisite to getting more out of data is the amalgamation of dissimilar data into a singular analytical source. Now, if getting to know a single database seems like a lot of work, getting to know several and finding a way of combining their contents could well be considered a Herculean undertaking. And frankly, it can indeed be a hard and an arduous process. Is it worth it? Any organization not convinced it is, should probably reconsider stockpiling data in expensive databases.

As illustrated throughout this and the remaining chapters, the most significant difference between information-savvy organizations and their data-rich but information-poor counterparts is the data analytical *know-how*. In other words, while virtually the same hardware and software technologies are available to all organizations; it is the power of the subsequent data exploration and utilization that determines the ultimate return on the overall data infrastructure investments. And it all starts with a solid grasp of the available data.

DATA FUNDAMENTALS

Broadly defined, data are facts. There are multiple ways of categorizing data: by source, type, usage situation, etc. From the standpoint of informational content, data can be broadly divided into an *events/behaviors* and *attributes* that describe or otherwise augment events and behaviors. Within the realm of risk management, the former can include accidents (events) and insurance claim fillings (behaviors), while the latter encompasses a broad spectrum of potentially explanatory factors, such as demographics or firmographics, weather readings or accident attributes; hence while event metrics record observed or observable occurrences, attribute variables are the potential causes, or at least correlates of those occurrences.

These rudimentary differences between event and attribute metrics are indicative of the informational value of the two data types: The former offer the basis for the historical count-based aggregate likelihood estimates (e.g., the likelihood that an U.S exchange traded company will incur a securities class action litigation), while the latter make possible more granular contextualization of likelihood estimates (e.g., the likelihood of incurring a securities class action litigation by an energy vs. a pharmaceutical firm), as well as enabling causal attributions, defined here as a delineation of identifiable event-describing characteristics.

Events

As the once ubiquitous paper file repositories of insurance claims, accident or employee records gave way to electronic databases, the detail, amount and the sheer extent of record keeping grew exponentially. Nowadays, in virtually all aspect of business – and life in general – events and behaviors leave an electronic imprint – a data record. Consider an example of an on-the-job employee accident and the subsequent processing of the resultant worker's compensation claim: The initial accident is entered into an appropriate electronic repository, along with numerous evidentiary details, such as time and place, cause and nature of an injury, initial treatment and diagnosis, etc. The claim is assigned to a handler (a claim adjuster) who manages the record communicating with the injured worker, reviewing requests for medical treatments, salary continuation payments, injury-related expense payments, etc.; all handler actions and activities are also recorded electronically (as adjuster notes in a diary system). Any other activity by other parties, such as medical examinations and the subsequent treatment, return to work activities or any legal actions are also captured electronically, all of which results in a web of ultimately interconnected (via a widespread use of a common record identification, such as Claim ID) but otherwise dispersed (due to be located in different files and, possibly, different databases) details of the aforementioned on-the-job accident.

Attributes

Within the confines of risk analytics, descriptive attributes that tend be associated with an event or a behavior of interest serve a dual purpose: Firstly, they offer more granular contextualization of likelihood estimates, which makes such estimates more tailored to individual firms. Secondly, descriptive attributes lend insight into the "why" behind the "what" in the form of correlates or root causes of the observed events or behaviors. The distinction between correlates and causes is not always clear, hence it deserves a closer look.

Ascertaining Causation

Given its central role in knowledge creation, the notion of *causality* or *causation* has been a subject of centuries-long debate among scientists and philosophers alike. At the core of the debate has been the line of demarcation separating cause-and-effect from just simple concurrence based relationships. Is factor A causing B, or do the two merely coincide? From the standpoint of philosophy of science an explanation has to meet four separate criteria, detailed in Table 7.1, before it can be classified as causal[1].

Table 7.1
Causality Criteria

Criterion	Description
Temporal Sequentiality	Changes in factor A to be used to causally explain factor B must precede in time the occurrence of changes in B. Thus an attributed action must precede the observed outcome before it can be considered a cause of it. It is an intuitively obvious and an easily established requirement in practical business analysis.
Associative Variation	Changes in factor A must be systematically associated with changes in factor B. In other words, in order to conclude that certain types of accidents cause higher losses, one must be able to observe systematic cost increases associated with these accidents. Again, a logical and usually relatively easy to meet requirement.
Non-Spurious Association	If A causes B, then there must be no factor C which, if introduced into the explanation would make the systematic A—B association vanish. Thus if work absenteeism is indeed one of the causes of higher workers' compensation claim frequency, factoring out another metric, such as length of employment, should not nullify the *absenteeism—claim frequency* relationship. Unlike the previous two requirements, this is a far more difficult condition to meet, primarily because data is not always available to make that determination and even when it is, its quality can vary considerably among sources.
Theoretical Support	If A causes B, is it consistent with an established theory X? If the aforementioned absenteeism indeed leads to higher workers' compensation claim frequency, what is the theory that explains that dependence? Since practical business analyses are typically not concerned with abstract theoretical explanations, thus this particular requirement is rarely satisfied, though it is worthwhile to keep it in mind.

As pointed out above, temporal sequentiality and associative variation have a very simple meaning and application, in spite of the somewhat foreboding names. Occurring in sequence (A followed by B) and doing so persistently is both intuitively obvious and relatively easy to demonstrate. For instance, if a certain behavior (such as absenteeism mentioned in Table 7.1) proceeds, time-wise, other behaviors, such as workers' compensation claims, and it is observed on recurring basis, that would generally constitute sufficient basis to attest to temporal sequentiality and associative variation.

It is less so with the remaining two causality thresholds: a non-spurious association and a demonstrated theoretical support. Even though many behaviors tend to be somewhat repetitive, the mere fact that they tend to be a part of a larger set of behavioral interdependencies makes the requirement of proving their non-spurious nature a difficult one. In addition, many of these activities are highly pragmatic—i.e., they do not espouse to adhere to specific general theories and their roots are often in fact, spurious ideas and decisions. Frankly, the pursuit of competitive advantage demands that firms take steps that are uniquely more advantageous to them then their competitors, rather than pursuing strategies that have been proven to work the same way for everyone else.

So what is the conclusion? Establishing causality in business analyses should reconcile pragmatic and scientific considerations, with an eye toward a practically-dependable, rather than theoretically-pure solution. This may sound almost blasphemous to some, but let's consider some of the hallmark differences between applied and scientific endeavors. First and foremost, business analyses are typically concerned with uncovering unique though sustainable sources of competitive advantage, in contrast to scientific investigations which almost always are focused on formulating and testing generalizable, i.e., universally true, knowledge claims. This means that business and theoretical analyses both share in a requirement of ascertaining temporal sequentiality and the associative variation of the potentially causal relationships, but it also means that in contrast to the theoretical pursuits, business analyses can conclude that the relationships of interest are causal without conclusively demonstrating a clear theoretical support or the non-spurious nature of the said association. In other words, a particular cause—effect relationship does not need to be universally true (meaning, equally valid for all other organizations) in order to be a source of competitively advantageous decisions by a particular organization—it only needs to be persistent, or hold up across time.

Secondly, scientific worthiness of findings is demonstrated through their generalizability and only implicitly through longitudinal stability, while the value of practical business analyses is demonstrated almost exclusively through longitudinal persistence of results. To a firm it matter little whether particular dependencies can be generalizable to other firms or industries (frankly, the pursuit of a competitive edge would argue the opposite), but it is tremendously important that these relationship hold as expected when resources are invested into future business initiatives, whether these are promotional programs or other capital expenditures. In other words, while theoretical research aims to create universally applicable knowledge, business research strives to uncover the few dimensions of knowledge that are uniquely applicable—i.e., advantageous—to a particular firm.

Thirdly, business analytics are contextualized by focus and data. Even the largest organizations only compete in a subset of all industries and their data and data analyses are a reflection of the scope of their operations. In other words, the focus of business analyses is the world in which the firm operates, while the focus of theoretical investigations naturally transcends any idiosyncratic industry or a set of industries. Thus the resultant knowledge claims—including causality—should be evaluated in the proper context.

DATABASES IN A NUTSHELL

Although we tend to associate databases with modern computer applications, as repositories of facts databases as such existed long before the advent of modern electronic computing. In a strictly definitional sense, a telephone book found in nearly every household is as much a database as Wal-Mart's 583^2 terabyte mega system. In other words, a database can range from a simple listing of your friends' phone numbers written down on a single sheet of paper to a large corporate or governmental computerized system.

Obviously, no one (at least as far as I know) needs a statistical analyst to analyze a database of their friends' or family's phone members. Thus in practical business sense, the notion of a database conveys a certain level of utility and technical sophistication that is typically not associated with just any informational reservoir. Hence in a more formal sense, business database could be defined as an electronically stored collection of facts requiring its own management system (i.e., DBMS) in conjunction with specialized query and analysis tools. Furthermore, due to its assumed size and complexity, business databases typically require specialized skills for ongoing reporting and knowledge extraction.

There are multiple ways of describing databases: by data type, purpose, content, organizational structure, size, hardware software characteristics, etc. From the standpoint of database analytics, the most pertinent aspects of a database are: 1. Scope, which considers differences between data warehouse and data mart; 2. Content, specifies the form of encoding, which can be text, multimedia or numeric; 3. Data model, which details the basic organizational structure of a database, known as a "data model", which can be one of three general types: entity-relationship, relational and object-oriented.

The Scope: Data Warehouse vs. Data Mart

Even limiting the database definition to business applications, database is still a very general designation. Overall, business databases can be grouped into the following two categories, briefly described in Table 7.2.

Table 7.2
Categories of Business Databases

Database Type	Description
Data Warehouse	Broadly defined as comprehensive data repositories focusing on enterprise-wide data across many or all subject areas. They tend to be subject-oriented (e.g., claimants, customers), time-variant (i.e., capturing changes across time) and non-updatable in the sense of new replacing the old (i.e., read-only and periodically refreshed with a new batch of data). Data warehouses are usually data, rather than task oriented, application independent (i.e., can be hierarchical, object, relational, flat file or other), normalized or not (database normalization is a reversible process of successively reducing a given collection of relations to a more desirable form) and held together by a single, complex structure. "Custom" database analytical initiatives typically source their data from a data warehouse, but the analysis itself almost always takes place outside of its confines.
Data Mart	These are specific purpose data repositories limited to a single business process or business group. Data marts tend to be project, rather than data oriented, decentralized by user area and organized around multiple, semi-complex structures. An example is a claims data mart containing current (open) and past (closed) workers' compensation claims, containing claimant's contact details, accident and injury type information, medical, indemnity and other costs, insurance coverage information, adjustor activities, treatment history and related details . Usually, a data mart contains a sub-set of the contents of a data warehouse, which makes it informationally more homogenous and application-ready. Data marts can serve as just data repositories or, in conjunction with business intelligence applications, can support ongoing performance dashboarding.

The term "database" is sometimes used to denote a data warehouse, other times a data mart. Even worse, it is not uncommon for an organization to expect data mart-like functionality from a data warehouse, simply because in view of some, a database is a database. Yet in the knowledge-creation sense, there is a vast difference between these two general types of databases. A *data warehouse* is a storage-oriented repository of data, inspired by an idea that it is both more cost effective and more convenient to store large volumes of data in a single

154

storage facility. A *data mart*, on the other hand, is usually focused on pre-determined subset of data and pre-determined functional utility, which emphasizes not only storage of data, but also easy retrieval and manipulation. The hierarchical data warehouse – data mart relationship is shown below.

Figure 7.1
Data Warehouse vs. Data Mart

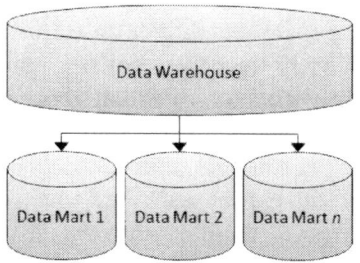

Database Content

Content-wise, there are a number of different types of databases, comprising several of distinct categories, detailed in Table 7.3.

Table 7.3
Types of Databases

Consideration	Description
Bibliographic	Used to organize published sources, such as books, journal or newspaper articles; contains basic descriptive information about those items; mostly used in library cataloging as reference sources, not analyzable with traditional statistical techniques discussed here.
Full Text	Contain complete texts of publications, such as journal or newspaper articles; examples include LexisNexis or Encyclopedia Britannica. Great qualitative sources of knowledge, full text databases can be sources of quantitatively-coded data, but are not directly statistically analyzable.
Multimedia & Hypertext	The most recent database type, largely responsible for the explosive growth of the World Wide Web; it supports creative linking of diverse types of data objects (text, pictures, etc.) into a single record; indirectly analyzable, though require considerable amount of preparation.
Numeric	Used to store digitally-coded data, such as events or behaviors, demographics or survey responses; a staple of business data capture and the focus of the analytical processes described in this book.

Bibliographic and full text databases are traditionally associated with library informational services, such as ABI/Inform or LexisNexis, containing summaries or full texts of publicly available published sources, such as newspapers, professional journals, conference proceedings, etc. In a business sense, they offer a referential source of information rather than ongoing decision support. Multimedia and hypertext databases are one of many Internet and the World Wide Web related informational innovations that tend to be used more as businesses communication/(i.e., promotional) vehicles, rather than sources of decision-guiding insights. Although at this point these type of databases offer limited utility in the context of risk management, the slow emergence of the Semantic Web may invalidate this conclusion.

The last of the four broad types of databases, numeric, is the primary decision support engine of organizational decision making. The content of numeric databases, such as the earlier described transactions, behavioral propensities or basic descriptors, coupled with the easy to analyze coding make these databases both statistically analyzable and informationally rich.

Data Models

Business databases that are designed to store event-tracking and augmenting data are almost always explicitly- or implicitly-numeric[3]. The information they contain can be organized in accordance with one of several data organizational models, which tend to fall into the three general categories:

1. *Entity-Relationship*: The most basic data model, it is built around parent-child hierarchical typology; it identifies basic organizational objects, such a claimant, age, injury type and specifies the relationships among these objects. It is the simplest and the oldest of the three models, which means it is relatively easy to up, but offers limited usability – its general logic is illustrated below:

Figure 7.2
Entity-Relationship Data Model

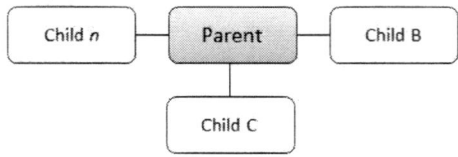

2. *Relational*: Represents facts in a database as a collection of entities, often called *tables,* connected by relationships in accordance with predicate logic and the set theory. The relational model is more supportive of automated, templated report generation, but is also more restrictive as the relationships need to be specified and programmed in advance. The term "relational" conveys that individual tables are linked to each other to enhance the descriptive value of a simple, flat data file – its general logic is illustrated below:

Figure 7.3
Relational Data Model

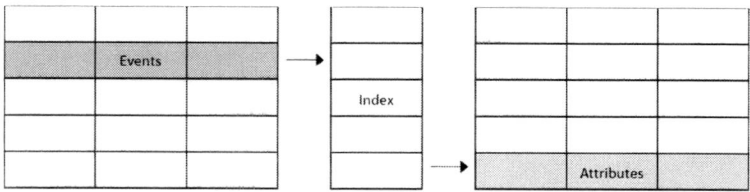

3. *Object-Oriented*: In many regards, this is the most evolved data organizational model, but it is also least analytically flexible. The data structure is built around encapsulated units – objects – which are characterized by attributes and sets of orientations and rules, all of which can be grouped into classes and super-classes, as illustrated in Figure 7.4. Although the individual objects exhibit a significant amount of usage flexibility, their preparation requires a considerable amount of programming.

Figure 7.4
Object-Oriented Data Model

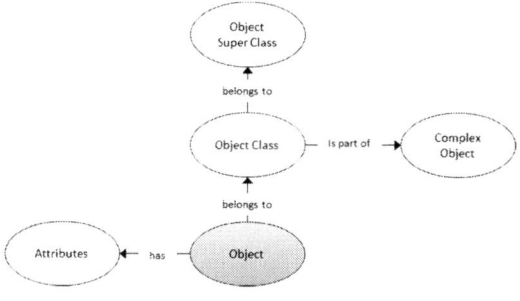

Database types and data model differences certainly contribute to the level of difficulty associated with developing a solid level of understanding of the fundamentals of database analytics. However, although these considerations have a significant impact on the database's querying and reporting capabilities, they exert only a relatively marginal impact on analytics. The primary reason for that is that querying and reporting are conducted within the confines of the database itself with the help of the database management system, or DBMS, while data analytics is usually carried out outside of the database. Thus the organizational structure of the database is of interest to database analysis only insofar as the identification and proper classification of the available data.

BUT IT IS NOT ABOUT THE HARDWARE...

Even the most advanced databases need significant amount of human-directed processing before their contents can become a source of value. Interestingly, the amount of effort and resources put into knowledge creation activities pales by comparison to how much is spent on hardware and related infrastructure: On average about 85% of all database-related expenditures are consumed by hardware (i.e., storage), about 10% is spent on software and only about 5% on the analysis of stored data. As a result, a typical scenario looks something like this: A mid-size or a large organization spends millions of dollars to erect complex and expensive data storage and management facilities, but stops short of committing comparable resources to harvesting the raw material locked away in various databases. Nor is our hypothetical organization overly concerned with the lack of compelling evidence to suggest that these expensive database assets are worth the investment...Once again, virtually all organizations have data, yet only a small sub-set of them are able to turn it into a source of competitive advantage.

Yet overtly, the reason organizations make database investments is to outwit their competitors, or at the very least, maintain competitive parity. Hence the database paradox: The larger, more complex and comprehensive a database, the less likely it is to give rise to competitive advantage. It is another way of saying that organizations tend to "choke" on the amount of data at their disposal. Quite often, large data volumes give rise to an even larger volume and array of reports, which tends to amount to nothing more than color-coding of raw data which is the practical consequence of reporting on outcomes without a clear cause-delineation. Untold man-hours are spent pouring over disparate pieces of information, many conclusions are reached, but ultimately, very little competitive edge producing knowledge is created and decisions continue to be driven more by intuition than by facts. Building and maintaining large corporate data reservoirs becomes a goal in itself, with the creation of competitively advantageous knowledge becoming an afterthought.

Obviously, not every organization falls into that trap. The now-famous Wal-Mart's data prowess helped to propel it to the elite group of the most dominant (as measured by revenue) and most influential (as measured by market power) organizations in the world. Perhaps lesser known but nonetheless equally illustrative of the power of intelligent data mining is the case of Progressive Insurance, an insurance organization that consistently maintains an average of 5-point combined ratio (a measure of profitability) advantage over the industry, due in large part to their investment in predictive analytics.

The Data—Information—Knowledge Continuum

Databases exist for two basic reasons: First, they enable an ongoing capture and storage of facts. Secondly, they serve as platforms for inferential knowledge creation. When both reasons are combined, databases become conduits for transforming data into information, then knowledge, ultimately giving rise to competitive advantage. Figure 7.5 below summarizes the *data→information→knowledge* progression, shown in the context of each of the step's incremental value to users, interpretational challenges and the level of benefit.

Figure 7.5
The Data—Information—Knowledge Continuum

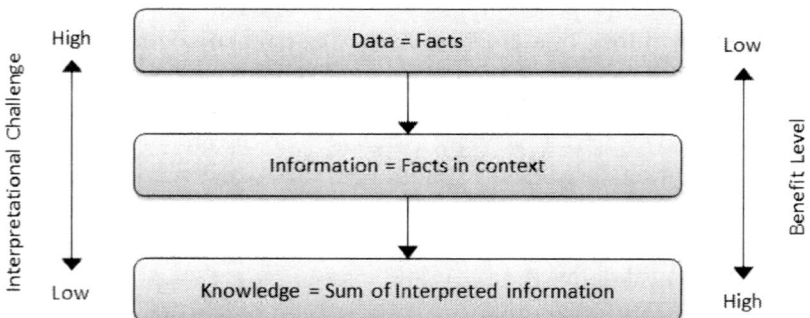

From the standpoint of users, raw data, which is simply a repository of digitally coded (in the case of business databases) known facts, represents the lowest level of utility. It is both the most interpretationally challenging (obviously, thousands or millions of seemingly random digits mean very little) and it embodies the least amount of user benefit, precisely because it does not clearly communicate anything…Regardless of its format, source or organizational model, raw data just about always presents a considerable interpretational challenge because of its sheer volume, cryptic nature and the lack of self-evident differentiation between important and trivial facts.

However, once the raw data are converted into information, the resultant interpretation becomes easier and it is of more benefit to users. Its

160

value increases as a result, but it still might be hampered by limited actionability. For example, translating individual claims (raw data) into period-specific frequency and severity summaries (information) certainly increases the benefit and lightens the interpretational challenge, but the resultant information is still of little benefit to decision makers as, in this case, it says little about any causes of the observed outcomes. In other words, while useful, information still needs additional refinement before the value of the database investment is truly maximized. In the example used here, that point is reached when the individual insurance claims (events) information is combined with explanatory attributes to ultimately give rise to knowledge of the reasons behind the observed event variability. In a more general sense, while *information* is the product of raw data summarization, *knowledge* is the result of explaining the variability of summarized outcomes.

Hence the value progression implied in Figure 7.5 can form a foundation for thinking about data analyses. The *data—information—knowledge* value continuum can be used to illustrate the most fundamental difference between database reporting and database analytics: The former enables the conversion of raw data into information, while the latter facilitates the creation of knowledge, which is the ultimate expression of the value of data. Figure 7.6 illustrates this distinction.

Figure 7.6
Data Value-Add Progression

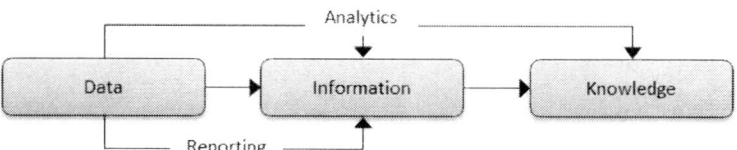

The informational value creation process outlined above carries important usage considerations surrounding large, corporate databases. At the most rudimentary level, databases can be used to support ongoing business performance reporting through performance "dashboards", usually built around a pre-selected set of metrics of most importance to the organization. Such reports are of particular interest to line managers with vested interest in keeping an eye on operational aspects of business. The format of these reports, as well as their content and frequency, tend to be shaped by factors such as data availability, industry characteristics and the organization-specific needs. In general, database reporting tends to be data type specific (e.g., claim reports are generated from detailed records, while adjustor effectiveness reports are based on a combination of claim development, activity timing and adjuster notes), making it difficult to "cross-pollinate" different pieces of information and altogether impossible to arrive at the next level of conclusions. In essence, basic data reporting provides important though generic information, which significantly reduces the value of those reports.

Going beyond the mere status quo reporting, a more robust analytical set of processes can help in translating disparate pieces of information into higher-level inferences, or knowledge. Of course, it is not quite as easy as it may sound: As pointed out earlier, the ability to distill large volumes of often somewhat dissimilar information into specific, competitively advantageous insights hinges on a combination of a forward-looking informational vision and a robust analytical skill set. Converting raw data into generic information can be handled, for the most part, with the help of highly automated, commercially available database tools. Funneling the still voluminous and almost always inconclusive information into unique knowledge cannot be handled by standardized, off-the-shelf database reporting applications for reasons ranging from extensive data preparation requirements to the intricacies surrounding multivariate model calibration and the need for drawing inferences that is beyond the capabilities of machine learning. In more technical terms, the conversion of information into knowledge quite often also necessitates the amalgamation of multiple (and otherwise disconnected) data sources into a single yet multidimensional causal chain, which in turn requires the establishment of cross-factor correlations, cause—effect relationships as well as the more technically obtuse interaction and nonlinear effects.

More on Reporting vs. Analytics: Tools & Applications

The simplest way to extract information out of a database is to query it. Querying involves relating individual data elements to create specific information. For example, to get at the "cost by region" information, the DBMS used to run the queries needs to divide all available sales into the appropriate regional "buckets", create region-by-region summaries and return appropriately formatted information. The speed and the agility of database querying capabilities vary across the type of data model used, with the entity—relationship model offering the lowest levels of querying speed and agility, while the relational model tends to deliver the highest levels of performance in that regard.

Database querying is a somewhat manual process, requiring some level of technical proficiency. For example, accessing of a relational database, which is arguably the most dominant data storage mechanism in business today, requires familiarity with querying protocols of the particular relational database type, such as Microsoft Access, Oracle, IBM DB2 or MySQL. Combined with the repetitively ongoing nature of many of business informational needs, much of the ad hoc database querying is usually replaced with standard, automated database reporting. Business intelligence tools commonly providing the automated reporting functionality rely on standard templates and pre-defined process to repeatedly generate the same set of reports, often in fixed time intervals. Thus rather than querying the database about period-by-period and/or region-by-region accident counts manually, an automated sales report is generated without the need for manual querying.

Unfortunately, such generic, standard database reporting processes are frequently confused with database analytics, so much so, that in the eyes of many, analytics = reporting. Although there are certainly similarities between these functions—both entail manipulating and translating raw data into the more meaningful information—there are sharp differences separating the two. Perhaps the most important is the type of data processing. Reporting relies primarily on summarization, tabulation and contrasting, all with the goal of generating basic *descriptive* conclusions about the underlying data. More analytically advanced data exploration often starts with basic descriptive analyses as well, though its ultimate goal typically entails forward-looking extrapolations and predictions. In other words, database analytics goes far beyond the status quo reporting by offering causal explanations and making decision-guiding predictions. In that sense, basic database reporting offers descriptive summaries of past events, while the inferential knowledge focused database analytics supports *probabilistic interpretation* of data, as illustrated by Figure 7.7 below.

Figure 7.7
Factual vs. Probabilistic Data Exploration

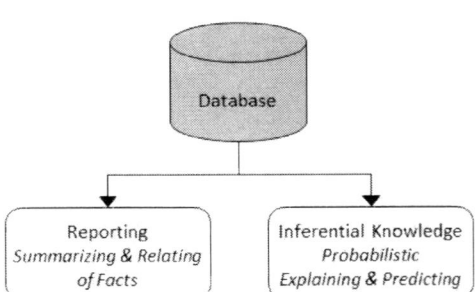

Different missions call for different tools. Database querying and reporting typically utilize the database's own DBMS capabilities, typically in the form of database reporting applications known as business intelligence tools. Their overall goal is to help to automate report generation while also deepening database exploration; operationally, business intelligence applications are a part of the DBMS and as such, operate within the database itself. Furthermore, the resultant reports are externally consumed and are not used to enrich the informational value of the database itself.

The necessary coupling of hardware and software applications that are required to support an operational database environment gave rise to a new class of database computational devices known as *database appliances*. The fundamental difference between a database appliance and a traditional stand-alone hardware and software approaches is that the former is a turnkey solution integrating the hardware and software components into a single unit, an appliance. The single unit performs all the functions of a database, a server and a storage device considerably faster[4] and thus might be preferred in situations where large volumes of standard reports need to be generated under tight time constraints. From the data analysis standpoint, the fundamental underlying assumption of this class of database devices is that it is desirable to analyze the contents of the entire database (i.e., to use all available records), and it is in the context of such "full database queries" that the greater speed of database appliances is most appreciated. However, as will be shown in the subsequent chapters, the database analytical process of translating data into competitive edge producing insights makes a heavy use of appropriately selected samples, which can be quite cumbersome in a database appliance.

Although the specific characteristics of a particular database management system may impact the speed and the ease of performing certain operations, data analysis and modeling are ultimately impacted far more by the power and the efficacy of the statistical analysis applications. The three most widely used systems—SAS, SPSS and R—are functionally independent of the DBMS and are in effect, open-ended methods of addressing data-related issues, rather than means of funneling data into pre-defined templates (although they can be incorporated in most database designs, including the aforementioned appliance and used for basic reporting). What differentiates these three leading systems from lesser-known applications is their depth and comprehensiveness, in particular as it relates to data processing, management and manipulation, statistical analysis and modeling, database scoring and output management.

From the standpoint of the resultant information, all data management systems, inclusive of the earlier discussed business intelligence as well as the data analysis and modeling applications, can be used for either descriptive or predictive purposes. The former is focused primarily on retrospective outcome summarization and tabulation, while the latter is typically tasked with forward-looking decision support. Although both tend to be labeled "analytics", it is more correct to refer to retrospective outcome summarization as "reporting" and forward-looking decision support as "inferential knowledge". As depicted in Figure 7.8 below, reporting functionality tends to be database-resident, as it is quite conducive to automation.

Figure 7.8
Database Reporting vs. Analysis

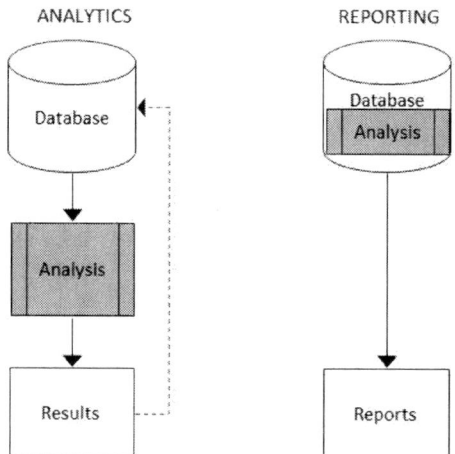

The Case of Data Mining

One particular aspect of database analysis called "data mining" does not fit in with the rationale outlined above. Broadly defined, *data mining* is an information extraction activity designed to uncover hidden facts contained in the data with the help of an automated system combining statistical analysis, machine learning and database technology (it should be noted that data mining can certainly be performed manually, but in the eyes of many, the term itself became synonymous with automated data pattern identification capabilities). So although data mining resembles database reporting in terms of its degree of automation, its methodological engine aligns it more closely with inferential knowledge discovery. At the same time, its goal of "roaming the database to find noteworthy relationships" differentiates it sharply from conventional database analytics focused on testing specific hypothesis in support the organizational strategy-driven informational needs. Overall, data mining is distinctly different from the objective-driven database analytical process described in this book, yet it is an alternative inferential knowledge creation avenue, as shown in figure 7.9 below.

Figure 7.9
Database Exploration Venues

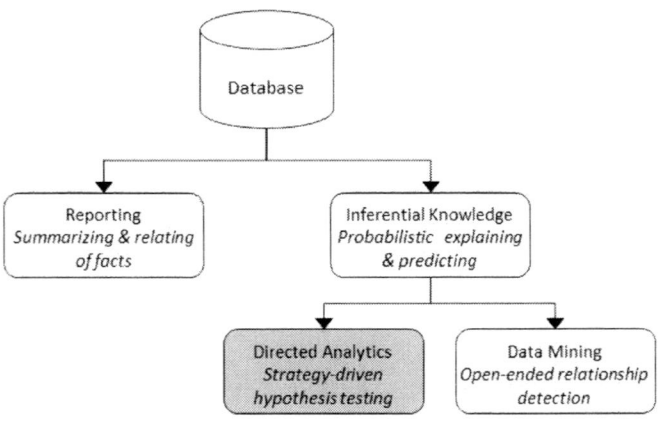

I should point out that data mining received a lot of attention over the past decade or so, particularly in the area of "enterprise data management." Leading software business applications developers, including IBM and SAS, invested in relatively complex systems built expressly to sift through large volumes of data in search of significant relationships. However, there are a couple of key hurdles that, to the best of my knowledge, have not been overcome.

The first one is methodological in nature. In order to differentiate between "significant" and "not significant" relationships, data mining applications employ established statistical significance tests (of which there are different types, tied to data characteristics), which as a group are a set of techniques for determining if a given relationship is spurious (i.e., it represents a chance occurrence) or persistent. As fully discussed in later chapters, the reliability of statistical significance tests is negatively impacted by sample size, which leads to practically trivial relationships (e.g., extremely small correlations or differences) being deemed as "significant", in a statistical sense, as the truly pronounced ones.

The second key shortcoming of automated data mining is of more pragmatic nature, reflecting the relative inability of such systems to deliver sustainable informational—and ultimately, competitive—advantage. The reason for that is that the bulk of risk management related data is not unique to a single organization, just as electronic transaction processing systems generating the data are not unique. Similarly, data mining applications are commercially available applications, which means that combining two relatively generic entities will likely lead to generic outcomes…

Single vs. Multi-Source Analysis

The explosive growth in the volume and diversity of data brought to light yet another important data-related consideration: single-source vs. multi-source analyses. Although rarely receiving much more than a cursory mention, this is a tremendously important consideration from the standpoint of creating competitively advantageous knowledge.

What constitutes a data type? For the most part, it is uniqueness and homogeneity – more specifically, to be considered distinct, data need a unique source, or a point of origin. For instance, adjuster notes are sourced from electronic diary systems while location metrics from GPS tracking – both of these data types are also homogenous in the sense that individual records have fundamentally the same informational content.

It follows that there are multiple types of data that are applicable to risk analytics. These include individual-level metrics such as demographics, psychographics, credit scores as well as accident attributes, including cause and nature of accident, type of injury and related. Another key risk analytics applicable data type are organization level metrics such as annual and quarterly public filings or credit ratings, as well as somewhat more esoteric indicators, such as corporate governance quotients or accounting accrual scores. In the vast majority of cases the analysis of these and other data types takes place in a single-source context, simply because it is less complicated than concurrent analyses of multiple, diverse data types. In some instances, single-source analyses are indeed quite appropriate, namely, when informational needs can be adequately met in that fashion. However, there are numerous instances where multi-source analyses would reveal insights that cannot be gleaned from single source explorations.

In the first chapter, as well as earlier in this chapter I touched briefly on the fact that the bulk of mid-size and larger companies have lots of data and majority of those companies also have considerable amounts of relatively generic information derived that data. Yet only a few of those organizations are able to convert those generic insights into unique and competitively advantageous knowledge – why? Among the reasons are the challenges associated with successfully bridging the generic information—unique knowledge gap is the lack of multi-source data analytical proficiency. That is because in contrast to basic reporting, which is primarily concerned with single data source analyses, converting generic information into action-guiding knowledge requires pulling together dissimilar (in terms of measurement characteristics, level of aggregation, etc.) data sources, a process known as multi-source analytics. Figure 7.10 below illustrates the essence of the aforementioned gap.

Figure 7.10
Multi-Source Analytics as a Driver of Unique Knowledge

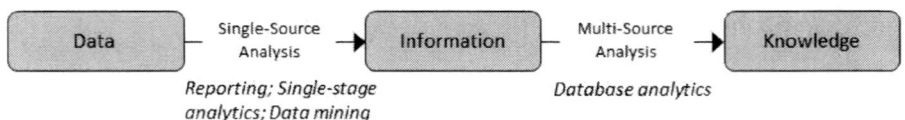

Reporting; Single-stage analytics; Data mining   *Database analytics*

FROM DATA TO KNOWLEDGE

Once again, though many organizations engage in data analysis, relatively few do so in a systematic fashion. Even today, data exploration tends to still be approached as an ad hoc, question-and-answer driven undertaking, where the wealth of data so often readily available is rarely adequately utilized. In many regards, organizations' sputtering data exploration efforts sometimes bear a close resemblance to the way many of us make attempts at staying fit: Starting strong with a solid New Year's resolution is followed by a gradual degradation of will and effort...We all like the idea of staying fit, just as every organization certainly revels in the vision of success, yet not all of us have the requisite discipline...And just as personal fitness is "10% inspiration and 90% perspiration", taking advantage of the abundant data resources requires some clarity of objectives, but the bulk of what's required is the process—i.e., the analytic know-how—and the persistency.

There is an often-told story illustrating the importance of the know-how (it's probably entirely fabricated, but nonetheless it illustrates the point quite well). It goes like this: A homeowner had a problem with a squeaky floor—specifically, there was one, relatively small spot that seemed to defy any repair attempts. He retained a long succession of craftsmen, but in spite of what seemed like a simple and a very contained problem, the floor kept on squeaking in spite of their repeat efforts. But as it tends to be the case (at least with some of us), the more the solution evaded the owner of the house, the more it became important to that homeowner to fix the squeak. And surely enough, eventually a yet another craftsman came to fix the problem and following a careful examination of the potential cause, hammered a handful of carefully placed nails and the floor stopped squeaking! The initial elation of the owner of the house to finally get the squeak fixed turned into dismay upon the receipt of the craftsman's bill of $1,020. He demanded an explanation and a breakdown of the total charge, following which he received an itemized bill which read as follows: $20-Nailing squeaky floor boards; $1,000-Knowing where to where to place the nails. This is the essence of the analytic know-how.

Of course, knowing what to do needs to be accompanied by access to adequate (meaning, informationally-rich) data. In spite of the apparent cross-industry segment differences, many of the risk management related challenges facing organizations in different industries are in fact quite similar: Quantifying the likelihood and severity of risk exposure related losses; mitigating exposures to individual risks through internal exposure-reducing efforts; and identifying the most economically-appropriate risk financing posture for risks where internal mitigation alone is not deemed sufficient. Although in principle most organizations in a given industry have access to similar data, some are more purposeful and systematic about data capture, though the exploding interest in using data to drive business decisions is beginning to erase those disparities.

Data Capture Infrastructure

Data capture is rarely a topic of boardrooms' discussions, even though it plays a significant role in shaping the quality of firms' informational proficiency. Not taking advantage of the otherwise readily available data can short-circuit even the best thought out strategies, as inadequate decision-aiding knowledge can impair the execution of plans, not to mention the validation of some of the strategic tenets in the first place. Frankly, unlike the task of crafting strategic plans, which is generally deemed to be intellectually and otherwise rewarding, getting "down and dirty" with data is simply not. Even though there is more than ample evidence at this point highlighting the knowledge advantage, the task of laying the requisite data capture foundation continues to be assigned relatively low levels of organizational priority. In short, data capture is a topic of considerable importance, in terms of its downstream consequences, but it tends to receive disproportionately little attention from the senior layers of organizations.

Probably the most common error is to entrust the data capture decisions to the IT department. Why should the overall data acquisition strategy, along with tactical decisions surrounding database model selection or data organizational schemas, be entrusted to those who will have very little to do with it, both in terms of conducting analyses and using the resultant insights? There are a number of considerations surrounding the initial data capture decisions that will have profound impact on the "usability" of the resultant database which might be of trivial importance from the IT infrastructure standpoint. It is a "butterfly effect", of sorts: Small changes in initial settings may have disproportionately large and even more important—and unintended—consequences later. A database may ultimately just be an aggregation of events, behaviors and attributes, but how it is all initially structured can have a lot to do with the ease of translating the potential contained in raw data into value associated with decision guiding knowledge.

8

Knowledge Creation: Analytic File

D ata capture can be either incidental or purposeful. It is incidental when it is a byproduct of ongoing business operations and it is purposeful when a priori determined metrics are captured with a specific informational need in mind. The bulk of the data used in assessing organizations' exposure to risk reflects the former – we do not necessarily set out to collect it and at times, we are not even aware that it is being collected. In some way, it is a bit like walking in snow—we leave behind clearly visible footprints not because we choose to, but rather because it is one of the consequences of walking in snow. Similarly, risk management systems accumulate large reservoirs of claims along with the accompanying details, even though the primary reason for the development of these systems is operational efficiency. In short, incidental data capture occurs as a result of particular activity not because someone intended to capture particular information.

Data that are not captured as a byproduct of other activities generally fall under the broad umbrella of purposeful data, the capture of which requires special effort and it is generally a result of a particular, express need. For instance, the management of a large retail organization may notice a sharp upturn in the frequency of "slip and fall" accidents among its customers, prompting an obvious question of why? In order to answer that question, risk management needs to turn to data for insights, but chances are that the requisite data is not readily available, thus necessitating additional data capture. In that situation, the management might opt to conduct an employee survey with the goal of eliciting potential contributors to observed trend. Such a survey would likely make use of Likert or semantic differential attitude/opinion measuring scales[1], as well as some open-ended questions (i.e., free-flow text) questions, all with the purpose of eliciting potential contributors to the observed outcomes. In addition, the organization may also choose to acquire data from outside sources, typically companies specializing in specialized types of data, such as weather (e.g., heightened snow precipitation could lead to an increase in "slip and fall" accidents), or demographics, or more specifically, geodemographics, which represents geography-based (using the Census Bureau-defined geographic hierarchy[2]) aggregation of the U.S Census data.

Looking beyond data acquisition, getting to the bottom of the aforementioned increase in the incidence of "slip and fall" accidents will necessitate combining of the differently-sourced data files, which will likely entail addressing several key file merge considerations. Though specific challenges one might encounter will depend on the particulars of the individual files, common issues include non-overlapping coverage[3]—defined as the proportion of events for which attribute values are available (see Chapter 7)—and the organizational schemas of the individual files.

ANALYTICAL DATASET CREATION

Some databases come "fully loaded" with a rich assortment of events of interest as well as supporting attributes, all properly organized and ready to be analyzed. A more common scenario, however, is a database in need of additional metrics and proper organization. In such cases it is more cost and time effective to create a database extract-based analytical dataset.

An *analytical dataset* is a subset of the database that has been enriched with the appropriate outside (to the database) data, properly organized and cleansed. In the data sense, it is the starting point for the analytical process described in this book. As previously mentioned, its creation involves three separate steps:
1. Extracting a subset of the database.
2. Enriching the resultant database extract.
3. Organizing and cleansing.

Extracting a Subset of the Database

As noted earlier, the most common database type today is one built around event-tracking information, where a "transaction" is any electronically-recorded event. The resultant data reservoirs can be very large, containing millions of individual records, along with hundreds or even thousands of variables. Having a lot to work with is a good problem to have, though it is still a problem which needs to be addressed.

On the one hand, large volumes of data can be helpful in assuring reporting accuracy, yet at the same time, size can be a hindrance in more advanced statistical modeling. One of the reasons behind it is obvious and requires little explanation: It is quite difficult and time-consuming to manipulate such large files[4], particularly when "large" refers to both the number of records as well as the number of variables. The second reason is somewhat less obvious, but it has more direct impact on the validity of findings: Large sample sizes have a potentially skewing effect on the robustness of statistical parameters and tests. In view of the potentially weighty implications of that dependence, a more in-depth explanation seems warranted.

Central to the estimation of many statistical parameters is the notion of standard error, which is an estimated standard deviation of a particular statistic. In the computational sense, there are multiple methods of calculating standard errors, depending on the type of statistic used, which in turn reflects different possible applications of this concept. In the realm of database analytics, probably the most frequent application of the notion of *standard error* can be observed in the context of sample mean estimation, the standard error of which is computed by dividing the sample standard deviation by the square root of the sample size. Interpretation-wise, the larger the sample size, the smaller the standard error, which is the crux of the sample size problem.

Although in and if itself the notion of standard error is of little interest to applied analytics, it is one of the key inputs into a frequently used process of *statistical significance testing*[5], the goal of which is to determine if the observed differences between means (such as the difference in occurrence rates or average costs) are factual or spurious. As the value of standard error decreases (which is a direct consequence of an increasing sample size), the ever-smaller, eventually trivial, differences are deemed "statistically significant". In other words, excessively large sample size artificially deflates the size of the standard error estimates which in turn increase the likelihood of "false positive" findings—i.e., ascribing a factual status to trivially small, spurious differences.

The practical consequences of this dependence can be considerable— almost disproportionately large given the somewhat obtuse nature of the concept. For example, an organization might be led to believe that it outperforms its peers in terms of the frequency or the average cost of its workers' compensation claims (i.e., the organization's frequency and/or severity are below the peer group's level and the difference is statistically significant), when in fact the analysis (when properly executed) might not support such conclusions. Hence this seemingly trivial notion might be the database analytics' version of the Butterfly Effect[6], which is why it demands a deeper treatment, presented later. But for now, let's concentrate on the delineation of effective database extract selection rules that can circumvent the aforementioned false positive problem.

Extract Selection Rules

The most important considerations in selecting a subset of an entire database are *representativeness* and *sizing*. The former speaks to the degree of compositional similarity between the database and the extract, while the latter spells out the minimum required number of records. Though different in terms of their focus, the two are highly interconnected. An extract-wide sample size is in a large part determined by the composition of the sample, specifically, the number of individual sub-segments and the nesting structure (i.e., how many tiers of sub-segments, or segments within segments, are there). The extract selection rules, therefore, should be framed in the context of the expected representativeness and sizing of the contemplated sample.

The often recommended—and used—*random selection* is actually rarely the best approach to take in selecting a sub-set of the total database. The reason behind that counterintuitive statement is that this otherwise convenient approach is likely to lead to over-sampling of large groupings and under-sampling of the small ones. The resultant sample distribution may showed a skewed, or an altogether invalid projection of the underlying population.

To mitigate the possibility of such undesirable outcomes, the *stratified sampling* scheme can be used instead. This sampling technique offers a higher likelihood of bringing about the typically desired random selection[7], by building the selection logic around appropriately defined unit of analysis[8] segments. The specific stratified customer database extract selection steps are outlined below in Table 8.1.

Table 8.1
Stratified Sample Selection Process

Process Step	Description
Step 1	Explicitly describe the content of the database by identifying: 1. Unit of analysis clusters (e.g., accident cost, etc.) 2. Descriptive variables and their quality (i.e., coverage) 3. Longitudinal depth (i.e., how far back does the data go?)
Step 2	Identify the most disaggregate unit of analysis cluster, e.g., what is the most narrowly-defined group to be used as the focus of analysis?
Step 3	Flag database records in accordance with cluster membership and determine the number of records per cluster.
Step 4	Select a random sample of 500-1,000 records from each of the clusters.
Step 5	Contrast the profile of the sample extract with the parent population by comparing the means and distributions of the descriptive variables outlined in Step 1. If differences > 1 standard deviation → re-sample.

An important consideration governing the appropriateness of the resultant sample is its *analytic adequacy*: Will it support the most detailed, in terms of sample composition, analysis? The general rule of thumb is to use the most narrowly defined group expected to be used in the ensuing analyses as the starting point and work up the level of aggregation chain to arrive at the final sample. Once selected, the sample extract usually needs to be enriched with additional, typically causal data to enhance its explanatory power.

Extract Data Enrichment

Additional data can be added to the selected sample either from other internal systems or from outside partners or data suppliers. However, one should not lose sight of the fact that since much of the data organizations capture are byproducts of their ongoing operations, there is usually a scattering of it throughout the various systems. Although many organizations have been trying to integrate much of that data into a single, so-called "360° view" data reservoirs, it tends to be a slow process and more often than not much of that data remains scattered across various internal systems.

At the same time, it is often beneficial to look outside of the organization for sources of potentially explanatory data. Although there are dozens of data suppliers specializing in data compilation and aggregation, the bulk of the third-party, risk management related data can be classified as either demographics (individuals) / firmographics (organizations) or physical / behavioral attributes.

As it regards the former, the U.S Census is the only source of comprehensive population demographics in the U.S; however, the Bureau is prohibited from making individual-level data available to non-governmental entities, though it is permitted to disclose geography-based aggregates and averages. The resultant descriptors, commonly referred to as *geodemographics*, are made available at the least aggregate grouping level, which is a census block (see endnote #2), an area which in urban setting typically corresponds to a city block bounded by streets. In total, as of the last U.S census the United States is divided into over 8 million individual blocks. It should be noted, however, that due to privacy considerations some of the Census data are only available at the more aggregate census tract level (as of the most recent census, the United States is broken down into 65,443 tracts). On the organizational side, providers such as Dunn & Bradstreet make available a range of general industry characteristics and financial performance metrics; in addition to the mass data suppliers, a number of smaller firms offer sample based estimates of the otherwise hard-to-quantify individual-level metrics, such as household net worth, or automobile registration[9].

The other commercially available and risk analytics related source of attribute data are physical and behavioral attributes. The former include weather details collected by the National Oceanic and Atmospheric Administration's (NOAA) network of 114 U.S and about 1,500 global stations or the global position system (GPS) sourced location data describing organizations, while on the consumer data side the three main consumer credit bureaus (Experian, Equifax and TransUnion) make available consumer credit and financial asset related estimates. Also worth mentioning public filings of companies by publicly traded (available through Standard & Poor's Compustat), which offer a comprehensive overview of financial and accounting metrics.

Quality—defined in terms of coverage and accuracy—varies across the types of data. Weather measurements, location details or public filings tend to be both comprehensive and accurate, while other data types, such as geodemographics or net worth estimates are either coarse (geodemographics) or considerably less precise (net worth estimates). As a result, the ultimate efficacy of any data source is highly situational.

Data Cleansing

Once properly structured, a dataset needs to be *cleansed* before any meaningful analysis can take place. According to a TDWI report, "Data Quality and the Bottom Line," poor data quality costs U.S businesses approximately $600 billion annually. Obviously, data quality related losses are inherently difficult to quantify, hence it is possible that an actual magnitude of these costs might be somewhat higher or lower. That said, even if the "true" losses are only 50% or so of the above estimate, it is still a significant enough problem to be given serious consideration. In a more abstract sense, it seems clear that adequate data quality controls should be a necessary component of the database analytics-driven knowledge creation processes, if the results are to be valid and reliable. The two key data quality due diligence steps are data cleansing and normalization. Technically, data normalization is a subset of data cleansing, but in view of both its importance and a certain degree of technical complexity it will be discussed as a stand-alone concept.

Data cleansing can be broadly defined as the process of "repairing" of the contents of an extracted dataset; *data normalization*, on the other hand, is the process of identification and removal of outlying and potentially skewing and influential data values and correcting for undesirable distributional properties by means of missing and derivative value substitution. The key elements of each are discussed next.

Data Normalization: Outlier Identification

An outlier is a value that falls outside of what is considered to be an acceptable range. Some outliers are illustrative of data errors, but others might represent accurate, though abnormally large or small values that are extremely rare. Depending on the size of the dataset (i.e., the number of records), outliers can be visually identified by means of simple two-dimensional scatterplots, or can be singled out by means of distribution scoring, which is the process of "flagging" individual records whose values on the variable of interest fall outside of the statistically defined norm, such as ±3 standard deviations away from the mean.

Visual representations of data, such as the aforementioned scatterplots, offer the simplest method of identifying outlying observations, as illustrated below by a plot of household weekly spending levels at a grocery store chain.

Figure 8.1
Sample Scatterplot

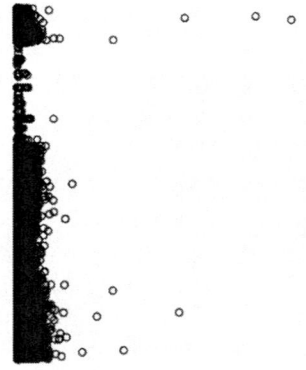

However, visual detection of outliers becomes practically impossible once the number of dimensions (i.e., defining variables) is greater than two and the data can no longer be easily shown as a simple two-dimensional plot. In addition, even when a two-dimensional representation is sufficient, there is an obvious difficulty associated with the reliance on the visual outlier detection: Where, exactly, is the line of demarcation separating outlying and acceptable values? As illustrated by the above chart representing real-life data, the most extreme—i.e., the furthest to the right in the above illustration—values are easy to classify as outliers, yet the closer those values get to the high density part of the distribution, the more difficult and arbitrary the decision becomes. Outlier treatment needs to be approached with caution, as eliminating too many or too few outlying values carries with it undesirable statistical and practical consequences. Also, excessive "value clipping" may reduce the variability in the data, which in turn may to diminish the informational value of subsequent analyses[10]. This is particularly important in the analysis of risk analyses, as many severe threats (such as storms) are extreme events.

The best way to circumvent the subjectivity of visual outlier identification is to use dataset flagging, which takes advantage of basic distributional properties of data to objectively identify not only the outlying data points, but those that may exert excessive amounts of *influence* on the analysis of data. In the context of database analytical applications, the influence of a particular database record is a function of that records deviation from the norm and its leverage, expressed as:

*Influence = Deviation from Mean * Leverage*

In terms of individual values, influence of a particular value is determined by estimating the standard deviation of actual values (deviation from the mean) from the mean value and the leverage of (potentially) outlying values. Leverage is an expression of "outlyingness" of a particular value, which is its distance away from the average value—the further away from the mean a particular value, the more leverage it has. Hence influence is simply a measure of the distance, expressed in terms of standard units, away from the center of the distribution.

The challenge associated with the above method—particularly in the sense of measuring the degree of non-conformity (i.e., the outlyingness of individual data points)—is the potential for *masking* of some outliers. In other words, since all data points, including any outliers, are used in computing a mean, it is possible that some of the "less extreme" outliers will be masked by an artificially inflated mean values. It is important to point out that the masking problem occurs with both the physical distance and magnitude difference based measures[11]. That said, a relatively easy fix is available: Prior to computing the mean of a variable, rank-order all sample records and exclude the lower and upper 5%-10% of the records, prior to calculating the mean. Doing so will prevent any potential outliers from effecting the mean and thus eliminate the masking problem outlined above.

The appropriately computed mean can then be used as the basis for quantifying the extent of deviation from an expected level for each of the records in the analytical dataset. Of course, there are typically a number of candidate variables to be used as basis for classifying a particular record as an outlier. To that end, it is recommended that, in terms of the earlier discussed event vs. descriptor variable types, primarily the former should be used as the basis for the outlier determination, because these measures present the greatest danger of individual customer record misclassification or group level mischaracterization.

The Outlier Identification Process

Regardless of the approach used, the definition of what constitutes an outlier will always carry with it a certain level of ambiguity, or at least subjectivity. Hence outlier identification is as much about the process as it is about thresholds. Putting in place a single and consistent, across time and applications, method for detecting and remedying outlying values will at the very least diminish the possibility of introducing a selection-related bias.

In risk related event or behavior databases, such as accident reports or insurance claims, the key metric of interest is a measure of severity, typically cost. In that situation, value outlyingness can be operationalized in terms of the number of standard deviation units the value of interest is greater or smaller than the appropriately computed mean value. (To be deemed "appropriately computed", mean calculation should exclude the two tail ends of the value distribution, typically 5% or 10% of the most extreme values.)

What remains is the setting of an *outlier threshold*—in other words, at what point an otherwise large value becomes an outlier? In thinking about this issue, consider the goals of the planned analysis and the general inner-workings of statistical methods to be used. Although both vary, within the confines of risk management a common objective is the estimation of the likelihood and the severity of a particular threat, which often makes use of a variety of regression methodologies. Regression parameters are evaluated in terms of their level of significance (see the *Behavioral Predictions* chapter for more details), which is ultimately tied to distributional properties, including the notions of standard error and standard deviation. The commonly used 95% significance level expresses the validity of an estimated parameter in terms of the likelihood of it falling within ±2 standard deviations away from the mean. Why not calibrate the acceptable value range to the anticipated level of precision? Using such an objective benchmark, only records falling outside the standard deviation-expressed range of allowable departures from the mean should be flagged as abnormal. This rationale can be translated into the 4-step process outlined in Table 8.2 below.

Table 8.2
Outlier Identification Process

Process Step	Description
Step 1	Compute the mean and the standard deviation of the variable of interest.
Step 2	Select the desired allowable limits; i.e., 3 standard deviations away from the mean = 95% of the values, 4 standard deviations away from the mean = 99% of the values, etc.
Step 3	Compute the maximum allowable upper values: *mean + upper allowable limit* and the maximum allowable lower values: *mean − lower allowable limit*.
Step 4	Flag as abnormal records falling outside the allowable range, both above and below.

Demonstrably outlying records should be eliminated from the analytical dataset. Before those are eliminated, however, it is worthwhile to discern if they are more-or-less randomly distributed across entity groupings, or concentrated in a particular group or groups. If it is the latter, the basic descriptive characteristics of the effected groups should be compared in terms of the before and after the outlier deletion. If significant differences are uncovered, such as mean differences in excess of one standard deviation, the sample-based analysis may not be representative of that group's entire population in the source database. The most obvious remedy is to re-draw that particular part of the sample or to exclude it from the extract if re-sampling is not feasible within the available timeframe. In addition, the reason behind the high outlier concentration should be investigated.

Data Repairing

One of the key criteria for evaluating the initial analytic quality of database extracts is the degree of completeness, which is usually expressed at an individual variable level. For instance, if 1,000 individual records were extracted, with each containing 100 individual variables, what is the proportion of missing to non-missing values for each of the 100 variables across all 1,000 records?

Frankly, it is rare for an extract data file to be 100% complete. First, organizations vary in terms of their data capture and maintenance proficiency. But even those that excel in that area still need to contend with the inevitable

181

"missing value" challenges. In other words, due to factors including human error, occasional technical glitches or imperfect data capture methods virtually all data types exhibit some degree of incompleteness. In general, events tend to have a smaller proportion of missing values than attributes, primarily because the former tend to record materially-important developments, while the latter capture additional descriptive details, which may not be as dutifully recorded.

The bulk of the analytic techniques discussed in the next chapter cannot proceed unless "data holes" are filled; otherwise, records containing missing values will be systematically eliminated (a process often referred to as pairwise or listwise deletion). These unintended deletions of missing data-containing records are obviously troublesome from the standpoint of maintaining an adequately representative, and possibly sufficiently large analytical dataset. Even if missing values are randomly scattered throughout the extract dataset, a (favorable) condition termed *missing completely at random* (MCAR), the analysis sample may become prohibitively small.

Another, even potentially more handicapping consequence of such unchecked elimination of missing value records is a systematic bias creation potential, which is a result of underlying—though usually not self-evident—communalities shared by missing value cases. This might be particularly evident in the context of the previously outlined stratified sample, where the overall universe of database records is comprised of several, clearly discernable sub-categories. In this case, it is possible that any missing value driven record deletion would impact some segments noticeably more than some others.

And finally, even if the effective (i.e., post-deletion) sample remains robust in terms of its size and unbiased in terms of its composition, the amount of variability in the data will certainly have been reduced, which may potentially adverse effect the robustness of findings (see endnote #10). In other words, since the amount of data variability is directly related to the explanatory and/or predictive power of data analyses (i.e., low variability attests to very few or very weak cross-record differences), reducing it runs the danger of diminishing the informational content of the data.

In view of these potentially significant missing value deletion consequences, the safest approach to dealing with missing data often turns out to be a reasoned *a priori replacement* strategy. However, for reasons detailed below it is not always possible to take this course of action and even when it is possible, it entails its own due diligence process. First and foremost, each variable needs to be assessed in terms of its usability—i.e., does its coverage warrant inclusion in the ensuing analysis, or should it be outright eliminated. For instance, a metric which is 90% populated will almost always warrant inclusion in future analysis; on the other hand, a metric which is 90% missing will almost warrant exclusion from any analysis. In practice, however, most variables will fall into that grey area of indecision that tends to span the middle ground between the two extremes. What then?

To some degree, the answer depends on the type of variable. Event recording metrics should be held to a higher standard of completeness simply because they are manifestations of factual developments which, in a statistical sense tend to serve as predictive targets that do not have clear proxies. A database record lacking the event information lacks the most fundamental classificatory dimension enabling it to be correctly categorized, which renders it informationally incomplete. Assigning any replacement value to such a record is tantamount to creating data, which run counter to analysis of objective data...Attribute data, on the other hand, can be held to a less stringent standard. As descriptive details, those variables are explanatory (rather than classificatory) in nature and usually have multiple proxies or substitutes—i.e., they are a part of a multi-attribute mix, rather than being a singular target. In other words, a record where some attribute values are missing may still make a positive informational contribution if its other attribute values are complete.

The question that arises, however, is what should be the upper limit of missing values (i.e., the proportion of missing) that should be deemed acceptable? There is no agreement among analysts (or among theoreticians, for that matter) as to what such a threshold should be and as a result, treatments vary widely across situations. That said, it is reasonable to assume that a missing value metric, which could be called "proportion of missing values" is a continuous, randomly distributed stochastic variable that could be examined within the notion of standard normal distribution. It also seems reasonable to conclude that basic distributional properties of the normal distribution can be used as bases for identifying an objective missing value evaluation threshold. In particular, the proportion of all observations accounted for by the set number of standard deviations away from the mean seems particularly appropriate, as it expresses the probability of the actual value falling within a certain range. Still, the decision of how many standard deviations away from the mean should constitute the outlier line of demarcation will always remain, at least somewhat, arbitrary.

Figure 8.2
Standard Normal Distribution

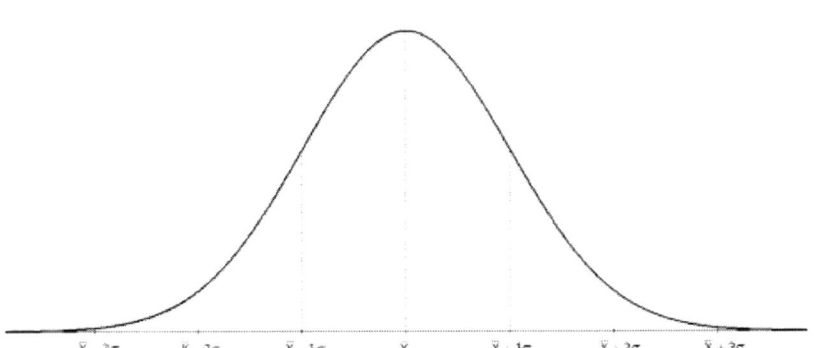

Consider the idealized depiction of the standard normal distribution shown above in Figure 8.2. Roughly ⅔ of all observations can be accounted for within ±1 standard deviation away from the mean ($\bar{X}$-1σ plus $\bar{X}$+1σ) which increases to about 95% of all observations within ±2 standard deviations and more than 99% within ±3 deviations away from the mean. Although 95% or even 99% would be the ideal standards, in practice, setting the threshold at such a high level would lead to the elimination of the vast majority of individual metrics. At the same time, recent analyses[12] indicate that any variable which has fewer than 32% of its values missing can still be "repaired" without significantly affecting its basic distributional properties. Hence, variables which have more than roughly ⅓ of their values missing should be excluded from further analysis.

The basic distributional properties of the standard normal distribution also offer value replacement hints: First and foremost, the practice of replacing all missing values with a single value (usually one of the measures of central tendency: the mean or the median) should be avoided as it tends to diminish the variability in the data, which can in turn lead to bias, unreliable effect estimates. A somewhat better value replacement strategy used by database analysts involves mimicking the generalized normal distribution proportions, which means randomly assigning either mean or median values to some, while mean/median + or – 1 or 2 standard deviations to others, in a proportion depicted in Figure 8.2 above. In a number of instances, however, particularly when missing values are not randomly distributed deletion of incomplete records might be a safer road to take.

Missing Data Imputation

    In instances where the deletion of missing value containing records is not a viable option, the most effective method of dealing with missing values is *value imputation*, which is the process of estimating the most appropriate replacement option. The imputation process can either result in physically replacing the missing value—i.e., substituting an actual value in place of the missing one—or just imputing the distributional characteristics, such as means and standard deviations, from the available data without actually physically replacing the missing values. Although this discussion is concerned primarily with the former, i.e., the physical value replacement, both approaches will be discussed to paint a complete picture of the available replacement options.

Table 8.3
Missing Data Imputation: Physical Replacement Options

Method	Description
Cold Deck Imputation	Perhaps the simplest approach to missing value imputation is to replace them with an externally derived constant. However, because a single value is imputed into numerous cases, this approach will lead to an artificial reduction in the variability of data, which is likely to bias coefficient estimates, ultimately diminishing the explanatory or predictive validity of findings.
Mean Imputation	Missing values are replaced with the commonly used measures of central tendency, such as the mean, estimated with non-missing values. Its main advantage is the conceptual and operational ease (SAS and SPSS have built-in functions). The disadvantages, however, are numerous. First of all, the true variance in the data might be understated, thus reducing the reliability of subsequent analyses. Secondly, the actual distribution of values is likely to be distorted. Thirdly, cross-variable relationships might be depressed because of a constant being added to numerous cases. Overall, this method produces results inferior to regression or model-based methods discussed below.
Regression-Based Imputation	Regression analysis finds the best fitting substitute for the particular missing value based on the relationship of the missing value variable with other variables in the dataset. Since the approach makes a better use of the available data, it is relatively efficient[13] (able to yield unbiased coefficient estimates while also being easy to implement), but also has several distinct disadvantages. First, it is considerably more complex as it requires the calibration of a multivariate statistical model; second, it reinforces the relationships already in the data; third, it diminishes the variance of the distribution unless stochastic values are added to the estimated values (which increases complexity); lastly, it makes an assumption that the missing value variable is highly correlated with other variables. Ultimately, empirical comparisons found it to be less efficient than probabilistic approaches (next).

185

| Probabilistic (Model-Based) Imputation | Although simple solutions are generally preferred, in the case of missing value imputation the more methodologically complex methods have been found to yield the most robust replacement values, while at the same time also being most efficient. There are two distinct model-based missing value replacement methods. The first is the *maximum likelihood estimation* which uses all available data to generate the correct likelihood for the unknown parameters. Although there are numerous maximum likelihood computational methods, in general, they are all based on the assumption that the marginal distribution of the available data provides the closest approximation of the unknown parameters. The good news is that the main statistical analysis systems already implemented the maximum likelihood methods for missing data; the bad news is these methods are quite computationally- intensive. |
| | The second of the probabilistic approaches is *Bayesian imputation*, which represents a probability-based way to estimate the conditional and marginal distribution for missing data. Computationally, it is based on a joint posterior distribution of parameters and missing data, conditioned on modeling assumptions and the available data. |

Table 8.4

Missing Data Imputation: Non-Replacement Options

Method	Description
All-Available Information	By expressly taking into account all non-missing data, this approach estimates the cross-variable relationships and maximizes the pairwise information available in the sample. Each correlation is based on a unique set of observations and each correlation is computed with a potentially different number of observations. The resultant correlations are representative of the entire sample and are used (in subsequent analyses) in lieu of the raw sample. Naturally, unless the missing values are truly randomly distributed, the correlations will be biased. However, even if the missing values are random, any of the correlations between X and Y can be inconsistent with other so-computed correlations due to dataset-wide interrelationships among all variables[14]. In other words, the range of values for any X—Y correlation is constrained by the correlation of X and/or Y to a third variable, Z, as shown below (based on Pearson's product-moment correlation coefficient r):

$$\text{Range of } r_{xy} = r_{xz}r_{yz} \pm \sqrt{\left(1 - r_{xz}^2\right)\left(1 - r_{yz}^2\right)}$$

Missing value imputation is an important consideration, likely to have a considerable impact on the robustness of analytic results; hence it demands careful consideration, particularly when choosing an approach. The first step in the data engineering process should always entail deciding between the outright elimination of the incomplete metrics and imputing the missing values. In many situations, particularly those involving large event-tracking databases that can easily absorb sample size reductions, eliminating poorly populated data might be the most appropriate corrective step to take, provided that the missing value case deletion would not be biased (i.e., systematically eliminate certain types of records, while keeping others). Empirical research almost universally found pairwise deletion (another term for missing value case elimination) to be the most efficient approach to missing values, and certainly the safest one from the standpoint of result validity.

If, however, throwing out missing value cases is not appropriate or feasible, the probabilistic methods, namely maximum likelihood estimation or Bayesian imputation should be employed as, again, empirical analyses found those methods to be the most efficient. The conceptually and operationally easier to tackle—and more frequently used—mean or median substitution should be avoided as much as possible. By artificially deflating the amount of variability contained in the dataset and distorting the distribution of values, these methods can introduce a considerable bias into the analysis, ultimately diminishing the validity of the results. Lastly, to further enhance the robustness of missing value imputations, the following approach is recommended[15]:

> Impute missing values using an appropriate model.
> Repeat the above process, n-number of times (usually, 3-5) to produce n-complete datasets.
> Perform the desired analysis on each dataset using complete-data methods.
> Average the resultant parameter estimates across the individual datasets to arrive at a single point estimate.
> Compute the standard errors of the estimates as follows:

$$SE_m = \frac{s}{\sqrt{n}}$$

where,

s is the standard deviation
n is the number of observations

METADATA

Somewhat tautologically defined, *metadata* is data about data. Operationally, it is a summary view of the individual variables contained in the dataset expressed in terms of the key statistical descriptors, such as value ranges and the corresponding central tendencies, the average amount of variability, as well as the assessment of coverage and accuracy. Although historically more familiar to academicians than to practitioners, the concept of metadata is gaining popularity among the latter as the amount and diversity of data contained in corporate repositories continues to grow to the point of becoming overwhelming. In the world of corporate databases, even the well-annotated ones, i.e., those accompanied by clear data model descriptions and comprehensive data dictionaries, are often just a hodgepodge of some-well and some-sparsely populated variables or discontinued, definitionally-amended metrics, with little indication as to what is analytically-usable and what is not.

The value of metadata is primarily in the time savings it can deliver. A priori knowledge of a dataset means being able to take the right data engineering steps, which in turn means focusing on appropriate techniques that can be supported by the available data. When the metadata information is not available, database analyses can becomes riddled with time-consuming and confidence-shaking corrective re-work, largely due to the underlying data challenges not having been discovered, and corrected, in a timely fashion.

Metadata Template

Although the type and the number of specific variables can differ considerably across datasets, the informational foundation of the metadata associated with each dataset is relatively constant. A general outline of a metadata template is shown below:

Figure 8.3
Sample Metadata Template

		Metrics						
		Mean	Median	St. Deviation	Min	Max	% Missing	Coding*
Events	Accident / Claim 1							
	Accident / Claim 2							
	Accident / Claim *n*							
Attributes	Cause of Accident							
	Nature of Accident							
	Injury Type							
	Treatment							
	Demographic 1							

* quantitative vs. qualitative

The sample template is shown at a relatively aggregate level, i.e., it illustrates variable types, rather than listing specific variables which are likely to differ across datasets. The focus of the metadata is on a comprehensive overview of the key characteristics of datasets as it relates to using the therein contained data as a foundation for the development of unique, competitively advantageous knowledge. To aid in specific statistical technique selection[16], data evaluation imbedded inside of a metadata template needs to differentiate between the two key data types discussed earlier: events and the augmenting attributes. As discussed earlier, key considerations such as those surrounding missing value treatment strategy are dependent on the general variable type.

The main focus of metadata is on the description of the basic distributional properties of the dataset with the help of measures of central tendency (mean and median), variability (standard deviation), and extremity (minimum and maximum). Combined, these evaluative statistics clearly describe the usefulness of individual variables as inputs into specific types of statistical analyses. Further adding to that assessment are the remaining two variables: coverage (% missing) and data type (coding). The former captures the degree of missing values, while the latter qualifies variables' informational content as either qualitative (i.e., nominally or ordinally scaled) or quantitative (i.e., intervally or ratio scaled) – high incidence (i.e., more than the 32% threshold cited earlier) of missing values can make an individual variable analytically unsuitable. On the other hand, high proportion of qualitatively-coded values, including 0-1 indicators (dummy-code values) or categories, such as 'under-18, 18-44, 45-65, 66+' age group categorization tend to limit the analytic usability of such-coded variables[17].

189

Using Metadata

Metadata is compiled—what next? Evaluate the usefulness of the individual dataset variables in the context of the analytic plan, discussed earlier. Is the available data of sufficient quality to support the knowledge creation goals laid out in the analytic roadmap? In short, the main benefit of clear and concise metadata information is to evaluate the availability and quality of raw materials (i.e., data) prior to launching data analysis/model building efforts. Doing so entails working backwards from the desired informational outcomes, as shown below in Figure 8.4

Figure 8.4
Using Metadata to Assess Analytic Preparedness

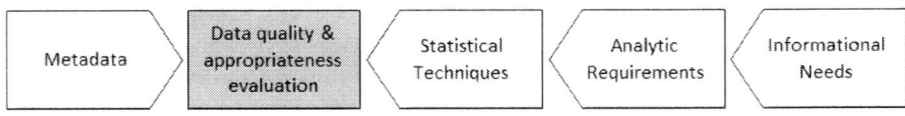

In order to bring about the desired informational end state—i.e., the sought after knowledge—data needs to exhibit the desired quality and statistical characteristics in order to be analyzable in a valid and reliable fashion, which underscores the importance of an a priori preparation of an explicit analytic roadmap. The data quality and appropriateness evaluation is a process of contrasting the informational needs-dictated analytic requirements and the realities of the available data. Hence, the distribution, quality and coding-constraints characterizing the available data (Metadata) are compared to Statistical Techniques' requirements, where the latter stem from Informational Needs-driven Analytic Requirements.

190

9

Knowledge Creation: Exploratory Analyses

What does it mean to "explore"? Conceptually, it is a fairly straightforward notion, but not so in the realm of data analytics, where exploratory analyses are perhaps the most difficult to define and frame aspect of the data analytical process. As discussed earlier, nowadays even fairly modestly sized companies have at their disposal overwhelming quantities and variety of data, which in itself creates a dizzying number of possible data exploration avenues. Technique-related methodological considerations add another wrinkle to an already challenging decision, as the same set of metrics can be explored using univariate or multivariate methods – furthermore, data derived effects can be looked at as stand-alone factors, factor interactions or a combination of both. In an operational sense it means choosing from among an array of methods that although similar in some regards tend to be quite dissimilar in terms of their applicability limits, which will ultimately produce somewhat different information.

Yet, exploratory research does not need to be an all-encompassing, overwhelming endeavor, uncertainty-ridden endeavor. As detailed in Chapter

4, the RPM process is ultimately focused on deriving decision-guiding knowledge that fulfills informational needs stemming from the organization's risk management objectives. That means that even the otherwise open-ended data explorations ought to be focused on topics that relate to those objectives. In addition, to further constrain the informational and methodological scope of that process, a clear distinction needs to be drawn between theory building research and business analytics.

There are a number of significant differences between theory building focused academic research and competitive edge oriented practical business analytics. First and foremost, the former seeks universally true generalizations, while the latter pursues entity (i.e., an organization) and situation (i.e., a specific business context at a point in time) unique insights. Hence the most important methodological considerations surrounding theory building research pertain to sample-to-universe generalizability, which is in sharp contrast to future replicability demands of applied business analyses. Though seemingly of more philosophical than practical importance, these differences in fact have a profound impact on the applicability of some of the more commonly used statistical techniques. As a result, the validity as well as the reliability of outcomes of analyses are, to a large degree, dependent on acknowledging (and taking appropriate steps) of these often fundamental incongruities.

Keeping the above considerations in mind, as used within the RPM process detailed in this book, *exploratory data analysis* (EDA) is defined to be an aspect of data analysis concerned with investigating and reviewing new or not previously analyzed data. It is also sometimes referred to as "data mining", in recognition of the fact that a common objective of initial data explorations is the identification of not-yet-known patterns and/or relationships in the data. Exploratory investigations may exhibit varying degrees of complexity and sophistication and generally make use of various numeric/statistical tests as bases for establishing the validity and reliability of its conclusions. One general approach is to "manually" sift through data in search of (statistically) significant relationships and patterns. For example, a correlation matrix of appropriately selected variables in conjunction with statistical significance tests can be used as the starting point in evaluating relationships among a number of metrics, based upon which, an analyst can uncover not-yet-known relationships.

Over the last couple of decades, certain aspects of "manual" data explorations exemplified above began to benefit from the explosive wave of data processing innovations. Of most interest to business analytics have been two particular sets of developments: *Automated data mining* and *data*

192

visualization. The former represents an attempt at leveraging the advancements in data processing and software technologies to develop stand-alone, self-operating automated data mining systems. These complex applications governed by sophisticated algorithms, such as genetic algorithms of neural networks and are intended to perform the job of an analyst by exploring data for hints noteworthy patterns and relationships.

A related, albeit substantively quite different of the two key data analytic innovations is represented by data visualization applications. Like the aforementioned automated data mining, these too are stand-alone software applications, but in contrast to data mining tools, data visualization systems require an active participation of the part of the analyst. Their goal is to replace some of the obtuse and frequently misinterpreted (and misunderstood) numeric tests with visual representations of the relationships found in data, all with the goal of making the results easier to consume by non-technical users. It follows that although not all relationships can be depicted visually, but a number of simpler, basic reporting functions can be handled quite effectively and elegantly in that format. After all, a picture is worth a thousand words (or numbers)…Figure 9.1 captures the different faces of exploratory data analysis.

Figure 9.1
Exploratory Analyses vs. All Data Analyses

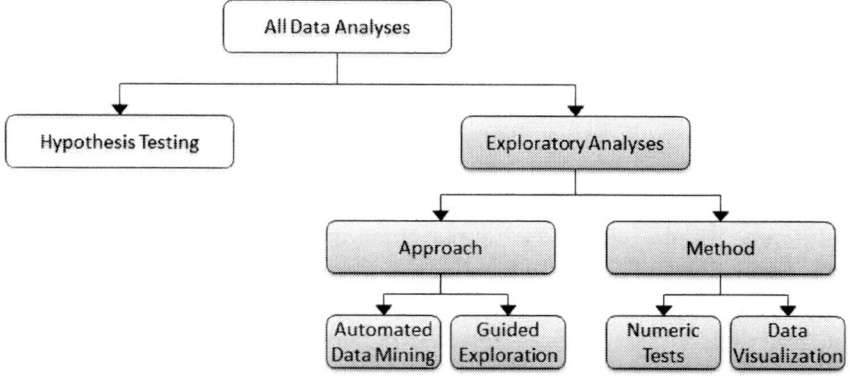

More on Data Exploration Techniques

Data exploration can take many forms, but in the broadest sense, it can entail either self-directed, open-ended exploration (i.e., automated data mining), or an analyst-driven, specific informational objective focused analysis (i.e., guided exploration). Unfortunately, these two philosophically and methodologically distinct approaches are at times used—at least name-wise—synonymously, which is problematic, considering that results both generate can be substantially different: The outcomes of automated data mining are in practice highly unpredictable, simply because this type of database exploration tends to entail the widest possible scope of searching a database for <u>any</u> (statistically significant) patterns or systematic associations. On the other hand, analyst-directed exploratory database analyses are, from the very beginning, focused on informational needs-implied relationships only. In other words, the former is usually driven by the question of "what's there?", while the latter is directed by the question of "what's there, that is related to the organization's risk management goals?" Considering that the RPM process discussed here is explicitly focused on organizational risk management goals, automated data mining does not offer an operationally-viable data exploration avenue.

First and foremost, as a mode of insight discovery, automated data mining is generally informationally unconstrained, as it considers "all possible", rather than just "informational need-related" relationships. In practice, it leads to lumping together of all statistically significant relationships, without regard for their business value[1]. Considering the typically large volumes of data (record-wise) coupled with a large number of available metrics, it is easy to see that any automated data mining tools[2] designed to sift through the contents of voluminous data repositories in search of any relationships are likely to generate an overwhelming number of "significant" relationships. Given the practical limitations of statistical significance tests (see the *Beware of Statistical Significance Tests* section later in this chapter), which offer the only objective means of identifying patterns and relationships in the data, it is often difficult to objectively differentiate between true informational nuggets and practically trivial informational tidbits. Also in a more theoretical sense, automated data mining is philosophically incongruent with the goal of organizational objectives-driven knowledge creation process, as it represents an *inductive*, (or *bottom-up*, to use a business vernacular) approach to the creation of knowledge. Directed exploratory analyses, on the other hand, represent a *deductive* (also called *top-down*) insight discovery mechanism. Although seemingly trifling, this distinction is actually quite critical in view of the database analytical knowledge creation processes described in this book.

As depicted in Figure 9.1, exploratory data analysis can also take on two distinctly different methodological directions: numerical/statistical testing based decision rule vs. visual/spatial data interpretation. In keeping with the belief that a "picture is worth a thousand words," spatially-based data exploration has steadily grown in popularity; however it is best suited for diagnostic rather than relationship-testing purposes. The main reason behind this conclusion is that the knowledge creation demands a relationship testing facility that can support an ongoing and unbiased assessment of the relationships of interest. Spatial data presentation delegates the task of identifying and assessing patterns and relationships to individual analysts, which confounds conclusions with subjective opinions, all of which may ultimately bias the results. In the end, objective, properly used and interpreted numerical tests are preferred over the more subjective visual data interpretation. Spatial data representation, however, is a potent knowledge communication tool and can be a very effective method of conveying otherwise abstract or complex relationships.

Summarizing the above discussion, it follows that in the context of the RPM process, exploratory data analysis is defined as a bottom-down process guided by the organization's risk management goals and tasked with identifying specific informational foundations to support the development of decision-guiding knowledge, as graphically depicted in Figure 9.2 below.

Figure 9.2
Exploratory Analyses

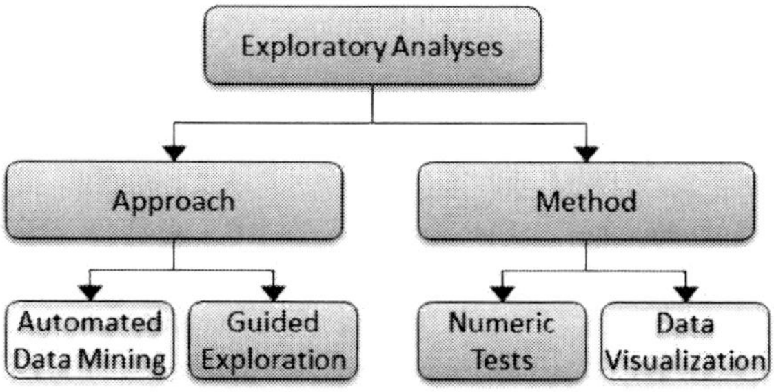

Data Exploration Process

The general outline of the exploratory data analysis process has been well-established for nearly four decades now[3], however, the specificity of risk management-targeted outcomes, coupled with the characteristics of modern databases (see Chapter 7) call for considerable modifications to the general exploratory data analysis approach. Specifically, the data exploration process needs to be constraint to the identification and quantification of specific data elements, as dictated by the specific informational needs stemming from the organization's risk management objectives. At the same time, the approach needs to be extended to also include the creation of meta analytic summary and index variables (see Chapter 8). The so-amended and framed exploratory data analysis (EDA) process can be broken down into a number of distinct steps, with each geared toward a specific end objective, as outlined in Table 9.1.

Table 9.1
Exploratory Data Analysis Process for RPM

Process Step	Description	Objective
Step 1	List the stated informational needs	Review previous findings
Step 2	Re-visit meta analysis	
Step 3	Assess the suitability of available data, with particular emphasis on the amount of variability	Examine the informational quality of the available data
Step 4	Graphically examine key variables	
Step 5	Univariate Exploration: Describe the dataset	Describe—Assess—Explain
Step 6	Bivariate Exploration: Assess relationships	
Step 7	Multivariate Exploration: Explain	
Step 8	Identify indexing and summarization requirements	

THE EDA PROCESS

The general exploratory data analysis (EDA) process detailed in Table 9.1 is comprised of eight distinct stages grouped into three aggregate categories: 1. Review of previous findings; 2. Examination of the informational quality of the available data; and 3. Analyses of data. The first of the three phases—the review of previous findings—offers an opportunity to "take inventory" of previous findings and assess their potential contributions to the current informational needs. The second phase—assessment of the informational quality of the available data—calls for a critical and thorough examination of the value of the data assets vis-à-vis the stated analytical objectives. The third and the final phase of the EDA process—analyses of data—encompasses a broad array of database exploration-centered, yet focused (on the organization's risk management goals) and an analyst-directed "looks" at the available data. As stated earlier, the overriding objective of the RPM-focused EDA process is the identification of data insights that have the potential to make material contribution to the stated informational needs.

EDA Part I: Review Previous Findings

Knowledge creation is a cumulative process. Even the most eye-opening and revolutionary insights ultimately exist within the realm of other, previously created knowledge. This is particularly important when an organization intends to build a comprehensive reservoir of decision aiding knowledge. It is so because unless proper steps are taken, these insight repositories can become nothing more than collections of unconnected, random tidbits of information lacking collective power. In other words, even though some of the individual pieces of information can shed insight onto specific issues, there is little-to-no informational synergy being created by their aggregate total.

The knowledge creation process, which is an inseparable part of the RPM process outlined in this text, emphasizes a purposeful and systematic accumulation of knowledge. Systematic knowledge accumulation, in turn, stipulates that each additional insight contributes something new to the already-in-place knowledge base, while at the same time, all insights are connected by an underlying theme. Recalling the earlier overview of the differences between automated data mining and an analyst-guided data exploration, exploratory analyses should be shaped by both the stated informational goals and the already on-hand information. However, as suggested earlier, these two quite

197

dissimilar elements do not present a "natural" fit, thus bringing them together can benefit from an objective evaluative framework.

The MECE framework (*m*utually *e*xclusive and *c*ollectively *e*xhaustive) is the most appropriate conceptual tool that can be used to jointly evaluate the already-on-hand information and the stated information gathering goals. Its basic premise is that the best way to approach an analytical (but not necessarily quantitative) problem is by identifying—within the confines of the scope of the analysis—all independent components in such a way as to provide a maximally complete coverage or an explanation, while avoiding double-counting. Hence the framework stipulates that each element of knowledge should be informationally non-overlapping with other ones, but collectively, all of them should exhaustively cover the informational demands of the organization's strategic objectives.

The use of the MECE evaluative framework can instill a certain amount of informational discipline by drawing attention to pieces of information that contribute the most, individually as well as collectively, to reaching the stated informational objectives. Since the importance or value of an individual piece of information can be highly situational—i.e., it can depend on what are the stated informational goals—it follows that individual data elements should not be treated as being universally important or universally unimportant. In addition, the MECE framework also promotes thoughtful accumulation of knowledge, by helping to differentiate between causally or otherwise related explanatory factors and spurious informational tidbits.

However, in order to yield robust results, the evaluative framework requires a high degree of definitional clarity. A definitionally-clear informational element is one accompanied by an unambiguous explanation of its interpretative meaning along with the detailing of its measurement, or operational qualities. Specifically, it is important to express the already available insights as well as the planned ones in maximally operational terms, which includes measurement properties (i.e., continuous vs. discrete), the unit of analysis and the acceptable value ranges, all with the goal of diminishing potential misinterpretations of individual informational elements. The importance of operational specificity carries far beyond the exploratory analyses presented in this section and will become even more evident in the context of segmentation and behavioral predictions overviews presented in the ensuing chapters. In the sense of technical analyses of data, the definitional precision matters for reasons ranging from effect specification to methodological appropriateness (i.e., making sure that metrics meet the distributional and other requirements of specific statistical methodologies).

198

Reconciling Stated Needs and Meta Analytic Insights

The key to any comparison is the establishment of robust and objective evaluative thresholds. Keeping in mind the MECE evaluative framework, meaningful communalities between the stated informational needs and the currently-on-hand insights (i.e., the results of meta analyses) requires an a prior assessment of the appropriateness of individual variables, followed by the determination of sufficiency of coverage of the combined variable set. The purpose of these two preliminary steps is to make sure the scope and contents of the raw inputs to be used in the analysis are both appropriate.

Appropriateness of Individual Variables

An appropriate variable is one that exhibits the desired value availability (i.e., % of missing values), scaling (i.e., the type of measurement), distributional (i.e., the shape of the frequency distribution) and interpretational (i.e., meaning) characteristics. The intent behind this evaluative dimension is to ascertain that the individual measures are statistically as well as contextually useful in the context of the informational needs-dictated ensuing analyses.

A single variable can be deemed analytically appropriate if it meets the following criteria:
> The proportion of its values that are missing are within the objectively allowed limits—i.e., the previously discussed norm of not exceeding about ⅓ of the total number of observations.
> Its measurement scale is appropriate given its anticipated usage— specifically, the measure is continuous, if necessary (remember that continuous variables can always be re-coded into discrete values, but discrete values cannot ever be converted into continuous ones).
> Its frequency distribution meets the requirements of the statistical techniques to be used, or the desired properties can be brought about through an appropriate transformation.

At the same time, a given variable can be deemed informationally appropriate if it meets the following criteria:
> Its meaning falls within the general scope of the stated informational needs.
> Recency-wise, it represents the most up-to-date level of insight.

MECE Considerations

The individual variables deemed appropriate based on the above criteria need to contribute incrementally to the explanatory power of the entire set. Operationally, this means that individually, measures should not exhibit excessive cross-variable collinearity[4]. This is a somewhat tricky area because it imposes seemingly contradictory statistical and informational requirements. In a statistical sense, non-trivial variable correlations (usually expressed as statistically significant at a chosen confidence interval, such as 95% or 99%, or ± 2 or 3 standard deviations away from the mean, respectively) are a necessary prerequisite of meaningful multivariate and cross-variable analyses, simply because absent those, the resultant models will lack any explanatory and/or predictive power. In an informational sense, however, as stipulated by the earlier-discussed Ockham's Razor, each individual variable is expected to make an incremental (i.e., unique) contribution to the overall explanation in order for it to not be deemed informationally redundant. In other words, while some level of variable correlation is absolutely necessary to enable explanatory analyses, too high a correlation may preclude some variables from being included in the analysis. Fortunately, steps can be taken to find an acceptable middle-ground and the next chapter will provide an in-depth discussion of the recommended diagnostics and remedies.

Sufficiency of Coverage of the Variable Set

The adequacy of the informational content of the entire variable set should be evaluated by considering the following two characterizations:

1. The availability of multiple indicators, which translates into two or more operationally distinct but informationally related metrics. The basic idea behind this requirement is to ascertain that the underlying informational constructs are measured with multiple indicators.
2. Distributional properties of specific variable sub-sets are aligned with individual informational needs. For instance, if the stated informational needs are focused on the exploration of high cost claims, the individual metrics should encompass a robust number of high cost claim-attributable values and the overall distribution of values should adhere to the requirements of statistical techniques that are to be used.

200

The availability of multiple metrics for each of the individual informational dimensions is important for a number of reasons. First of all, it is necessary to explaining or predicting a particular phenomenon, since any such analyses are multivariate in nature (e.g., regression analyses require, at a minimum, two or more variables, one to be the target and one or more to be predictors). In other situations, multiple metrics are required to ascertain the construct's convergent validity, which is the degree to which multiple indicators produce similar results, lending credence to subsequent interpretations.

Assessing distributional properties of individual variable cohorts is important primarily from the standpoint of technical data analysis. Many of the commonly used statistical techniques, such as Pearson's product-moment correlation, regression or analysis of variance require at least some of the input variables to be continuous and normally distributed. Hence it is important that the metrics available to support individual informational needs exhibit properties required by statistical techniques that are best suited to generate the desired insights.

MECE Considerations

As is the case with other aggregate evaluative schemas, such as SWAT analysis, there is a certain subjectivity that is inherent to the MECE framework. It is another way of staying that effort should be taken to minimize any potential analyst bias. An obvious step that can be taken in that regard is the cross-analyst triangulation, akin to the Delphi method[5]. Multiple analysts should each come up with an independent assessment, following which they should be shown the results of other analysts' conclusions and given an opportunity to revise their own. Several iterations should produce convergence or near-convergence and in case of the latter, an open forum discussion can be used as the mean of reaching the final solution.

EDA Part II: Assess the Informational Quality

It is important to look beyond "what are the available metrics", to "what would be the ideal metrics", given the demands of the informational needs at hand. In other words, how adequate is the currently available variable set? In practice it is rare for the data currently-on-hand to leave nothing to be desired. More often than not, the informational needs pose questions that go beyond the currently available metrics, implying other data. However, other types of insights may be imbedded in the currently available raw data, though not expressly listed among the current metrics. Instead, it may be derived from the already-on-hand data either by means of *indexing* or *combinatorial* means. In other words, some of the already available raw metrics can be used to create new raw metrics, which then can be added into the currently-on-hand dataset. In effect, the amount of data, in terms of the raw metric count as well as the informational scope that is available at any given time can be increased with the help of some carefully thought out steps. As a matter of fact, as shown in Figure 9.3, the gap separating the current and the ideal variable sets can be narrowed through intelligent harvesting of the not immediately evident informational content of the available raw data.

Figure 9.3
Desired vs. Available Data

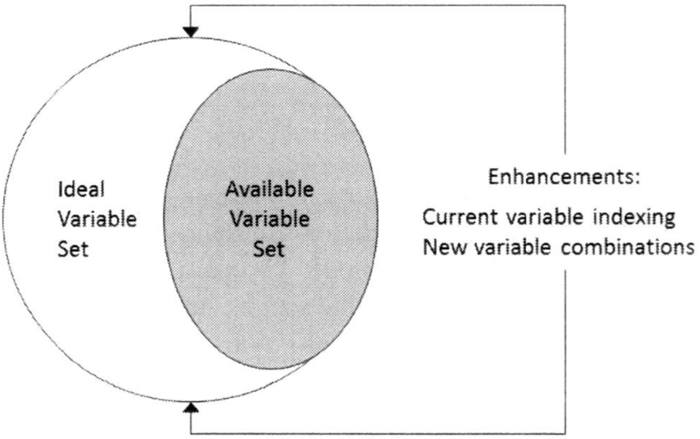

Current variable indexing is a process of re-expressing raw metrics in a more immediately usable descriptive qualities, as exemplified by value indicators (e.g., high, medium, low) derived from numeric data or the so-called "flags" (e.g., "yes" vs. "no" indicators) inferred from other metrics. It is important to keep in mind that indexing frequently takes the form of discrete indicators, thus to the degree to which it might be possible the appropriateness of the qualitative measurement scale should be considered in the context of the contemplated analyses prior to committing to a particular measurement scale.

On the other hand, as implied by its name, *new variable combination* simply refers to creating brand new measures through joining of two or more of the existing ones. In the informational sense this amounts to developing higher-order insights from more disaggregate raw components; alternatively, somewhat dissimilar metrics can be combined into new measures yielding different insights. In contrast to the previously discussed indexing, newly created variables are typically more likely to be continually distributed, leading to fewer usage restrictions.

Graphical Examination of Data

It is important to not lose sight of the fact that not all variables in a particular dataset are equally important from the informational content standpoint. In a more technical sense, some metrics that are informationally important could lack statistical robustness. Specifically, they could manifest poor measurement precision or inadequate amount of variability, both in univariate and multivariate contexts. Thus any dataset evaluation should be guided by a dual objective: One, to differentiate between theoretically critical and the lesser theoretically impactful metrics; two, to assess the statistical quality of the crucial pieces of data.

Always a good time-saving idea, this type of pre-analyses due diligence may be a necessity when dealing with event-tracking databases, often populated by a staggering number and variety of metrics. The determinants of what constitutes an "important" vs. "less important" metric are obviously highly situational, though in general any data element deemed essential to understanding events are behavioral outcomes, or those explaining cross-group or -type differences should always be considered important. On the other hand, variables offering primarily profiling or descriptive insights, such geodemographics discussed earlier, are usually less important, largely because—as shown in later chapters—their explanatory and predictive power tends to be considerably lower.

Again, the key reason for differentiating between the more and less critical metrics is to focus the attention on the former to enable an efficient assessment of their basic statistical qualities. In other words, do these important variables exhibit the desired statistical properties, given the informational needs at hand and the contemplated analytical methodologies? The quickest and perhaps the easiest method of answering such questions is through graphical examination of the data. Made possible (and quite easy) by the proliferation of powerful statistical analysis packages designed for personal computers, carefully selected data graphs can lead to a quick "thumbs up" or "thumbs down" assessment of the individual metrics. I should point out that graphical description of data is certainly not limited to univariate (i.e., single variable) depictions, but it is arguably most potent in those cases, as higher-order contrasts (i.e., multi-variable relationships) are more effectively evaluated with the help of mathematical tests.

The starting point in assessment of any variable should be the characterization of the shape of its distribution, because as discussed later, many key statistical procedures are built around certain distributional assumptions, most frequently, the ubiquitous standard normal distribution discussed earlier. The easiest approach to assessing univariate distribution is to simply graph it. The cleanest (and likely the easiest) way of doing so is through the use of a *histogram*, which represents the frequencies of occurrences of data values within categories. Figure 9.4 shows an example of a histogram. The individual bars represent frequency counts, thus the taller the bar, the higher the count of that particular value.

Figure 9.4
Sample Histogram

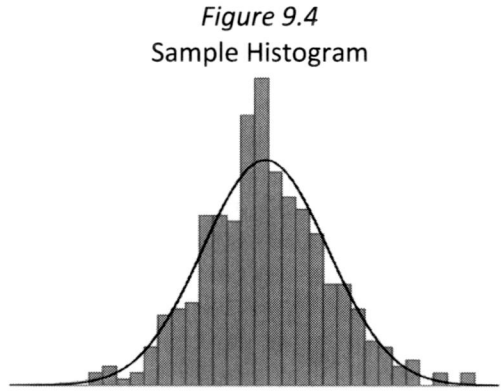

To aid in the assessment of the (statistically defined) normality of a particular univariate distribution, it is helpful to add to the barred histogram an outline of the normal distribution, shown as the darker-colored bell shape curve in Figure 9.4. Technically, the normal curve represents the expected distribution, to be contrasted with observed valued depicted by the individual bars[6]. In the above example, the distribution appears to be approximately normal, with the operative term being "approximately." It is rare to come across a distribution which has exactly the shape shown by the idealized bell curve and more importantly, it is not statistically necessary. Most of the commonly used techniques, such as regression and other related (i.e., general linear model) methods discussed in subsequent chapters are relatively robust with regard to some departure from normality.

Of course, as the difference between the ideal and actual distributions grows, the robustness of the analytic results will tend to diminish, which means that it is important to single out a relatively "hard" threshold beyond which a particular variable should be no longer considered normally distributed. Unfortunately, a histogram-based visual distributional assessment leaves that determination to more-or-less qualitative judgment of an analyst. However, given the importance of accurately discerning the distributional qualities of at least the key database metrics, if a particular distribution raises doubts regarding its shape, one of the available numeric goodness-of-fit tests should be used to assess its level of normality. The χ^2 (chi squared) test is among the easiest to implement univariate normality diagnostics.

The chi squared test measures the goodness-of-fit between the *observed* and *expected* (under the normal distribution) frequencies. In the context of Figure 9.4, for every bar (observed), which represents a single data category, and line (expected) intersection, the test determines if any differences represent persistent dissimilarity or are mere random, non-systematic fluctuations. The tests requires the ability to compute the cumulative distribution function, which is the probability that the variable takes on a value that is less than or equal to the expected value. Its computation, however, is relatively straightforward:

$$\chi^2 = \sum_{i=1}^{k} \frac{(O_i - E_i)^2}{E_i}$$

where,

O_i is the observed frequency for category i
E_i is the expected frequency for category i

The *observed* frequency reflects the actual counts contained in the data—on the other hand, the *expected* frequency is computed as follows:

$$E_i = N(F(Y_u) - F(Y_l))$$

where,

F is the cumulative distribution function for the distribution being tested
Y_u is the upper limit for class i
Y_l is the lower limit for class i
N is the sample size

The results of the χ^2 test are interpreted in the familiar p-value expressed significance test format, as the test is defined for the following general hypotheses:

H_o: The data follow normal distribution
H_a: The data do not follow normal distribution

A statistically significant result leads to the rejection of the null (H_o) hypothesis and a corresponding acceptance of the alternative (H_a) hypothesis, which ultimately leads to the conclusion that the variable of interest is not normally distributed.

It should be noted that there are multiple other tests that have been developed and used to detect departures from normality, the best known of which include the Kolmogorov-Smirnov and Anderson-Darling operationalizations. In general, though, these tests adhere to a more-or-less similar evaluative logic. The latter, which is used frequently in the financial sector, is a modification of the former, giving more weight to the tail-end of the distribution than its parent (Kolmogorov-Smirnov). Unlike the chi squared test discussed earlier, however, these two tests are restricted to continuous distributions.

EDA Part III: Describe—Assess—Explain

Although data visualization is gaining in popularity, the bulk of the more in-depth data exploration and virtually all of the more complex hypotheses testing remains numeric. All too often, however, the numerical data analyses do not go far enough in translating the usually somewhat abstract results into more meaningful insights. Many analysts find it difficult to look beyond *how* a particular analysis was carried out to *what* the results mean to the organization. The appropriateness and robustness of employed methodologies will certainly always be of critical importance, but to users, the clarity of results in terms of business implications will carry a lot more meaning. In short, in order for results of analyses to yield highly impactful and advantageous knowledge, analytic findings cannot be confounded with analytic methodologies in a way that impedes users' understanding.

These considerations are particularly important in the context of the actual (exploratory) data analytical continuum of *describe—assess—explain*. Although throughout this section, as well as the rest of this book, a number of computational formulas are presented, the overall objective is to develop an

206

intuitive level of understanding of the subject matter being discussed, to enable one to move beyond technical details in presenting their findings. Hence the scattering of technical details is geared toward the identification of the most effective methods of solving a particular problem, with the ultimate goal of bringing to bear the most insightful and advantageous knowledge. An added benefit of this approach is that the ensuing discussion will not get bogged down in an encyclopedic delineation of every conceivable approach available, but instead will be focused on the few that were proven to generate the most valid and reliable outcomes.

Unlike the previously discussed EDA Parts I and II, which were focused on preparatory considerations, this part of the exploratory data analytical process is focused on the actual exploration of the available data: The *describe* step is focused on revealing the basic facts about the data, such as the average claim cost or the frequency of claim filings; the *assess* step captures the goal of developing a fundamental understanding of patterns of relationship in the data (i.e., it expands the *what-is* of the *describe* step to include *why-it-is*); lastly, the *explain* step brings to bear the final building blocks that are needed to transform the more-or-less generic information into unique and thus far more valuable knowledge. In practical business terms, the culmination of the three-step process is the delineation of root causes behind either the observed failure or the success of a particular action, with the goal of fostering a more effective future deployment of organizational resources.

Describe: Univariate Distributional Properties

Data exploration necessitates examining the resultant cleansed data in the context of their informational content. Doing so entails computing several basic univariate descriptors, all of which is necessary to validly describe the informational content and analytic usability of the individual metrics. The choice of the descriptive metrics is primarily a function of individual variables' measurement scale, specifically, whether it is discrete or continuous. Discretely-coded data, often referred to as *categorical* or *qualitative* (the latter not to be confused with qualitative research or conclusions) assume only values that represent distinct categories that can be nominal (such as "male" and "female" for gender) or rank-ordered (such as "small", "medium" and "large" for size). Whether expressed as "strings" (words or alphanumeric values, which represent a combination of letters and digits) or as "digits", discrete data can assume any value, so long as it is not fractional. In the vast majority of applied business situations, categorical variables have a finite number of values, although that is not theoretically required.

On the other hand, a *continuous variable* is one that takes on an infinite number of possible values, usually bounded by two extremes[7]. Thus in contrast to categorical metrics where only integer or integer-equivalent (i.e., non-fractional) values are permissible. In this case, any value is possible so long as it falls within the range-defining end points, usually referred to as the maximum and minimum values. Common examples include incurred claim cost; individual's age, weight or wealth; or even derived metrics, such as litigation propensity or absenteeism proneness. In a practical sense, these otherwise advantageous (from the standpoint of data analyses) basic properties of continuous variables' can potentially complicate the interpretation of results, particularly in the sense of differentiating between statistically and practically significant findings.

In view of the differences between their respective distributional properties, it is intuitively obvious that continuous and categorical variables cannot be subjected to the same types of mathematical manipulations, such as division or multiplication. Due to its lower informational content, categorical data presents far fewer analytic options than does its continuously-coded counterpart, which naturally limits its informational value. (Keep in mind that, as previously mentioned, continuous metrics can always be re-coded into categorical ones, but the reverse is not possible; that said, any continuous-to-categorical conversion will lead to an irreversible loss of information as a direct result of diminished variability of the resultant data.) The practical consequences of the impermissibility of some basic algebraic operations, such as division required to compute average values can place rather severe limitations on the informational value of categorical data. For that reason, careful due diligence is urged when contemplating data capture or variable coding and when possible, preference should be given to continuous measurement.

In view of this fundamental computational schism separating the categorical and continuously coded metrics, different statistical technique will be applicable, depending on the measurement characteristics of individual metrics. In general, categorical variables are described in terms of *counts* and *frequencies*, while continuous variables are best characterized with the help of measures of *central tendency*, a departure from the average and the range, which measures the spread between the smallest and the largest values.

Categorical Variables

Considering that discrete variables are comprised of a finite—and usually manageable—number of distinct categories, the most effective univariate analytical method involves numeric or graphical (such as the histogram depicted in Figure 9.4) frequency distribution review. However, just because the number of categories is finite, does not mean that it is small. For instance, "location" is a categorical (specifically, nominal) measure, yet in many instances, such as in the case of a large retailer, the number of locations can be quite large. Either numeric or graphical frequency distribution will yield a large number of categories making the output somewhat difficult to interpret.

An easy corrective step to take is to create groupings of categories. Using the retail locations cited above, it would be advisable to lump individual stores located in a geographically-distinct area, such as a state, into a smaller and thus more manageable number of categories. An added benefit of taking that step is that it will help to limit the amount of noise in the data, since low frequency categories contribute disproportionately more to the unexplained variability in the dataset then they do to the explanatory power of most statistical models. In addition, some statistical techniques may require re-coding of the categorical variables into so-called *dummy variables*, which in effect converts a single, multi-category metric into multiple binary ones, where the number of resultant metrics is equal to the original number of categories. Dummy-coding can be quite tedious in instances where the number of categories is high, but it will usually enhance the parsimony of the resultant statistical model.

Continuous Variables: Measures of Central Tendency

There are three commonly used measures of univariate central tendency: the average, the median and the mode. The *average* depicts a typical value in a particular distribution. Computationally, there are multiple ways of calculating averages, with the *mean* being the most commonly used one[8]. There are several different mean formulations: arithmetic, geometric, harmonic or weighted. The *arithmetic mean*, also referred to as a "straight" or a "simple" mean, is obtained by summing two or values and dividing the resultant by the number of items. The *geometric mean* is defined as the nth root of the product of all values in a set of numerical data, where n is the number of values in the dataset. Although somewhat more computationally involved, the geometric mean is more resistant to extreme values than the more interpretationally straightforward arithmetic mean. The *harmonic mean* is yet another method of computing the average while minimizing the influence of extreme values and it is defined as the quotient of *n* divided by the sum of the reciprocals of all the values in a set of numerical data, where *n* is the number of values in the dataset.

Most statistical applications rely on a simple arithmetic mean, computed as follows:

$$\bar{x} = \frac{\sum_{i=1}^{n} x_i}{n}$$

where,

> $\bar{x}$ is the estimated mean
> x_i is an individual observation *i*
> *n* is the number of cases

Median and mode are the two alternatives to the mean as the measure of average or typical values. A *median* is the middle number in a set of ordered data, usually found with a simple formula:

$$(n + 1) / 2$$

where,

> *n* is the number of records

In the event a sample contains an odd number of records, the median of that sample will be one of the actual values contained herein; otherwise, if there happens to be an even number of records in a particular sample, the resultant median will be computed as the mean of the two middle values.

The last of the three measures of central tendencies is the *mode*, which is simply the actually observed value that happens to appear in the largest number of records, or put differently, it is an observed value with the highest frequency of occurrence. In contrast to both the mean and the median, the mode is likely to not be unique.

Continuous Variables: Measures of Variability

In a statistical sense, the best way to think about measures of central tendency is to think in terms of the expected value of a random variable. Hence, if one were to guess the most likely value that is to be assumed by a random variable, the "best guess" would point toward one of the earlier discussed measures of central tendency. Given that, if one were to compute the difference between, let's say, the mean of a particular variable and each actual value, the difference (known as the residual), aggregated across all records would yield the measure of variability contained in the data. Hence, the amount of variability in the data can be simply expressed as:

$$Variability = \sum_{i=1}^{n}(observed - mean)$$

However, there is a caveat: Given that the mean will fall more-or-less in the middle of the distribution, roughly half the values will be larger than it and half smaller, thus if added, the positive and negative deviations from the mean will cancel each other out, all of which would result in zero (0) variability (or a very small value close to 0). Simply squaring both the positive and negative values will eliminate the canceling effect and lead to a real number based variability estimate, which offers a convenient way of circumventing the apparent computational flaw. The resultant measure is called *variance*, which is denoted as s^2 and computed as follows[9]:

$$s^2 = \frac{\sum_{i=1}^{n}(x_i - \bar{x})^2}{n - 1}$$

where,

x_i is an individual observation
$\bar{x}$ is the mean
n is the number of cases

The most practically compelling interpretation of variance is that it is indicative of the explanatory power of a particular variable: The larger the variance, the more likely is the variable to contribute to the resultant explanation. That is because large variance is indicative of significant cross-record differences, which is a necessary prerequisite for any metric to have strong predictive power. In addition, variance also gives rise to another useful statistic—the *standard deviation*—which is a more effective way of comparing the levels of variability across variables. Methodologically, standard deviation is simply the square root of variance, denoted by s^9 and computed as follows[10]:

$$s = \sqrt{\frac{\sum_{i=1}^{n}(x_i - \bar{x})^2}{n - 1}}$$

211

where,

x_i is an individual observation
$\bar{x}$ is the mean
n is the number of cases

Standard deviation is an important metric because it illustrates the amount of variability contained in a particular variable—the larger the standard deviation, the more variance there is in a particular variable. Variables with very small standard deviation are informationally poor because they contribute little to the cross case differentiation (this is in contrast to parameter estimates, where small standard deviation is desirable as it is an indication of stable estimates). As noted earlier, small variance can significantly reduce the predictive or explanatory power of otherwise intuitively important metrics. However, because its computation involves squaring of the residual ($x_i - \bar{x}$), both the standard deviation as well as its "parent", the variance are particularly effected by extreme values, which can be a cause for concern, but also underscores the importance of solid data due diligence efforts.

Continuous Variables: Measures of Dispersion

The last key univariate distributional characteristic is the *range*, which is simply the spread between the smallest and largest values. Again, because it measures the absolute distance between the extremes, it can be more informative to use an interval range, such as the frequently used quartiles. *Quartiles* are empirically selected points that divide an ordered distribution into four parts, each containing one quarter of all scores. Examining the percentage of all cases falling into each of the four quartiles sheds additional light on the magnitude of spread depicted by the range. A large range accompanied by a condensed quartile distribution (i.e., very few cases falling into quartiles 1 and 4) is informationally poorer than an equally large range accompanied by a more evenly balanced quartile distribution.

Univariate analyses usually require a relatively tedious variable-by-variable examination of the descriptive characteristics of data, such as the average or the range of values, which tends to narrow the focus to a relatively small sub-set of all available data. As previously suggested, the choice of variables to be included in the analysis sub-set is largely subjective and driven by the analyst's level of experience. When it comes to event-tracking databases, there tends to be a short list of candidate metrics, including, in the case of risk management systems, measures of incurred cost (total, medical, etc.), reserves or personal characteristics such as age, income, or the length of employment.

Lastly, univariate data analysis is an outcome-oriented undertaking, which means it can lead to a virtual avalanche of status quo tidbits while offering little-to-no explanatory diagnostics. In fact, its implicit assumption of individual metric *orthogonality*, or independence, means that cross-variable comparisons can be potentially misleading as otherwise spurious associations are interpreted as cause and effect. For instance, a side-by-side comparison of seemingly related factors, such as employee wages and the injured worker claim's total incurred value (for workers' compensation claims) can suggest that an increase in the latter was caused by the former, where in fact the said increase might have been driven by a different—and unaccounted for—set of factors, such as the nature of the accident or the type of injury. Hence, while univariate analyses can shed light on *what-is*, these methods cannot offer reliable and conclusive insights into the reasons behind the observed outcomes.

Assess: Bivariate Relationships

Potential relationships first suggested by univariate profiling might be initially investigated with the help of bivariate analyses, which assess the persistence and generalizability of pairwise relationships. For instance, a concurrent increase in the length of employment and the claims' total incurred cost may be suggestive of a potential relationship, a positive one in this case, between these two outcomes measures, thus affirming the validity of the initial, exploratory findings.

Although methodologically straightforward, analyses of associations can be riddled with hidden traps, as illustrated by the *Simpson's paradox*, according to which the direction or strength of the relationship changes when data is aggregated across natural groupings that should otherwise be treated separately. In other words, one should be cautious when searching for "globally valid" relationships—it might be better to assess multiple associations framed in the context of more homogenized population. Furthermore, few if any databases offer anything other than a subset of all possible data that might be related to a particular phenomenon, in addition to which, the available data may vary in terms of its accuracy. Moreover, a threat that is particularly potent in the context of bivariate analyses is the potential presence of *intervening* or *moderating factors*, where an outside variable moderates a particular bivariate or conditional relationship where the strength or direction of the relationship changes across the values of a third variable.

Keeping an eye on these and other potential traps, there are two general approaches to quantifying bivariate relationships: 1. simple cross-tabulation and 2. correlation analysis. When both variables are discrete, *cross tabulation*, or crosstab for short, is usually the easiest method of assessing the relationship between the two. On the other hand, when both measures are continuous, quantifying their *correlation* is the most effective method of assessing their relationship. In fact, a correlation coefficient can be computed for virtually all random variables, regardless of their scaling properties (i.e., continuous as well as categorical ones) – that said, correlating discrete variables can be tricky given the multiplicity of esoteric and rarely used tests, so much so that a crosstab might offer the best combination of methodological robustness and the ease of interpretation.

Cross Tabulating Discrete Variables

Bivariate χ^2 (chi square) analysis is the simplest approach to quantifying bivariate relationships with the help of cross-tabulation. Since crosstabs involve the construction of matrices, where variables are usually expressed as columns and individual categories as rows, it is obviously advantageous to keep the number of categories relatively low[11] (at this point, we are only concerned with bivariate, or 2x2 designs, thus the number of variables would obviously always remain low). The goal of the test is simple: to determine if there are *non-spurious associations* between the specified variables. It is important to point out that the test is binary—i.e., it can confirm or reject the presence of relationships, but it yields no information regarding the strength of the association. However, as shown below, there are supplemental methods of discerning that information.

In a statistical sense, χ^2 is a nonparametric test, which means that it places no distributional requirements on the sample data. That said, however, in order to yield unbiased estimates, the test requires the sample to be random, data to be reported as raw frequencies (not percentages), the individual categories to be mutually exclusive and exhaustive and the observed frequencies to meet the minimum count requirements (the often-cited rule of thumb calls for a minimum cell[12] size of 5 frequencies—in practice, however, a minimum sample size 50 is more reasonable to assure the robustness of business analyses). The test itself is relatively simple—it compares the difference between the observed and expected frequencies in each cell to determine if significant patterns of similarities (i.e., a relationship) exist between the two variables; it is computed as follows:

$$\chi^2 = \sum \frac{(O-E)^2}{E}$$

where,

        O is the observed value
        E is the expected value

The χ^2 test will determine if any two variables are related—however, it is not indicative of the strength of the relationship. A separate measure—Cramer's V—was developed for cross-tabulations larger than 2x2 to quantify the strength of χ^2-significant relationships. That measure is computed as follows:

$$\text{Cramer's V} = \sqrt{\frac{\chi^2}{N(k-1)}}$$

where,

        χ^2 is the value of the previously computed chi square statistic
        N is the total number of observations
        k is the smaller of the number of rows or columns

Thus in situations where there are more than five cells (i.e., at least one of the variables has more than two categories) the strength of the relationship can be computed. The resultant Cramer's V coefficient is interpreted the same way as the commonly used Pearson's product-moment correlation coefficient, discussed next. Of course, since its computation involves taking of a square root, the phi values will always be positive, ranging from 0 to +1.

Bivariate Analyses of Continuous and Mixed Variables

As detailed above, the informationally richer continuous data yields more breadth of bivariate analytical insights – what about situations where one of the variables is continuous while the other is discrete? There are different methods available for assessing bivariate relationships of continuously measured and mixed (continuous + discrete) pairwise variable comparisons, all of which fall under the general umbrella of *correlation analysis.*

The term "correlation" has a rather broad usage. Aside from bivariate correlation which is the focus of this section, there are several other expressions of correlation-based associations. Regression analysis produces a measure of *multiple correlations*, which is the correlation of multiple independent variables with a single dependent variable. In addition, there is the *partial correlation*, which is the measure of association of two variables controlling for the impact of other variables; there is also a similarly named *part correlation*, which is similar to partial correlation except that the impact of other variables is only controlled for one of the two correlation measures. Lastly, there is also the *canonical correlation*, discussed in more detail below. All of these are special purpose variants of the general bivariate correlation and will be discussed throughout this book as appropriate, however, in this chapter the focus is on the general discussion of the bivariate correlation.

Technically, correlation is a concurrent change in value of two numeric variables, which represents the degree of relationship between those variables. As it is intuitively obvious, the correlation-expressed relationship can be either positive, when an increase in one is accompanied by an increase in the other, or negative, which is when an increase in one is accompanied by a decrease in the other. A numeric result of correlation analyses is a correlation coefficient, which is a metric expressing the strength of the relationship between the two variables of interest, ranging from +1 (perfectly positive correlation) to -1 (perfectly negative correlation) and centered on 0, which denotes a lack of relationship. In the context of knowledge creation, correlation represents an informational improvement over univariate analyses because it begins to explain the phenomenon of interest, which goes a step beyond just summarizing the observed status quo.

In spite of its widespread usage, there is a healthy amount of confusion surrounding the notion of correlation analysis. The bulk of the misunderstanding centers on the scope, or more specifically, the number of items being correlated; a close second is the choice of a specific formulation.

Overall, correlation is bivariate, which means that it can only be computed for two entities at a time, as a simultaneous assessment of multi-variable (i.e., 2+) relationships would be methodologically complex and practically limiting, primarily because it would necessitates the use of conditional expressions and/or interaction terms[13]. That said, it is important to point out that correlations can be computed for a set of two individual variables, as well as for two sets of variables (i.e., for correlation purposes, an entity can have very specific operationalization or it can represent a summary). Both cases, conceptually speaking, will result in bivariate relationships as there are ultimately only two entities involved, yet in the methodological sense there are two distinctly different approaches that need to be employed.

In the case of two individual variables being correlated, an approach generally described as the *bivariate correlation* should be used, while a different methodology known as the *canonical correlation* should be employed with summary-based (i.e., the previously mentioned sets of metrics) operationalizations. It should be noted, however, that in practice the use of canonical correlations is relatively infrequent in business analyses and virtually non-existent in analyses of large event databases. The reason for that is that since the canonical correlation is primarily of value in quantifying relationships between two sets of metrics, where each set is intended to measure the same underlying (and usually unobservable) construct[14], it is obviously of little value to the analyses of observed outcomes. Thus beyond this brief mention, canonical correlation will not be discussed here any further and the term "bivariate correlation" will denote a relationship between two individual variables only.

In terms of specific formulations there are multiple methods of computing correlation coefficients, the bulk of which were devised to address specific data requirements. Table 9.2 offers an enumeration of the different correlation formulations.

Table 9.2
Coefficients of Correlation

Correlation Measure	Description	Application
Pearson's product-moment (r)	Both variables are continuous & normally distributed; relationship is linear	The most commonly used formulation
Spearman's rank (rhea)	Both variables ordinal or one ordinal and one interval	The most commonly used substitute for Pearson's r
Kendall's rank (taut)	Both variables ordinal or one ordinal and one interval	A less frequently used alternative to Spearman's rhea
Polyserial	Interval and ordinal variables (3+ categories) and the latter reflects underlying continuum; bivariate normality required	The preferred method used to correlate interval and multichomous ordinal variables
Polychoric	Both variables are dichotomous or ordinal, but reflect underlying continuous variables; bivariate normality required	The preferred method to correlate two dichotomous or ordinal variables
Biserial	Same as polyserial, but the discrete variable is dichotomous (2 categories) and it reflects underlying continuum	Rarely used (polyserial used in its place); coefficient can be greater than 1.0
Tetrachoric	Same as polychoric, but both variables are dichotomous	Mostly in theoretical research employing structural equations
Rank biserial	An ordinal variable is related to a truly dichotomous variable (no underlying continuity)	Rarely used in practical research
Point biserial	An interval variable is correlated with a truly dichotomous	Can use Pearson's r formula
Phi	Both variables are dichotomous	A substitute for Pearson's r used with dichotomies

Largely due to computational and display convenience, bivariate correlation coefficients are typically computed for multiple pairs of relationships and presented in a matrix format. In addition, correlations are standardized, i.e., the original units of measurement are replaced with mean=0 and standard deviation=1, which makes coefficients directly comparable in spite of any original scale differences[15]. Figure 9.5 shows an example of a simple correlation matrix.

Figure 9.5
Sample Correlation Matrix

	factor_1	factor_2	factor_3	factor_4	factor_5	factor_6	factor_7
factor_1	1	.987	-.166	-.260	-.072	-.312	.797
factor_2	.987	1	-.153	-.242	-.054	-.329	.798
factor_3	-.166	-.153	1	.535	.199	-.139	-.113
factor_4	-.260	-.242	.535	1	.268	-.142	-.213
factor_5	-.072	-.054	.199	.268	1	-.022	.013
factor_6	-.312	-.329	-.139	-.142	-.022	1	-.362
factor_7	.797	.798	-.113	-.213	.013	-.362	1

The intersection of a specific row and a column pinpoints a correlation coefficient computed for that particular pair of variables. For instance, the value for Factor_3 and Factor_4 is 0.535, which is a moderately strong positive correlation. The same variables appear in the matrix' rows and columns, which means that the diagonal values represent correlations of individual variables with themselves, which will always be equal to 1 since a variable is perfectly correlated with itself[16]. Thus a half of the matrix shown in above is redundant because correlations are non-directional, i.e., factor_1 x factor_2 correlation is functionally the same as factor_2 x factor_1 correlation – i.e., it would suffice to only show values above or below the diagonal, as depicted in Figure 9.6.

Figure 9.6
Non-Redundant Elements Only

	factor_1	factor_2	factor_3	factor_4	factor_5	factor_6	factor_7
factor_1	1						
factor_2	.987	1					
factor_3	-.166	-.153	1				
factor_4	-.260	-.242	.535	1			
factor_5	-.072	-.054	.199	.268	1		
factor_6	-.312	-.329	-.139	-.142	-.022	1	
factor_7	.797	.798	-.113	-.213	.013	-.362	1

However, as pointed out earlier, there is more to computing a correlation coefficient than choosing between a bivariate and a canonical correlation. The proliferation of the "point and click" computing capabilities has the unfortunate side effect of fuzzing the distinctiveness among the different correlation coefficient formulations. By far the most commonly used formulation—Person's product-moment correlation coefficient—tends to be the default in popular statistical packages, but it is certainly not the only formulation that should be considered, and even more importantly, it carries specific data distributional (normal vs. non-normal) and relationship type (i.e., linear vs. non-linear) requirements, the violation of which will significantly limit the reliability of the resultant statistic. The two other bivariate correlation coefficients—Spearman's and Kendall's rank correlations—do not make specific data or relationship type requirements, which makes them suitable substitutes under certain circumstances.

Somewhat complicating the picture are the mixed-scale correlations, particularly where one variable is measured on a metric scale (i.e., interval or ratio) while the other one is measured on a non-metric scale (i.e., nominal or ordinal). There are two approaches to dealing with such situations:

1. Re-code the metric into a non-metric variable and use Spearman's rank correlation coefficient if the result is an ordinally-scaled variable and use the polychoric correlation with dichotomies (see Table 9.2). This takes advantage of the fact that continuously measured variables are informationally richer, which means they can always be reduced into categorical ones, simply by breaking out their continuous values into discrete ranges. Of course, the re-coding process tends to be arbitrary since most continuous scales do not have natural discrete break points.

2. The second approach is to replace the product-moment correlation with amended formulations which account for scale differences. As shown in Table 9.2 there are multiple coefficients available: the *biserial, polyserial, polychoric, point biserial, phi,* etc. In general, the choice of the appropriate formulation is primarily a function of the type of measurement scale and its constancy between the variables being correlated. Specifically, different computational methods should be used when both variables have the same scale characteristics—such as both are ordinal or nominal—versus when their measurement scales are different, such as one is ordinal and the other is nominal. Figure 9.7 below offers a simple decision rule to be used when choosing among the available correlation formulations.

Figure 9.7
Correlation Coefficient Types

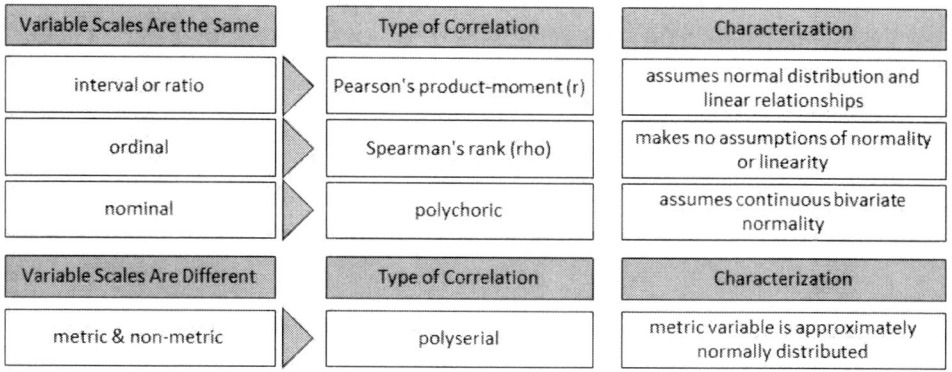

Variable Scales Are the Same	Type of Correlation	Characterization
interval or ratio	Pearson's product-moment (r)	assumes normal distribution and linear relationships
ordinal	Spearman's rank (rho)	makes no assumptions of normality or linearity
nominal	polychoric	assumes continuous bivariate normality

Variable Scales Are Different	Type of Correlation	Characterization
metric & non-metric	polyserial	metric variable is approximately normally distributed

To select an appropriate formulation, start out by identifying the measurement scale of each of the variables to be correlated. As discussed earlier, a random variable can be nominal, ordinal, interval or ratio. *Nominally scaled* variables carry no ordering or magnitudinal information whatsoever—they are simply labels intended primarily for convenience. Although their informational value is quite limited, the biserial correlation coefficient can be used to quantify their relations to a metrically measured variable. An *ordinal scale* is informationally richer as here the individual categories are rank-ordered, although it is still limited insofar as it contains no information about the cross-category spacing (i.e., spacing is not assumed to be equal or have any other numerical properties). An even richer source of information is the *interval scale*, which in addition to being rank-ordered is also assumed to be equally-spaced (i.e., the distance between adjoining pairs of values is constant across the entire value continuum, which means that the measurement distance between values 1 and 2 is the same as the distance between values 2 and 3, 4 and 5, etc.). Lastly, the *ratio scale* contains all of the informational characteristics of the other three scales, in addition to which it also has a rational point of origin, such as age or income.

If both variables are measured with either an interval or a ratio scale (they could both be the same, or one interval <u>and</u> the other ratio) and their distributions are approximately normal <u>and</u> their relationship is assumed to be more-or-less linear, Pearson's product-moment correlation will yield the most robust estimate of the their relationship. If, on the other hand, either of those conditions is not met—i.e., the variables are not either interval or ratio, at least one is not normally distributed or their relationship is believed to not be linear, Spearman's rank correlation is the appropriate choice[17]. An example of a typical output depicting a correlation matrix, using Pearson's product-moment method is shown below.

Figure 9.8
Two-Tailed Correlations with Significance Tests

		factor_1	factor_2	factor_3	factor_4	factor_5	factor_6	factor_7
factor_1	Pearson Correlation	1	.987**	-.166*	-.260**	-.072	-.312**	.797**
	Sig. (2-tailed)		.000	.011	.000	.272	.000	.000
	N	235	235	235	235	235	235	235
factor_2	Pearson Correlation	.987**	1	-.153*	-.242**	-.054	-.329**	.798**
	Sig. (2-tailed)	.000		.019	.000	.408	.000	.000
	N	235	235	235	235	235	235	235
factor_3	Pearson Correlation	-.166*	-.153*	1	.535**	.199**	-.139*	-.113
	Sig. (2-tailed)	.011	.019		.000	.002	.033	.084
	N	235	235	235	235	235	235	235
factor_4	Pearson Correlation	-.260**	-.242**	.535**	1	.268**	-.142*	-.213**
	Sig. (2-tailed)	.000	.000	.000		.000	.029	.001
	N	235	235	235	235	235	235	235
factor_5	Pearson Correlation	-.072	-.054	.199**	.268**	1	-.022	.013
	Sig. (2-tailed)	.272	.408	.002	.000		.737	.839
	N	235	235	235	235	235	235	235
factor_6	Pearson Correlation	-.312**	-.329**	-.139*	-.142*	-.022	1	-.362**
	Sig. (2-tailed)	.000	.000	.033	.029	.737		.000
	N	235	235	235	235	235	235	235
factor_7	Pearson Correlation	.797**	.798**	-.113	-.213**	.013	-.362**	1
	Sig. (2-tailed)	.000	.000	.084	.001	.839	.000	
	N	235	235	235	235	235	235	235

** Correlation is significant at the 0.01 level (2-tailed).
* Correlation is significant at the 0.05 level (2-tailed).

As shown in Figure 9.8, aside from the correlation coefficient itself there are several other pieces of information included in the output, all playing a distinct though somewhat different role in the evaluation of the correlation results.

The first is the effective sample size. An *effective* sample size is the actual number of cases used in the particular analysis, which is contrasted with a *nominal* sample size, which is the total number of cases in the dataset. Under certain circumstance, most notably a persistent missing value problem, the effective sample size can be quite smaller than the nominal one, which at some point may diminish the robustness of the findings. What then is the minimum acceptable sample size? There is no single concrete minimum, as that usually dependent on multiple factors, most importantly the amount of variation in the data. That said, the best general guideline to minimum sample sizing can be derived from the Central Limit Theorem, which states that whenever a random sample is taken from any distribution, the sample means will be approximately normally distributed, which seems to imply that beyond a certain point sample size expansion may not be necessary. The proverbial $64,000 question is, of course, what is that threshold? As a general rule of thumb, it is believed that fewer than about 30 observations calls for nonparametric analysis, while more than 30 but fewer than 50 observations should be treated with caution. In other words, a sample size of as few as 50 records may be sufficient. As previously discussed, normal distribution is a requirement of Pearson's product-moment correlation; hence attaining an appropriately sized sample is important to the validity of the statistic.

In practice, however, prohibitively small sample sizes are relatively rare, given the size of most databases. Interestingly, the sample size "over-abundance" is a more likely challenge as too large a sample size can lead to an artificial inflation of statistical significance, a commonly used though controversial measure of the non-spuriousness of correlation and other coefficients. This is an important consideration and as such is discussed in more detail in the subsequent section.

Lastly, a proper assessment of a correlation coefficient also involves a choice between a one- and a two-tail test. A *one-tail test* is used to identify events that are different only in one direction in reference to the average—such as customer spending levels that are considerably above the average. In that sense, a one-tail test would not differentiate between the average and extremely small values, as it is focused on detecting only abnormally large values. A *two-tail test*, on the other hand, can be used to identify values that are either significantly greater or smaller than the expected or average values. Naturally, the two-tail test is informationally richer because it can detect unexpected events on both ends of the continuum—those significantly larger as well as significantly smaller than the average or expected values.

It is also necessary to specify the level of *statistical significance.* Technically, the significance level of a test is the maximum probability of incorrectly rejecting a true null hypothesis, which is also known as the Type I error[18]. Since the null hypothesis typically stipulates that there are no differences between the entities being tested, the concept of statistical significance is in fact a measure of the amount of risk an analyst is willing to accept in concluding that noteworthy differences exist where in fact there are none. In the context of correlation analyses, significance testing is used to assess the degree to which the reported bivariate correlations are manifestations of enduring relationships are a mere product of random chance. However, statistical significance testing suffers from some severe deficiencies, which are particularly evident in the context of database analytics. Given the pivotal role of significance testing in virtually all sample-based analyses, the limitations of significance testing deserve a more exhaustive treatment, presented in the next section.

Beware of Significance Tests!

Statistical significance tests (SST) are a hypothesis testing tool, the purpose of which is to identify universally true effects. SST's secondary and closely related objective is that of generalizing sample-based insights onto a larger population. Although principally a theory development method, significance testing has in recent years been adopted to promotional program measurement where it gained quick acceptance as the impact validation standard.

Operationally, SST utilizes any of the known distribution statistical difference tests, such as F, t, or χ^2 to compare observed to expected effects with the purpose of distinguishing between spurious and persistent relationships. While the statistics utilized in significance testing (i.e., the above referenced F, t, or χ^2) are themselves methodologically sound, their program measurement applications tend to outstretch their usability limits leading to misapplications and misinterpretations. Some of it is due to simple user error, but a considerable share of SST misuse can be attributed to fundamental lack of fit between theory testing and typical business objectives.

Although rarely compared "side-by-side", theory testing and applied knowledge creation processes differ on some very important dimensions. Perhaps most importantly, theory testing aims to uncover universally true knowledge claims, while business analytics focus on the identification of sustainable competitive advantage. It follows that significance testing is used as a sample-to-population generalization tool for scientific theory building purposes, and as a now-to-future or longitudinal replicability tool for applied knowledge creation. This is a critical distinction as it gives rise to one of the more common SST application errors discussed later in this text.

Another common SST misapplication stems from its dependence on sample size. Sample size and the likelihood of detecting statistical significance are highly correlated, so much so that at a moderately large sample size even inordinately trivial differences can become statistically significant, while not being statistically significant at a smaller sample size (everything else being the same). For a variety of reasons that are not important at this moment, theory testing research typically utilizes small sample sizes leading to limited sample size distortion. The opposite, however, is true for most applied business endeavors which depend on large scale (i.e., large sample size) for business viability, resulting in a considerable sample size distortion.

Expected precision of estimates is yet another albeit more subtle theory testing vs. applied business knowledge creation distinction. In short, while theory development is primarily concerned with the identification of universally true relationships and less so with the exact quantification of the magnitude of effects, business analyses are almost single-mindedly focused on quantifying the impact of actual or contemplated courses of action. It is a matter of pragmatism: The goal of business actions, such claims handling policy changes, is to benefit a particular organization only; hence it is of little concern to business analyses if a particular relationship is not generalizable to other users. In fact, from the standpoint of a particular organization, the lack of cross-user generalizability is actually a preferred outcome.

Putting the above pieces together suggests that when applied to a large scale database analytical initiatives, statistical significance testing is of questionable value for three key reasons: First, extremely small treated vs. control differences are likely to be found statistically significant even if their magnitude renders them practically inconsequential, which will then give rise to the previously discussed statistical vs. practical significance divergence, ultimately leading to SST misapplication. Secondly, significance testing does not support future replicability generalizations, which means that we cannot use the results from today's test as basis for forming expectations regarding tomorrow's rollout; again, an issue of central importance to promotional program measurement. Thirdly, cause attributable effect cannot be expressed as an exact quantity, which although not a show-stopper is still less than ideal, particularly when the range of effects encompasses both positive and negative values.

Those are not trivial differences. Significance tests are computationally relatively straightforward and highly suggestive of normative applicability limits. At the same time, the goals of the theory building and practical applications focused analyses are oftentimes quite different. The interaction between the significance tests' applicability limits and the different (i.e., theoretical vs. practical) applications of those tests are sufficient to question the wisdom of unqualified significance testing usage in business applications. SST's sample size dependence (i.e., the likelihood of a given relationship being deemed "statistically" significant increases as the sample size gets larger, everything else being the same), inability to support longitudinal conclusions (i.e., offering an objective quantification of the probability of future replicability of current relationships) or the basic incommensurability of scientific and business objectives (i.e., seeking universally true generalizations vs. future replicability) all highlight the dangers of blind SST reliance by business analysts.

Faced with these shortcomings of an otherwise key methodological element, analysts grew accustomed to drawing a line of demarcation between the statistical and practical significance. In effect, it has become a commonplace in applied business analytics to expressly differentiate between the "statistically significant results we accept" (i.e., the results that are deemed both statistical and practically significant) and the "statistically significant result we do not accept" (i.e., the results that are statistically significant but at the same time are assumed to be practically insignificant). Let's pause for a minute: Isn't there something unsettling about the manifestly *quantitative* statistical significance tests having to be *qualified* in order to become of value to business analyses? By extension, isn't it equally unsettling that the task of differentiating between "important" and "not important" statistically significant results—for those who believe in the validity of such split—be a matter of a subjective judgment? And finally, if significance testing is indeed a robust and objective program impact validation tool, why is there even a need to arbitrarily accept some of its "significant" findings while rejecting other equally statistically "significant" findings?

Explain: Multivariate Analyses

Although potentially insightful, bivariate correlation is, well, only bivariate. In many business contexts the development of true understanding requires the assessment of an interplay of multiple factors, which in tech talk translates into multivariate (i.e., multi-variable) analyses. Oftentimes, even making more sense out of the observed correlations requires a broader, multi-variable analyses as it is common for two key variables to be correlated due to being jointly driven by a third factor. Furthermore, as previously noted, correlation is non-directional, as reflected in an often-cited adage of "correlation is not causation." Length of employment and claim costs might be correlated, but from a business standpoint a more pertinent question is: Does the length of employment really cause the total cost of claims to rise? Consider Figure 9.9 below:

Figure 9.9
Correlation and Dependence

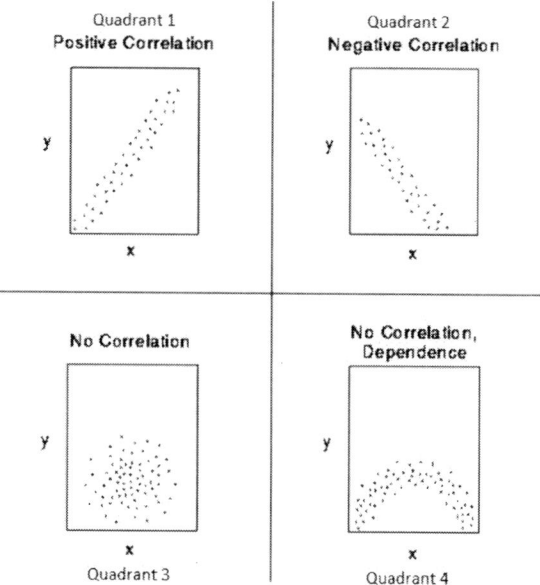

The four quadrants depicted above suggest that aside from the presence of either a positive (Quadrant 1) or a negative (Quadrant 2) relationships, the correlation analysis can also reveal that there is no linear relationship between the variables of interest (Quadrant 3), but what it cannot detect is a non-linear relationship suggesting a *dependence* of one variable on the other (Quadrant 4). Overall, the bivariate correlation illustrate above can be quite helpful in shedding light on the existence of a potential X-Y relationship, but it falls short of offering even a minimal amount of *causal* explanation—in other words, is X causing Y, or is Y causing X?

Generally, the type of relationship depicted in Quadrant 4 is reflective of curvilinear effects, which are most effectively explored—in a causal sense— with the help of multiple regression analyses and more specifically, by computing higher-order effects. Only focusing on the two variables X and Y, where the value of Y is believed to depend on the value of X, the Y-X dependence can be tested as shown below:

$$y = \alpha + \beta x_1 + \beta x_1^2 + \varepsilon$$

where,

α is an intercept term (practically interpretable only when the β terms equal 0)

βx_1 is a test of linear dependence of X on Y

βx_1^2 is a test of curvilinear dependence of X on Y

ε is an error term, or the unexplained residual

Another common analytical data exploratory challenge involves describing interactions taking place in the context of dependence analysis. As mentioned earlier, a correlation between X and Y can be a result of both X and Y being impacted by yet another factor, Z. For instance, the cost of an on-the-job accident (Y) can be a function of the injured worker's age (X), as well as pre-existing health conditions (Z). The assessment of an interaction between these two predictors (X and Z) involves computing a new variable that is a multiplicative combination of X and Z, technically known as an interaction term. As a result, to test the dependence of Y on X and Z, inclusive of potential X-Z interactions, the resultant multiple regression model needs to specify the following set of dependencies:

$$y = \alpha + \beta_1 x_1 + \beta_2 x_2 + \beta_{12} x_1 x_2 + \varepsilon$$

where,

α is an intercept term (practically interpretable only when the β term equals 0)

$\beta_1 x_1$ is linear dependence of X on Y

$\beta_2 x_2$ is linear dependence of Z on Y

$\beta_{12} x_1 x_2$ is multiplicative dependence of X and Z on Y (X-Z interaction)

ε is an error term, or the unexplained residual

The above implicitly assumes that X, Y and Z are all continuous, which is obviously not always the case. Factorial analysis of variance (ANOVA), a special case of regression analysis, is perhaps the best known analytical tool for tackling that problem. The inner-working of ANOVA is somewhat different from that of the above outlined regression: In essence, ANOVA carries out a number of tests, where the means of the dependent variable, such as incurred claim cost, are compared across a number of different factors (individual categories of independent variables, such as cause or nature of accident designations) and their levels. The end objective is to pinpoint statistically significant[19] interactions between specific factor-level conjoints and the dependent variable of interest.

The so-operationalized pursuit of maximally complete explanation typically brings to the forefront the notion of informational domain specification, the goal of which is to answer the basic question: Is the available data sufficient to generate a complete explanation of the phenomenon of interest?

Informational Domain Specification

Throughout the Risk Profile Measurement process detailed in this book there are several "transitions" where the objective, well-codified science of data analysis intersect the subjective and rarely-codified art, or perhaps more correctly stated, intuition of the analyst. Correctly specifying the informational domain is likely the pinnacle of that intersection.

In everyday terms, *informational domain specification* (IDS) is the process by means of which the analyst selects and arranges specific (raw) data elements to form a conceptual model, based upon which specific (statistical) analyses and tests will be carried out, all with the goal of answering the questions posed by the stated informational needs. IDS itself represents an intersection of several competing considerations: First, the scope, in terms of the selected variables, needs to be sufficient. Second, the selected variable list needs to be non-redundant and operationally comparable (i.e., variables that are to be related to each other on the same plain of abstraction need to expressed at a comparable level of aggregation). Third, the model needs to exhibit a certain level of parsimony—in other words, throwing every conceivable metric into the mix is undesirable from both the statistical (introduction of numerous, albeit spurious correlations tends to detract from finding a clear solution) and interpretational (describing an outcome in terms of an excessively large number of "important" factors in some way defeats the purpose of conducting the analysis) points of view.

In terms of the outcomes of the IDS process, the informational domain can be just-, over- or under-specified. Ideally, an informational domain is *just-specified*, which is accomplished when a sufficient number of non-trivial explanatory variables are available. Of course, knowing whether or not that is the case is in many regards "half the battle." First of all, no single, objective appropriate number of variables benchmark exists, largely because the number of metrics is not important per se, so long as the resultant solution is manageable and maximally explanatory. In other words, the number of explanatory variables is sufficiently but not excessively large when it yields a statistically exhaustive explanation, i.e., the model explains the vast majority of the variability in the data, while at the same time, it is small enough to be parsimonious[20] and practically actionable. Given the obvious difficulty of balancing the number of variables and the amount of explanation contained in the model, more often than not a domain is either under- or over-specified.

An *under-specified informational domain* is one that yields too few non-trivial explanatory variables, which translates into insufficiently small amount of the variability in the data being explained by the model (which means that any predictions made based on such a model are likely to be unstable as well as inaccurate). On the other hand, an *over-specified domain* is one that depends on an excessively large number of trivial, yet correlated explanatory factors, for the explanation of the variability in the data. This is typically an indication of either a relative scarcity of truly explanatory data, or a poor data management strategy, such as making use of too many disaggregate metrics.

In practice, informational under-specification diminishes the explanatory power and reliability of information, simply because under-specified explanations are spurious, or chance-driven. Over-specified explanations, on the other hand, are interpretationally cumbersome because they employ an excessively large number of practically unimportant factors. Under-specification is most often a function of data scarcity, which in many instances is hard to remedy. Over-specification is usually a function of flawed variable retention rationale, such as the use of too many disaggregate metrics or over-reliance on statistical significance testing[21], which is used frequently as a variable inclusion or retention standard. Excessive dependence on statistical significance tests increases the likelihood that variables of negligible importance will be included alongside highly explanatory factors, particularly as the sample size increases. As large sample size analyses are becoming a commonplace due to the proliferation of large databases coupled with rapid gains in data processing technologies, the frequency of the significance testing induced informational over-specification increases, which is a cause for concern, especially in the context of transforming large volumes of data into a manageable number of decision-guiding insights.

Although much of the informational domain specification is situational, as it depends of the specific characteristics of data, there are a number of general steps that can be taken to increase the likelihood of it being just-specified. The key strategies are detailed in Table 9.3.

Table 9.3
Informational Domain Specification Strategies

Consideration	Description
Metric Aggregation	Event-tracking and other databases usually are made up of variables that exhibit various degrees of aggregation, or specificity. Since some of the data is a byproduct of operations, such as risk management systems, while other data are purposefully acquired and still other data types represent third-party estimates, such as geodemographics, the resultant metric mosaic may be quite dissimilar in terms of its basic informational properties. Homogenizing the individual metrics' levels of aggregation can be a relatively complex task, as it may entail computing summary measures for detailed, indicator-level metrics. Nonetheless, combining detailed metrics into more aggregate, summary-level variables will have the desirable effect of reducing the number of explanatory variables while retaining the bulk of the original metrics' informational content.
Indexing	As it is used in the risk profiling process outlined in this book, indexing refers to assigning of pre-determined labels to database records with the goal of delineating distinct and non-overlapping categories. In some regards, indexing leads to the creation of "shadow" variables, which are typically used as basis for record grouping and homogenization of analytical subsets, such as identifying and subsequently selecting (for analysis) only certain types of accidents. The resultant metrics are almost always categorical which, as previously discussed, may limit the usability of such metrics in certain contexts. At the same time, indexing expands the informational domain by creating new predictors.
Transforming	Nominally, variable transformations, the goal of which is to amend the underlying distributional properties of the individual measures (such as correcting for skewness with the goal of bringing about approximate normality) offers a yet another possible IDS aiding strategy. Within the confines of risk analytics, however, this approach is rarely appropriate, primarily because it leads to the attenuation of the effects (such as large losses) that form the ultimate target of the analysis.

CONFIDENCE INTERVALS

More often than not, business analyses are focused on delineating fairly specific informational outcomes, which in statistical jargon are known as *point estimates*, or single numbers that can be regarded as sensible values for a particular parameter. For example, when projecting the expected future cost of a risk-related event, such as a natural storm or litigation, organizations are interested in single-value estimates. Though understandable from the business standpoint it can nonetheless be troublesome from the analytical perspective, primarily because single-value estimates are often methodologically implausible. The reason for that is that in the vast majority of cases the underlying data are imperfect, which means that any inferences drawn from such data need to explicitly account for that imperfection, which is best accomplished with the use of confidence intervals.

A *confidence interval* is a range of most likely values for an estimated parameter. We expect that range to encompass the "actual" population parameter of interest, such as the population mean, with an a priori decided upon degree of certainty, which is a reflection of our willingness of being wrong. For instance, the commonly used 95% confidence interval is a reflection of the analyst's willingness to accept a 5% chance (or 1-in-20) of being wrong in his/her conclusions. The willingness of being wrong is usually shown as α, hence $\alpha = 0.05$ is synonymous with 95% confidence interval.

Interval-based estimation is important because random sampling error and other noise in the data essentially guarantee a certain level of imprecision of estimates. For example, if we were to compute an average cost for a particular set of insurance claims (i.e., a sample), the resultant estimate would more than likely be somewhat smaller or larger than the "true" (i.e., actual) average cost for the population as a whole. Consequently, if we were to draw multiple samples from the population, each sample would yield a somewhat numerically different estimate. Hence, in order for us to obtain a meaningful estimate of the average cost of the entire population of claims, we should express our sample-based estimate as a range, rather than a single (i.e., a point) estimate.

Given that virtually all data used in risk analyses contains some degree of noise, the above reasoning applies to estimates stemming from descriptive analyses described in this chapter. In other words, rather than exact values— i.e., point estimates—range of most likely values—i.e., confidence intervals— should be reported and used in describing the phenomenon of interest. As far as the aforementioned degree of certainty, the choice is highly situational. It has become customary to "default" to 95% degree of certainty, but there is nothing magical about that particular choice. 90% and 99% confidence intervals are also used in theoretical research, usually to highlight a marginal or a particularly pronounced, respectively, relationship. In applied business research, analysts at time compute 80% (1-in-5 chance of being wrong) confidence intervals – is it too low? There is no single answer, as it dependents on what one considers to be an acceptable chance of drawing an incorrect conclusion.

To compute a confidence interval for the population; two-sided:

$$Lower\ Limit\ =\ \bar{X}\ -\ t_{1-\frac{\alpha}{2}}(n-1)\frac{s}{\sqrt{n}}$$

$$Upper\ Limit\ =\ \bar{X}\ +\ t_{1-\frac{\alpha}{2}}(n-1)\frac{s}{\sqrt{n}}$$

To compute a confidence interval for the population; one-sided:

$$Lower\ Limit\ =\ \bar{X}\ -\ t_{1-\alpha}(n-1)\frac{s}{\sqrt{n}}$$

$$Upper\ Limit\ =\ \bar{X}\ +\ t_{1-\alpha}(n-1)\frac{s}{\sqrt{n}}$$

where,

$\bar{X}$ is the estimated mean
n is the sample size
α is the desired confidence level
s is the standard deviation
t is the upper critical value of the t-distribution (with n-1 df)

Interpretation

The interpretation of the confidence interval is couched in terms of probability, but will differ depending on which of the two probability schools of thought an analyst subscribes to: A Frequentist will interpret a 95% confidence interval as follows: 95% of the time the intervals computed using the same sampling procedure will capture the true value of the unknown quantity, while the remaining 5% of the time they will not. Stated differently, 95% of all possible random samples selected from the same population can be

233

expected to result in an interval that will capture the true value of the underlying population, as long as the calculating procedure remains unchanged. However, we cannot know if a single interval would fall in the 95% correct or the 5% incorrect portion.

A Bayesian interpretation is somewhat closer to the "everyday" usage of the confidence interval notion. It holds that for any of the calculated intervals, we can be 95% certain (or confident) that the interval contains the "true" value of the unknown quantity, again, assuming invariance of the measurement procedure.

Looking beyond the philosophical differences, the width of the confidence interval is a reflection of its precision, where a tighter interval (i.e., smaller range between the upper and lower limits) suggests higher precision of the estimate. That said, there are two distinct factors that impact the precision of confidence level estimates: significance level and sample size. The higher the desired level of confidence, i.e., the closer it is to 100%[22], the wider the resultant lower—upper confidence limit range. On the other hand, the sample size has the opposite effect on the precision of estimates: The larger the sample size, the higher the resultant precision—i.e., the narrower the confidence interval range. The latter conclusion is probably a bit less intuitively obvious than the former, however, it should become clear upon a closer examination of the confidence interval computational formulas presented earlier. In essence, both the upper and lower confidence intervals are a product of three distinct elements: the mean, level of significance factor and the standard error[23]. The standard error, as discussed earlier (and illustrated in the one- and two-side confidence interval formulas), is computed by dividing the standard deviation by the square root of sample size—i.e., the larger the sample size, the smaller the resultant standard error, everything else being the same. A smaller standard error will in turn translate into a smaller up and down deviation from the mean, hence a narrower confidence interval range.

10

Knowledge Creation:
Predictive Analytics

W hat is the reason companies succeed? Why do some organizations prosper in the same environment where others struggle? Obviously, this is not an easy question to answer. Authors Tom Peters and Robert Waterman famously tackled that topic in their 1982 book *In Search of Excellence*, in which they spelled out eight communalities shared by excellent organizations, in effect asserting that those factors were the key drivers of success of companies. Their book was certainly a publishing success (it quickly became one of the best-selling business books of all time, with 3 million copies sold in just the first four years), but their conclusions were just as quickly shown to be flawed[1].

More recently, Thomas Davenport and Jeanne Harris suggested that the extensive use of *analytics*, defined as statistical analysis of data used to analyze business problems, has a positive and a measurable impact on the quality of decisions such as customer management, supply chain and financial performance. In their 2005 book, *Competing on Analytics: The New Science of Winning*, Davenport and Harris assert that a number of high performing organizations are deriving their competitive strategies from data-driven insights. In other words, the quality of decision guiding information is one of the drivers of success.

As far as I can tell, Davenport and Harris' book has not sold anywhere near the number of copies of *In Search of Excellence*, but I think it nonetheless contains more true kernels of knowledge. *Competing on Analytics* offers compelling evidence for something we have known for several decades, namely, that rational decision-making, or one where objective and logically consistent rules are used to solve problems, will yield measurable gains. Not only is this an intuitively compelling idea, but it has been formally taught under the umbrella of "decision sciences" as a part of business curriculum for the past several decades. I should note that my goal is not dismiss the idea that a momentary inspiration can occasionally produce impressive results—I am merely suggesting that effective, ongoing management is primarily the product of perspiration, not inspiration. And methodical exploration of the available data is one of its tools of trade.

On a more micro level, making sound decisions in a competitive setting resembles the game of chess, insofar as the ability to estimate the most likely response to one's "move" is one of the strongest determinants of the final outcome. This line of thinking is best exemplified by the famed "machine vs. man" chess match, in which an IBM-developed chess-playing computer, Deep Blue, defeated the world chess champion Garry Kasparov in 1997[2]. In the vast majority of cases, business contests are far less dramatic and take far longer to be decided, but nonetheless it all boils down to skillful and purposeful utilization of not just available, but appropriate information. As I mentioned in the opening chapter, virtually all organizations have data – the difference-maker is the efficacy with which the otherwise generic data is used. This is particularly true in the area broadly described as "predictive analytics", which has become a major contributor to organizational risk management efforts and as such, it plays a key role in the Risk Profile Measurement process detailed in this book.

PREDICTIVE ANALYTICS

Although it may not be immediately obvious, business (and thus risk) analytics can be thought of as an operational outgrowth of the *scientific method*, which is a broadly defined mode of inquiry. It is based on gathering empirical evidence, through observation or experimentation, which is then used to test hypotheses that have been formulated in adherence to specific principles of reasoning. As such, the scientific method is the mean to an end; a broadly defined knowledge building mechanism, the goal of which is to derive universally true generalizations which can be used to explain the past and predict (in the sense of probabilistic estimation) the future. Although business analytics makes very heavy use of the tools of science, our focus is rarely—if ever—on building universally true generalizations. The essence of competitiveness suggests that not only is it not necessary for business analysts to pursue universally true generations—it could even be seen as being counterproductive.

Within the realm of risk management, the goal of data analyses is to estimate the probability and severity of outcomes of importance to the well-being of an organization. In recent years, data analytical efforts directed at making such predictive estimates of outcomes or phenomena of interest to organizations became synonymous with terms such as "predictive analytics" or "data mining".

In applied business settings, the terms *data mining* (DM) and *predictive analytics* (PA) are at times used interchangeably, which is incorrect. Both in terms the underlying methodologies as well as the applied business outcomes, these two data analytical approaches are quite dissimilar. The most fundamental difference between DM and PA is that the former is exploratory in nature, while the latter is confirmatory. Stated differently, data mining is synonymous with data exploration, which is an open-ended (i.e., not aimed at validating of any specific relationships) search for any relationships that can characterize a particular data set. In short, it is akin to saying: "I would like to find out if data I have available to me contains any insights that I could use to inform my decisions; I don't have any preexisting beliefs regarding the possible existence or nature of those relationships." Although often associated with highly automated database analytic applications (such as SPSS Modeler or SAS Enterprise Miner tools), DM can also employ more manual and "traditional" approaches such as bivariate or canonical correlation, cross-tabulation, multidimensional scaling, cluster analysis, factor analysis and a number of other analytic tools. Specific method notwithstanding, data mining is a retrospective exercise geared toward uncovering any relationships or associations that might be imbedded in data.

Unlike data mining, predictive analytics is focused on parameterization of specific relationships. It is akin to saying: "I believe that certain factors, such as accounting accruals, stock price volatility and the frequency of restatements play a role in the likelihood and severity of securities class action litigation; I would like to empirically verify my suspicion and if I am right, to quantify the impact of those factors on the likelihood and severity of securities class actions." In a technical sense, *predictive analytics* is the deployment of multivariate mathematical modeling techniques to quantitative data with the goal of estimating future outcomes. As noted earlier, it is a confirmatory approach, which is to say that its goal is to provide an empirical substantiation of suspected relationships. In contrast to the open-ended nature of DM, PA is focused on estimating the future state of previously identified relationships or interdependencies. Hence it follows that under most circumstances, predictive analytics should build upon the exploratory findings of data mining.

In a somewhat more obtuse theoretical sense, data mining can be viewed as a theory building tool, while predictive analytics as a theory testing mechanism. In practice, this distinction translates into period vs. ongoing usage, respectively. Within the confines of the RPM Framework described in this book, where analytical objectives are shaped by stated risk management objectives, data mining is effectively reduced to conformation (or rejection) of those objectives-implied relationships. Simply put, the RPM Framework is confirmatory in nature, which points to predictive analytics as the dominant methodological mechanism.

Keeping the preceding in mind, in the context of risk management, predictive analytics yields two broadly defined and interrelated sets of outcomes:

1. *Future States' Parameterization.*
   Forecasting of future states—objectively estimating of likelihood and/or severity of individual risk types.
2. *Drivers of Risk Enumeration.*
   The delineation of the most pronounced influencers of the future state estimates (above), along with their respective elasticities.

Future States' Parameterization

The starting point in any analytical exercise is data. More specifically, it is an in-depth assessment of its contents and limitations, which is a necessary prerequisite to determining the degree to which the available data "falls in line" with the stated organizational goals-implied informational needs. Assuming that sufficient (both in terms of quality as well as quantity) data are available, quantitative analyses are deployed to parameterize the relationships and outcomes of interest. Parameterization is a broadly defined process of numerically estimating the impact of theorized risk drivers or expected future values of outcomes of interest. Very simply, it involves estimating values of individual coefficients representing the impact of risk drivers or expected values of future states of interest. The former are exemplified by specific measures believed to precipitate or at least contribute to specific risk-related outcomes, such the nature of injury associated with casualty claims or precipitous stock price decline raising the possibility of securities litigation, while the latter typically represent the likelihood of those outcomes—i.e., the said casualty claims securities class action litigation.

Hence it follows that there are two distinct parameterization focal points: 1. Input, or risk driver parameterization or 2. Outcome parameterization, as illustrated below in Figure 10.1.

Figure 10.1
Predictive Analytics

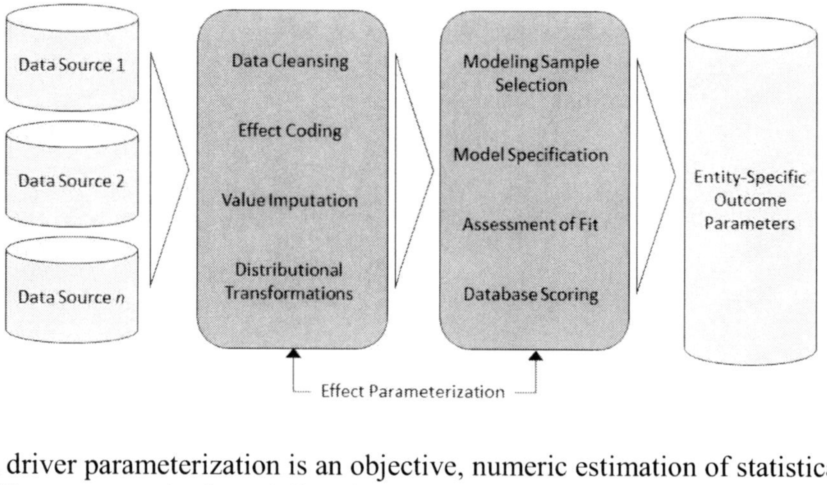

Risk driver parameterization is an objective, numeric estimation of statistical significance, magnitude and direction of each potential risk predicting factor. As noted earlier, the RPM process is built around the notion of "prediction by explanation", which is to say that past outcomes (such as accident claims, in terms of their occurrence as well as magnitude) are explained with the help of the available descriptive (such as demographics or behavioral profiles) and causal (such as nature of accident, cause of accident, type of injury) metrics, utilizing multivariate statistical models. Multivariate statistical methodologies, such as regression models, are used to distill a (typically) large list of potential contributors to observed outcomes—such as claim frequency and severity—into a smaller set of factors that are systematically associated with those outcomes. Furthermore, the relative and absolute impact of each of those factors is also estimated. Altogether, this comprises the "explanation" part of the aforementioned "prediction by explanation" approach. In practical business terms, it constitutes risk driver parameterization.

Outcome parameterization is the objective, numeric estimation of likelihood and/or severity of specific future states. This is the second part of the "prediction by explanation", which is that of making forward-looking predictions, or estimating the likelihood and/or severity of specific, risk-related outcomes. It is a continuation of the "explanation" part of the process discussed earlier, insofar as applies the explanation of past outcomes to the future. Operationally, it entails the development of database scoring algorithms, the details of which are outlined in later chapters.

From the statistical point of view, the data analytical rationale utilized in the "prediction by explanation" process illustrated in Figure 10.1 is graphically depicted in Figure 10.2. Understanding of this rationale is important not only from the standpoint of establishing a solid knowledge base of how the conclusions were estimated, but it also carries important model efficacy testing implications, discussed later.

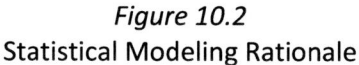

Figure 10.2
Statistical Modeling Rationale

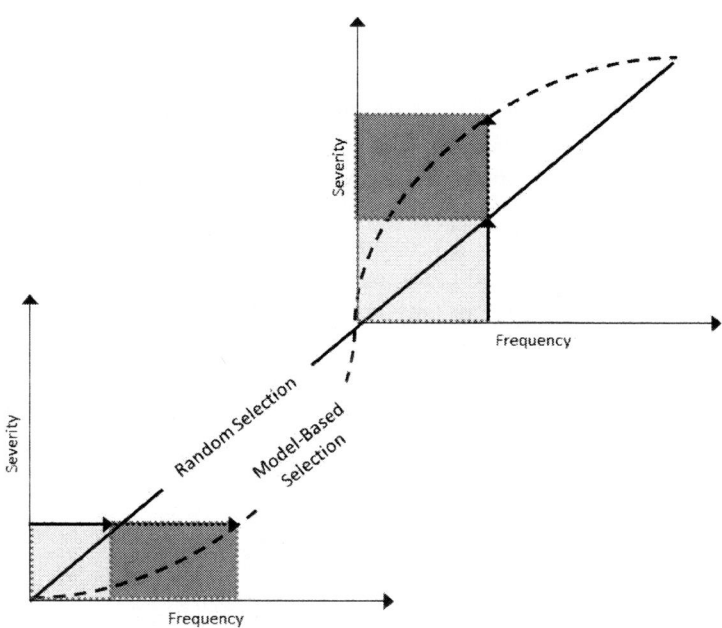

The two X-Y coordinates graphs above connected with the straight, solid line (labeled "Random Selection") show that, on average, a certain proportion of companies (let's say 20%) will account for a proportional share of claims (in this case, 20%), as denoted by the shaded regions in both graphs. The goal of statistical models is then to skew these proportions, in the manner shown by the dotted line (labeled "Model-Based Selection"), so that fewer selections will encompass a larger or a smaller number of cases. Those gains and losses are shown by the extensions to the shaded regions in both graphs. Here, the intersection of dotted curve and the dotted arrow (extending from the shaded area), show the amount of "lift" generated by the model. Lift, in the case of this type of statistical models, represents an increase in classification accuracy, over the "no model" selection. In terms of subsequent performance measurement, a well-performing model is one that can attain the greatest degree of skewing, which is where a relatively small proportion of the total number of companies (let's say 20%) can account for a disproportionately large share (let's say, 60%) of total claims.

241

More on Multivariate Modeling

Multivariate modeling techniques are ideally suited for "crunching" large volumes of historical data, simultaneously considering all available metrics and distilling the universe of the available measures to a handful of persistent and empirically validated indicators of outcomes of interest. In the broadest terms, multivariate statistical models can be categorized as either *predictive* or *descriptive* in nature. The former encompass the varying specifications of the dependent outcome vs. independent variate relationship, where the independent variate is a function comprised of a combination of multiple variables and the dependent outcome is the focus of explanation and the subsequent prediction. The latter are methods built around mutual interdependence and as such can only be used for descriptive, rather than prescriptive purposes. As suggested by the above definitions, predictive statistical techniques are the quantitative core of predictive analytics.

There are many different multivariate statistical models, each with its own type of analysis and applicability; with some of the more commonly used methods, or families of techniques, including:

> *Multivariate analysis of variance (MANOVA).*
> Those methods extend analysis of variance methods to cover cases where there is more than one dependent variable and where the dependent variables cannot simply be combined.
> *Discriminant or canonical analysis.*
> The goal of those methodologies is to determine if a set of variables can be used to distinguish between two or more groups.
> *Regression analyses.*
> A broad family of statistical techniques, including linear, log-linear, ordinal, logistic, logit, probit, among others; overall, regression models attempt to estimate how some variables respond to changes in other variables.
> *Neural networks.*
> These are highly automated, "black box" approaches, which is to say are built around a set of decision algorithms that cannot be easily explained and/or are not transparent in terms of their problem-solving logic.

All of the above techniques can be broadly categorized as "dependence methods." A *dependence technique* expressly attempts to explain or predict one variable (called a dependent variable) with the help of one or more independent variables. In other words, it seeks to assess the degree to which specific measures (independent variables) cause changes in outcomes of interest (dependent variable). The nature of causal, or dependence relationships can be either linear or non-linear, with the latter taking on a variety of different forms, which are generally dictated by the slope and the number of inflection points of the line describing the relationship. Given the infinite number of potential non-linear curves, a number of established statistical methodologies are based on specific, generalizable distributions, or types of dependence shapes.

As mentioned earlier, the single most important goal of multivariate statistical models is to make a prediction with regard to likelihood or the severity of outcomes of interest. A prediction, or more realistically, an estimate of future outcomes, is a product of impact-weighted multivariate preponderance. Within the realm of risk analytics, estimates are based on the proportion of multiple, statistically significant risk indicators that point toward either the high or the low end of the risk continuum, as illustrated below.

Figure 10.3
Impact-Weighted Multivariate Predictors

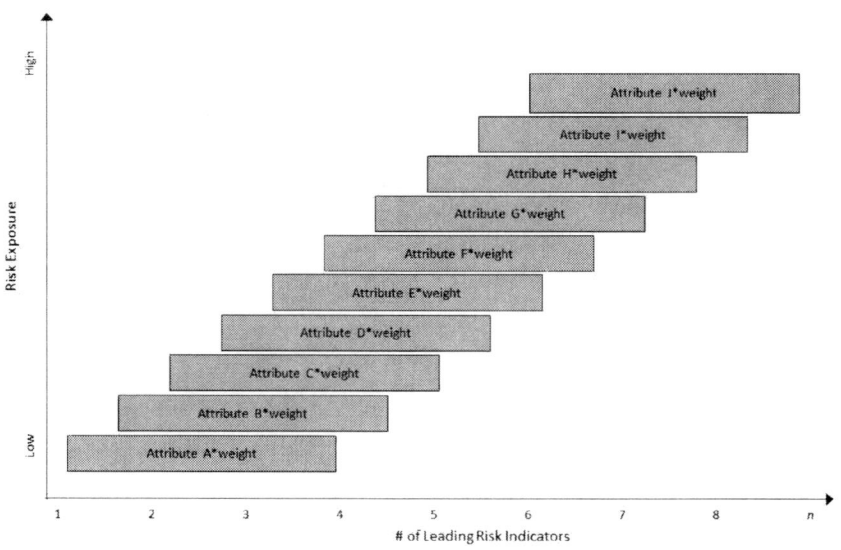

243

As shown in Figure 10.3, the overall likelihood or severity prediction is an additive function of individual, impact-weighted and statistically significant risk factors (though not shown, the predictive equation would also commonly include a constant term, which tends to enhance the accuracy of resultant estimates). From the methodological standpoint, there are two key issues that need to be addressed in the context of multivariate quantitative prediction: 1. variable coding and value adequacy (missing value proportion), and 2. model specification. Both are summarized in Table 10.1 below.

Table 10.1
Key Multivariate Modeling Considerations

Consideration	Description
Variable Coding	The vast majority of data is collected as a byproduct of business operations, which means that it is not always ideally suited for multivariate models. Aside from the degree of coverage (or looked from the flip side—the proportion of missing values), variables may be captured as multi-attribute composites (e.g., a *cause of accident* metric being a compilation of multiple potential codes) or as "yes vs. no" indicators, rather than frequencies. It is important to emphasize that those are not necessarily flaws, but rather impediments to robust data analyses (in other words, data can be perfectly usable 'as-is' for a number of other applications), nonetheless, specific steps may need to be taken to ensure the data's appropriateness for predictive modeling.
Model Specification	The degree to which a particular statistical model accounts for the bulk of the causes—in a relatively parsimonious fashion—behind the outcomes of interest reflects the strength of its specification. In other words, the focus of model specification is to ascertain to what degree the final multivariate statistical model "explains the most with the least." Admittedly, it is a far more esoteric consideration than the above discussed variable coding, but as discussed later, nonetheless an important aspect of risk modeling.

Impact Quantification

Operationally, risk can be expressed as a product of probability and severity, where Risk = (Likelihood of Occurrence) * (Economic Severity). In the realm of statistical analyses (or more specifically, statistical decision theory), risk is usually expressed as a product of parameter estimates computed for a set of observable indicators, often referred to as "drivers of risk." Hence the likelihood of occurrence is usually estimated as a probability of an undesirable event (i.e., risk factor) taking place, while the economic severity tends to be expressed as an estimate of the cost associated with that particular event. For methodological and practical purposes, these two dimensions of risk are usually estimated independently, and to the degree to which the two are indeed orthogonal, the overall "expected value of risk" (in the context of a particular type of risk) can be estimated by computing the product of likelihood and severity (in the event the two are highly correlated, likelihood and severity should not be combined in this manner).

The aggregate expected risk value can, however, be misleading. Let's consider two hypothetical events, A and B. Event A carries an estimated cost of $1MM, while event B carries a cost of $10MM. At the same time, Event A exhibits 90% chance of occurrence, while Event B exhibits only 9% chance of occurrence. In terms of their expected values, both risks are estimated at $900,000, though a reasonable (i.e., somewhat risk averse) individual would certainly be more comfortable with the Event B. The point here is that it ultimately might be more useful to present risk type specific exposure in terms of the severity and likelihood dimensions being shown separately, to make sure the maximum amount of information is presented to the decision maker.

Prediction Intervals

As noted earlier, sample based statistical inference is built upon an assumption of a certain degree of imprecision, which is largely a consequence of sampling variability and data incompleteness. The earlier discussion of descriptive analyses incorporated a notion of confidence intervals used to estimate the expected range of values of present characteristics. In a similar fashion, forward-looking predictions also entail a certain degree of imprecision which is expressed in the form of prediction intervals.

Prediction intervals represent an attempt at determining the most likely range of values for a quantity that is being predicted; it is a critically important part of any prediction is an assessment of how much a predicted value will fluctuate due to the noise in the data. Absent that information, it would be infeasible to draw cross-prediction comparisons or to compare the expected to target value. Prediction interval statistics are computed as follows:

Simultaneous prediction intervals for k future observations; two-side intervals:

$$Lower\ Limit = \bar{X} - t_{1-\frac{\alpha}{2k}}(n-1)s\sqrt{1+\frac{1}{n}}$$

$$Upper\ Limit = \bar{X} + t_{1-\frac{\alpha}{2k}}(n-1)s\sqrt{1+\frac{1}{n}}$$

Simultaneous prediction intervals for k future observations; one-side intervals:

$$Lower\ Limit = \bar{X} - t_{1-\frac{\alpha}{k}}(n-1)s\sqrt{1+\frac{1}{n}}$$

$$Upper\ Limit = \bar{X} + t_{1-\frac{\alpha}{k}}(n-1)s\sqrt{1+\frac{1}{n}}$$

Prediction intervals for the mean of k future observations; two-side intervals:

$$Lower\ Limit = \bar{X} - t_{1-\frac{\alpha}{2}}(n-1)s\sqrt{\frac{1}{k}+\frac{1}{n}}$$

$$Upper\ Limit = \bar{X} + t_{1-\frac{\alpha}{2}}(n-1)s\sqrt{\frac{1}{k}+\frac{1}{n}}$$

Prediction intervals for the mean of k future observations; one-side intervals:

$$Lower\ Limit = \bar{X} - t_{1-\alpha}(n-1)s\sqrt{\frac{1}{k}+\frac{1}{n}}$$

$$Upper\ Limit = \bar{X} + t_{1-\alpha}(n-1)s\sqrt{\frac{1}{k}+\frac{1}{n}}$$

where,

$\bar{X}$ is the estimated mean
n is the sample size
k is the number of future observations
α is the desired confidence level
s is the standard deviation
t is the upper critical value of the t-distribution (with n-1 df)

Requirements & Interpretation

Both types of statistical intervals—confidence and prediction—make two basic assumptions about the underlying data: independence and normality (both of which were discussed in more detail in the *Understanding Data* chapter). It is important to check, ahead of the parameterization, the distributional properties of the measures of interest as well as to ascertain the independence of the individual records used in the estimation process. Interpretation-wise, the meaning of prediction intervals parallels that of confidence intervals, which were discussed in the previous chapter.

Degree-of-Similarity Modeling

Within the realm of predictive analytics there is one general approach that is particularly well suited to the goals of risk analytics—it is known as the *degree-of-similarity modeling*. Data requirements-wise, it leverages historical outcomes (e.g., claims) and their potentially causal influences; logic-wise, it is built upon the idea of discerning the difference between outcome-homogenous groups of entities, such as high vs. low cost claims, or companies that incurred securities litigation vs. those that did not, and then using the patterns of learned differences as the basis for making forward-looking estimates.

The most often used contrasts (group-based comparisons) are binary, such as the simple dichotomy of yes vs. no, high vs. low; although multichomous contrasts are certainly methodologically and otherwise viable. The sampling considerations discussed earlier are, of course, of paramount importance to ascertaining the adequacy of representativeness of the groupings, as are the numerous statistical adequacy notions, also discussed in the *Understanding Data* chapter. The foundations of the degree-of-similarity approach are highly pragmatic, insofar as considerable weight is placed on factors that differentiated the desired vs. undesirable past outcomes; furthermore, the interpretation of the results tends to be intuitively obvious, as it is framed in a probabilistic context. In other words, the modeled degree of similarity to observed outcomes, such as the filing of an insurance claim, represents a probabilistic estimate of the likelihood of its future occurrence – the generalized modeling process is shown in Table 10.2.

Table 10.2

The Degree-of-Similarity Modeling Process

Step	Description	Decision
Modeling Samples Selection	Select representative samples	The sample sizes should be at least 50% higher than required to allow for future pruning;
	Quantify distributional similarity between the two samples	Weak test: Prepare side-by-side histograms (for the two samples), showing actual value labels and conduct visual, qualitative inspection of pairwise degrees of similarity. *Although not ideal, the weak test provides a "quick and dirty" look at the two samples and can be used effectively to identify metrics on which samples are grossly dissimilar.*
		Strong test: The logistic regression based "look-alike" modeling requires the predictor metrics to be either normally distributed or dummy-coded (for categorical variables). Hence a more robust alternative to a direct side-by-side distributional comparison is a normative contrast, where both samples' distributional properties are expressly assessed. If both samples are deemed "normal" in accordance with a priori established criteria, then they should be considered functionally identical. *A more objective and methodologically robust approach, the strong test should be used whenever possible.*
Model Building	Identify appropriate set of predictors	Assess the collinearity of predictors;
		Assess the appropriateness of individual variables' level of aggregation ;
		Review input data requirements, such as indicator variable coding for discrete variables;
	Fit the model / calibrate model coefficients	Review model's classificatory accuracy—the confusion matrix for logistic regression;
		Assess model's goodness-of-fit indicators—the pseudo R^2 statistic;
		Assess model's explanatory parsimony—review the predictive variate for number of predictors and assess the individual predictor's incremental explanatory contribution.

248

ADDITIONAL MODELING CONSIDERATIONS

Making behavioral predictions, as embodied in the notion of Predictive Analytics, carries a number of unique model-building considerations, some of which are frequently overlooked. The most salient of those considerations are detailed below.

Data vs. Statistical Effects

Any discussion of behavioral predictions needs to include an explicit differentiation between *data* and *statistical effects*. The key difference between the two is that the former exists independently of any modeling endeavors, while the latter is inextricably connected with a specific analytic exercise. A *statistical effect*, on the other hand, is a metric which is created with a specific analytical purpose in mind—i.e., it does not exist prior to, and often outside of, specific analytical endeavor.

Conceptually, data and statistical effects should be approached differently. Data can explored for the insights it hides, in which case little-to-no theoretical foundation is necessary. It can also be used in a prescriptive or predictive manner, in which case it is necessary to have at least a general theoretical model in mind, spelling out the presumed relationships.

Statistical effects, on the other hand, require a foundation of sound theoretical reasoning, largely due to practical considerations. Also, in contrast to data, which for most part is a manifestation of certain observable outcomes, such as product sales, statistical effects are intended to capture the intangible component of the forces shaping those outcomes, such as the interdependence of sales and promotional spending or the diminishing productivity extra promotional spending. In short, statistical effects represent means of modeling, or replicating reality with the goal of understanding (and quantifying) the impact of specific business actions. Although in theory there can be an infinite number of statistical effects, they tend to fall within the four basic categories: indicators, indices, interactions and velocitators.

Indicators

These typically dichotomous measures are used to denote the presence or absence of an event, trait or a phenomenon of interest. Often referred to in practice as "flags" or "dummy-coded variables", they are most frequently expressed as nominal measures, which means their analytic applicability is

249

relatively constrained (see the *Understanding Data* chapter for more detail). Coding-wise, indicators can be numeric (e.g., 0-1) or non-numeric (e.g., yes-no), though interpretation-wise the two connote the same meaning.

Indices

Most types of event-tracking databases entail repetition, whether it is multiple accident claims logged by the same claimant or repeat measures of certain outcomes, such as financial reports submitted to the SEC on quarterly or annual basis. Either way, this translates into a need to capture frequency counts of certain events or other occurrences. For instance, to be able to determine the number of claims filed by a single entity, such as an employee for workers' compensation claims or a shopper for general liability claims (for a retailer), it is necessary to link unique entity identifiers, such as social security numbers with claim numbers. Indices are metrics designed especially for the purpose of providing such frequency counts. In contrast to indicators, they are almost always numerically-coded and measured on either interval or ratio scales, which makes them more statistically versatile.

Interactions

What if the above mentioned indices and indicators were not sufficient to explain the variability contained in the data, yielding a statistically poor model fit and an inadequate amount of predictive power? One of tactics that can be used to improve the model's performance, without dramatically increasing the number of variables (which would take away from the model's parsimony, discussed earlier) is to introduce measures of cross-variable interactions and non-linear effects.

In general, behavioral models utilizing dependence methodologies, such as regression, are based on the assumption of predictor independence. For the most part, this is of course a sound idea, as its goal is to eliminate redundancy among individual metrics, which ultimately leads to greater parsimony. Unfortunately, sometimes it results in relatively weak (prediction-wise) models, simply because the assumption that the outcome of interest is largely shaped by a set of mutually independent factors simply does not reflect reality. *Interaction terms*, which represent the combined effect of two or more factors[3] can be introduced to enhance the predictive power of a behavioral model. However, since an interaction term can employ measures that are already included in the model as stand-alone predictors, the inclusion of these terms will typically violate the assumption of predictor independence mentioned earlier[4]. (In a technical sense, behavioral models meeting the assumption of predictor independence are "additive" which allows for an assessment of cumulative power of the otherwise singularly measured metrics; adding-in interaction terms will often result in "non-additive" models.)

Methodological considerations aside, interaction effects can yield informationally invaluable insights, simply because they capture what are often quite pronounced real-life interdependencies. For instance, the likelihood of a publicly traded organization becoming a target of securities class action litigation could be expressed as a function of a couple of known indicators, such as downward stock price volatility and aggressive accounting accruals, each expressed as a singular effect. The resultant likelihood score would then be a product of the sum of these two stand-alone factors. What the score would not capture would be any potential interactions between the downward stock price volatility and accounting accruals. In other words, it would not at all contemplate the following consideration: What will be the effect of the joint movement of the downward stock price volatility and accounting accruals? What happens (to the said likelihood score) when both metrics increase or when both decrease, simultaneously? Such insights could be invaluable to effective risk mitigation efforts; hence interaction effects should always be considered an important part of behavioral model development.

In terms of model specification, interaction terms introduce an added level of complexity for a couple of distinct reasons. First, their inclusion changes the character of the model from the conceptually more straightforward additive formulation to the more involved multiplicative formulation. Additive model tend to easier to evaluate, in terms of the statistically expressed goodness-of-fit, and to interpret. Secondly, the addition of interaction terms increases the level of difficulty of the previously discussed model specification. However, the additional specification complexity will then tend to diminish the model specification error. Specifically, inclusion of interaction, or product[5] (as they are also called) terms will generally diminish the model under-specification by lessening of the omitted variable bias.

As suggested earlier, the inclusion of interaction terms can draw criticisms from some methodologists because it tends to increase collinearity (inter-correlations among predictor variables) in the resultant model, though there is no evidence suggesting that it reduces the robustness or validity of the model. That said, when considered from the standpoint of developing a knowledge base of competitively advantageous insights, the tradeoff between a more realistic (i.e., all-encompassing) explanation vs. greater collinearity, when there is no compelling evidence suggesting that the latter diminishes the robustness, seems to point to the appropriateness of erring on the side of including interaction terms.

Velocitators

Many statistical models used in the industry are built around the idea of linear or constant effect of predictors on outcomes of interest. For instance, an organization-specific likelihood of securities class action litigation is a product of a slew of balance sheet, income statement and firmographic factors, including revenue and debt variability, downward stock price volatility, etc. The resultant effect estimates are commonly linear in nature, which is in direct contradiction to the frequently observed law of diminishing marginal returns[6]. Although such an oversimplification can "tolerable" from the standpoint of exploratory, descriptive analyses, it can yield dubious recommendations in the context of promotional mix allocation and related business planning.

Operationally, linear relationships hold certain effects to be constant across the range of values, which can be unrealistic. For instance, when expressed linearly, a 10% drop in the stock price might increases the securities class action likelihood by 5% which, when linearly extrapolated, would then lead to the conclusion that a 20% stock price drop will lift the class action likelihood by 10%, 30% drop will push the said likelihood up to 15% and so on. In other words, the relationship between stock price volatility and the likelihood of securities litigation can be curvilinear, not linear, as shown below.

Figure 10.4
Linear vs. Curvilinear Effects

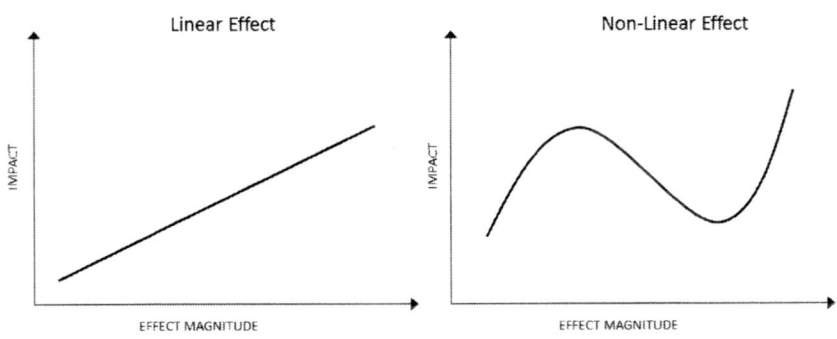

252

At the same time, it is important to note that the linear-effect-induced interpretational error does not necessarily need to be inflationary in nature, as just as easily it can lead to understanding of certain propensities. For instance, in the context of securities class action[7] mitigation, the initially small impact of a relatively (monetarily) small net income restatement might increase exponentially as the value of the said restatement grows. Here, expressing the initially computed class action probability linearly would lead to understating of the potential consequences of net income restatements.

In view of the significant shortcomings of only considering linearly-expressed relationships, a yet another category of statistical effects is necessary to capture any non-linear effects that might better describe the interrelationships imbedded in the data. Velocitators are a type of statistical effect designed expressly to capture the degree to which certain measures have a non-constant or non-linear impact on the outcomes of interest. Similarly to the previously discussed interaction terms, the inclusion of velocitators adds to the analytical complexity of behavioral models, but the added complexity might be worthwhile in view of informational gains.

The Role of Effect Types in IDS

Capturing and correctly coding statistical effect-coded the real life business interactions is critically important to the ensuing behavioral analyses. The degree to which any model can capture—and henceforth, explain—reality is highly contingent on the sufficiency of model specification. Of particular importance are the efficacy of the business relationship-to-statistical effect translation and the adequacy of the scope of model coverage.

The efficacy of the business relationship-to-statistical effect translation is a reflection of the accuracy with which individual variables and cross-variable interrelationships are both operationalized adequately. As pointed out earlier in the discussion of Informational Domain Specification (IDS), a model can be over-, under- or just-specified. An inadequate operationalization of individual variables and/or cross-variable interrelationships can lead to model under-specification. Under-specified models are characterized by poor explanatory and classificatory power, which in turn is evidenced by poor fit or low explained variance (such as relatively small R^2 in linear or pseudo-R^2 in logistic regression models) and low predictive accuracy.

The adequacy of the scope of model coverage is a reflection of the model's inclusion logic—which variables and relationships are explicitly embodied in the model? Simply put, it is a measure of the degree to which what is included within the scope of the model provides enough "raw materials" to answer the questions posed by the stated informational objectives. In the context of the Informational Domain Specification, inadequate scope of coverage can manifest itself either in the form of model under-specification or over-specification (although in practice, under-specification is far more common). Outcome-wise, the evidence of an inadequate scope of model coverage is a bit less self-evident that is the evidence of the above discussed efficacy of the business relationship-to-statistical effect translation. Primarily, it is made visible by a potential gap separating the informational content of the model results and the stated informational objectives: If the results of the model do not meaningfully contribute to the stated business needs, it is likely that the underlying model's scope is not sufficiently broad.

Some Practical Considerations

Recall the earlier discussion of Informational Domain Specification. As noted there, the inclusion of statistical effects requires the foundation of a solid theoretical reasoning, primarily for the very practical reason of containing a possible effect proliferation. An average event-tracking database contains hundreds of raw metrics, which potentially could give rise to thousands of potential statistical effects (indicators, indices, interactions and velocitators). For instance, let's estimate the number of potential interaction effects for a database containing 100 individual metrics. To do so, we can use the following factorial formula:

$$\text{Number of Potential Interactions} = \frac{n!}{k!(n-k)!}$$

where,

    k is the number of 2-way interactions
    n is the number of raw metrics

Solving the above equation for $k = 2$ (2-way interaction) and $n = 100$ (100 individual raw variables), we arrive at 4,950 potential interaction terms! Needless to say, that number does not include indicators, indices or velocitators and for that matter, it only accounts for 2-way interactions. Clearly, without an a priori rationale focusing the attention on a specific subset of all of the potentially available statistical effects, even a moderately sized (in terms of the number of raw metrics) dataset would result would spur an overwhelming proliferation in the number of analyzable measures.

Predictive Reliability of Indicators

In the *Beware of Statistical Significance Tests* section I warned against over-reliance on statistical significance tests (SST), particularly when constructing longitudinal generalizations. SST have been frequently—and incorrectly—used to validate numerous data-supported business decisions by attesting to the robustness of analytically derived estimates. Within the realm of risk management, likelihood estimates are of particular interest, given the importance of accurately quantifying the chances of a particular adverse event materializing.

In general *likelihood models* are statistical methods of quantifying the probability of occurrence of specific events, such as the probability of shareholders of a publicly traded company filling a securities class action, in general, as well as in response to a particular event, such as a precipitous stock price decline. These types of models play a dual role: First, they offer a unit-of-analysis specific (i.e., individual publicly traded companies) assessment of likelihood of specific action. Second, likelihood models also to bring to light the most pronounced drivers of actions of interest, which in turn contributes to "risk mapping" discussed in earlier chapter. It is here where statistical significance tests can be of considerable value, if used properly.

Significance tests estimate the probability that an observed relationship could be a result of a mere chance, rather than an indication of an enduring association. In other words, significance testing offers the means of attesting to the generalizability of sample based findings and/or conclusions. Since these tests are based on inferences, their conclusions will always be probabilistic—i.e., based on the degree of confidence, rather than absolute certainty. Over the years, a three-tiered significance level became widely accepted: $\alpha = .01\%$, which corresponds to 1% probability of the observed relationship arising purely out of random chance; $\alpha = 5\%$, which corresponds to 5% probability of the observed relationship arising purely out of random chance; and $\alpha = 10\%$, which corresponds to 10% probability of the observed relationship arising purely out of random chance[8]. Stated differently, a conclusion of statistically significant relationship can have 1-in-100 ($p = .01\%$), 1-in-20 ($p = 5\%$) or 1-in-10 ($p = 10\%$) chance of being incorrect. This means that in the context of a large, multivariate model, different metrics can be significant at varying numerical levels. A common practice is to choose one of the three thresholds ($p = 5\%$ being the most commonly used) and evaluate all potentially explanatory indicators in relation to that singular threshold. In the academic

255

theory building sense this is a very rational and an appropriate approach, but it is not necessarily so in the context of applied business analyses. Here is why:

Let's say that a particular likelihood model singled out a dozen of individual drivers of risk (of the aforementioned securities class action litigation). Let us further assume that some of those indicators are highly significant, i.e., $p \leq .01\%$ (telling the analyst that the likelihood of those relationship being spurious is less than 1-in-100), some others are somewhat weaker, but nonetheless still significant, i.e., $.01\% > p \leq 5\%$ (again, telling the analyst that the likelihood of those relationships being spurious is approximately 1-in-20), with the remaining group registering as statistically significant, but at the lowest of the three previously mentioned levels, i.e., $5\% < p \leq 10\%$ (telling the analyst that the likelihood of those relationships being spurious is about 1-in-10). Let us then say that only a single significance threshold is used, which is quite typical. Unless the most restrictive of the three significance cuff-off values is used (i.e., $p \leq .01\%$), metrics manifesting considerably dissimilar levels of reliability will be lumped together into a single category, which in turn may lead to equal reliance (in the business decision making process) on metrics exhibiting otherwise distinctly differently levels of reliability.

Imagine confronting a choice of two potential courses of action: Option 1 has a 1-in-100 chance of leading to damaging consequences; Option 2 has a 1-in-10 chance of leading to damaging consequence. Assuming that no other differences exist between Options 1 and 2, which one would you choose? Clearly, this is a rhetorical question, since no rational person would pick Option 2. Why then treat quantitatively quite dissimilar insights as equally reliable?

There is an obvious alternative to the fuzzing of the otherwise important cross-indicator reliability differences: Construct a three-tier indicator reliability table, as illustrated in Table 10.3. Statistically significant metrics are grouped into three tiers, corresponding to the three generally accepted thresholds of $p \leq 0.01$ (1-in-100 false positive chance), $p \leq 0.05$ (1-in-20 false positive chance) and $p \leq 0.10$ (1-in-10 false positive chance). In addition, standardized estimate of each metric's contribution to the explained variability (e.g., partial R^2 for linear regression) is also provided to round off the overall assessment of all statistically significant metrics' predictive power.

Table 10.3
Three-Tier Indicator Reliability Assessment

Metric	Predictive Reliability			Explanatory Power
	Tier I:	Tier II:	Tier III:	Standardized Estimate of Contribution
	False Positive: 1-in-100	False Positive: 1-in-20	False Positive: 1-in-10	
Metric A				
Metric B				
Metric C				
Metric *n*				

Once again, the importance of this step lies in increasing the business efficacy of the otherwise abstract statistical findings. To the degree to which individual predictors vary in terms of SST-related reliability, their usefulness as, for instance, target population selection tools will also vary accordingly. For example, a likelihood indicator falling into Tier I (1-in-100 false positive chance) offers considerably higher levels of targeting utility than indicators falling into Tiers II or III.

QUALITATIVE ANALYSES OF RISK

In his book *Blink*, Malcolm Gladwell describes rational, though subconscious instantaneous decision making process. According to the author, "When you meet someone for the first time, or walk into a house you are thinking of buying, or read the first few sentences of a book, your mind takes about two seconds to jump to a series of conclusions...those instant conclusions that we reach are really powerful and really important and, occasionally [emphasis added], really good[9]." *Blink* paints a very compelling picture, but leaves a key question unanswered: Assuming that the "blink-of-an-eye" rational decision making process really takes place as frequently as Mr. Gladwell asserts, but outcomes are, according to the author, only occasionally correct, is there a way of knowing when those instinct-like conclusions are worth relying on? What if fewer than a half of these instantaneous, subconscious "hunches" turn out to be correct—how much stock should I put in these subliminal conclusions? This brings to mind the old advertising adage—"We know that half of the advertising spending is wasted, we just don't know which half... "

Mr. Gladwell goes to great lengths to avoid using the term "intuition", but it is hard for me, and I imagine many others who read the otherwise well-written, entertaining book, to not see what he describes as just that—basic intuition, which sometimes turns out to be correct and other times not. I do, however, agree with the author that there is value (in the context of business decision making) in considering conclusions of our instantaneous, subconscious thinking, but only if those conclusions are cross-validated against other, equally knowledgeable individuals. This can be accomplished via the Delphi method, which is a technique for qualitatively estimating outcomes, such as the probability and severity of certain types of risks, for which "hard" or quantitative data is not readily available.

When No Hard Data Exists

Not all that is worth knowing is knowable. There are a great many types of risks for which likelihood and severity estimation are quite difficult, primarily because of a scarcity of the appropriate data. Recall Table 3.1 containing a typology of downside risks. By far, the most numerous of the three broad categories of risk are the External, Not Controllable Risks. Although virtually all of those risks can have a profound impact on earnings of an organization, no robust, objective data exists for most, which begs the question: "How can we evaluate the impact on earnings of risks for which no reliable, quantitative data exists?" The answer is qualitative data analysis.

Qualitative analyses attempt to extract and interpret meaningful patterns from non-numeric data. Whereas in quantitative analysis numbers and what they stand for are the material of analysis, qualitative analysis deals in words and other non-numeric symbols. Hence unlike the former, which employs a wide range of highly structured and standardized mathematical formulations, qualitative data analyses are guided by fewer universal rules and standardized procedures. And lastly, the role of an analyst in quantitative analysis is to remain an objective outsider so that analysis is separate and largely independent of the analyst (i.e., multiple analysts conducting the same type of analysis on the same data set should arrive at substantially the same results), in qualitative analyses, the analyst cannot be separated from the analysis. Stated differently, results of qualitative data explorations are to a large degree a reflection of analysts' subjectivity.

One of the more effective methods of reducing the potentially biasing effects associated with the analysis—analyst confounding is the use of multiple loop-like rounds of revisiting the data as additional questions emerge, new connections are brought to the surface or more complex, deeper understanding of the material develops. Throughout the resultant iterations, the analyst should continue to search for emerging themes or patterns as well as deviations from the observed patterns, hints of a need to collect additional data and any evidence of the emerging themes corroborating the findings of any other, previously conducted analysis.

There are two general types of qualitative analysis: *intra-case analysis* and *cross-case analysis*. It should be noted that the definition of "case" is situational—it could be a single individual, a session made up of a group of individuals (such as a focus group) or a particular site, such as a manufacturing facility or a retail location. With that in mind, intra-case analysis will focus on the identification of themes or patterns within a single case, such as a particular retail store. Inter-case analysis, on the other hand, will focus on identifying a pattern of commonalities across a number of individual cases, for instance, across a number of different store locations.

When considering qualitative analysis, it is important to make an explicit distinction between the analysis of qualitative data and the estimation of qualitative outcomes. There is a fundamental difference between these two otherwise similar concepts: Qualitative data analysis is a process incorporating somewhat distinct set of activities focused on collection of data, the analysis of data and lastly, drawing conclusions from the findings of the analysis. The important part of this process is that data are collected independently of the analysis—in other words, data collection and data analysis are independent of each other. That is not the case with qualitative outcome estimation. Here, the analysis and the collection of data are indistinguishable from one another. Another way of looking at the difference between the two is that in the case of qualitative data analysis, data source and data analysis are represented by two, typically independent sets of individuals: those who contribute data and those who analyze it. In the case of qualitative outcome estimation, data is contributed and analyzed by the same individual. This is an important consideration, one that will play a key role in selecting the optimal qualitative risk analytical techniques.

One of the most important aspects of any analysis—be it qualitative or quantitative—is objectivity. Surely, there are those who on some occasions may have a uniquely accurate insight into certain types of risk exposures. The problem is that the only way to ascertain the accuracy of an atypical viewpoint is inherently retrospective—in other words, it requires looking back and comparing it against competing estimates. Hence at the time at which a given projection is being (subjectively) made, there is simply no way of (objectively) ascertaining the reliability of it, which means "uncoupling" of the data capture and analysis functions of qualitative research is particularly important. In the context of risk analytics, the qualitative analytical approach that best meets these demands is the Delphi method.

Delphi Method

Delphi[10] method is a systematic, interactive forecasting which relies on a panel of independent experts. It was developed at the beginning of the cold war to forecast the impact of technology on warfare. In 1944, General Henry Arnold ordered the creation of the report for the U.S. Air Force on the future technological capabilities that might be used by the military. Two years later, Douglas Aircraft Company started Project RAND[11] (*R*esearch *AN*d *D*evelopment) to study "the broad subject of inter-continental warfare other than surface". Delphi method was developed with that purpose in mind in late 1950s and has since been adapted to a variety of business applications.

Delphi method works as follows: The carefully selected experts answer questionnaires in two or more rounds. After each round, a facilitator provides an anonymous summary of the experts' forecasts from the previous round as well as the reasons they provided for their judgments. Thus, participants are encouraged to revise their earlier answers in light of the replies of other members of the group. It is believed that during this process the range of the answers will decrease and the group will converge towards the "correct" answer. Finally, the process is stopped after a pre-defined stop criterion (e.g. number of rounds, achievement of consensus, stability of results) and the mean or median scores of the final rounds determine the outcomes. Delphi is based on the principle that forecasts from a structured group of experts are more accurate than those from unstructured groups or individuals.

In terms of its philosophical underpinnings, Delphi method is based on the notion of *successive approximations*, which is a method of estimating the value of unknown quantity via repeated "re-shaping" of the original estimates, as depicted in Figure 10.5.

Figure 10.5
Successive Approximations of the Delphi Method

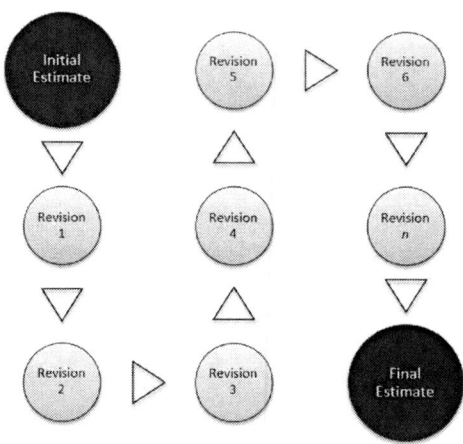

The process of successive approximations is used extensively in computational mathematics, behavioral psychology, educational research, health treatment and other areas where repeated interactions with the outside (to a respondent) environment are deemed beneficial to shaping of the final outcome. It has proven itself to be an effective method of arriving at a "most reasonable" estimate in situations where potentially large disparities in judgment exist. The outcome of the Delphi process is a "stress tested" product of subjectively generated insights of a group of experts. In the context of enterprise risk management, it will be the most dependable and stable estimate of risk for which no reliable, quantitative data exists.

TEXT DATA

An important, though often largely inaccessible (for large scale analyses) source of data is *text*, defined here as words treated as data. In contrast to numerical data, the bulk of which is a product of machine-to-machine communication, textual data is a result of human communication, which means it is ubiquitous and analytically challenging. There are numerous reasons for why textual data is analytically challenging, but they can be reduced to two primary factors, which are structural variability and volume. The former encapsulates the intricacy of human communication – the interweaving of explicit and implicit elements, structured vs. unstructured modes, the multiplicity of meanings associated with many commonly used terms, to name just a few. The latter is self-evident, though perhaps it might be instructive to more explicitly define that quality: The World Wide Web contains more than 7 billion indexed pages[12]; Google, the widely recognized online search leader (accounting for about half of all internet searches) grows its search database by more than 100 million searches per day; Facebook alone sits atop of more than 30 petabytes[2] of data...There are numerous examples that attest to the rapid growth and the sheer size of what has come to be known as "big data"; the rather unimaginatively named repositories of largely text data that are too large to be managed using traditional database management and analytical tools.

Although text data sources that are both available to business organizations and pertinent to management of risk are not quite on the scale of Google's, Facebook's or Twitter's, business organization nonetheless have access to large volumes and diversity of text data. Countless reports, insurance policies, litigation fillings or electronic diary-captured claim handlers' notes, just to name a few sources, contain a wealth of potentially action-directing insights. Historically largely inaccessible, these often quite extensive repositories of data can now be explored due to significant advances in text mining technologies.

Structured vs. Unstructured Data

Much like typical numeric data files discussed in the *Understanding Data* chapter, text data files are two-dimensional matrices, where columns demark individual variables and rows delimit successive cases. Given that, a key consideration in machine-aided analysis of text is the organizational composition of data files, with a particular emphasis on the relationship between successive rows and individual columns in the data matrix. Within the confines of the successive rows vs. individual columns layout, text files can be categorized as either structured or unstructured.

Structured data follows a repeatable pattern where each successive data record (row) mimics the layout of the previous one and columns demark distinct variables. Form-based information, such as warranty cards that accompany household appliance purchases are a good example of this category of text – each purchaser completes the same type of information captured in the same manner. Naturally, given the fixed and repeatable format of structured data files, it stands to reason that so-formatted files are far more amendable to machine processing, though at the same time, the informational value of outcomes of those analyses might be somewhat limited. Why? Structured data files' computer processing malleability is rooted in their layout – as mentioned earlier, to be considered "structured", a text data file has to follow a basic two-dimensional matrix layout where columns contain distinct fields and rows enumerate successive data records. Given that, the only truly meaningful difference between structured text and numeric data is that the individual data fields (i.e., variables) comprising the former contain text rather than digits. Although somewhat less obvious, it also means that the informational content of those fields tends to be skewed toward categorical, rather than syntactical substance[13] (think of the warranty cards that usually accompany household appliance purchases and the type of information that those cards attempt to collect). As a result, the output of the analysis of structured text tends to be limited to the identification of patterns and/or communalities across records, which is obviously worthwhile, though at the same time only represents a fairly small subset of the informational content of text-encoded communications. Hence, the task of reliable machine-aided analysis of structured text data is a fairly manageable one, but the resultant insights tend to be fairly limited.

Unstructured data, which are by far the most common form of text files[14], do not adhere to a recognizable layout schema. The layout of individual records comprising unstructured data can be characterized as being amorphous and lacking discernible organizational schema – it is non-repeatable in the sense that each successive record is independent of the previous one and any similarity is coincidental; furthermore, individual columns do not delimit distinct and repeatable variables. Examples of unstructured or free-flowing text abound, as most of the written human communication, ranging from books, newspapers and including technical documents such as insurance policies or accident reports, tend to fall within that category. The lack of structure coupled with the inherent ambiguity of "natural" (meaning, used in human communication) language makes unstructured data quite difficult to deal with algorithmically, primarily because, in principle, each data record is different from all other records, both in terms of the layout as well as content[15]. The upside to the absence of a rigid organizational schema is that unstructured text tends be syntactically-rich, which means that although it is possible to focus the mining efforts on the identification of cross-record patterns and communalities (as is the case with structured text), the true value in analyzing unstructured text often lies in surmising the "deeper meaning" hidden in what and how is being communicated. However, it can be a daunting task, primarily because natural language depends heavily on common sense knowledge, which is the understanding of the implied meaning of expressions that goes beyond technical definitions of individual terms. This is one area where precision-demanding machine processing is – in spite of over-promising terms such as artificial intelligence – far inferior to human mind. Thus, unlike the relatively manageable task of categorizing structured text, unstructured textual data is exceptionally hard to encode logarithmically, which means it does not succumb to traditional data analytic techniques.

Given the considerable differences separating structured and unstructured text, it follows that there are a number of different methods that can be used to machine-process large volumes of text data. Broadly referred to as "text mining", these techniques are summarized next.

Text Mining Approaches

As noted earlier, text data are very common – by some estimates, a typical business organization has anywhere between two and ten times more textual than numeric data. Analysis of textual data, which is overwhelmingly exploratory in nature, is commonly referred to as *text mining*, which itself is considered a subset of a broader category of *data mining*[16]. As applied business analytic notions, both data and text mining tend to be associated with machine-aided processing, primarily because of the computer applications first introduced in the 1990s by companies like SAS, SPSS[17] or IBM; though in principle, those terms apply to all exploratory analyses, whether or not aided by machines. Thus, an analyst using a computer-based application to explore a large repository of text data, such as customer comments posted on a brand's website, or a researcher reading a transcript of a focus group are both examples of text mining. Naturally, "manual" – reading and summarizing by humans – mining of text or other data is only operationally feasible when the quantity of data is fairly small.

Process-wise, mining of textual data entails four distinct steps: 1. retrieval, 2. summarization, 3. structural mining and 4. digitization. *Retrieval* pertains to searching for records of interest that are hidden in large repositories, such general or topical databases; the outcome of the retrieval efforts will usually take the form of an extract. *Summarization,* on the other hand, involves condensing of otherwise large quantities of (textual) data; its outcome typically takes the form of an abstract or a synopsis. *Structural mining* is probably the broadest, as well as most complex aspect of text mining as it involves converting voluminous text data into (statistically) analyzable, categorized metadata[18]. Depending on the combination of purpose and the type of data (discussed below), structural mining can mean searching for pre-determined expressions or attempting to surmise the deeper meaning hidden in the syntactic structure of text. Lastly, *digitization* refers to the process of number-coding of metadata, or converting non-numeric data values into numeric ones. The ultimate goal of that conversion is to facilitate amalgamation of form-dissimilar (i.e., text vs. numeric), but complementary-in-meaning text mining derived insights and already digitally-coded numeric data, with the goal of enabling *multi-source analytics*[19].

Function-wise, text mining can be performed with several different outcomes in mind, such as: 1. *summarization*: identifying co-occurrences of themes in a body of text; 2. *categorization*: reducing of documents' content to pre-defined categories; 3. *clustering*: reducing of documents' content to emergent (i.e., based on documents' content, rather than being pre-defined) categories; 4. *visualization*: re-casting of textually-expressed information into graphics; 5. *filtering*: selecting sub-sets of all information, based on pre-determined logic. It is important to note that though quite dissimilar the individual text mining functions can be viewed as complements, as each delivers a distinctly different end user informational utility.

Method-wise, mining of text data can take the path of either frequency count and tabulation or natural language processing. The *frequency count and tabulation* approach itself can take one of two paths: 1. "tagging" of a priori identified expressions, or searching a body of data for specific expressions or terms that have been spelled out in advance of the search; or 2. "term funneling", where instead of using a priori lists, the starting point of the analysis is the generation of comprehensive frequency counts of all recurring terms. The former – *tagging* – requires a substantial amount of knowledge on the part of the analyst, to the degree to which specific expressions or terms have to be identified as important ahead of the search; as such, it is deductive in nature, which is to say it is focused on answering specific questions

265

stemming from hypothesis formed at the outset of analyses. Furthermore, simply searching for terms that have been identified as important beforehand is not conducive to uncovering new "truths", as the focused mechanics of deductive search make it difficult, if not practically impossible, to notice unexpected results. The latter of the two frequency and tabulation data mining approaches – *term funneling* – requires no prior knowledge hence in contrast to tagging it is inductive in nature, but it can produce overwhelming large quantities of output (tens of thousands of terms and/or expressions), which in turn will demand a substantial amount of post-extraction processing. It follows that it is not only time-consuming, but also likely to infuse potentially large amounts of the earlier discussed *rater bias*, effectively reducing the objectivity of findings. Overall, their differences notwithstanding, tagging and term funneling are focused strictly on pinpointing of terms without considering the context or the way in which those terms are used. In other words, using the frequency count and tabulation method, it might be difficult, if not outright impossible to distinguish between positively and negatively-valenced lexical items[20].

The second broadly defined approach to text mining – *natural language processing* (NLP) – attempts to remedy the limitations of the frequency count and tabulation methodology by attempting to extract insights from the semantic[21] structure of text. The NLP is an outgrowth of computational linguistics (itself a part of a broader domain of artificial intelligence), which is statistical and/or rule-based modeling of natural language. The goal of NLP is to capture the meaning of written communications in the form of tabular metadata amendable to statistical analysis – as such, it represents an inductive approach to knowledge creation, well adept at uncovering new "truths." Given the significantly more ambitious goal of natural language processing, namely, objectively summarizing and extracting the meaning of nuanced human communications, the level of difficulty associated with this endeavor is significantly higher, which means that the reliability of findings will typically be proportionately lower.

Although NLP clearly offers a potentially deeper set of insights, it is also fraught with difficulties which directly impact the validity and reliability of the resultant findings – on the other hand, the comparatively more superficial frequency count and tabulation is straightforward to implement and can deliver a fairly consistent – keeping its limitations in mind – set of insights. All considered, both text mining approaches have merit and in order to gain a better understanding of the applicability of both methods, a more in-depth overview of presented next.

Frequency Count & Tabulation

As outlined earlier, the goal of frequency count and tabulation approach to text mining is to identify, tag and tabulate, in a given body (known as "corpora") of text, pre-determined terms and/or expressions. Conceptually, it can be thought of as a confirmatory tool as it is focused on finding concepts that are already (i.e., prior to search) believed to be important, rather than identifying new ones – i.e., pinpointing concepts that were not previously believed to be important. As a result, the efficacy of the frequency count and tabulation approach is highly dependent on prior knowledge, as manifested by the completeness of the a priori created external categories.

However, even the most complete external schemas in no way assure robust outcomes as the search or the mining process itself can produce incomplete findings due to ambiguity stemming from wording or phrasing variability and the potential impact of synonyms and homographs. The *word* or *phrase variability* is a syntax (principles and rules used in sentence construction) problem stemming from the fact that the same term or an idea can oftentimes be written in somewhat different ways. A common approach to addressing word or phrase related variability is to use the so-called "stemming algorithms" which reduce words to their Latin or Greek stems with the goal of recognizing communalities. *Synonyms*, which are yet another potential source of search ambiguity, are terms that have a different spelling but the same or similar meaning, while *homographs* are terms that have the same spelling but different meaning. The most common approach to addressing those sources of possible confusion or ambiguity is to create external reference categories, which are de facto libraries of terms delineating all known synonyms and homographs for all a priori identified search terms. Clearly, a rather substantial undertaking…

Process-wise, the frequency count and tabulation approach to mining textual data makes use of *text transformations,* defined here as the process of translating words into digits, where each word is an attribute defined by its frequency of occurrence[22]. This process is built around a notion of "bag-of-words" – a transformation-simplifying assumption which posits that a text can be viewed as an unordered collection of words, where grammar and even the word order are disregarded. Considered in the context of the two types of textual data discussed earlier – structured and unstructured – text transformation can take on somewhat different operational meanings: Transforming structured data typically involves supplanting textual fields with numerically-coded and a priori delineated categories, which effectively translates textual expressions into numeric values. In that context, it is a relatively straightforward process because structured textual data tends to exhibit relatively little ambiguity, due to heavy reliance on pre-determined lexical categories[23]. At the same time, the process of transforming unstructured data is considerably more involved because of an open-ended nature of that source of data – in principle, terms appearing in unstructured data can be thought of as unconstrained choices, as opposed to those representing selections from a pre-determined (i.e., closed) menu of options, as is often the case with structured text. A direct consequence of unconstrained nature of unstructured text is a far greater need for *disambiguation*, which is resolving of potential conflicts that tend to arise when a single term or an expression can take on multiple meanings. Conceptually, disambiguation is somewhat similar to the earlier discussed notion of term/phrase variability, but operationally it is quite a bit more complex as it necessitates anticipating the potential conflicts ahead of knowing what terms can appear in what context.

Overall, the frequency count and tabulation approach to text mining entails a considerable amount of analyst input, while at the same time its primary focus is on the identification and re-coding (from text into digits) of identifiable and definable terms and expressions, all while skipping over any deeper meaning that might be hidden in the semantic structure of text. As noted earlier, this broadly defined approach offers, in principle, no clear way of contextualizing or otherwise qualifying search-identified terms, beyond merely pinpointing their occurrence and counting the sub sequent recurrences. Looked at as a sum of advantages and disadvantages, frequency count and tabulation method can be an effective approach to extracting numerically-analyzable details out of the otherwise inaccessible textually-expressed data, but overall it is not an effective mean of discovering new knowledge.

Natural Language Processing

Perhaps the most obvious limitation of the frequency count and tabulation approach to text mining is the embrace of the bag-of-words idea, which leads to lumping together of stem-related but differently-valenced terms (i.e., the same term used in the positive vs. negative context). Stripping away of grammar linking together individual – i.e., merely counting the recurrence of terms without regard for their order or a broader context – inescapably leads to loss of information, which in turn diminishes the quantity and the quality of the resultant insights. Hence an obvious (and challenging) path to substantially enriching the depth and the breadth of newly discovered knowledge is to set aside the limiting bag-of-words assumption and to expressly consider the syntactical structure of text, which means to process what is known as "natural language".

Broadly conceived, *natural language* is human communication which is distinct and different from "constructed languages", best exemplified by computer programming or mathematical logic. In general, natural language can be spoken, written or signed, though text mining is obviously only concerned with the written aspect of it – more specifically, unpremeditated descriptions of states, outcomes and/or phenomena that comprise textual data. Formally defined, *natural language processing* is an exploratory process of extracting meaningful insights out of the semantic structure of a body of text. Approach-wise, NLP it can take one of two broadly defined forms: 1. supervised machine learning-based automated classification, or 2. unsupervised mining. At their core, both types of methodologies expressly consider words, word order and grammar in trying to discern generalizable rules that can be applied to distilling large quantities of text into manageable sets of summarized findings; however, they are quite different in terms of operational mechanics.

The first of the two NLP approaches, *automated classification,* can be thought of as a "pseudo-exploratory" methodology as it is a type of supervised learning where an algorithm (a decision rule) is "trained" using a previously classified text. The training task is essentially that of establishing generalizable rules for assigning topical labels to content, where the efficacy of the resultant algorithm is, to a large degree, dependent on balancing of two important, though somewhat contradictory notions of accuracy and simplicity[24]. There are two distinct schools of thought as it regards the development of automated text classification systems: 1. *knowledge-based*, which relies on codification of expert-derived classification rules; and 2. *learning-based*, where experts supply classified examples rather than classification rules. Within the realm of the marketing database analytics process detailed in this book (as well as the broader context of marketing analytics), knowledge-based systems are generally deemed more workable, primarily because the requisite training inputs are more obtainable[25] (under most circumstances, it is prohibitively difficult to compile adequately representative classification samples that are required by learning-based systems). It is important to note that to be effective as a classification tool, the initial algorithmic learning cannot be overly tailored to idiosyncrasies of the training file (a condition known as "overfitting"), as doing so will lead to poor generalizability – yet, it needs to be exhibit adequate classificatory accuracy (hence the need to balance the two somewhat contradictory notions of accuracy and simplicity).

Unsupervised mining, the second of the two general types of machine learning techniques, can be thought of as a purely exploratory methodology (in contrast to the above-described pseudo-exploratory automatic classification). However, even the purely exploratory text mining mechanisms do not represent, in a strict sense of the word, truly independent machine-based processing of human communications. These method leverage similarity / difference heuristics, such as hierarchical clustering techniques, that are informed by text records' content which are emergent from data, rather than being based on learning from already classified text. That said, it is important to note that although the mining itself is unsupervised, the general rules within which it is conducted are governed by explicit vocabulary control, which typically takes the form of an a priori constructed (by human experts) thesauri. The individual terms comprising a particular thesaurus are commonly noun phrases (i.e., content words), with the meaning of those terms restricted to that most effective for the purpose of a particular thesaurus, which in turn is shaped by the context of the search (e.g., a search of a database of customer comments might be focused on pinpointing drivers of brand users' satisfaction and/or dissatisfaction). In terms of *lexical inference*, or deriving meaning from grammar-connected word combinations, the human expert-provided thesaurus also needs to expressly define three main types of cross-term relationships: equivalence, which is critical to resolving synonym-related ambiguity, and hierarchy as well as association, both of which are necessary to extracting semantic insights, or imbuing meaning to multi-term expressions.

Regardless of which of the two general machine learning approaches is taken, the goal of natural language processing is to extract kernels of meaning out of textual data. In the vast majority of cases it is used with semantically-rich unstructured text, although in principle it could also be employed with unstructured text. In practice, however, the frequency count and tabulation text mining techniques discussed earlier is more appropriate – and probably more effective, all considered – to use with the categorization-friendly structured text.

Natural language is, at best, a probabilistic science yielding a moderate degree of success; at worst, it can be a frustrating endeavor. In general, the quality of outcomes is highly dependent on the nature of data and the desired utility of findings – the more constrained, focus-wise, the data, the better the quality of outcomes. The reason for that is that is that under those circumstances, the variability between inputs (e.g., classification rules, examples or thesauri) provided by human experts and raw data is minimized. It is hard not to come to an obvious conclusion: In contrast to numerically-encoded data, which can be analyzed with the expectation of highly valid and reliable results, analyses of the often highly nuanced and context-dependent text data cannot be expected to yield comparable (to the aforementioned numeric analyses) levels of result efficacy. In fact, the very task of objectively assessing the validity of text mining results is fraught with difficulties, not the least of which is the scarcity of evaluative benchmarks. More specifically, whereas the results of numeric analyses can be cross-referenced in a manner suggesting possible inconsistencies, the use of such evaluative methods is rarely feasible within the confines of text mining.

11

Knowledge Creation:
Evaluating Alternatives

Exploratory and predictive analyses discussed earlier offer means of discovering new and verifying pre-existing knowledge, but do not provide means of comparing the efficacy of competing courses of action, which is an important limitation from the standpoint of ongoing risk management. One of the key functions of corporate risk managers is the selection of the most economically appropriate risk response mechanism – for instance, should the organization purchase commercial insurance coverage or should it self-insure? Or, what is the most likely impact on the likelihood and severity of a particular threat that can be expected from implementing different risk mitigation solutions?

Although the above questions are fairly straightforward, deriving robust and reliable answers can be challenging due to a number of reasons, with perhaps the most significant one being invariant factor composition of the competing courses of action. That said, many of the key difficulties can be overcome with the help of *experimental designs*, which is a group methodologies designed to aid in the task of carrying out sound what-if contrasts.

EXPERIMENTATION

Experiments are one of two primary means of gathering empirical information (observation is the other one) to serve as bases for hypothesis testing. They entail willful and purposeful manipulation of factors of interests while controlling for potential extraneous influences; as such, experiments require a clear delineation of the factors to be studied and their interactions, as well as the means and the scope of the control mechanisms. Operationally, this translates into separate, appropriately sized and selected (i.e., assigned to specific groupings, or cells, as discussed later) *test* and *control* groups and appropriate control mechanisms, or means of preventing the emergence of competing explanations.

Under most circumstances, experimentation is the most effective method of quantifying the magnitude of a specific action. It is the only method offering a methodologically clean and interpretationally robust means of separating effects of the action of interest from other concurrent and possibly confounding actions. Considered from the standpoint of hypothesis testing, *action—result* effect estimation usually involves directional hypothesis tests[1] as the end objective of a test is to ascertain whether the action of interest had a positive impact on the focal outcome, such as sales level.

However, the design and (particularly) the implementation of experimental contrasts also tend to be quite demanding of the business user and under some circumstances, it may be impossible to implement[2]. Still, considering the operational importance of many risk management decisions, obtaining robust, objective decision-guiding insights may certainly be worth the extra effort. With that in mind, setting up a robust test involves distinct steps outlined in Table 11.1 and more expressly discussed in the ensuing sections.

Table 11.1
Test Design Steps

Consideration	Description
Experimental Design Development	This is the conceptual process of developing a test plan. It is at this stage that the analytic plan is "translated" into a testable and measurable entity. Arguably, it is the most difficult part of the measurement process. The outcome of it is a testing/measurement blueprint.
Sampling Requirements Assessment	The overall process of explicitly contrasting the design-mandated sampling/sample requirements with available data. The outcome of this process is a set of explicit sample selection guidelines, and experimental design amendments, if its requirements cannot be met by existing data.
Effect Estimation	An explicit, numeric assessment of the impact of experimental stimulus or stimuli on the population of interest. It can take either of two forms: 1. *Effect size estimation*. Quantification of the degree of change (increase or decrease) determined by contrasting the impact of the experimental stimuli on both test and control groups. It is ideal for ROI assessment; however, it requires a robust sample size. 2. *Rank-ordered effect estimation*. Directional-only assessment, i.e., it estimates whether one quantity is larger or smaller than another only. It utilizes analysis of variance; it is ideally suited for response rank-ordering; sample size requirements are considerably lower than #1 above.

Experimental Design

There are a large number of potential test designs depending on the number of comparative factors, type of comparisons and sampling constraints. In the context of experimental test design, a *factor* is defined as a stimulus the impact of which is being investigated, while a *factor level* is a specific value or a range of values for the said stimulus. A simple, single factor experiment may test the impact of different "return to work" programs on the overall cost of on-the-job accidents. In that scenario, the overall "return to work" program would be a factor and the individual variants of that program would represent individual factor levels – the goal of the experiment would then be to compare average accident cost (or more specifically, the cost of worker's compensation)

274

for each factor level in a manner that would control for the potentially confounding impact of various extraneous factors, such as accident severity or workers' age. Of course, to the degree to which "return to work" programs represent only one of multiple cost mitigation strategies that are typically available, it is likely that the aforementioned experimental design would include more than a single factor to allow the decisions makers to pinpoint the most effective cost mitigation strategy.

From the methodological point of view, there are numerous experimental design schemas and evaluative techniques that could be utilized to tackle the hypothetical problem outlined above. The otherwise diverse experimental design variety can be grouped into three general types of designs summarized in Figure 11.1 below:

Figure 11.1
Generalized Types of Experimental Test Designs

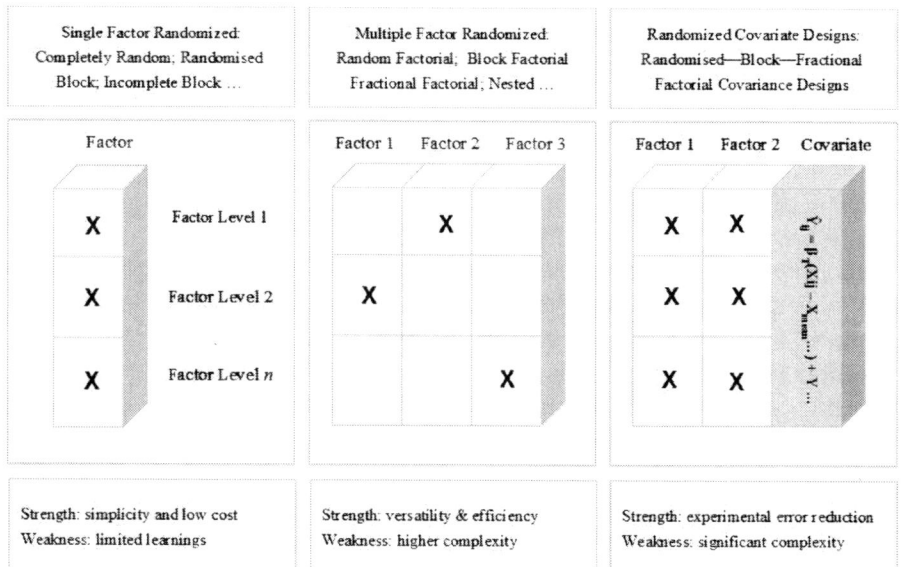

Single Factor Randomized: Completely Random; Randomised Block; Incomplete Block ...	Multiple Factor Randomized: Random Factorial; Block Factorial Fractional Factorial; Nested ...	Randomized Covariate Designs: Randomised—Block—Fractional Factorial Covariance Designs

Strength: simplicity and low cost Weakness: limited learnings	Strength: versatility & efficiency Weakness: higher complexity	Strength: experimental error reduction Weakness: significant complexity

The first category of test designs is the *Single Factor Randomized* group, exemplified by test designs such as Completely Random, Randomized Block or Incomplete Block. The common link connecting all of these test types is that their goal is to assess the impact of only a single action—i.e., a factor and the experimental subjects are randomly assigned to individual test cells. In business terms, the Single Factor Randomized family of test designs only allows the manipulation of a single promotional component, such as either frequency or the type of an offer, but not both. Also, as illustrated above, this group of test designs is complete, meaning that each cell representing a factor level has subjects assigned to it (denoted by "X").

Overall, a single factor test is usually appropriate in situations calling for very specific, narrowly defined insights, which means these types of designs will be overly restrictive for broader questions (i.e., ones requiring the assessment of several different elements) as they would require separate experiments for each factor, which is both impractical and does not allow for the assessment of cross-factor interactions. One final and important characteristic of this family of test designs is that task of controlling for extraneous sources of variability, which is critical in eliminating undesirable competing explanations for any potentially significant relationships, is handled outside of the test itself by either the previously mentioned random subject assignment or by *blocking* of said influences. The latter is typically accomplished by holding constant, across all cells, the values of the variable to be blocked. Computationally, the Single Factor Randomized designs are analyzed with the help of analysis of variance, or ANOVA procedures readily available in most statistical packages.

A natural extension of the single-factor designs is the *Multiple Treatment Randomized* group of experimental designs. Exemplified by Random Factorial, Block Factorial or Fractional Factorial, this family of test designs efforts the simultaneous assessment of multiple factors and factor levels. Constraints on the resultant number of cells are more practical then theoretical in nature, as increasing the number of cells has to be accompanied by a proportional increase in the overall sample size, not to mention the increasing treatment and tracking costs and difficulty. At the same time, being able to assess the impact of multiple factors simultaneously is attractive both from the standpoint of timeliness and efficiency, as well as the possibility of quantifying cross-factor interaction effects or synergies.

A possible solution to the potentially large number of cells associated with a multi-factor design can be offered by a *Fractional Factorial* design, illustrated in Figure 11.2 (center), which allows the investigator to reduce the number of cells by selecting only a representative sample of all cells. Depending on the specifics of the design, as little as 10% or 20% of all cells can be used to generate learnings that can be generalized to the full test matrix. However as it usually is the case, this gain too come at a price: cross-factor interaction effects cannot be computed with a Fractional Factorial design, which means that a more manageable design will prevent the investigator from uncovering potential synergies. In a fashion similar to single-cell designs, the potentially confounding influence of extraneous factors is controlled for outside of the test itself, but means of either randomization or blocking, or both. Computationally, the Multiple Factor Randomized designs are analyzed with the help of multiple analysis of variance, or MANOVA procedures.

The final and the most methodologically complex type of an experimental test design are the *Randomized Covariate* designs. These are multi-factor, complete (i.e., all delineated factor levels have experimental subjects assigned to them) designs that offer additional means of dealing with extraneous influences. In addition to the outside-the-experiment blocking and randomization, the Randomized Covariate designs enable the analyst to eliminate (or at least diminish) any undesirable outside influences by means of regressing their effects prior to carrying out the planned test contrasts. Computationally, Randomized Covariate designs are analyzed with analysis of covariance, or ANCOVA for single-factor studies or multiple analysis of covariance, or MANCOVA for multi-factor designs.

Sampling Requirements Assessment

Sample adequacy is a critically important area that often receives insufficient levels of consideration. The general process describing selecting of an analysis sample from a data repository (i.e., data warehouse) has been outlined the *Knowledge Creation: Analytic File* chapter. In the realm of experimental test design, a more micro view of sampling comes into play, as sub-sets of the overall analysis sample need to be assigned to individual experimental cells. In this context, the two considerations of most importance are sample composition and sample sizing.

In general, the impact of sample composition is primarily felt in the context of result utilization and/or application as well as the proper attribution of the test effects. Hence it is important both from the standpoint of generalizing the findings as well as containing the sources of extraneous variation. The former impacts the usability of results, as it usually arises when the population of interest is comprised of two or more *analytically-distinct* segments[3]. If such segments are not properly recognized, i.e., the analysis sample under- or over-represents some vis-à-vis the others, the results of the analysis might not be equally applicable to all, in other words, might not be generalizable.

The latter of the sample composition related considerations, the containment of the sources of extraneous variation, impacts the robustness of the analysis itself. Specifically, it helps to eliminate alternative explanations to which the observed effects might be attributable. It addresses the critical part of any experimental design, which is that the goal of subsequent analysis is not only to quantify the magnitude of effects, but also to precisely identify the source of the observed effect, which is to attribute results to a particular action.

The importance of *sample sizing* is a bit more straightforward, insofar as it reflects the adequacy of the available sample size to arrive at statistically sound conclusions. The primary concern here is, once again, twofold: First of all, to delineate the *effective* sample size, which is the estimation of the minimum required number of subjects/responses at the most disaggregate level of analysis. Secondly, it is to identify an objective record-to-group assignment method.

The *effective* sample size is the actual number of records used as inputs into analyses, in contrast to the *nominal* sample size which is the number of records available for analyses. The former is almost always smaller that the latter, due primarily to missing values, as many commonly used statistical techniques exclude records containing missing values. Thus it is possible that an initially robust sample size may be reduced to a prohibitively small effective sample size in a context of a specific statistical technique, which in turn may lead to unstable, biased effect estimates. When determining the minimum required effective sample size attention should be focused on the ratio of the number of usable records (i.e., those without any missing values) to the number of variables. A minimum ratio of 4:1, i.e., four usable records for every one variable, is recommended. It is important to keep in mind that the sample size determinations should be made at the most disaggregate level of analysis, which in the context of effect quantification means the most narrowly-defined business action—outcome contrasts. Of course, this is a situational determination as the type (and thus a number) of metrics used will obviously vary across different analyses.

Devising an objective record-to-group assignment method is considerably more complex than identifying the minimum acceptable effective sample size. Record-to-group allocations have to be carried out in a way that will support an unambiguous effect interpretation, operationalized as attributing the observed effects to specific stimuli. The task may be further complicated by the presence of multiple response groups or two distinct sets of stimuli, or both. In other words, the goal of incremental impact quantification is often to contrast the productivity of two of more in-practice programs and/or to assess the impact on two or more types of consumers. The following generalized example outlines the recommended approach to determining an objective record-to-group assignment.

Effect Analysis

There are several ways of quantifying the magnitude of individual factor level comprising an experiment – however, similarly to experimental design types, those can be grouped into two general categories: cross-sectional and longitudinal contrasts. Broadly defined, *cross-sectional* contrasts aim to quantify differences across groups at a point in time, while *longitudinal contrasts* attempt to discern differences that arise out of the passage of time. Under many circumstances, the former tend to offer a "cleaner read", or a more accurate assessment, primarily because it is generally easier to control for extraneous variability that arises out of cross-group, as opposed to cross-time differences.

Analyses of experimental effects touch upon two important, though frequently misapplied notions of *point vs. interval estimation* and *statistical significance*. As discussed earlier, statistical significance tests are often used in conjunction with point estimates to "attest" to the tangibility of measured effects. All too often, these two concepts are used erroneously.

Statistical Significance Testing & Effect Measurement

One of the most common misapplications of the statistical significance testing in business analytics is exemplified below using a simple, two-group contrast.

Example 1: Reporting Effects Lacking Statistical Significance

Group A Avg. Cost:	$2,143
Group B Avg. Cost:	$2,071
Cost Variance:	$72
Desired Confidence Level:	$\alpha = 0.05$ (95%)
Observed Significance Level:	0.29

As shown in the above example, Group A's average cost of $2,143 appears to be $72 higher than Group B's average cost of $2,071, suggesting a material difference between the two groups' costs. The level of significance, however, is 0.29, which is considerably below the desired 95% level and in general considered "not statistically significant."

The example presented above highlights a common practice of quantifying and reporting as "real" results lacking statistical significance, despite their ostensibly spurious nature. Specifically, I am referring to the above shown Cost Variance of $72, which is being reported as a tangible value, in spite of clear lack statistical significance. The dependence of effect magnitude estimation on statistical significance is not acknowledged as evidenced by presenting the two as independent insights, leading some into believing that there is a tangible difference between the two groups, just not statistically significant one. Interpretations like that are self-refuting, as there simply are no instances of differences being both "real" in the sense of representing a genuine distinctiveness, while at the same time not being statistically significant. Any evaluative metric (such as "average cost" used in Example 1) lacking statistical significance should be reported as zero and only as zero. Reporting actual effect magnitudes for not statistically significant results leads to erroneous inferences, as it is easy to look past the abstract *level of significance* detail and focus instead on the reported magnitudinal difference. Hence, whether one agrees with the logic of SST or not, using it to validate cross-group comparisons necessitates its correct application, the core of which is an inseparability of effect estimates and their levels of significance. Thus only statistically significant effects should be quantified and reported as real; all not statistically significance results should be reported as 0.

A quick methodological note: The above reasoning is reflective of the hypothesis testing logic, which is the SST's scientific parent. Whether it is explicitly stated or merely implied, virtually all experimental contrasts entail testing of some type of cross-group equality hypotheses[4]: The no-difference, or null hypothesis is either upheld or rejected – if it is the latter, the alternative hypothesis[5] is accepted, concluding the presence of one or more differences. Statistical significance tests are a mechanism used as basis for making the "reject" vs. "accept" decisions, thus they play a central role in the hypothesis testing process. (It is worth pointing out here that the hypothesis testing logic itself is not beyond reproach as it is built around the assertion that any two sample means are expected to be equal, an assertion that itself is hard to reconcile with such basic statistical concepts as random error; this topic, however, falls outside the scope of the present discussion.)

The basic decision rule governing hypothesis testing is quite simple: If, using Example 1, Group A Average Cost ≠ Group B Average Cost and the resultant difference (Cost Variance here) is statistically significant, the null hypothesis is rejected; otherwise it is accepted. If the two group-specific costs are different but the difference is not statistically significant, the null hypothesis is accepted as true which then effectively imposes the conclusion that the apparent difference (e.g., the Cost Variance of $72) is nothing more than a sampling error. As such, it is not a "real" difference, but merely a spurious consequence of data noise and it should be treated as such.

Another commonly encountered example of misinterpretation of results of experimental contrasts is ascribing of "exactness" to results that should be interpreted as a range, which is illustrated by Example 2.

Example 2: Ascribing Statistical Significance to Exact Values

Group A Avg. Cost:	$2,143
Group B Avg. Cost:	$2,071
Cost Variance:	$72
Desired Confidence Level:	$\alpha = 0.05$ (95%)
Observed Significance Level:	0.01

In contrast to Example 1, the Cost Variance depicted above is a clearly statistically significant (at 99% or $\alpha = 0.01$). Much like before, however, this too illustrates a misapplication of significance testing, albeit more subtle one centering on interpreting SST in the context of exact values, technically referred to as *point estimates*.

In short, statistical significance can only be ascribed to a range of values (technically known as a *confidence interval*) and not to a specific value (i.e., a *point estimate*). This is a manifestation of the impact of data noise, known as *random error*, on statistical techniques in general and significance testing in particular. Simply put, SST is not precise enough to substantiate the validity of an exact value, such as the difference between Group A and Group B being equal to, exactly, $72. Hence, to correctly interpret the information presented in Example 2, the $72 should be restated as a range. Assuming the lower end of the range (i.e., lower confidence limit) of, let's say, $62 and the upper end of the range (i.e., upper confidence limit) of, let's say, $82[6], the correct interpretation of the Example 2 data would state that we can be 99% confident that Cost Variance falls in the range of $62 to $82. This is in contrast to what appears in Example 2, which states that we can be 99% confident that Cost Variance is $72, which is incorrect.

The above examples highlight an interesting interplay between significance testing and impact measurement objectives: SST application and interpretation limits at times run counter to business informational needs. Typically, the ultimate metric of success is the business action's return on investment, ROI, which requires SST-validated effect quantification. For obvious reasons, decision makers are interested in an exact ROI estimate, rather than a range of values. Nonetheless, only range-based estimates are permissible within the context of significance testing, which imposes a stringent and at times difficult to accept limitation.

Confidence Intervals vs. Credible Intervals

In the *Risk Profile Measurement* chapter I addressed some of the high level differences between the two main approaches to probability: the Frequentist and Bayesian views. The former is both more computationally objective and interpretationally straightforward insofar as it is all about the data. Past occurrences are the basis for making forward-looking estimates; the job of the analyst is to merely carry out the computations. Inferences based on the Frequentist approach are essentially past occurrences fitted to an empirically validated distribution and subject to the confidence interval considerations highlighted in examples 1 and 2 in the previous section.

Bayesian approach is considerably different. Broadly speaking, it is a system for describing uncertainty by computing probabilities which are both objective and subjective at their root. Bayesian inferences start with (subjective) prior beliefs, which are updated using (objective) data to ultimately give rise to posterior beliefs. Not surprisingly, leveraging both the subjective and objective insights Bayesian inferences do not fit the conventional conception of confidence intervals – in fact, "confidence interval" is a concept that is associated with the Frequentist approach, while Bayesian statistics use a conceptually similar, but operationally distinct notion of "credible intervals."

As discussed earlier, confidence interval is a range that is calculated from a random sample of an underlying population, such that, if the sampling was repeated numerous times and confidence intervals were re-calculated from each sample (using the same method), the population parameter would be contained within the resultant range. On the other hand, *credible interval* is simply a posterior probability range, which, in contrast to confidence intervals incorporates problem-specific, contextual information embodied in prior beliefs.

Both the confidence and the credible intervals have noteworthy limitations: While the former is limited by the projectability of past trends (i.e., the degree to which the past may not be indicative of the future), the latter is constrained by the validity of individual's beliefs and the adequacy of peer group selections (i.e., are those asked to provide input truly experts in the area of interest?). At the same time, both approaches have distinct strengths: Frequentist probability is a robust tool when (relatively) accurate quantitative data is readily available; the outcome of interest is a relatively high frequency event; and no major disruptive events took place during the analytic timeframe[7]. Bayesian probability is an equally useful tool when the outcome of interest is characterized by low frequency (e.g., major earthquakes, terrorist attacks, etc.); the quantitative data is sparse or not available altogether; and any past "trends" cannot be reliably projected forward.

It follows that these two approaches are generally not substitutable—i.e., it is not advisable to use one when circumstances call for the other. It also means that, for the most part, Frequentist and Bayesian-derived estimates cannot be cross-validated in the true sense of the word. These are two different methods of reducing decision ambiguity that are most effective under, essentially, non-overlapping set of circumstances outlined above.

12

Knowledge Creation:
From Findings to Knowledge

The point made repeatedly throughout this book is that analytics is about the creation of unique, competitively advantageous knowledge. In business sense, it means transforming raw, generic data into unique insights capable of shedding explanatory light on past outcomes and directing future courses of action. As a result, the bulk of the ideas outlined in earlier chapters were directed toward the "how-to" of effective analytics, which, as illustrated in Figure 1.4, makes up the lion's share of the knowledge creation process discussed here. However, from the practical standpoint, putting the resultant knowledge to work is just as important. After all, having the knowledge that is not used is of little business value since it is unlikely to lead to any tangible benefits.

Although not as self-evident, putting data-derived insights to work is also quite important from the standpoint statistical analyses for a couple of distinct reasons: First and foremost, it makes possible the in-practice validation of analyses-derived recommendations. For instance, the efficacy of predictive models can be calibrated by contrasting the expected (i.e., model-predicted) to actual outcomes, such as the number of on-the-job accidents. Second, the utilization of analytic outcomes is a necessary prerequisite to the expansion of the organization's knowledge base via *successive approximations* of reality.

Expansion of the Knowledge Base

Consider Figure 12.1 below, showing an outline of the now-familiar RPM analytical process.

Figure 12.1
The RPM Analytical Process

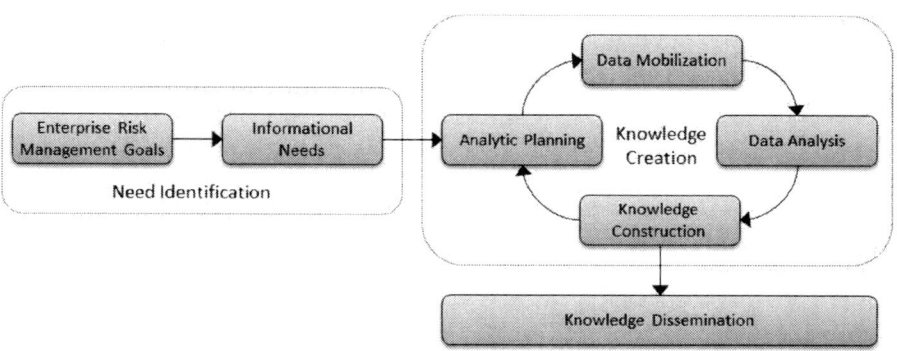

As depicted by the process flow shown above, the RPM process detailed in this book culminates in the dissemination of enterprise risk management-inspired and ensuing data analysis-derived knowledge. It is important to note that knowledge creation is an ongoing process, as one set of findings will typically raise additional questions or will lead to re-thinking of the original assumptions or the analytic plan. In a conceptual sense, the best way to think about the *ongoing learning loop* characteristic of the RPM analytical process is to consider the notion of *successive approximations* mentioned earlier. The basic idea conveyed in this frequently invoked idea (in fields as diverse as behavioral psychology and electrical engineering) is that empirical data analyses do not instantaneously yield the best insights, but rather deliver progressively more accurate estimates, with each subsequent estimate representing an improvement over the previous one (and thus in the existing knowledge base). Hence, the growing body of empirically-derived and in-practice-tested insights will lead to progressively more accuracy and depth in the generated knowledge, which will ultimately evidence itself in superior decision making.

DEPLOYMENT

To give rise to decision-guiding knowledge, results of empirical analyses usually need to be "translated" into action terms. That means not just a mere conversion of numerical effect estimates into applicable business terms, but also proper framing of these results in terms of (any) applicability limits. In general, no empirical results are universally and indefinitely true and applicable, which means that the deployment of these learnings needs to encompass explicit usability limits. It might sound somewhat counterintuitive, but excessive reliance on rigid, standard measures assessing the decision-making-worthiness of analytic insights should be avoided. In particular, the use of statistical significance tests as the basis of differentiating between important and trivial insights needs to be approached especially cautiously (see the *Beware of Significance Tests!* section in the *Knowledge Creation: Exploratory Analyses* chapter).

Also important is a proper framing of numerical coefficients. Recall the two examples highlighting an improper use and interpretation of statistical coefficients discussed in the previous chapter: Example 1 illustrated the often-seen tendency to report as valid effects lacking (statistical) significance, while Example 2 brought to light the even more commonly observed tendency of ascribing statistical significance to exact (point estimates, in statistical jargon) values. Both can have a profound impact on the validity and the reliability of the resultant knowledge and both are highly dependent on the application of statistical significance tests.

Tests' Applicability Limits

Although the proliferation of their usage might suggest a universal acceptance of the statistical significance tests (SST) as an effect validation standard, that is not at all the case. In fact, it is hard to think of another statistical concept that continues to generate as much controversy among methodologists. Though widely used on the one hand, significance tests' validity and credibility continue to be questioned on numerous, mostly methodological grounds[1]. Given the earlier discussed differences between scientific and practical research (e.g., the search of universal generalization that characterizes the former vs. the pursuit of longitudinally-sustainable effects that tends to dominate the latter), it is reasonable to suspect that at least of the scientifically limiting aspects of SST can be managed within the narrower context of business, and particularly, risk analytics. This can be accomplished by assessing the "goodness-of-fit", in the manner of speaking, between the stated informational needs and the of statistical significance tests' limitations. Better characterized as applicability limits, they include sample size dependence along with four distinct fallacies: replicability, exact quantity, representativeness and impact. From the standpoint of applied risk analysis, keeping each of these limitations in check presents the best approach to curtailing the undesirable aspects of SST, while at the same time retaining the objectivity that comes with using those tests as the basis for differentiating between spurious and material effects.

Sample Size Dependence

What is the impact of sample size on the validity of SST test and what can be done about it?

It is apparent from SST formulations that the likelihood of detecting statistically significant differences increases as a direct function of sample size[2], so much so that the initially statistically insignificant differences can gain statistical significance with relatively modest sample size increases. In general, keeping everything else the same and doubling the sample size will lead to more-or-less doubling of the probability of finding statistically significant results; tripling the sample size will lead to approximately tripling the probability of finding statistically significant results, etc.[3] In many instances, a sample size of several hundred records will lead to inordinately trivial differences becoming statistically significant.

To avoid falling into the sample size trap, make sure group-level sample sizes are in the range of 150 – 500 usable records for the most disaggregate record grouping. If any of the group-level sample sizes are in excess of 500 records, select a smaller subset of 500 or fewer records using a random, stratified or other appropriate sampling technique.

Replicability Fallacy

Should statistical significance be used to project the expectancy of current trends into the future?

In spite of misperceptions to the contrary, statistical significance testing does not support longitudinal generalizations. If a particular risk mitigation step generated statistically significant frequency of severity

287

decreases, it is not correct to ascribe any confidence (in a statistical sense) to the expectation of that program generating similar results when replicated in the future. SST is limited to generalizing sample-based results onto the population from which the sample was drawn at a given point in time—and that's all.

For example, if we started out with a population of 5,000 claims from which we selected a random sample of 500 to be included in a trial claim management program, we could generalize any statistically significant results onto the original universe of 5,000 claims. We could not, however, draw any conclusions regarding future replicability of the results, which is a considerable limitation from the practical point of view. The reason future-pointing generalizations are not plausible is due to the test statistics' cross-sectional rather than longitudinal emphasis. In other words, the t-test, χ^2 or the F-test (used to detect persistent vs. spurious differences between/among group means or proportions) utilize cross individual and single point-in-time information—not cross-individual and cross-time information. Consequently, significance testing supports sample-to-population, but not today-to-future generalizations. This is an example of SST application and interpretation limits running counter to business users' informational needs and it is one of several reasons for why significance testing is not a universally applicable tool.

To avoid the replicability fallacy, do not use statistical significance testing as basis for making result replicability claims; use it only to generalize sample-based findings onto a larger population (from which the sample came) but without any future-pointing implications. We might have reasons to believe that similar-to- current results can be expected in the future, but SST should not be used to substantiate those claims.

Exact Quantity Fallacy

Should the results of a statistical significance test be applied to an exact quantification of the magnitude of an effect?

This topic has already been covered in a sufficient level of detail earlier in this discussion, thus the current remarks are a summary of the previously made observations (see *Example 2: Ascribing Statistical Significance to Exact Values*, discussed earlier). As noted there, it is common to interpret statistical significance in the context of what is technically referred to as "point estimates". In spite of it being a relatively common practice, statistical significance cannot be ascribed to an exact value—it can only be associated with a range of values known as a *confidence interval*. This means that it is incorrect to associate confidence levels (e.g., 90%, 95% or 99%) with a specific numerical quantity, as doing so will likely produce misleading or outright inaccurate results.

Representativeness Fallacy

Should statistical significance be used to verify the representativeness of a sample?

Again, despite common misperceptions to the contrary, statistical significance testing does not measure the degree to which a sample represents the population (from which it was drawn). The only way to make that determination is to develop a carefully constructed sampling plan and take appropriate sample-to-population cross validation steps. All too often, however, there is a tendency to use the results of significance testing to validate the sample representativeness, which is erroneous.

Impact Fallacy

Should statistical significance be used as a proxy for business importance of results in question?

Frequently, the term "statistical" is dropped and the results are described as being "significant", rather than merely "statistically significant." Particularly in the business context the former might be taken to mean "being of practical relevance and/or importance", which is a considerably stronger characterization than warranted by the outcomes of significance tests, especially when put in the context of the previously discussed SST's sample size dependence.

UPDATING

As emphasized throughout this book, in order to deliver the most value to an organization database analytics should be viewed as a process, rather than a singular event. Consequently, the results should be additive, with each set contributing to a progressively more robust organizational knowledge base, which in turn brings the organizational decision makers ever closer to an optimally effective business decision-making model (recall the earlier discussion of successive approximations).

In contrast to most of the procedures and approaches that comprise the Risk Profile Measurement process detailed in this book, the task of updating the firm's knowledge base with results of successive database analytical "cycles" is somewhat softer in a procedural sense, while at the same time it is highly dependent on the type of analysis driving a particular update cycle. Overall, the importance of cycle-specific updating is a function of the expected stability of findings, with the need to update being inversely related to said stability—i.e., the more stable the results, the lower the update need. Consider Figure 12.2 below.

Figure 12.2
General Types of Updatable Analyses

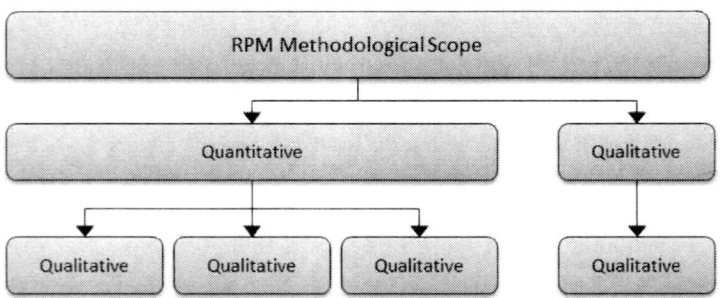

The RPM framework leverages two general types of statistical methodologies: quantitative and qualitative. The former is comprised of three distinct types of analyses: *Exploratory Analyses, Predictive Analytics* and *Alternative Evaluation* (technically known as experimentation); the latter leverages a singular technique known as *Delphi Method.* As detailed in earlier chapters there are considerable methodological and informational differences among these techniques, thus it follows that each methodology will exhibit a somewhat different set of update requirements.

It seems intuitively obvious that exploratory analyses will yield the most stable (consistent across time) results, which translates into lowest update frequency. Under most circumstances, general descriptive insights stemming from exploratory analyses have a relatively long "shelf life", as they tend to take the form of longer term, enduring trends. Furthermore, the results—in terms of insights—are cumulative in nature, as subsequent analyses may uncover additional, previously unknown insights without invalidating earlier generated learnings. As such, the results of exploratory analyses are largely strategic in nature, informing policy decisions and thus relatively slow-changing.

Predictive analytics, as a family of data analytical approaches is somewhat different with regard to results. First and foremost, the focus of predictive analytics is highly tactical, which is in keeping with their primary benefit being that of directing specific action steps, as opposed to informing broader policy decisions. Consequently, the requisite update frequency is also higher, which means that predictions have shorter "shelf life" (e.g., think of credit scoring or bond rating systems, which tend to be updated quarterly). Lastly, the more recent behavioral predictions tend to replace the older ones, which is in stark contrast to exploratory analyses.

To a large degree, alternative evaluation / experimentation tends to mirror predictive analytics, though it is also distinct in some important regards. On the one hand both provide guidance to decision makers, while on the other hand the type of guidance each of the two offers is quite different. Predictive analytical solutions tend to be focused on a specific, typically singular outcome (e.g., likelihood of incurring a securities class action), while alternative evaluation, as implied by its name, is primarily concerned with multi-item comparisons.

Lastly, the results of Delphi Method-derived learnings are somewhat more challenging to describe in terms of frequency of updates. In terms of its overall purpose (in the context of the RPM process), the goal of Delphi Method is to generate predictions for outcomes for which no readily available quantitative data exist—in that regard, Delphi Method is very similar to predictive analytics. On the other hand, the process of arriving at those qualitatively generated outcomes is not permissive of high re-computing frequency that is characteristic of predictive analytics for a variety of reasons, not the least of which is that the "data" – i.e., subjective expert beliefs – simply does not either rapidly or in regular intervals. Table shows a summary of the key update considerations discussed in this section.

Table 12.1
Update Decision Criteria

Type of Analyses	Update Action	Frequency
Quantitative		
Exploratory Analyses	Adding to the "catalogue" of observed patterns & relationships. *Action:* Accumulation	Low
Predictive Analytics	Adding new and/or refresh of existing record-level propensities. *Action:* Replacement	High
Alternative Evaluation	Adding new "action-response" results to the existing catalogue. *Action:* Accumulation	High
Qualitative		
Delphi Method	Revising the previous estimates, without substantially altering the composition of the expert group. *Action:* Replacement	Low

13

Knowledge Dissemination

To a varying degree, organizational decision making is hierarchical, the result of which is that managers' informational needs tend to reflect their individual scopes of responsibility, hence what constitutes useful information can take many different forms, depending on one's scope of responsibilities. Hence it follows that the goal of effective knowledge dissemination should be twofold: First, to identify specific shared need target audiences, and secondly, to design the "right" informational content and presentation for each audience type. Doing so is the necessary prerequisite to transforming generic information into decision-guiding knowledge.

In practice, custom-fitting information to end users' needs entails determining the appropriate level of detail and the scope of coverage, and then matching the so-delimited slice of the total available information with the audience most likely to benefit from those insights. The lack of alignment between the end users' specific informational needs and the scope, coverage and the delivery format can significantly diminish the value of data analyses-derived insights. The most brilliant and innovative analyses won't yield much value unless they are expressly incorporated into the decision making process.

In short, the key to effective knowledge sharing is the understanding of "who needs what." Overall, those with more tactically focused, narrower responsibilities usually need more disaggregate, detailed insights, while those with broader, more strategic responsibilities will be better served by more summarized and contextualized insights. Still, not all analyses-sourced insights can be easily aligned with distinct stakeholder groups and the need for some information may cut across functional and hierarchical organizational layers. Furthermore, business organizations themselves have been steadily making more information available to more internal stakeholders with the hope of increasing its level of utilization—for instance, key risk exposure related metrics that used to be made available only to senior-most managers are now routinely communicated to a broad range of middle and even staff managers. Given all those considerations, the key aspect of organizational knowledge creation is shaping the often diverse and esoteric analytic outcomes into easy-to-consume, maximally understandable to all decision inputs. Although there are numerous tools that can be employment in that process, the two information structuring and delivery mechanisms that have a nearly universal applicability are *management dashboards* and *scorecards*, which represent two of many examples of business intelligence applications.

Business Intelligence Applications

The 1990's witnessed a strong growth and a proliferation of business intelligence (BI), which are computer applications designed expressly for the purpose of disseminating data-derived insights. The origin of the first BI systems can be traced to enterprise data warehousing projects embarked on by most large organizations throughout the 1980's and 1990's with the goal of bring together multiple data systems and to develop user interface tools to support data analyses and reporting.

The bulk of the BI systems can be categorized as either *model-* or *data-driven*. Model-driven systems are built around data modeling capabilities, such as optimization algorithms, predictive models, decision simulations or decision trees. As such, these systems are geared toward drawing inferences and generalizing beyond the confines of the available data—in other words, they are focused on the prescriptive aspects of the analysis of data.

Data-driven systems, on the other hand, are constructed around the more conceptually straightforward data mart or data warehouse-based summarizations, typically utilizing on-line analytical processing, or OLAP engines. As such, these applications do not attempt to draw inferences from data, but merely try to summarize it, which means that data-driven systems tend to be primarily descriptive in nature.

Regardless of the underlying data processing capabilities, all BI systems ultimately produce standardized (i.e., fixed format, template-based) reports. Once structured, a standardized report template is usually re-produced on a periodic (most often weekly or monthly, but also as frequently as daily) basis, conveying snapshots of a fixed set of initially chosen operational metrics, such as the frequency of accidents or the cost of a particular group of claims, giving the organization an easy access to the key up-to-date metrics. Though beneficial to some users some of the time, by-and-large, the BI systems-originated reports are ultimately nothing more than collections of ad hoc, unconnected informational tidbits devoid of *cause—effect* type of conclusions. Stated differently, the basic BI functionality offers insights into "what-is", but leaves the question of "why" unanswered. Consider a periodic claims report capturing monthly or quarterly cost and frequency levels. Such reports certainly provide a convenient summary of outcomes of interest, but at the same time say nothing about the underlying causes of the observed outcome. As a result, decision makers are often very well informed about the levels and trends of various business outcomes, but know comparatively little about the factors influencing those outcomes.

Beyond Reporting

The lack of an explicit assessment of causal factors coupled with the focus on highly disaggregate analyses (i.e., detailed metrics) and a skew toward completeness (i.e., inclusion of all available metrics) severely limit the ultimate value of basic BI reports. In a sense, these reports emphasized quantity over quality – rather than "telling a story" they tend to provide "data-dumps." Also, these reports are usually constructed with no particular audience in mind, to the degree to which they are shaped by what is available (in terms of data) rather than what might be needed...

The underlying reasons point to a mix of business considerations and technical specifications. In terms of the former, vendors were trying to recoup their development costs as rapidly as possible, hence mass standardization, and the resultant generic information structure was a logical choice. In terms of the latter of the two reasons, at least the early BI applications were designed around somewhat limiting and inflexible treatment of input data matrices. More specifically, the reporting functionality was usually built around row (cases), but not column (metrics) summarization, which placed considerable limitations on within-application data manipulation, which in turn constrained the assessment of the underlying causal factors. As a result, standard BI reports simply did not have the capabilities that were needed to draw a clear line of differentiation between important and trivial metrics, or between persistent and spurious associations.

INFORMATIONAL REFINEMENT

The earliest precursor of what is now known as *dashboards* began to appear in the mid-1980's, and it was then known under the moniker of *executive information systems* (EIS). True to their designation of "executive", the EIS' circulation was typically limited to the very highest levels of organizations' management, such as CEO or Chairman of the Board. Consequently, their success was limited, in large part because their readership was so limited, but also because their data analytical foundations were still relatively immature. However, a couple of decades amount to an eternity in the information field, and so a lot has changed since the early EIS days. First and foremost, the next generation of what used to be known as executive information systems are no longer targeted at just a handful of the very top managers—in fact, the qualifier "executive" is rarely used in reference to dashboards and scorecards, both of which were pushed down through the organization to provide relevant information to area managers, rather than just the top two or three executives. Secondly, the scope of both has been expanded to cover a broader cross-section of a particular decision domain, all while being expressly focused on decision-guiding, persistent effects, while foregoing lesser important details.

Figure 13.1 depicts the relationship between basic BI reports discussed in the previous section, dashboards and scorecards, in term of their respective level of detail and the informational scope.

Figure 13.1
Scope vs. Detail

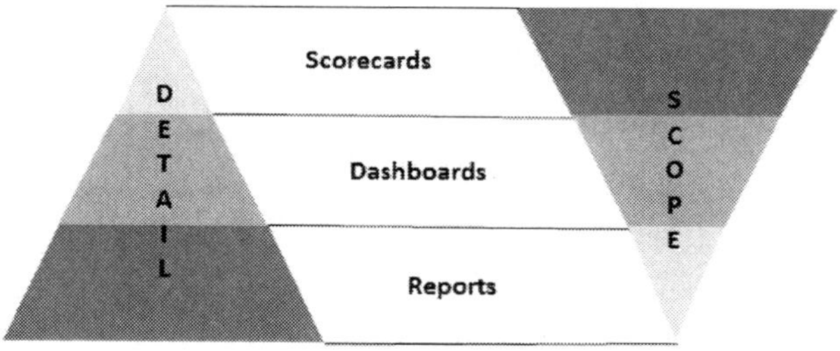

As shown above, the progression from detail-oriented, basic database reports toward the more summarization-oriented dashboards and scorecard entails an increase in the informational coverage, which is accompanied by reduction in informational detail. It is important to note that the detail vs. scope interdependence shown above is meant to illustrate the differences in the type of utility offered by each of the three information reporting mechanisms, which is to say that in some situations detailed reports might yield the desired utility, while other situations might call for a dashboard or a scorecard. That said, it is also important to note that from the standpoint of (risk management related) knowledge creation, dashboards and scorecards offer significantly greater levels of informational refinement.

Dashboards vs. Scorecards

While there are a number of distinct similarities between dashboards and scorecards, there are also clear differences. In terms of similarities, both dashboards and scorecards rely heavily on data integration and visualization, which is a consequence of broader scope (data integration) and diminished level of detail (visualization). Difference-wise, dashboards and scorecards are distinct in terms of how data is integrated and for what purpose, which means that choosing between the two demands clear delineation of their usage and application differences.

Perhaps most importantly, dashboards are focused on the *what* of business outcomes, while scorecards are geared toward communicating the *how*. In other words, dashboards communicate performance and scorecards chart progress, which ultimately means that the former are more tactically-focused, while the latter are more strategic. More specifically, the difference between these two modes of information visualization is most evident in the context of their purpose, inputs and the visual format.

Purpose-wise, the overall goal of a dashboard is to display performance-related information, while the goal of a scorecard is to show progress made against stated organizational objectives. It means that while the former is a performance monitoring tool, the latter can be considered a performance management instrument. In a typical risk management context, this difference parallels the distinction between loss tracking and tabulation (dashboard) and the overall performance of the entire risk management program (scorecard).

Input-wise, dashboards tend to be built around singular events described in terms of event-applicable, thus possibly idiosyncratic metrics, while scorecards tend to offer a cross-event, summary views emphasizing performance proxies often referred to as *key performance indicators,* or KPIs. In risk management terms, the distinctiveness between these two types of inputs parallels the difference between a single risk reduction initiative and the overall risk control, which implies cross-sectional (i.e., cross-initiative) vs. longitudinal (i.e., cross-time) comparisons. In that context, tracking of a distinct risk control initiative calls for a dashboard, while compiling a summary of broader risk management efforts is best accomplished with a scorecard.

The third of the key dashboard—scorecard points of differentiation is the use of information visualization. This is an important consideration given that roughly 70% of the sense receptors in the human body reside in our eyes, which makes us particularly adept at processing properly structured visual stimuli (hence the expression "a picture is worth a thousand words..."). On that note, though both dashboards and scorecards take advantage of visual display of information, the latter tends to make a more extensive of it. Given that the amount of information that needs to be "packed" into a scorecard can be considerable, especially for a larger organization with a diverse range of risk exposures, "catching the eye" of the reader can be a critical step in successfully disseminating analytical insights. A sample scorecard shown in Figure 13.2 illustrates that point.

Effective Presentation

To be effective as a communication mechanism, both dashboards and scorecards need to exhibit several distinct characteristics. Overall, these characteristics can be grouped into *visual* and *content design* considerations.

Most notably, the design of scorecards and dashboards needs to be intuitive and personalizable, which means that their construction ought to be guided by a combination of informational parsimony and visual simplicity. Furthermore, it is important to make an appropriate use of visual cues, such as color and universally understood symbols, and, whenever possible, combine singular informational elements into patterned displays. Consider the following scorecard example, illustrating the SampleCo's exposure to securities class action litigation (SCA):

Figure 13.2
Sample Scorecard

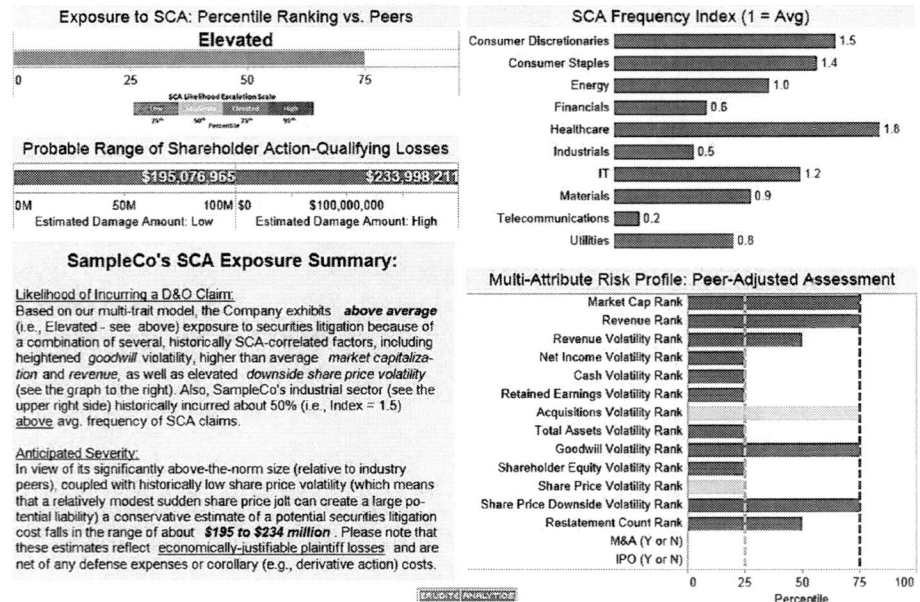

SCA Exposure Scorecard: SampleCo

Depicted above is a sample dashboard template designed to communicating the summary of the different facets' of SampleCo's SCA exposure – the one-page document is divided into several simple, visually-oriented sections:

> *Exposure to SCA*: Captures the aggregate view of the probability, measured in relation to peer companies, of incurring an SCA claim; this is the likelihood dimension of risk.

> *Probable Loss Range*: A range-based estimate of the expected cost associated with the aforementioned SCA claim; this is the severity dimension of risk.

> *SampleCo's Exposure Summary*: A short narrative highlighting the key likelihood, severity and risk driver findings.

> *Risk Profile*: A graphically-expressed delineation of the key risk drivers.

> *SCA Frequency Index*: An aggregate, industry-wide enumeration of past SCA filings frequencies.

300

The example shown above is one of the many potential dashboard designs. Its goal is to illustrate the key design considerations mentioned earlier, most notably the informational parsimony, visual simplicity and intuitive design. In general, scorecard and dashboard templates should be tailored not just to individual organizations, but to the informational needs of specific audiences within an organization. Thus the same fundamental information might be circulated throughout the organization in several different formats, all with the goal of increasing its utilization. At the same time, reporting templates should exhibit a fair amount of cross-time stability to aid in longitudinal comparisons, thus enabling more accurate longer-term performance trending.

THE NORMATIVE REPORT DESIGN FRAMEWORK

As much as an eye-catching and easy to "see" design is critical to capturing the intended stakeholders' attention, powerful informational content is a necessary prerequisite to assuring the desired impact. The Normative Report Design Framework discussed in this section offers a universally applicable, structured set of considerations that can be used to guide the development process. The framework is built around the three distinct, interlocking dimensions of *function, focus* (i.e., what to report) and *method* (i.e., how to report).

Function

Insofar as the development of decision-aiding knowledge is concerned (which is the stated purpose of this book), a report can serve one of two key functions: 1. to aid in assessing and communicating the outcomes of interest; and 2. to be a vehicle for compiling aggregate overviews of groups of outcomes. What are the "outcomes of interest"? Conceptually, it is relatively straightforward question – obviously, within the realm of risk management, the earlier discussed likelihood and severity of upside and downside risk comprise the outcomes of interest. However, as discussed in the *Knowledge of Risk* and *Risk Measurement* chapters, the list of potential threats is very long…Do all individual threats comprise the aforementioned outcomes of interest? The short answer is no, simply because not all threats are, well, equally threatening. That is an important consideration and it needs to be taken into account when designing dashboards and scorecards – sometimes, less is more...

To be deemed "of interest", a particular exposure needs to be decision-pending and have a designated, or at least stipulated, decision maker. Put in the context of the risk response options discussed in the *Knowledge of Risk* chapter (see Figure 2.5), this means accept-avoid-transfer-reduce choices need to be made, hence insights that shed light on the appropriateness of the individual response options, and/or more specific considerations pertaining to an already selected alternative (e.g., if the transfer of risk, via a commercial insurance placement, is the choice, how much coverage should be purchased?) would clearly be "of interest." On the other hand, for risks which are effectively ignored (there numerous external threats that simply cannot be managed, in the sense of taking measurable and meaningful likelihood or severity reducing steps – just think of political or economic risks) .

The second of the two aforementioned two key report functions is that of providing an aggregate overview. The fundamental idea here is this: Whether it is internal resource allocation or external activities, such as procurement of insurance coverage, there is an implicit competition among individual risk types. Given that, it is quite important to be wisely selective when compiling a listing of specific risk items that should be closely considered and reviewed—as mentioned repeatedly throughout this book, the goal of the analysis of data is to, ultimately, yield competitively advantageous, decision aiding knowledge. With that in mind, the role of dashboard and scorecard reports is to offer robust and objective summative conclusions in a manner that informs and guides.

Focus

Once the structure of a dashboard or a scorecard has been designed, reports need to be populated with the "right" information. The essence of that consideration is the tailoring of outcomes of data analyses to the specifics of the user—decision conjoint: Who is the user of information and what does that user need to know in order to make better decisions? In a more operationally clear sense, that translates into three distinct considerations: 1. user group's needs, 2. materiality of content and 3. completeness of conclusions.

User Group's Needs

It is intuitively obvious that user groups within an organization are going to differ, quite considerably at times, in terms of their informational needs. Senior executives' needs are rarely the same as those of risk managers', both in the sense of scope as well as detail, just as the informational needs of the latter will generally differ from those of claim managers. At the same time, all organizational stakeholders have a vested interest in the effectiveness of the organization's risk management efforts, though they all may contribute quite differently to it success. Hence it follows that the informational content should reflect those differences.

Consider the distinction between generic information and competitively advantageous knowledge discussed earlier: Information can be broadly defined as data in context, while knowledge as the sum of interpreted information. The difference between the two is essentially the degree of usability to decision making, with knowledge offering a greater level of utility by virtue of the fact that it is of more help in selecting the right course of action.

It follows that the content (i.e., the specifics of what is included) of a report is a function of what a particular user or a user group would like to know and what is knowable in view of the data analytic results on hand. Within the confines of risk management, the overriding consideration guiding knowledge creation and dissemination is to provide the greatest amount of risk protection at the lowest possible economic cost. At an operational, or a function management level this may translate into, for instance, better on-the-job accident claim cost forecasting. Here, a decision-guiding scorecard would be constructed around knowledge of which recently filed claims are most likely to develop adversely, thus directing cost-reducing efforts by the way of taking the "right" claim management steps against the "right" claims. At a higher, capability management level, a scorecard utilizing the same underlying information would communicate more aggregate insights, such as the most appropriate amount and type of risk transfer and the most appropriate risk reduction steps. Lastly, at an executive management level, the decision aiding knowledge might take the form of compelling evidence (course of action + anticipated impact) to suggested a more effective resource allocation strategy.

Materiality of Content

The informational content of a dashboard or a scorecard needs to demonstrate an appreciable impact on the decision making process of each user group. In other words, the content of a report has to be *material*, which is defined here as the degree to which any analysis-derived insights enhance the uniqueness and/or the depth of the stakeholders' knowledge.

The materiality of content is a manifestation of the theme of one of the earlier chapters (*Risk Measurement*): Not everything that is knowable is worth knowing and not everything that is worth knowing is knowable. Few things accumulate as quickly as seemingly interesting, but decision-wise inconsequential information, so much so that it is not unusual for organizations to struggle to find the few useful nuggets in an avalanche of spurious tidbits. Admittedly, the distinction between "important" and "trivial" can be somewhat arbitrary[1], at least initially. However, as analysts become more familiar with informational needs of different constituent groups and the latter more intimate with what is analytically discernable, the quality of the content should improve rapidly.

Completeness of Conclusions

To paint an informationally complete picture, the report's coverage of its insights and any definitions of their interpretational boundary should be sufficient to make a positive contribution to the quality of its users' decisions. In that sense, the report's completeness is a function of its scope, boundary and the time interval covered. Under more circumstances, the scope of a scorecard should be narrower than the scope of a dashboard. In general, it is advantageous to limit the scope of the former to either a single risk management initiative (e.g., an analytical early warning system for the identification of specific claims most at risk of adverse development) or a relatively homogenous set of initiatives. The scope of a dashboard will necessarily be broader to accommodate cross-initiative comparisons, but it too should be limited to somewhat similar types of activities. Mixing and matching fundamentally dissimilar risk management initiatives carries a strong possibility of erect barriers to meaningful cross-initiative comparisons by diminishing the number of viable evaluative factors (due to reducing all comparisons to a common-to-all aspects).

Method

How information is "packaged" has significant bearing on its end user utility. As it is often the case, there are numerous, situation-dependent influences that defy an easy categorization or a generalization – still, there are discernable factors that exert a strong impact on the ultimate, decision-aiding impact of any dashboard or scorecard report. Within that context, of particular interest from the standpoint of report construction are: accuracy, reliability, clarity and cross-sectional and longitudinal comparability.

Accuracy

Without the doubt, accuracy is the single most important aspect of any type of information. Inaccurate conclusions can lead to a wide range of undesirable consequences, from missed opportunities (strategic risk) to inappropriate amount of coverage (property damage or executive liability) to misallocation of risk management resources (ongoing claims management).
To be deemed accurate, a dashboard or scorecard-reported insights have to stem from correct interpretations of unbiased analyses of robust data. In a more operational sense, correctness of conclusions means that the

underlying data has been evaluated in terms of its credibility, representativeness and size; any statistical method related assumptions (such as those relating to distributional properties of data) have been validated and met; the margin of error of findings is not wide enough to potentially influence conclusions (for instance, the confidence interval for action attributable effects does not include "0" in its range); and the shown conclusions are valid interpretations of the data and can be replicated, if needed. To be sure—these are considerable burdens. They impose a considerable level of discipline on the data analytical process and those responsible for the individual steps as well as the overall endeavor. The data analytical process described in this was to a large degree inspired by the desire to attain high degree of correctness of findings—to assure the said accuracy, each step ought to be sufficiently documented and the overall process peer-reviewed.

Reliability

Closely related to the notion of accuracy, reliability also ranks prominently among the report-defining characteristics. Definition-wise, reliability is a supposition that the underlying facts and analytical processes that form the basis for findings and conclusions contained in a report were compiled, analyzed and disclosed in a way that could withstand quality review.

In the context of sample-based business analyses, the notion of reliability takes on particular significance. Most organizations under most circumstances have a relatively limited interest in sample-only findings; instead, are interested in the degree to which these findings can be extrapolated onto a larger universe. For instance, it would be deemed as encouraging that the analysis of a sample of 1,000 fully developed workers' compensation claims suggests the potential of reducing the total cost of those claims by 20% or more, but ultimately, it is the degree to which those findings hold true for the entire universe of current workers' compensation claims that would be of interest to the organization. In that sense, the reliability of findings stands to mean "generalizability" of sample-based results, which in contrast to the earlier discussed accuracy of findings (which are binary in nature—i.e., are or are not true) should be expressed in terms of "degree of".

Let's consider the aforementioned sample of 1,000 workers' compensation claims. If the confidence interval-expressed action-attributable effect includes '0' in its range, e.g., it ranges from '0.3%' on the low end to '-20.2%' on the high end, the generalizability (and thus the reliability) of these findings should be called into question. In other words, the range of the estimated impact spans from a small possibility of a slight gain (0.3% increase) to a considerable decrease (-20.2%). In this example, a mere fact that the estimated range of effects includes "0" is enough to warrant calling the reliability of these findings into question.

Clarity

A lesson that many analysts find hard to remember is that oftentimes it is not just *what* the results are, but *how* we communicate them. Any scorecard or dashboard reported insight should be informationally unambiguous and interpretationally understandable to its stakeholders. Although as argued earlier, information should be tailored to the user type-specific needs (in order to become competitively advantageous knowledge), in principle, any user group tailored report should be understandable to any other user group. There is a vast difference between the usability and the understandability of results— just because a particular finding is not directly of interest to a specific audience does not mean that it should not be understandable to that audience.

Recall the two examples discussed in the *Knowledge Creation: Evaluating Alternatives* chapter, which outlined two of the more commonly seen misapplications of statistical significance tests (presenting as tangible sample-based differences lacking statistical significance and attributing statistical significance to point estimates). Once aggregated to the dashboard or scorecard level, such fairly technical considerations would likely be hidden, which means that the users of the information would not a clear understanding of those dependencies, instead taking the interpreted information as being true on its face value. As suggested earlier, accuracy is the most important consideration that goes into preparing informational summaries and conclusions, thus the importance of clearly stating any limitations or dependencies simply cannot be overstated.

Cross-Sectional & Longitudinal Comparability

For most organizations, scorecard and dashboard based reporting is an ongoing process, where each set of reports captures a snapshot (both section- and time-wise) of risk management activities. It follows that it is important for an individual scorecard to be comparable with other scorecards, as well as an individual dashboard to be comparable with other dashboards. To ensure the ongoing comparability of each of these two types of reports demands cross-sectional and longitudinal standardization.

Longitudinal standardization is the invariance of the key report elements with regard to the passage of time—in other words, a dashboard or a scorecard report prepared today should be built around the same key elements as the same type of report prepared in the past. On the other hand, cross-sectional standardization demands that reports encapsulating different promotion types could be compared in terms of their key outcomes. Simply put, it calls for a constant (across individual analyses) set effect measurement and outcome measures.

Index

A

acceptance · See risk, response
additivity · 109
algorithms · 19
alternative risk transfer · 67
analyses types · 295
analysis · 193
analytic planning · 142
analytical dataset · 175
analytics · 237
Anderson-Darling test · 208
ANOVA · 230
applicability limits · 289
approximately normal · 206
arithmetic mean · 212
asset · 31
automated data mining · 196
average · 211
avoidance · See risk, response

B

Bayesian networks · 127
Bayesian probability · 284
behavioral core · See data, content
biserial · 220
bivariate analyses · 215
bivariate correlation · 218
Bowman Paradox · 48
business analytics · 239
business intelligence systems · 297
butterfly effect · 176

C

canonical correlation · 217, 218
Capital Assets Pricing Model · 72
captive insurance · 66
categorical variable · 209
causal augment · See data, content
causation · 151
cause-attributable effect · 25
Central Limit Theorem · 224
chi square · 216
chi square test · 207, 216
cognitive dissonance · 2
collinearity · 202, 253
comparative assessment analysis · 70
competitive advantage · 88
competitive parity · 69
confidence interval · 234, 283
confidence intervals
    interpretation · 235
continuous variable · 209, 211
contract · 66
control group · 275
correlation · 217, 218
    coefficients, types · 220
correlation analysis · 217
correlation coefficient types · 223
correlation matrix · 221
COSO framework · 73
    alternatives · 85
    impact · 77
    limitations · 77
credible intervals · 284
cross-case analysis · See qualitative
    analysis
cross-sectional contrasts · 281
cross-tabulation · 215
cultural theory · 70

D

dashboard · 301
data
    asset · 31
    census-derived · 178
    cleansing · 179
    collection · 173
    competitive advantage · 33
    content · 149
    extract · 178
    mining · 167, 239
    normalization · 179
    quality · 14
    representativeness · 14
    visualization · 195
data exploration
    factual vs. probabilistic · 164
data exploration process · 197
data laden · 12
data mart · 155
data warehouse · 155
database appliance · 165
database paradox · 160
database querying · 164
database reporting · 164
databases
    types · 156
data-information-knowledge continuum · 161
deductive · 196
degree-of-similarity modeling · 249, 250
Delphi approximations · 124, 128
Delphi method · 124, 262, 294
dependence · 229
dependence technique · 244
disambiguation · 87
discrete variable · 210
dispersion · 214
dissemination · See risk analytical process
downside risk
    definition · 97
dummy-coding · 211

E

effect attribution · 25
effect estimation · 276
effective cost of coverage · 66
effective sample size · 280
effects
    linear vs. non-linear · 254
elasticity · 118
electronic transaction processing · 15
entity- specific estimation · 120
epistemology · 7
equality hypotheses · 282
exact quantity fallacy · 291
exchange risk · See risk, exchange
executive information systems · 300
experimental test designs · 277
explanation-based prediction · 120
explanatory analyses · 136
exploratory analyses · 194, 196
exponential growth · 2

F

factor · 276
factor level · 276
fractional factorial · 278
frequency, expected · 207
frequency, observed · 207
Frequentist probability · 284
F-test · 226

G

Galileo affair · 12
general systems model · 140
goodness-of-fit · 207

H

hedging · 67

histogram · 206
homogeneity · See data, types

I

impact fallacy · 292
impact quantification · 246
imputation · 187
   non-replacement · 188
   physical replacement · 187
incidental · See data, collection
independence · See severity-likelihood
   independence
indexing · 204, 233
indicator reliability · 258
indicators · 251
indices · 252
inductive · 196
influence · 181
information
   applicability · 22
   availability · 22
information type categorization · 111
informational advantage · 5
informational domain specification · 231,
   256
   just-specified · 231
   over-specified · 232
   under-specified · 232
informational parity · 23
informational precision · 134
inputs · See general systems model
interaction · 230
interactions · 252
inter-rater reliability · 128
interval scale · 223
intervening factor · See moderating factor
intra-case analysis · See qualitative
   analysis

K

Kendall's rank · 220

key performance indicators, KPIs · 301
knowledge · 162
   base · 19
   codifiability of · 5
   competitive · 19
   components of · 6
   creation · 8, 199
   definition · 5
   explicit · 7, 9
   pursuit of · 30
   tacit · 7, 10
   teachability · 6
knowledge creation · See risk analytical
   process
knowledge leaders · 22
known vs. knowable · 57
Kolmogorov-Smirnov test · 208

L

latent construct · 128
latent construct measurement · 127
learning loop · 288
logistic regression · 250
longitudinal comparability · 310
longitudinal contrasts · 281
look-alike modeling · 250
loss · 45

M

machine learning
   automated classification · 271
   unsupervised mining · 272
management dashboards · 25
materiality · 307
mean · 211
   arithmetic · 211
   geometric · 211
   harmonic · 211
MECE framework · 200
median · 212
meta analysis · 9, 27, 57

metadata · 190
   template · 190
metric aggregation · 233
missing completely at random · 184
missing values substitution · 183
mode · 212
model specification · 246
moderating factor · See intervening factor
Modern Portfolio Theory · 75
multiple correlations · 217
multiple treatment randomized · 278
Multi-source analytics · 169
multivariate analyses · 228
multivariate distribution · 106
multivariate modeling · 57, 122, 244
   descriptive · 244
   predictive · 244

N

natural hedge · 67
need identification · See risk analytical
   process
nominal scale · 223
non-spurious association · 216

O

Ockham's Razor · 26, 202
one-tail test · 225
ordinal scale · 223
orthogonality · 215
outcome · See general systems model
outlier identification · 183
outlier threshold · 182
outliers · 179
output · See general systems model

P

pairwise deletion · 184

parameterization · 240
partial correlation · 217
Pearson's product-moment · 220
phi · 220
planning · 140, 141
point biserial · 220
point estimate · 234, 283
point vs. interval estimation · 281
policy setting · 63
polychoric · 220
polyserial · 220
prediction intervals · 247
predictive analytics · 123, 137
predictor independence · 252
principle of parsimony · See Ockham's
   Razor
probabilistic interpretation · 164
probability
   Bayesian approach · 104
   conditional · 103
   definition · 103
   estimation · 102
   frequentist · 104
   joint · 102
   marginal · 102
   multivariate · 105
process · See general systems model
profiling · 86
propensity model · 257
purposeful · See data, collection

Q

qualitative analysis · 261
qualitative outcome estimation · 262
qualitative variable · 209
quantitative variable · 209
quartile · 214
querying · 163

R

random error · 283

randomized covariate · 279
range · 214
rank biserial · 220
ratio scale · 223
record-to-group assignment · 280
reduction · See risk, response
regression analysis · 229
regression parameters · 182
relationships, bivariate · 215
reliability · 127, 128, 309
replicability fallacy · 290
report design framework · 305
reporting · 162
representativeness fallacy · 292
risk
    activities · 56
    analytical process · 40, 51
    causal view · 50
    components, main · 49
    definition · 41
    downside · 47, 91, 95
    estimation · 98
    exchange · 43
    exposure · 53
    management · 55
    mapping · 51, 56
    response · 52, 58, 112
    types · 60
    typology · 91
    upside · 47, 91
    vs. uncertainty · 44
risk analytical process · 131
risk dimensions
    probability · 48
    severity · 48
risk exposure · 48
risk management
    enterprise risk management · 72
    ERM typologies · 73
risk modeling process · 121
risk profile · 116
    example · 89
risk profile management · 61
Risk Profile Management · 85
risk profiling · 88

definition · 89
risk response
    acceptance · 112
    avoidance · 115
    reduction · 115
    transfer · 114
RPM analytical process · 288

S

sample composition · 279
sample size · 175
    effective · 224, 280
    nominal · 224, 280
sample size dependence · 290
sample sizing · 280
sampling
    random · 177
    stratified · 177
scientific method · 239
scope of model coverage · 255
scorecards · 301
severity · 108
    attribution · 108
    projectability · 108
    recency · 108
severity--likelihood indepedence · 109
significance
    practical · 228
    statistical · 228
Simpson's paradox · 215
single factor randomized · 277
Spearman's rank · 220
standard deviation · 213
standard error · 176, 189, See error
standard normal distribution · 186
statistical effect · 251
statistical modeling rationale · 242
statistical significance · 176, 225, 281
statistical significance testing · 257
statistical significance tests · 226
strategic objectives · 136
strategic risk · 93

successive approximations · 287, See
   Delphi method
summarization · See text mining
syntax · 269

T

test group · 275
tetrachoric · 220
text mining · 266, 267
   approaches · 267
   disambiguation · 270
   homographs · 269
   natural language processing · 268, 270
   synonyms · 269
   text transformation · 269
textual data · 264, 266
   structured · 265
   unstructured · 265
theory laden · 12
theory testing · 226
total cost of risk · 15
transactional data · 15
transfer · See risk, response
t-test · 226
two-tail test · 225
Type I error · 225

U

uncertainty · 44
uniqueness · See data, types
upside risk · 93, See risk, upside
   definition · 94
utility · 43

V

validity · 127, 129
validity, types · 129
variability · 212
variable appropriateness · 201
variable coding · 246
variable indexing · 204
variable set sufficiency · 202
variance · 213
velocitators · 254
volatility · 98
   semi-standard deviation · 102
   semi-variance · 101
   standard deviation · 100
   variance · 99

Bibliography

Ayres, I. (2007). *Super Crunchers: Why Thinking-By-Numbers is the New Way To Be Smart.* New York: Bantam Books.

Babcock, C. (2006, January 9). Data, Data Everywhere. *Information Week* .

Baker, S. (2008). *The Numerati.* New York: Houghton Mifflin.

Banasiewicz, A. (2005). Marketing Pitfalls of Statistical Significance Testing. *Marketing Intelligence and Planning Journal* , 23(5), pp. 515-528.

Black, F., & Scholes, M. S. (1973). The Pricing of Options and Corporate Liabilities. *Journal of Political Economy* , 81(30, pp. 637-654.

Bowman, E. (1980). A Risk/Return Paradox for Strategic Management. *Sloan Management Review* , v. 21, pp. 17-13.

Bowman, E. (1982). Risk Seeking by Troubled Firms. *Sloan Management Review* , v. 23, pp. 33-42.

Churchland, P., & Sejnowski, T. (1992). *The Computational Brain.* Cambridge, MA: MIT Press.

Daniel, L. (1998). Statistical Significance Testing: A Historical Overview of Misuse and Misinterpretation with Implications for Editorial Policies of Educational Journals. *Research in the Schools* , 23-32.

Davenport, T. H. (2006). Competing on Analytics. *Harvard Business Review* , January, pp. 98-107.

Davenport, T. H., & Harris, J. G. (2007). *Competing on Analytics: The New Science of Winning.* Boston, MA: Harvard Business School Press.

Davenport, T. H., & Harris, J. G. (2007). *Competing on Analytics: The New Science of Winning.* Boston, MA: Harvard Business School Press.

Drucker, P. F. (2001). *The Essential Drucker: The Best of Sixty Years of Peter Drucker's Essential Writings on Management.* New York: HarperCollins.

Dyche, J., & Levy, E. (2006). *Customer Data Integration.* Hoboken, NJ: John Wiley and Sons.

Fisher, R. (1925). *Statistical Methods for Research Workers.* London.

Gladwell, M. (2005). *Blink: The Power of Thinking Without Thinking.* New York: Brown and Company.

Hair, J. (1998). *Multivariate Data Analysis.* Upper Saddle River, NJ: Prentice Hall.

Henkel, R. E. (1976). *Tests of Significance.* New York: Sage.

Hubbard, D. (2007). *How to Measure Anything: Finding the Value of Intangibles in Business.* New York: John Wiley and Sons.

Huberty, C. (1987). On Statistical Testing. *Educational Researcher* , 16, 4-9.

Hunt, S. D. (1991). *Modern Marketing Theory: Critical Issues in the Philosophy of Marketing Science.* Cinncinnati, OH: South-Western Publishing.

Jeffrey, R. C. (1992). *Probability and the Art of Judgment.* Cambridge University Press: New York.

Kirk, R. E. (1982). *Experimental Design: Procedures for the Behavioral Sciences.* Monterey, CA: Brooks/Cole Publishing.

Kolmogorov, A. N. (1950; 1933, original). *Foundations of the Theory of Probability.* Berlin.

Lam, J. (2003). *Enterprise Risk Management: From Incentives to Controls.* New York: John Wiley and Sons.

Levitt, S. D., & Dubbner, S. J. (2005). *Freakonomics: A Rogue Economist Explore the Hidden Side of Everything.* New York: HarperCollins.

Likert, R. (1932). A Technique for the Measurement of Attitudes. *Archives of Psychology* , 140, pp. 1-55.

Mardia, K. (1970). Measures of Multivariate Skewness and Kurtosis with Applications. *Biometrika* , 57, pp. 519-530.

Markowitz, H. (1952). Portfolio Selection. *Journal of Finance* , 7(1), pp. 77-91.

Neter, J., Wasserman, W., & Kutner, M. (1990). *Applied Linear Statistical Models.* Boston, MA: Irwin.

Niven, P. (2006). *Balanced Scorecard: Maximizing Performance and Maintaining Results.* New York: John Wiley and Sons.

Peters, T. J., & Waterman, R. H. (1982). *In Search of Excellence: Lessons from America's Best Run Companies.* New York: Warner Books.

Pfeffer, J., & Sutton, R. I. (2006). *Hard Facts, Dangerous Half-Truths & Total Nonsense: Profiting from Evidence-Based Management.* Boston, MA: Harvard Business School Press.

Porter, M. E. (1980). *Competitive Strategy.* New York: Free Press.

Quinn, J., Anderson, P., & Finkerstein, S. (1996). Managing Professional Intellect: Making the Most of the Best. *Harvard Business Review* , March-April.

Rogers, E. (1962). *Diffusion of Innovations.* New York: Free Press.

Rosenblum, B., & Kuttner, F. (2008). *Quantum Enigma: Physics Encounters Consciousness.* New York: Oxford University Press.

Rubin, D. (1987). *Multiple Imputations for Nonresponse in Surveys.* New York: John Wiley and Sons.

Sagan, C. (2006). *The Varieties of Scientific Experience.* New York: The Pinguin Press.

Sharpe, W. F. (1964). Capital Asset Prices: A Theory of Market Equilibrium under Conditions of Risk. *Journal of Finance* , 19(3), pp. 425-442.

Slywotzky, A. J., & Drzik, J. (2005). Countering the Biggest Risk of All. *Harvard Business Review* , April, pp.43-51.

Smith, A. (1991; original, 1776). *An Inquiry into the Nature and Causes of the Wealth of Nations.* Amherst, NY: Prometheus Books.

Switzer, F., Roth, P., & Switzer, D. (1998). Systematic Data Loss in HRM Settings: A Monte Carlo Analysis. *Journal of Management* , 24(6), pp. 763-779.

Tabachnick, B., & Fidell, S. (1996). *Using Multivariate Statistics.* New York: Harper Collins.

Thompson, M., Ellis, R., & Wildavsky, A. (1990). *Cultural Theory.* New York: Westview Press.

Tukey, J. (1977). *Exploratory Data Analysis.* Reading, MA: Addison-Wesley.

Endnotes

Chapter 1

[1] The 12-fold threshold was reached using a very long stretch of thin paper, resembling toilet paper, using what is known as "single direction folding." A number of people, however, questioned the validity of this mark, believing that a "proper" folding approach entailed folding a sheet in half, turning it 90° and then folding it again. Using the "proper" folding method, it has been shown that a single sheet of thin paper can be folded 11 times, with the first 8 folds accomplished manually and the remaining 3 with the help of mechanical equipment (a steam roller and a fork lift).

[2] *see* Rosenblum, Bruce and Fred Kuttner, *Quantum Enigma, Physics Encounters Consciousness.*, Oxford University Press, 2008.

[3] Quinn, J.B., P. Anderson, and S. Finkelstein (1996), "*Managing Professional Intellect: Making the Most of the Best*", *Harvard Business Review, March-April.*

[4] A Greek philosopher and mathematician, born around 428 B.C and a founder of the Academy of Athens, the first institution of higher learning in the western world.

[5] The processes governing making the said choices are subjects of an interdisciplinary field known as "decision theory", which is concerned primarily with goal-directed behavior in the presence of options, under the assumption of non-random selection. In a very broad sense, decision theories fall under two general umbrellas: normative and descriptive. A *normative decision theory* is a theory about how decisions should be made, and a *descriptive theory* is a theory about how decisions are actually made. Obviously, the availability of decision-guiding knowledge is essential to each of the two sets of theories.

[6] Microwaves are very short wavelength/frequency electromagnetic waves, much smaller than those used in radio broadcasting.

[7] Purposeful; derived from the Greek word *telos*, meaning *end* or *purpose.*

[8] The trial and the resultant abjuration of Galileo before the Holy Congregation of the Catholic Church at the convent of Minerva on June 22, 1633.

[9] See Churchland, Patricia S. and Terrence J. Sejnowski (1992), *The Computational Brain*, MIT Press.

[10] Even while a given insurance policy is in effect, the contingent capital it provides is typically not recognized as an asset on the organization's balance sheet.

[11] An insurance company established with the objective of underwriting only the risks emanating from its parent company; it is discussed in more detail in the next chapter.

[12] Perhaps the most familiar to most of us example of event-tracking data is the *point-of-sale*, or POS, transaction recording taking place in a retail setting. A customer paying for his/her purchases creates multiple event-tracking records, with each item comprising the shopping basket creating a separate electronic record.

[13] In principle, the term "algorithm" is sufficiently broad to include virtually all statistical techniques. However, as used here, *statistical techniques* refer to general problem solving methods readily available to anyone, while *computational algorithms* denote custom-built computational methods. For example, cluster analysis is a statistical technique widely-used for grouping customers into segments; it is typically included in many of the popular statistical analysis software packages (e.g., SAS or SPSS) and as such readily available for anyone to use. A proprietary approach to customer value quantification, developed "in-house" and not readily available to others is an example of a computational algorithm.

[14] Most notably, the difficulty of integrating these typically special application oriented systems with the growing number of other applications.

[15] In fact, a typical report layout is somewhat reminiscent of a car dashboard (hence the name), given the heavy reliance on dials and gauges as means of communicating the information. See the *Knowledge Dissemination* chapter for an example of a management dashboard report.

[16] *Entia non sunt multiplicanda praetem necessitatem,* Latin for "entities should not be multiplied unnecessarily"; it is often paraphrased as "All things being equal, the simplest solution is the best. William of Ockham was a 14th Century Franciscan friar and logician.

[17] These include standard POS (point-of-sale) transaction recording systems; third-party data vendors, such as AC Nielsen in consumer packaged goods or RL Polk in automotive industries; or Standard & Poor's Compustat (quarterly, annual and ad hoc SEC filings submitted by all publicly-traded firms) tracking financial metrics across all industries; etc.

[18] This is particularly the case with event-tracking data, where the *recency* of behavioral outcomes is one of the key factors in deriving robust explanatory/predictive insights. It is a manifestation of the intuitively-obvious notion that behaviors are most influenced by factors and events closest to them in time.

[19] See Thomas H. Davenport, *"Competing on Analytics", Harvard Business Review, January 2006, pages 98-107.*

[20] $469.2 billion in 2013.

Chapter 2

[1] Business entities which carried on business and were subject to legal right existed as far back as ancient Rome; the oldest, as it is believed, business corporation in the word is the Stora Kopparberg mining company in Sweden, dating its origins back to 1347.

[2] I am differentiating between "man-made" property, such as buildings, and "natural" property, such as land, because the latter is obviously not damageable.

[3] Douglas Hubbard, *How to Measure Anything: Finding the Value of Intangibles in Business*, pg. 46, John Wiley & Sons, 2007

[4] Two relatively recent events illustrate that point: the Financial Crisis of 2007-08 (also known as the Great Recession) and the Superstorm Sandy both directly impacted Lower Manhattan, home to some of the world's largest financial service organizations, yet only the former threatened the very survival of the said companies.

[5] A notion describing the degree to which a particular operationalization diverges from other, conceptually distinct, operationalizations – in other words, does it just sound differently, or is it indeed different?

[6] .9 * $10,000 vs. .1 * $1,000,000.

[7] Bowman, E.H, 1980, "A Risk/Return Paradox for Strategic Management," Sloan Management Review, v. 21, 17-31.
Bowman, E.H., 1982, "Risk Seeking by Troubled Firms," Sloan Management Review, v. 23, 33-42.

[8] A branch of applied mathematics and electrical engineering concerned with the quantification of information. Its origins date back to the publishing of C. Shannon's seminal work "A Mathematical Theory of Communication."

[9] Obviously, this is a bit of an oversimplification, as the coverage limits, the attachment point, terms & conditions and price are often jointly-determined.

[10] Under certain, limited set of circumstances, insurance coverage could yield some residual value; perhaps the best example of that are the so-called "membership credits" available to policy holders of industry mutuals, such as those formed by electric utilities.

[11] This is an example of a "pure captive"; a captive can also serve the needs of multiple entities, in which case it will be broadly referred to as a "group captive." The latter can still take on different forms such as "industry captive", "association captive", or "risk retention group captive", in addition to "rent-a-captive." Recently, a yet another form of a captive started to take hold, the so-called "program business captive", which is structured expressly as a profit center for the parent company.

[12] With that in mind, the majority of captives purchase re-insurance to protect against that possibility. Furthermore, that particular risk should be considered in the context of counter-party risk associated with the procurement of coverage from a commercial carrier, best illustrated by the liquidity crisis at AIG in the latter part of 2008 and early 2009.

[13] Sourced from BusinessDictionary.com

[14] The view expressed in this book is that cost-benefit analysis is not an adequate evaluation framework for making risk acceptance decisions, for a variety of reasons. Philosophically, the widely used cost-benefit technique tends to give undue prominence to quantifiable manifestations of risk, which are not necessarily the most significant. Practically, even focusing on the overtly quantifiable aspects, the validity of estimates of what constitutes costs and benefits is often suspect. What is the cost of accepting the regulatory risk of stricter carbon emission standards? What is the benefit of this course of action? Given that the majority of risks that organizations tend to accept are those that are hard to measure, both in terms of likelihood and severity, it is

borderline naïve to believe that traditional cost-benefit analysis can yield objective and robust conclusions.

[15] Thompson, Michael, Richard Ellis and Aaron Wildavsky, *Cultural Theory*, 1990, Westview Press.

[16] Markowitz, Harry (1952), "Portfolio Selection", Journal of Finance, 7 (1), pp. 77-91.

[17] Sharpe, William F. (1964), "Capital Asset Prices: A Theory of Market Equilibrium under Conditions of Risk", Journal Finance, 19 (3), pp. 425-442.

[18] Black, Fischer and Myron S. Scholes (1973), "The Pricing of Options and Corporate Liabilities," Journal of Political Economy, 81(3), pp. 637-654.

[19] Sponsored jointly by: the American Accounting Association, the American Institute of Certified Public Accountants, Financial Executives International, The Institute of Internal Auditors and the Institute of Management Accountants (formerly, the National Association of Accountants)

[20] An international standard-setting body, founded in 1947 and composed of representatives from various national standards organizations.

[21] Issued by Basel Committee on Banking Supervision, based at the Bank of International Settlements in Basel, Switzerland. Committee consists of representatives from central banks and regulatory authorities of the G10 countries, plus others (specifically Luxembourg and Spain). The committee does not have the authority to enforce recommendations, although most member countries (and others) tend to implement its policies.

Chapter 3

[1] *Statistical adequacy* is a function of numerous considerations which include the type of estimation methodology used, the desired precision of the resultant estimates and the type of data; those and other considerations are discussed in more detail in later chapters.

[2] The various frictional elements, such as taxes (which favor debt, because interest payments on debt are not taxable), imperfect information and transaction costs all add up to a conclusion that an optimal financial structure of an organization contains a mixture of debt and equity. This is the general rationale used by equity firms when evaluating public companies as possible targets for buyouts.

[3] Of the remaining 40%, 27% was attributed to operational failures (such as cost structure, poor project delivery or channel/supplier challenges) and the last 13% to compliance failures (e.g., SOX, SEC violations, fraud).

[4] Slywotzky, Adrian J. and John Drzik, "Countering the Biggest Risk of All", Harvard Business Review, April 2005.

[5] It has become a matter of common practice to use the terms "probability" and "likelihood" interchangeably. I will adhere to this practice in discussing the topics relating to probability estimation, however, I would like to point out that, technically, these two concepts are somewhat distinct. According to R. A. Fisher, the father of

modern statistical analyses, "probability" is the inference of sample occurrences drawn from assumptions regarding the population; "likelihood", on the other hand, is inference of population characteristics from sample characteristics (ref., "Statistical Methods for Research Workers", R. A. Fisher, 1st edition, 1925). In applied business analytics we are concerned with the latter, as we typically use the knowledge derived from the analysis of a sample to make projections regarding the larger population. Given that, using the two terms interchangeably will not adversely impact the quality or the substance of analyses.

[6] Jeffrey, Richard C., *Probability and the Art of Judgment.* Cambridge University Press, 1992, pp. 54-55.

[7] The earliest known contribution in this area is attributed to an accomplished Italian Renaissance mathematician, astrologer and…gambler, Gerolamo Cardano (1501-1576).

[8] *Analytical Theory of Probability*, published by Pierre Simon de Leplace in 1812 is believed to be the first major work blending calculus with probability theory.

[9] Kolmogorov, Andrei N., *Foundations of the Theory of Probability*, 1950. (Originally published in German in 1933.)

[10] While some events are characterized by a single point in time loss, others entail multi-year payment streams comprised of amounts that may not be known ahead of time. For example, a workers' compensation claim which includes ongoing medical treatment may take a number of years to "fully develop" (i.e., account for all costs) and there is generally no way of knowing the costs of medical treatment in advance.

[11] On average, there are about 200 of securities class action suits filed in federal courts annually (following the passage of the Private Securities Litigation Reform Act of 1995, these claims can no longer be filed in state courts).

[12] Of the nearly 3,000 securities class action claims filed since the PSLRA of 1995, only seven were resolved by a jury; the rest were either dismissed or settled.

Chapter 4

[1] In the example used here, there is adequate data to support entity-specific analyses, which means that the belief that group-level analyses are adequate is unwarranted.

[2] *Measurement theory* is a branch of applied mathematics, often used in data analysis. Its basic premise is that measurements (defined as a process of assigning numbers or other symbols to entities in such a way that relationships of those numbers or symbols reflect relationships of the attributes of entities being measured) are not the same as attributes being measured, thus in order to draw conclusions about attributes one must take into account the nature of the correspondence between attributes and their measurements.

Chapter 5

[1] It is quite common for a high proportion, 50% or higher, of workers' compensation claims to have no or negligible indemnity or medical costs. In fact, most manufacturing, retail or other organizations exhibiting high workers' compensation or general liability claim frequency see a very clear Pareto Effect (80-20 rule), where a relatively small proportion of claims account for a very large share of the overall cost.
[2] Assuming that the outside, data-append vendor has already been identified and the requisite purchase and usage agreements have already been put in place, the actual acquisition of the outside data requires the preparation of a file that is to be appended, transmitting the file to be appended to the vendor, data appending by the vendor followed by the review and validation of the added metrics.
[3] As detailed later in this book, data append match rates can range from a high of about 80% or so to a low of about 2%, depending on the type of data.

Chapter 7

[1] Hunt, Shelby D. (1991), *Modern Marketing Theory: Critical Issues in the Philosophy of Marketing Science*, South-Western Publishing, Cincinnati, OH, pp. 86-89.
[2] Charles Babcock, "Data, Data Everywhere," Information Week, January 9, 2006.
[3] Explicitly-numeric data are coded as digits; implicitly-numeric data are coded as alphanumeric (a combination of digits and letters) characters that are convertible into digital format. For instance, "gender" is often coded as "F" for females and "M" for males, which can be easily converted into a numeric format, such as "1" and "2", respectively.
[4] According to one vendor of database appliances, Netezza, its Netezza Performance Server delivers 10-50 times the performance (measured in processing speed) of traditional data warehouse systems as offered by Oracle, IBM or Teradata. The performance gains are generally attributed to multiple, micro data processing units replacing a single, central CPU based batch processing. It should be pointed out, however, that the greatly increased processing efficiency can make certain other operations, such as selecting of a representative database sample, somewhat more cumbersome.

Chapter 8

[1] *Likert scales* are psychometric measures (in fact, they are the most commonly used social research scales) seeking to elicit "the degree of agreement" (such as strongly agree, somewhat agree, neither agree nor disagree, somewhat disagree, strongly disagree) attitudinal responses. They are named after Rensis Likert (Likert, Rensis, "A Technique for the Measurement of Attitudes", Archives of Psychology, 1932, v. 140, p. 1-55). Semantic differentials are a different type of attitudinal measurement

scales—their goal is to measure the connotative meaning of objects or concepts; the connotations are in turn used to derive attitudes.

[2] The Standard Hierarchy of Census Geographic Entities (from least to most aggregate) is as follows: Census Blocks – Block Groups – Census Tracts – Counties – States – Divisions – Regions – Nation. Geodemographic data usually represents the lowest level of aggregation – the Census Block.

[3] For example, the outside vendor-sourced geodemographic variables have an average "hit rate" of anywhere from about 5% for certain special interest metrics, such as magazine subscription propensity, to about 50% for general purpose metrics, such age, house ownership, etc. The coverage will be far lower for direct-capture survey information, mostly due to high costs, which can run in excess of $10 per completed survey.

[4] The recently-emerged notion of "big data" is a case in point: It is a term used to describe a collection of data that is too large and complex to be processed using traditional or standard database management applications.

[5] An in-depth discussion of the applicability of statistical significance testing to marketing will be presented in the next chapter.

[6] In a nutshell, it means that small changes in the initial conditions can have disproportionately large impact on the system—i.e., a butterfly flapping its wings can set off a chain of events that can ultimately cause a hurricane. This colorful notion became a common moniker for a branch of mathematics known a *chaos theory* (which has its roots in meteorology, or the study of weather patterns, thus the label seems somewhat appropriate).

[7] It should be noted that the *stratified sampling* scheme also relies on random selection, but in pre-specified proportions. In contrast to *purely random* selection, stratified sampling breaks the entire database down into distinct segments (such as customer type groupings) called strata, following which, a representative, random sample is selected from each strata.

[8] A "unit of analysis" is the basic database record, such as an individual claim.

[9] The evolving legislative landscape continues to shape and redefine the organizations' access to consumer data, largely in response to mounting privacy considerations. For example, the Shelby Act severely restricts the access of companies to consumer auto registration data compiled by R.L Polk and Company from state automotive registries.

[10] Both *explanatory* and *predictive* analyses of data rely on variable variability to yield theoretically and practically meaningful results – in other words, if explanatory variables do not exhibit strong cross-case value differences, there is generally little chance of finding statistically significant results.

[11] Physical distance-based outlier identification typically utilizes the so-called *Mahalanobis distance*, which relates the arithmetic mean of the data and the sample covariance matrix as basis for identifying outlying data points. On the other hand, an approach based on a difference of magnitudes quantifies the discrepancy between the

sample-wide average and a record-specific actual value which is then evaluated in the context of the allowable upper and lower intervals.

[12] These analyses used regression-based missing value imputation processes to fill-in randomly created missing values (i.e., the values were deleted for the purpose of the experiment), the results of which were then validated via ascribed-to-actual comparisons.

[13] e.g., Switzer, F.S., Roth, P.L., and Switzer, D.M. (1998), "Systematic Data Loss in HRM Settings: A Monte Carlo Analysis", Journal of Management, 24(6), 763-779.; Rubin, D.B (1987), *Multiple Imputations for Nonresponse in Surveys*, New York, John Wiley.

[14] This particular limitation would be circumvented if the variables of interest, i.e., the X and Y metrics being correlated, had no relationship (operationally, 0 correlation) with other variables. Although theoretically possible, that is extremely rare in practice.

[15] Rubin, D.B (1987), *Multiple Imputations for Nonresponse in Surveys*, New York, John Wiley and Sons.

[16] In multivariate statistical analysis events are usually *dependent variables*, i.e., variables being explained, while attributes tend to play the role of *independent variables*, i.e., the drivers of the observed behaviors.

[17] Since the informationally-richer quantitatively-coded variables can always be re-coded into qualitative ones, quantitatively-coded variables do not face such limitations. However, since the process of quantitative-to-qualitative re-coding results in permanent informational reduction as the information richer quantitative variable is reduced into information poorer qualitative one, the quantitative-to-qualitative re-coding is non-reversible. It goes without saying that qualitatively-coded variables cannot be re-coded into quantitatively-coded ones.

Chapter 9

[1] Statistical significance tests are in principle a "pass-fail" mechanism, which means there is no implicit "degree" of significance that might be attributed to individual relationships, in spite of the evident numeric differences across individual tests (i.e., significant at .01 vs. .001). As a result, once a given relationship is deemed to be statistically significant, its level of a significance test-imputed importance is the same as that of all other (statistically significant) relationships.

[2] Among the most commonly used data mining techniques are *fuzzy query and analysis, case-based reasoning, neural networks* and *data visualization*. Fuzzy, in contrast to crisp, query and analysis tries to extract the intent from a relatively vague semantics of a database query (e.g., finding "good" customers vs. identifying all customers whose spending is greater than a specified threshold); case-based reasoning allow to identify records that are similar to specified targets; neural networks attempt to emulate human brain's learning processes to extracting insights out of raw data; data

visualization offers graphical interpretation of complex relationships in multidimensional data.

[3] Tukey, John (1977), *Exploratory Data Analysis,* Addison-Wesley, Reading, MA.

[4] Collinearity is an excessively high correlation between predictor variables in multiple linear regression. This concept will be discussed more fully in the next chapter.

[5] The *Delphi Method* is a structured process for collecting and distilling knowledge from a group of experts, hence it is also sometimes referred to as the "jury of executive opinion." The basic idea behind this particular method is that in areas where the development and/or validation of objective scientific laws is not possible, human judgment can be considered a legitimate and useful decision making input. The term "Delphi" refers to the hallowed site of the most revered oracle in ancient Greece (which in the opinion of some, is an unfortunate choice of a label).

[6] Since *histograms* show categories of data, continuously measured variables typically need to be grouped into categories to allow the frequency of data values to be tabulated. Not doing so will distort the appearance of the graph making it unreadable due to a very large number of distinct values appearing with very low frequency. There are no set ways of grouping continuous variables, as the best method is in part a function of the type of data. For instance, behavioral data (e.g., captured by UPC code readers or other POS systems), could be divided into a number of equally-sized categories by subdividing the range of values into the chosen number of categories. On the other hand, survey-captured data, such as employee attitudes could be easily categorized by summing scale responses (e.g., although the commonly used Likert scale is assumed to be continuous, responders select specific categorical responses on the agree—disagree continuum).

[7] It may seem somewhat counterintuitive that a range defined by stated end-points would have an infinite number of values but the basic idea here is that any interval bounded by extremes can still be divided into ever-smaller sub-sets.

[8] Technically, it is also important to distinguish between a *sample* and *a population* mean. Sample mean is the actual computed value based on the data contained in a particular dataset or a database. The population mean, on the other hand, is a more abstractly defined expected value of a random variable. In database analytics the term mean is synonymous with sample mean.

[9] Assumes it is computed in a sample (as opposed to the population).

[10] Sample standard deviation; it can also be expressed as a square root of variance.

[11] SAS and SPSS do not have a limit on the number of categories, thus it is possible to end up with very large matrices.

[12] A cell is a unique *conjoint*, or a combination, of a variable and a level. For instance, a 2x2 test would be comprised of 4 individual cells, as there are 2 variables each with two levels.

[13] Some of that rationale is evident in what is known as *partial correlation*, which is (still) a bivariate relationship, but one that is computed net of the effects of one or more

326

of the potentially confounding variables. In that sense, partial correlation should be treated as a special case of the general bivariate correlation.

[14] Examples include such well-known, yet elusive concepts as intelligence, expertise or satisfaction, all of which are typically measured with multiple-indicator survey studies (largely because it is believed that no single item is a perfectly reliable measure of those constructs). Thus when multiple items are all intended to measure the same underlying concept, ascertaining the relationships between those items is obviously of informational value to researchers. However, more methodologically robust approaches, such as the *confirmatory factor analysis* are now the preferred method of studying those relationships.

[15] *Standardization* involves subtracting means from the original values and dividing the residual by the standard deviation.

[16] There are a few notable exceptions to that rule in the context of *structural equations modeling* (SEM) techniques, but these techniques fall outside of the scope of this book.

[17] *Kendall's tau* is also an appropriate choice and will typically yield practically the same results (both Kendall's and Spearman's correlations carry out the same computation, just by somewhat different means). In the past, Spearman's coefficient tended to be the preferred Kendall's because it is computationally less taxing, though that is obviously a moot point currently. That said, Spearman's has more recognition, thus it is preferred.

[18] A *Type II error* entails incorrectly accepting a false null hypothesis. The previously discussed prohibitively small sample size is among the more common causes of the Type II error.

[19] In contrast to the earlier-detailed three-prong shortcomings of tests of statistical significance associated with exploratory data analyses, applying SST tests to causal analyses discussed here generally raises concerns only in terms of the effective sample size and the resultant potential of deeming as significant relationships whose significance is inflated the sample size used in the analysis.

[20] See the *principle of parsimony* discussed in the opening chapter.

[21] For an in-depth discussion of misapplications of statistical significance tests see Banasiewicz, Andrew (2005), "Marketing Pitfalls of Statistical Significance Testing", Marketing Intelligence and Planning Journal, vol. 23(5), pp. 515-528.

[22] Although the level of confidence will asymptotically approach 100%, it will never reach it, as the only way of being 100% certain of a particular value is by accounting for each and every element in the population. Sample based analyses can yield highly accurate projections, but not absolute certainty.

[23] Upper Confidence Interval = Mean + (Level of Significance Factor * Standard Error)
   Lower Confidence Interval = Mean – (Level of Significance Factor * Standard Error)

Chapter 10

[1] Just two years after the book's initial publishing, a Business Week article, "Oops, Who's Excellent Now?" (November 5, 1984) observed that of the 43 "excellent" companies, about a third were in financial difficulties just five years following Peter's and Waterman's research.

[2] The match, played on May 11, 1997, was won by Big Blue 2-to-1 (with three draws).

[3] In practice, *interaction terms* are often limited to bivariate (two-variable) terms as higher-order interactions become quite cumbersome to interpret. Also, pragmatically speaking, the higher the number of variables linked together to form an interaction term the lower the likelihood that such multi-way interactions will turn out to be statistically significant.

[4] There is an ongoing controversy among methodologist regarding the tradeoff between adhering to the assumption of *predictor independence* at the cost of poorer model fit vs. effectively violating that assumption (by means of introducing interaction effects of variables that are already in the model as stand-alone predictors) but at the same time enhancing the model's goodness-of-fit. In applied business analyses the latter choice is preferred.

[5] This name reflects that, mathematically, interactions represent a *product* of n stand-alone metrics; i.e., a two-way interaction is a product of variable1 x variable 2.

[6] Probably the best-known (among non-economists) economic principle which suggests that each additional unit of input (holding everything else to be unchanged) will produce less and less additional output.

[7] These are typically investor-filed civil lawsuits, predominantly in federal courts, asserting fraudulent behavior on the part of officers and directors of publicly traded companies which then led to investor loss (a "class" represents a group of investors banding together for the purpose of jointly pursuing retribution). The much-publicized Enron, WorldCom and Tyco scandals represent examples of large securities class actions.

[8] Applied business analyses at time make a use of lower levels of significance, such 80%, which most of the time is in response to the desire to show as "significant" a compelling explanatory factor, which falls short of one of the traditionally used significance thresholds. This is a potentially dangerous practice, particularly when coupled with a large sample size. Given that the probability of finding statistically significant relationships increases as a function of sample size, also lowering the probability of interpreting as significant otherwise spurious associations will greatly increase the likelihood of coming to an unsupported (by the data) our outright erroneous conclusion.

[9] Excerpt from the author's online blog, Gladwell.com.

[10] The name "Delphi" is derived from the Delphic oracle, the most important oracle of the classical Greek world. The creators of this method (Rand Corporation) were not

happy with this name, because it implies "something smacking a little of the occult", but the name stuck nonetheless.

[11] Now RAND Corporation, a non-profit think tank.

[12] www.worldwidewebsize.com.

[13] Discussed in more detail later, *syntax* refers to the arrangement of words in sentences which, together with the meaning of the individual words, gives sentences their meaning.

[14] Consider the earlier-mentioned examples of the largest repositories of textual data – Facebook's social networking, Google's search or the Library of Congress databases – the overwhelming majority of the individual files comprising those gargantuan databases is made up of free-flowing text lacking discernible structure.

[15] As is well-known, the primary advantage of machine processing is speed, not creativity. The vast majority of computer processing algorithms are designed to apply the same processing logic to all cases (rows of data) – when that is not the case, i.e., when input files do not follow a pre-determined and recurring structure, the otherwise highly efficient algorithms' performance degrades rapidly.

[16] The "mining" label is meant to connote *exploratory* focus; in general, data mining is focused on search for patterns and/or relationships in typically very large databases, such as UPC scanner-originated purchase databases amassed by retailers. With that in mind, text mining can be viewed as a subset of data mining, as it focuses on search for patterns and/or relationships in text data.

[17] SPSS is now a subsidiary of IBM.

[18] Data about data; the term (metadata) is quite broad as it is used in a wide array of contexts. Within the confines of executive risk-related text mining, its meaning is synonymous with "meta content".

[19] The so-called "360° view of customers", "customer focused" or "customer centric" approaches to customer relationship management, or CRM, rest upon organizations' ability to compile a singular data analytical infrastructure, where different aspects of customer knowledge are all "tied together". The ultimate goal of multi-source analytics is to yield a complete (or as complete as possible, given all available data) understanding of consumer behavior, which means linking of consumers' opinions/attitudes (the bulk of which are text-coded), demographics as well as other salient motivational factors with product and service purchases (which tend to be numerically-coded) and other marketplace behaviors.

[20] Consider, for instance, a term such as "price discount" – in a broader context, it could be used to communicate that a price discount had no impact on purchase intent or the opposite. Obviously, the ultimate informational value of the "price discount" term is highly dependent on the context in which the term was used.

[21] *Semantics* is the study of meaning, focused on establishing the relationship between words, expression or symbols and what they stand for; *linguistic semantics* is the study of language-based communication.

[22] In a broader sense, text can be transformed into a wide variety of other media, such as pictures, video, etc. In fact, in educational research, "text transformation" is used in the context of enhancing printed text to aid in students' efforts to comprehend the meaning of text.

[23] Many database applications make heavy use of libraries of terms that are used to describe a particular condition, state or an outcome. In effect, the structured textual data represents selections made from a pre-defined listing of applicable terms.

[24] A key simplicity related consideration is reflected in the notion of "overfitting", which is a condition where the algorithm is too tailored to the specifics of the training data and does not generalize well to new data.

[25] Knowledge-based classification systems are usually built around phrasal pre-processing and pattern matching that is guided by tailored (to a specific subject area) classification rules; given that, expert-imbued knowledge provides the basis for probability-expressed matching.

Chapter 11

[1] A non-directional hypothesis test involves determining if a phenomenon of interest has any impact, positive or negative, on the focal outcome.

[2] For example, the current regulations require that all individuals whose credit was queried need to be made a credit offer as a result, which precludes setting aside a random control group.

[3] Analytically-distinct segments are sub-groups that are expected, based on past analyses or theoretical considerations, to exhibit somewhat unique behavioral or attitudinal patterns. What comprises an analytically-distinct segment can vary across situations or the type of investigation.

[4] Although the "no difference" null hypothesis, where treated buy rate = control buy rate, is probably most common as it requires no specific a priori knowledge, the test-control relationship can also be expressed directionally, e.g., "policy change-exposed group's accident rate > control group's accident rate" or "treated – control rate ≥ x%", although it is rarely done so for reasons of operational efficiency or lack of sufficient a priori knowledge.

[5] This is more globally referred to as *falsificationism,* according to which knowledge claims cannot be definitively proven as being true (since it would take an infinite number of tests), thus the best we can do is to fail to reject the claim(hypothesis) in question, leading to its tentative acceptance, at least until contrary evidence is presented.

[6] These are arbitrary numbers used only to illustrate the concept; confidence interval can be easily calculated with formulas available in most basic statistics textbooks.

[7] The most typical disruptive events are those representing regulatory or legislative changes directly impacting the phenomenon of interest. For instance, the passage of the Private Securities Litigation Reform Act of 1995 was a trend-disrupting event in

the area of executive liability because the Act fundamentally altered rules regarding pleading, discovery, liability and class representation.

Chapter 12

[1] See Banasiewicz, A. (2005), "Marketing Pitfalls of Statistical Significance Testing", Marketing Intelligence and Planning Journal , 23(5), pp. 515-528.

[2] The basic logic of significance testing involves comparing actual (such as the observed difference between treated and control buy rates) to expected (statistically derived) values based upon which a test statistic (such as *t-test*) is computed along with its respective probability, i.e., the *p* value. Expected values are arrived at by means of dividing the total amount of variability by sample size, which means that the larger the sample size the smaller the expected value. It can be easily shown that as the sample size increases, the magnitude of the expected value will continue to diminish. Naturally then, as a given observed value (e.g., buy rate differential) is compared to an ever smaller expected value, the likelihood of the former being deemed "statistically significant" will continue to increase.

[3] This is due to an increase in a number of error degrees of freedom which is a direct function of sample size.

Chapter 13

[1] Recall the discussion of the limitations of significance testing (*Beware of Significance Tests!*) and the basic characteristics of tests of association discussed in earlier chapters. The size of the analytical universe used in many, if not most practical business applications will tend to be relatively large, which in turn will result in relatively small, magnitude-wise, associations being deemed statistically significant, the net effect of which will be a potentially large pool of associative factors characterized by large differences in the magnitude of effects. In short, an analyst will need to, more or less arbitrarily decide which of the multiple statistically significant associative factors warrant inclusion in a dashboard or a scorecard.

CPSIA information can be obtained at www.ICGtesting.com
Printed in the USA
BVOW02s0302260815

415054BV00007B/32/P